Fodor's

ESSENTIAL NORWAY

EVA HARR

Welcome to Norway

One of the world's most beautiful countries, Norway has long been a popular cruising destination, famed for its stunning fjords. Formed during the last ice age's meltdown when the inland valleys carved by huge glaciers filled with seawater, fjords are undoubtedly Norway's top attractions. But while they are Norway's most striking and dramatic scenic features, there is much else to see, from the vast expanses of rugged tundra in the north to the huge evergreen forests along the Swedish border, from fertile coastal plains in the southwest to the snow-covered peaks and glaciers of the center.

TOP REASONS TO GO

★ **The fjords:** Norway's iconic waterways are known for their majestic beauty.

★ **The great outdoors:** Hiking, biking, skiing, sailing—there's something for everyone.

★ **Midnight sun:** The sun never drops below the horizon in summer.

★ **Northern lights:** Witness this spectacle between November and February.

★ **Dining out:** From new Nordic cuisine to hearty traditional dishes.

★ **Wildlife viewing:** Animal life is abundant, from herds of reindeer to pods of humpback whales.

Contents

MAPS

Chapter 1

EXPERIENCE NORWAY

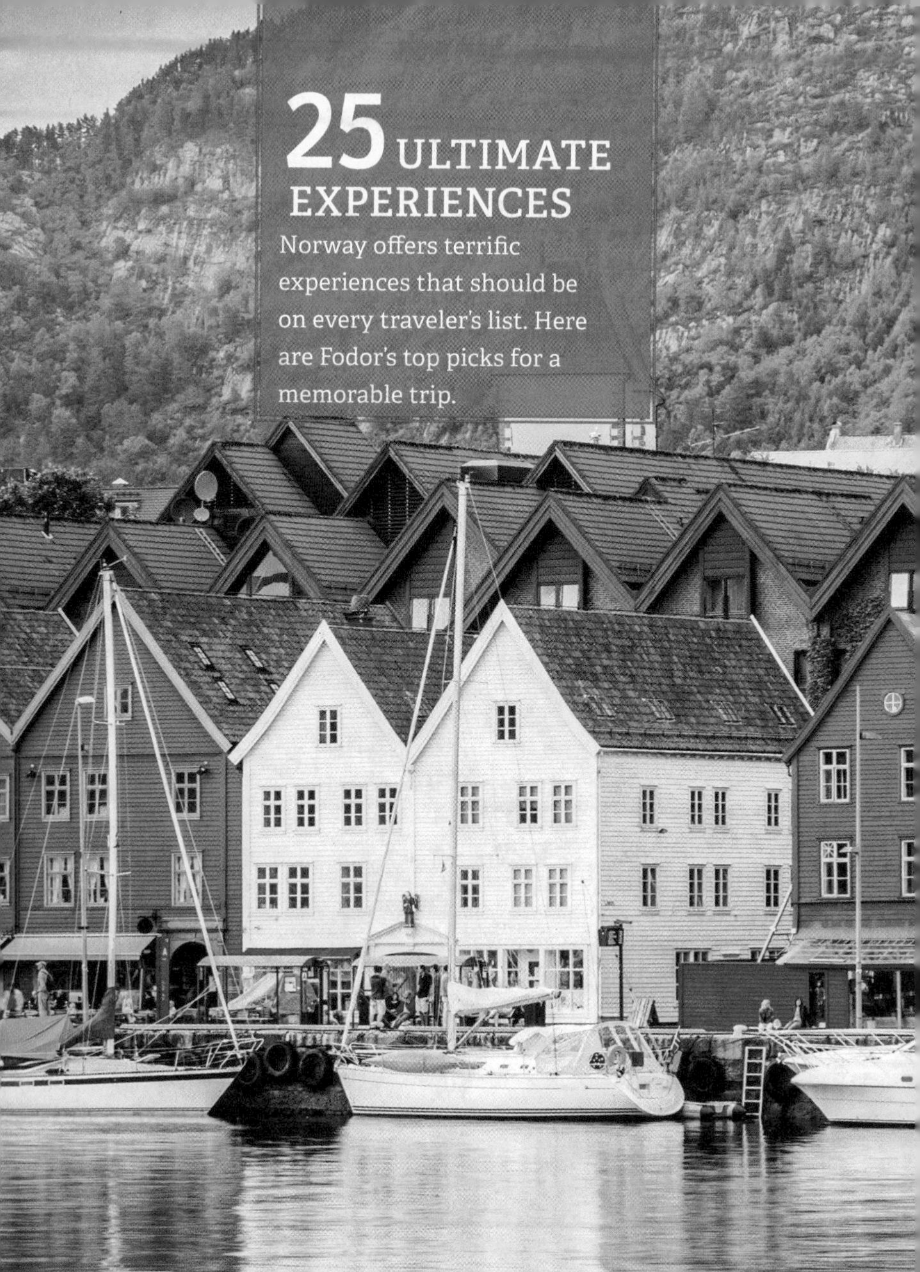

25 ULTIMATE EXPERIENCES

Norway offers terrific experiences that should be on every traveler's list. Here are Fodor's top picks for a memorable trip.

1 Visit Bryggen

The colorful wooden buildings of the old Hanseatic wharf in Bergen are a UNESCO Heritage Site, with a history that makes them much more than popular postcard motifs. *(Ch. 7)*

2 Explore Svalbard

Svalbard's main settlement, Longyearbyen, might only have 2,000 inhabitants, but it offers a good selection of hotels, restaurants, cafés, and bars. *(Ch. 11)*

3 Cruise the Coast

The former post and freight boats of the Hurtigruten line have been transformed into modern cruise vessels that take you on amazing voyages. *(Ch. 7, 8, 9, 10)*

4 Cross-Country Skiing

One of the best places to learn cross-country skiing is Lillehammer—a 2.5-hour drive from Oslo and the site of the 1994 Winter Olympics. *(Ch. 6)*

5 Stavanger's Old Town

A stroll through Old Stavanger, made up of 173 wooden buildings dating from the 18th and 19th centuries, is a half an hour well spent. *(Ch. 5)*

6 Experience the Northern Lights

Millions of visitors flock to the north between September and March to catch a glimpse of the northern lights, especially to the city of Tromsø. *(Ch. 10)*

7 The Kjerag Boulder

Seasoned hikers who really want to get their heart rates up should consider tackling the extremely challenging, 12.5-mile round-trip trek to the boulder at Kjerag. *(Ch. 5)*

8 Visit Geirangerfjord

Geiranger is Norway's most famous fjord, a UNESCO World Heritage Site, and the inspiration for the fictional Arendelle in Disney's *Frozen*. *(Ch. 8)*

9 The Midnight Sun

The sun doesn't set in Longyearbyen from late April to late August, during which you can observe the sun going around the horizon without ever dipping below. *(Ch. 11)*

10 Drive Trollstigen Road

The 11 hairpin turns of western Norway's Trollstigen, known as the "troll's footpath" in Norwegian, make a lasting impression. *(Ch. 8)*

11 The North Cape

The continent's northernmost point is North Cape, on the island of Magerøya. The photo ops are particularly striking in the evening light of summer's midnight sun. *(Ch. 10)*

12 Ride with Flåmsbanen

The thrilling train ride between the mountain communities of Flåm and Myrdal boasts some particularly scenic views. *(Ch. 8)*

13 Try Brown Cheese

Brown cheese is a Norwegian culinary specialty made from whey, cream, and both cow and goat milk, and it has the color and flavor of caramel.

14 The Lofoten Islands

With mountains, fjords, rugged coastlines, sandy beaches, and lots of farmland, the landscapes of this Arctic archipelago seem the embodiment of Norway. *(Ch. 9)*

15 See the Royals

The royals make official public appearances at many events and celebrations throughout Norway each year. They're known to be quite down-to-earth. *(Ch. 3)*

16 Ride a Cable Car

In the land of fjords and mountains, you're sure to stumble upon a cable car or two; few can compete with those from the Fjellheisen in Tromsø. *(Ch. 10)*

17 Experience Polar Night

Over a period of four weeks to four months, depending on the specific northerly location, the sun doesn't rise at all in parts of Norway. *(Ch. 10, 11)*

18 A Night in a Cabin

The most scenic locations for authentic cabin stays are the Lofoten Islands and along the route between Geiranger and Ålesund. *(Ch. 8, 9)*

19 Relax on the Rooftop of the Opera House

Oslo has plenty of popular hangouts, but few have the fantastic views afforded by the rooftop of the Opera House. *(Ch. 3)*

20 Hike Pulpit Rock

The narrow plateau set at almost 1,970 feet above Lysefjord affords stunning views—if you dare to look down, that is. *(Ch. 5)*

21 Hike to Trolltunga

Those who can handle the challenging 13.5-mile round-trip trek will be rewarded with one of Norway's most impressive mountain views. *(Ch. 8)*

22 Go Whale-Watching

Between November and January, herring schools migrate to the fjords of Troms County. And where there's herring there are whales, particularly orcas and humpbacks. *(Ch. 10)*

23 Celebrate National Day

National Day is Norway's biggest cultural event of the year, and visitors are more than welcome to join the celebrations on May 17. *(Ch. 2)*

24 Art Nouveau in Ålesund

Ålesund's abundance of Art Nouveau buildings, built after a 1904 fire destroyed most of the city center, continues to charm Norwegian locals and visitors alike. *(Ch. 8)*

25 See the Stave Churches

Only 28 of these impressive, early medieval churches still exist in Norway. Borgund Stave Church is one of the best preserved in the nation. *(Ch. 6, 8)*

WHAT'S WHERE

1 Oslo. Norway's capital city has reoriented itself in recent years, looking to its underused waterfront for inspiration. The Oslo Opera House was the beginning of a renaissance, with new neighborhoods like Aker Brygge and Tjuvholmen making this one of Europe's most vibrant cities.

2 Oslofjord. The fjord that makes Oslo such an exciting city is also home to Viking ruins, fortified towns, and bohemian artists colonies that provide a glimpse into the region's rich heritage.

3 Southern Norway. Nicknamed Norway's Riviera, the extreme southern tip of the country is one lovely village after another, many of them dotted with 18th- and 19th-century wooden houses that huddle at the water's edge.

4 Central Norway. Some of Europe's tallest peaks punctuate this largely unspoiled region, making it a prime destination for skiing, snowshoeing, and other outdoor activities. The national parks here boast some of the most breathtaking scenery.

5 Bergen. The country's second-largest city preserves the past with sights like beautiful Bryggen, the row of clapboard buildings facing the wharf that call to mind the country's seafaring days.

6 Western Fjords. The best way to see Norway's western coast is by boat, plying the waters of brilliant blue fjords where the mountains seem to rise at impossible angles. And don't forget spectacular train rides like the Flåmsbana.

7 Trondheim to the Lofoten Islands. The coastal community of Trondheim is leading the charge with New Nordic cuisine, winning international awards. It's a great stop along the way to some of the country's most stunning islands.

8 Northern Norway. The nighttime skies in this remote region are full of color, thanks to the amazing northern lights. In summer there's nearly endless sun.

9 Svalbard. Halfway between the mainland and the North Pole, the frozen tundra of Svalbard is barely inhabited, except if you're counting Arctic foxes, Svalbard reindeer, and the elusive polar bears.

80°N
10°W
0°
10°E
20°E
30°E
40°E
50°E
Norway
Longyearbyen
SVALBARD
ARCTIC OCEAN
Barents Sea
NORWEGIAN SEA
Hammerfest
Kirkenes
Alta
Tromsø
Murmansk
Finnsnes
Harstad
Svolvar
Bodø
Rovaniemi
Mo i Rana
Lulen
RUSSIA
Namsos
FINLAND
Steinkjer
Trondheim
Vaasa
SWEDEN
Ålesund
Molde
NORWAY
Sundsvall
Tampere
Vangsnes
Lillehammer
HELSINKI
Hamar
Bergen
OSLO
St. Petersburg
Drammen
Haugesund
TALLINN
STOCKHOLM
Stavanger
ESTONIA
Pskov
Kristiansand
LATVIA
1
2
3
4
5
6
7
8
9

What to Eat and Drink in Norway

SKOLEBOLLER
"School buns," which feature a custard filling and grated coconut, are so called as they were once a common lunch for schoolchildren. Today, they're a must for anyone with a sweet tooth, so it's a good thing that you can find them in pretty much any café.

BROWN CHEESE
Thought to have been created by a milkmaid named Anne Hov in the 19th century, *brunost*—a sweet, caramelized goat cheese with a tannish or brownish color—is still a Norwegian staple, often used to fill breakfast or lunch sandwiches or to top afternoon waffles. There are plenty of regional variations, so don't be surprised if the owner of a local restaurant insists that you sample some made at a nearby dairy.

REINDEER
Many of Norway's indigenous Sami people still herd reindeer, and you simply can't visit northern Norway without trying reindeer meat. It's traditionally served with mashed potatoes and cranberry or lingonberry sauce, though on special occasions such as Sami People's Day (February 6) or during Tromsø's street food festival, SMAK (third week of September), you can also find it dried or prepared as kebabs and sausages.

KING CRAB
Originally at home in the Bering Sea of Alaska and eastern Russia, king crabs were introduced to the Barents Sea by Soviet scientists in the 1960s, and the crustaceans quickly made their way to Norway. Now they're a staple of Norwegian fine dining, served in steaming bowls of soup or simply with some bread and mayonnaise.

FISH SOUP
You'll find this creamy soup made with hunks of cod and lots of vegetables anywhere in the country, though Norway's second-biggest city, Bergen, offers its own version with salmon, halibut, or even shrimp in addition to cod. It's a hearty wintertime staple that definitely warms you up after a day outside in the cold.

FISH CAKES
Ubiquitous in roadside diners and on ferries, Norwegian fish cakes are slightly smaller and thinner than other varieties and are commonly made from cod and served with potatoes or in a bun.

FÅRIKÅL
You can't visit Norway in autumn without tasting *fårikål*, a stew of mutton and cabbage that is the unofficial national dish. Commonly served with potatoes and bread on the side, the stew goes well with beer.

LAPSKAUS
A stew with beef or pork, vegetables, and potatoes, *lapskaus* originated in northern Germany before being adopted by Scandinavian and even English kitchens. What is now a staple of Norwegian home cooking goes exceptionally well with any of the local craft beers.

LEFSE

Lefse is a very thin and versatile potato flatbread. The most common preparation is to spread butter, sugar, and cinnamon over it, roll it up, and cut it into pieces. Nordland County, in the country's upper reaches, has a thicker version called *møsbrømlefse* that's made with brown cheese.

MEATBALLS

Thicker and less round than their Swedish counterparts, Norwegian meatballs are another staple of home cooking and are generally served with mashed potatoes and brown gravy. Everyone's grandmother has their own recipe.

STOCKFISH

Stockfish is air-dried cod that's commonly served with vegetables and potatoes. The dish originated in northern Norway, particularly the Lofoten Islands, where cod is caught each winter and then hung to dry on wooden racks throughout the spring.

LUTEFISK

Translating to "lye fish," lutefisk is, as its name suggests, made from aged stockfish and lye. The gelatinous dish, which takes about a week to become edible after the lye treatment, isn't for everyone. For Norwegians, however, it's a Christmastime tradition. The dish goes well with white wine.

RIBBE

It might be easy to forego lutefisk at Christmastime, but you won't be able to resist *ribbe*, another holiday favorite. This roast pork belly needs several hours in the oven, but once it's formed its golden crust and is served on the table with potatoes, sour cabbage, and lingonberry sauce, chances are you won't want anything else for Christmas dinner ever again.

PINNEKJØTT

On Christmas Eve, most Norwegian families serve either ribbe or *pinnekjøtt*, which translates to "stick meat" and which consists of lamb or mutton ribs served with potatoes.

SMALAHOVE

If you're in rural western Norway around Christmastime, don't be surprised if you find yourself staring at *smalahove*—and, possibly, having it stare back. The dish consists of boiled sheep's head (the brain is usually removed) served with potatoes and mashed rutabaga. Lucky for you, it goes well with *akevitt* (aquavit), Norway's traditional distilled spirit.

Must-Sees in Oslo for Art Lovers

MUNCH MUSEUM
The Munch Museum is dedicated entirely to Norwegian expressionist painter Edvard Munch, who is best known for his work *The Scream*. Stolen from the museum in 2004 and subsequently recovered, this famous painting is just one in a collection of over 1,200 paintings.

KRAGSTØTTEN
Kragstøtten refers to both a viewpoint that takes in all of Oslo and the on-site statue of 19th-century Norwegian road commissioner Hans Hagerup Krag. Krag developed the roads in northwestern Oslo's hilltop Holmenkollen district, which is now home to the ski jump and ski museum.

PEER GYNT SCULPTURE PARK
Northeastern Oslo's Peer Gynt Sculpture Park is dedicated to the play of the same name by Norwegian playwright and poet Henrik Ibsen. The park's 20 sculptures depict the storyline act by act and were designed by several contemporary artists.

VIGELANDSPARKEN
Although its formal name is Frognerparken, this central Oslo park is commonly referred to as Vigelandsparken, owing to its collection of 20th-century works by local sculptor Gustav Vigeland. Many of his 212 granite and bronze creations dot the vast grounds. The highlight, though, is the roughly 46-foot monolith showing all stages of life.

EKEBERG'S SCULPTURE PARK
Combining both art and nature, Ekeberg's Sculpture Park, in the hills east of central Oslo, couldn't be more Norwegian. Many of its 40 sculptures (to date) are positioned in ways that make the surrounding landscape part of the art.

TJUVHOLMEN SCULPTURE PARK
Like Ekeberg's Sculpture Park, Tjuvholmen Sculpture Park in Frogner makes use of Oslo's stunning scenery—in this case, the fjord. Designed by Renzo Piano, in collaboration with Denmark's Louisiana Museum of Modern Art, the park has seven sculptures by contemporary artists.

VIPPA
Situated in a former warehouse by the Vippetangen port and the Oslofjord, the Vippa food court highlights street food from all over the world, from Norway to Eritrea and Syria to China. The exterior is also a draw, thanks to a mural that depicts the capital's key sites.

THE NATIONAL MUSEUM
The new National Museum of Art, Architecture, and Design (opening in 2020) is shaping up to be the largest of its kind in the Nordic countries, exhibiting examples of both art and design from antiquity through today.

THE TIGER
Norwegians call Oslo the Tiger City, and the 15-foot-long bronze tiger in front of Oslo's central train station is perhaps the capital's most photographed sculpture. Designed by Norwegian artist Elena Engelsen, who specializes in sculpting exotic animals, it commemorates the city's 1,000-year anniversary, which was celebrated in 2000.

THE HOLMENKOLLEN TROLL
If you head up to the Holmenkollen district, watch for the Kollentrollet (Holmenkollen Troll). Although he's situated in the woods, the 23-foot concrete figure is easy to find. He was designed by Norwegian sculptor Nils Aas, who also developed the sculpture of King Haakon VII on the 7 June Square in downtown Oslo.

Natural Wonders to Experience in Norway

SOGNEFJORD
As Norway's deepest (almost 4,300 feet) and longest (127 miles) fjord, Sognefjord is a must see. Equally impressive is the fact that 12 other fjords branch off from it, including the well-known Nærøyfjord, a UNESCO World Heritage Site, and Aurlandsfjord, home to the scenic Flåm Railway.

SVARTISEN
Although Svartisen is at the Arctic Circle, Norway's second-largest glacier is very accessible thanks to its lower elevations. What was once a single large formation has separated into two parts, one to the west and the other to the east. The glacier is almost 5,300 feet above sea level at its highest point.

MARMORSLOTTET
Not many visitors know about Marmorslottet (Marble Castle), but if you're heading to Svartisen glacier, you should also check out this formation less than an hour from Mo i Rana. The water is a deep, icy blue—appropriate given its glacial origins.

DOVREFJELL NATIONAL PARK
Together Dovre and Dovrefjell-Sunndalsfjella national parks cover some 770 square miles in south-eastern Norway. The region is home to wild reindeer, as well as Norway's only population of wild musk ox, which were imported from Greenland in the first half of the 20th century. Today, safaris take you to see these giants up close.

GLOPPEDALSURA
In the lunar-like landscape of Gloppedalsura, some of the boulders are as big as cars; others are the size of buildings. They're all remnants of an ancient rockslide that's thought to have been the largest in northern Europe. Because this granite was originally formed from magma, Gloppedalsura is also part of the Magma Geopark.

SALTSTRAUMEN

Saltstraumen, close to the city of Bodø, has the world's strongest tidal current. Each day, during high and low tides, vast amounts of seawater are forced through the tiny, 492-foot-wide, roughly 2-mile-long strait separating mainland Norway from the island of Straumøya.

JOTUNHEIMEN NATIONAL PARK

Jotunheimen National Park is a haven for hikers, climbers, and skiers. Its roughly 1,300 square miles encompass northern Europe's greatest concentration of peaks over 6,500 feet, including 8,100-foot Galdhøppingen, Norway's highest mountain.

JOSTEDALSBREEN

Jostedalsbreen is the biggest glacier not only in Norway, but also in continental Europe. It stretches across almost 200 square miles and has dozens of branches. One of the most popular is Briksdalsbreen, which is near Olden and is accessible on guided tours in "troll cars" (aka buggies).

VETTISFOSSEN

The 900-foot Vettisfossen is Europe's highest free-falling, unregulated waterfall. Situated in Jotunheimen National Park, Vettisfossen has been protected since the 1920s and is only accessible from Utladalen via a steep (it rises roughly 1,000 feet), 7.5-mile round-trip hike.

HARDANGERVIDDA

At an average height of 3,600 feet, Hardangervidda is Europe's largest (almost 3,300 square miles) high-altitude plateau. It's also part of the biggest national park in the Nordic countries, stretching from western to eastern Norway across the three counties of Hordaland, Buskerud, and Telemark.

Architectural Masterpieces in Norway

STEGASTEIN VIEWPOINT
Designed by the architectural team of Todd Saunders and Tommie Wilhelmsen, the 98-foot-long, 13-foot-wide, steel-and-wood Stegastein viewing platform protrudes from the side of a mountain roughly 2,100 feet above sea level. It's a popular stop for visitors traveling by Flåm Railway.

NIDAROS CATHEDRAL
The world's northernmost medieval cathedral has cultural as well as historical significance. Built over the course of 230 years (between 1070 and 1300), it was originally established to honor King Olav II, who became St. Olav after his death in 1030. It's also the site of his grave.

HELLEREN I JØSSINGFJORD
Historians believe that the Helleren i Jøssingfjord site at Jøssingfjord in southwestern Norway was first inhabited in the 16th century. Situated beneath a 197-foot-long, 33-foot-high mountain overhang, the site is, indeed, a spacious, shielded spot.

ARCTIC CATHEDRAL
Situated in front of Mt. Storsteinen, the Arctic Cathedral, Tromsø's most famous landmark is a parish church that was designed to impress by Norwegian architect Jan Inge Hovig in 1965. Thanks to its 11 rooftop triangles, it's said to resemble either icebergs and/or the typical northern Norwegian cod-drying racks.

LOEN SKYLIFT
Loen Skylift is Norway's steepest cable car line, with an average ascent of 45 degrees. It's also relatively speedy, traveling from the lower station in Loen up 3,600 feet to Mt. Hoven in just five minutes. Despite pricey tickets, the cable car is a major draw. The skylift dangles you almost 560 feet above the ground, and the journey is well worth conquering any fear of heights you may have.

ATLANTIC OCEAN ROAD BRIDGES
Atlantic Ocean Road—a 5-mile stretch of Norwegian Road 64 connecting the mainland with Averøy Island—has been cited on lists of the world's best road trips. It was built in the 1980s and has a total of eight bridges, including Storseisundbrua, the longest (850 feet) and highest (75 feet).

NORTHERN LIGHTS CATHEDRAL
Designed by the Norwegian LINK architectural firm and completed in 2013, it is an intriguing example of contemporary Norwegian design. The church is open year-round; be sure to step inside to see its altar and organ backed by light installations that evoke the aurora borealis.

UNDER RESTAURANT
Translating to both "underneath" and "wonder," Under is Europe's first subaquatic restaurant. Panoramic windows enable you to view the maritime flora and fauna while enjoying the best cuisine that Norway has to offer.

SNØHETTA VIEWPOINT
The large Norwegian Wild Reindeer Centre Pavilion, more commonly known as Snøhetta Viewpoint, offers panoramas of Mt. Snøhetta and Dovrefjell-Sunndalsfjella National Park. The building is open from June until mid-October and can be reached via the hiking trail from the Snøhetta parking lot or the train station at Hjerkinn.

HOPPERSTAD STAVE CHURCH
Hopperstad Stave Church was built in 1130, making it one of Norway's oldest. It was restored in the late 19th-century by Norwegian architect Peter Andreas Blix, who used Borgund Stave Church, with its triple nave, as inspiration and who discovered the remains of an older, 11th-century church on the site.

Unique Things to Bring Home From Norway

CLOUDBERRY JAM
Similar in shape to raspberries, cloudberries have a unique sweet-and-sour taste and are very rich in vitamin C—in fact, the indigenous Sami people are said to have survived harsh Arctic winters thanks to their consumption of the fruit. The berries are tricky to find and must be hand harvested each summer, so jams, liqueurs, and other items made from them can be expensive.

CAVIAR IN A TUBE
Norwegians are very fond of their "tube food," and although it might initially seem strange, consider this: in a country where people love to spend their free time hiking or skiing in the mountains, easy-to-carry food that doesn't easily spoil (tubes can be stored at room temperature for up to two weeks) makes sense. Breakfast and lunch spreads—from caviar to cream cheese in a variety of flavors—as well as mayonnaise and other condiments all come in tube form.

TROLL FIGURES
Every souvenir store in Norway sells troll figures in various shapes, sizes, and, well, levels of ugliness! As cliché and kitschy as the dolls might seem, note that trolls are intrinsic to Norwegian culture. Indeed, folk tales about them have been passed down through generations thanks in part to two friends named Asbjørnsen and Moe. In the 19th century, Norway's version of Germany's Brothers Grimm traveled the country to collect folk tales, including one detailing how a boy named Ashlad outsmarted a troll. Unlike the smiling, Norwegian-flag-holding, Viking-helmet-adorned souvenir versions of the creatures, those in folk tales are usually depicted as dangerous (albeit a little dumb) and very ugly.

CHEESE SLICER
In the early 20th century, a carpenter from Lillehammer named Thor Bjørklund came up with the idea, inspired by the tree slicers he used in his line of work. He patented the product in 1925, and it quickly became an important export—despite attempts to ban it on the part of Norwegian cheese makers, who feared its use would result in people consuming less cheese.

WOODEN COFFEE MUGS
During hikes in the Norwegian mountains, you might spot people pouring their coffee from flasks into wooden mugs. Quite common all over Norway, Sweden, and Finland, the mugs are generally made from birch, although the Sami people sometimes use reindeer horn. Regardless, they're excellent examples of traditional craftsmanship.

SELBU MITTENS
Knitwear has been part of Norwegian culture for centuries, and it seems as though every region has its own traditional patterns. One of the most famous, however, is the Selbu pattern that's used for woolen mittens. As its name suggests, it hails from the town of Selbu, close to the major city of Trondheim, and it was developed

roughly 150 years ago by a woman named Marit Emstad. The black-and-white mittens featuring an eight-point star are now a symbol of Norway, with souvenir shops everywhere selling countless variations.

MARIUS SWEATERS

Developed in the 1950s and, hence, comparatively new, the Marius pattern used for sweaters has, nevertheless, become the most knitted in all of Norway. And Marius sweaters are so thick, you'll often see people wearing them without a jacket even in winter. Traditionally hand knit of high-quality wool, these sweaters can also be expensive. If cared for properly, though, they will last for years, so think of them as investment pieces.

AKEVITT

If you want something with a little bite to put in your wooden Norwegian mug, pick up some akevitt (aquavit). Made from potatoes, Norway's traditional distilled spirit is 40% alcohol by volume and comes in clear (aged three to six months) or brown (aged up to several years) versions. There are also varieties infused with dill, cardamom, sweet cumin, and other herbs or spices. It's often served together with beer and generally accompanies authentic Norwegian dishes.

KVIKK LUNSJ

Kvikk Lunsj translates to "quick lunch," and this milk-chocolate bar made by the Norwegian company Freia is definitely a lunchbox staple. Think of it as the Norwegian version of Nestle's KitKat bar—only better, as any Norwegian will tell you! Kvikk Lunsj is available in literally any supermarket.

MACKEREL IN TOMATO SAUCE

Before it was Norway's oil capital, the western Norwegian city of Stavanger was the country's fish-canning center. The last cannery closed in 2008, but canned fish is still a staple of the Norwegian diet. Back in the day, the emphasis was on sardines, but these days, mackerel in tomato sauce is popular, particularly at lunch.

ROSEMALING CRAFTS

Rosemaling, the decorative folk painting popular in some of the country's most far-flung communities during the 19th century, has been revived today by artists interested in the country's artistic heritage. Wooden plates, bowls, and vases are popular items, and they will easily fit in your luggage.

What's New in Norway

OSLO'S WATERFRONT EXPANDS

Oslo is not a city that rests on its past accomplishments—even if you've visited in the past few years, the ever-changing waterfront and growing skyline reveal a city that is always moving forward. The Oslo Opera House, which opened in 2008, turned out to be marking the beginning of a brand-new era. The development of Aker Brygge and Tjuvholmen have transformed what was once a rusting shipyard into the city's hippest destination, either for an afternoon stroll along the waterfront promenade or an evening on the town in any of the dozens of trendy bars and restaurants. Formerly in a dowdy location in the city's eastern reaches, the new Munchmuseet (Munch Museum) is taking its rightful place not far from the Opera House. Also new on the scene is a strikingly modern Nasjonalmuseet (National Museum), also a stone's throw from the fjord.

TOURISM TURNS TO THE ARCTIC CIRCLE

Norway's tourism industry focused for many years on the southern half of the country, with most foreign visitors headed to the cities of Oslo and Bergen and the spectacular waterways of the western fjords. This was due, in a large part, to itineraries like "Norway in a Nutshell" that heavily promoted this part of the country. In recent years—and in a large part thanks to gorgeous photos posted on Instagram—northern Norway has rapidly made it on to many people's bucket lists because of the unspoiled wilderness and easy access to the northern lights above the Arctic Circle. While the Lofoten Islands used to be many a local's favorite summer holiday destination, the islands have seen an increase in international tourism that has proven difficult for this small archipelago to manage. Many visitors now turn away from the Lofoten Islands and towards nearby Senja, an island halfway between Tromsø and Lofoten, that is now also experiencing a rapid increase in tourism of its own, for better or worse.

THE NORTHERN LIGHTS ARE THE LATEST CRAZE

What most visitors to northern Norway have in common is a desire to admire the spectacular northern lights. (A BBC documentary featuring actor Joanna Lumley, called *Joanna Lumley in the Land of the Northern Lights*, kicked off the craze, and it shows no signs of slowing down.) Those who haven't seen the brilliant colors of the aurora borealis are dying to go north, while those who have already experienced them want to head back for more. Northern lights safaris where visitors pile into all-terrain vehicles to seek out the best vantage point can now be found all over the Arctic Circle. The main hub is in the northern city of Tromsø, but you'll also have plenty of options in Bodø, Alta, Kirkenes, and the Lofoten Islands. While these trips are a bit on the pricey side, they can pay off on overcast nights when operators transport you to the spots with the least amount of cloud cover. Before getting your hopes up, keep in mind that you should spend at least four nights above the Arctic Circle for the best chance at actually seeing this phenomenon. The northern lights are notoriously shy.

CRUISE SHIP TOURISM ANGERS LOCALS

Similarly to northern lights tourism, cruise ship travel has experienced a major boom in recent years. In the summer of 2019, Bergen had many days when 10,000 cruise ship passengers disembarked into the small city center. Nearby Stavanger planned to welcome 100 more cruise ships in 2020 than it did in 2019. In the popular western fjords region, the tiny waterfront village of

Flåm, gateway to the UNESCO World Heritage Site of Geirangerfjord, is experiencing up to 1 million visitors a year. With these huge numbers, it shouldn't come as a surprise that many locals have had enough. News reports of residents complaining about the crowds are becoming a summer tradition, and pollution from the ships is becoming more and more of a problem. The capital city of Oslo has already planned new regulations to allow cruise ships to use locally generated electricity while in port, enabling them to turn off their pollution-belching engines. Flåm has banned older ships with higher emission levels from visiting its port entirely.

INCREASED FOCUS ON CLIMATE CHANGE

All signs point to an eco-friendly shift in Norway's economy and tourism industry—not just because of pollution from the growing cruise industry, but also because of the unexpected challenges of drier and warmer summers across the entire country, including above the Arctic Circle. Climate change is very visible in Norway, with the weather becoming even more unpredictable. Sustainability has been embraced by many businesses (your hotel is likely to promote its eco-friendly practices) and welcomed into many Norwegian households little by little. Oslo is one of many cities pledging to become carbon neutral, whole communities turn out for annual beach-cleaning events, and school children raise their voices at "Fridays for the Future" demonstrations.

NEWER NORDIC CUISINE

The green movement has made its way into the country's restaurant scene. Traditionally a farming and fishing country, Norwegian cuisine has long been characterized by its meat, fish, and dairy products, though an ever-growing concern for the environment has prompted increased interest in vegetarianism and veganism. While Oslo is still where you'll find most of the country's organic restaurants, it's now much easier to find meat-free and gluten-free options as you travel outside of the capital. The New Nordic culinary movement, with its focus on locally sourced, seasonally available ingredients, has also left its mark in many Norwegian cities, so don't worry about finding the best Norwegian cod, salmon, or other seafood on the menu. But now you're likely to find healthier versions of the typical fish-and-potatoes meal that was a staple in many restaurants for so many years.

TOLL ROADS

One effort of the Norwegian government to reduce the country's carbon emission levels has involved setting up more toll stations in cities, much to the dismay of many locals. It's a much-discussed political topic, particularly in the run-up of municipal and county elections. Time will tell how many of the toll stations remain in the future, but the fact of the matter is that going for a road trip is going to cost you a bit more.

Planning a Road Trip in Norway

With a total coastline of 25,148 km (15,626 miles), Norway is a challenge for road-trippers. The breathtaking fjords in the western part of the country are an irresistible draw, but then there are the quaint fishing villages along the southern coast to consider, along with the rough-and-tumble islands up north above the Arctic Circle. And who wants to miss two of Europe's most fascinating cities, modern Oslo and historic Bergen? What's the best way to see them all in one thrilling trip?

WHERE TO START YOUR TRIP

Hitting the road in Norway requires narrowing down your trip to one or two regions so that you actually get to experience one of the most beautiful places on Earth. While it's possible to drive the entire length of the country, you'd be spending four or more days on the road just to get all the way north and back again. With rental cars in Norway, you're looking at hefty fees if you want to return the car in a different location. It's best to start in one easily accessible city and from there focus on a relatively compact area to explore in-depth—for instance, from Bergen you can easily reach the western fjords, and from Oslo the southern coast is a short drive away. For something a bit farther afield, Bodø makes a great gateway to the Lofoten Islands.

HOW MUCH TIME TO ALLOCATE

When planning an itinerary, you need to keep in mind Norway's rather conservative speed limits (topping out at 80 kph, or about 50 mph) and the fact that highways like you find back home are few and far between mean that you'll cover less ground than you might think each day. The country's curvy mountain roads and sinewy routes along the edges of fjords see to that. Instead of seeking out the fastest way between two points, you might look for the prettiest way to get there, often one of Norway's National Tourist Routes. Always allocate some extra time for several spontaneous photo ops. Many journeys require you to take a ferry or two to get to your destination, adding an extra 30 minutes to an hour to your trip.

WHEN TO GO

June to August have the most reliable weather of the year, which is why you'll encounter so many other road-trippers who've had the same great idea. Make sure to book your accommodations well in advance, especially near the most popular destinations. Spring is lovely, with little snow on the ground at lower elevations but plenty still in the mountains, making spring skiing a popular activity here. Fall sees fewer travelers on the road, but most ski resorts haven't yet opened for the season and many summer attractions have already closed. Winter is cold and dark, with precious few hours of sunlight, making it the hardest season for hitting the road.

KEEP IN MIND

Even if the forecast looks fine, roads can close without warning due to floods, avalanches, or icy conditions, potentially leaving you stuck in the middle of nowhere for a few hours. Also keep an eye out for wildlife, particularly moose and reindeer, but also the occasional sheep on the loose—particularly where you'd least expect them. And remember that fjord crossings add extra time to your itinerary. But if you plan carefully and watch out for changing conditions, a drive through Norway will be the trip of a lifetime.

What to Pack

A trip to Norway requires a little extra thought as you're packing. In a country with ever-changing weather conditions, it pays to dress in layers. This is true no matter what time of year, whether you're skiing in the towering peaks around Lillehammer in winter or driving along the coastal road near Kristiansand on the hottest day of summer.

CLOTHING

It's a common expression in Norway that there's no such thing as bad weather, just bad clothing. Do as the locals do and be prepared for the weather to change without warning. Your base layer should keep you warm and dry no matter what the weather conditions—lightweight athletic undergarments that wick away moisture in the summer and thermals in winter work well. Wool is generally the best material to keep you warm, and a woolen sweater or a fleece jacket will come in handy no matter what time of year. (That includes summer, when night-time temperatures often drop more than you'd expect.) Your outer layer should always be waterproof and windproof and well insulated, especially if you're headed into the mountains or to the northern coast. Don't forget a hat, scarf, and gloves if you're here in fall, winter, or spring. In summer, a good rain jacket and hiking pants pay off, and not just when trekking in the mountains. They're also a must-have item when visiting the rain-prone areas around Bergen and the western fjords.

One thing you won't have to worry about is dressing up, as Norwegians tend to favor casual clothing except on the most formal occasions. A sweater tends to be fine for most establishments, even in more formal restaurants. A stylish scarf or pashmina is a great way to dress up any outfit, and in Norway you'll fit right in.

FOOTWEAR

If you're planning to hit the trails in Norway, high-quality hiking shoes or boots are important for preventing serious injuries. Most trails, especially in the mountains, are characterized by bare rocks that can be slippery when wet, so you need soles with a good grip. While you might encounter many locals wearing rain boots in the cities, it's better to invest in a good pair of waterproof hiking shoes versatile enough to accompany you on any city explorations. It will save you a ton of space in your suitcase. If you're not hiking, a pair of comfortable walking shoes will do for most trips. Make sure they're waterproof, or you may end up with wet feet after a sudden deluge. Leave the heels at home, as they won't be much use either in the countryside or in the cities where you'll encounter lots of cobblestone streets.

EQUIPMENT

A waterproof daypack is a must no matter what time of year. In the summer, especially when you're headed to the mountains, bring insect repellent and plenty of sunscreen. (If the sun does decide to show, it's actually pretty strong and often burns travelers who are fooled by the gentle breezes and cool temperatures.) If you're going to travel by long-distance ferry or drive on curvy mountain roads, you might want to bring medication for motion sickness. Last but not least, a reusable water bottle goes a long way, especially since Norway's tap water isn't only free and healthy, but also tastes delicious.

Did You Know?

Central Norway's Jostedalsbreen National Park is home to the Jostedal Glacier, the largest in Europe.

Chapter 2

TRAVEL SMART NORWAY

Updated by
Barbara Woolsey

★ CAPITAL:
Oslo

POPULATION:
5.4 million

LANGUAGE:
Norwegian, Sami

$ CURRENCY:
Norwegian krone

COUNTRY CODE:
47

⚠ EMERGENCIES:
110 (fire), 112 (police), 113 (ambulance)

DRIVING:
On the right

ELECTRICITY:
230 volts; plugs have two round prongs

TIME:
6 hours ahead of New York

WEB RESOURCES:
www.visitnorway.com

AIRPORTS:
Oslo (OSL), Bergen (BGO), Kristiansand (KRS), Sandefjord (TRF), Stavanger (SVG), and Trondheim (TRD)

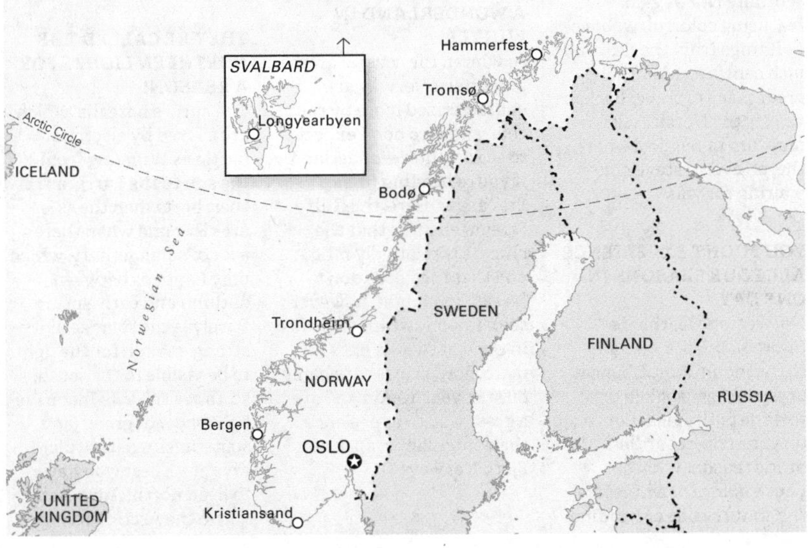

What You Need to Know Before You Go

Are you planning to see the northern lights or experience the beauty of the west coast? Will you be exploring touring Oslo or other Norwegian cities? Before visiting, there are a few things you should know to get the most out of your time in Norway.

OSLO IS THE LEAST QUINTESSENTIALLY NORWEGIAN PLACE—WITH A COUPLE OF EXCEPTIONS
Norway's capital has glitzy skyscrapers and an international feel. That being said, if you know where to look, the city also has some of the traditional architecture featured in those online images of the country's quaint villages. In central Oslo, the area around the two streets of Damstredet and Telthusbakken is picturesque and quintessentially Norwegian, featuring colorful, wooden buildings from the 18th and 19th centuries. Another great place to travel back in time is the Norsk Folkemuseum in Bygdøy, where there's even a stave church waiting for you.

YOU MIGHT EXPERIENCE ALL FOUR SEASONS IN ONE DAY
Norwegian weather is unpredictable, especially in the mountains. Chances are, you'll get soaked or feel the chill at least once on your trip, regardless of the season. Whether you're going for a hike in the countryside or heading out to sightsee in town, you'll need to plan ahead—which means layering up. For a base, choose clothes made of wicking fabric to pull moisture away from your skin, followed by a woolen or other knit layer for warmth and a water- and windproof jacket. Also, mind your footwear, especially if you're visiting the mountains, where hiking shoes with a good grip are a must on Norway's steep, rocky trails.

NOT ALL OF NORWAY IS A WONDERLAND IN WINTER
In winter, the coastal areas of western Norway are characterized more by rain than snow, so don't expect to see a winter wonderland if you're heading to, say, Stavanger. Here, the Gulf Stream ensures that the climate is relatively mild and that the fjords don't freeze. You might, however, see a few snowcapped peaks in the distance. What's more, fjord cruises are being offered year-round and are a great way to experience the winter landscapes of Fjord Norway.

EATING OUT IS EXPENSIVE
If you're visiting Norway on a budget, you might want to book accommodation with kitchen access, so that you can prepare most meals yourself. Otherwise plan on allocating between 150 and 400 NKr for dinner. Although lunch is usually the cheapest meal, there are huge differences between different restaurants, so it pays to shop around. Sandwiches and pastries at kiosks and cafés can cost as little as 30 NKr and as much as 100 NKr; in restaurants, the midday meal can be between 80 and 180 NKr with drinks. If you opt for the latter, ask about specials: most restaurants offer at least one cheap lunch dish, often a soup and/or salad, both with bread. Regardless of the meal, patronizing off-the-path establishments rather than those along main pedestrian streets and near big sights will save you money.

THEY'RE CALLED THE *NORTHERN LIGHTS* FOR A REASON!
The aurora borealis, which are caused by electrical particles traveling from the sun to the Earth, are at their best when the skies are clear and when there's a lot of solar activity, which only happens between autumn and early spring. Rarely is the solar activity strong enough for the lights to be visible in the south, so, to see the awe-inspiring light show of green (and sometimes even purple) rays at its best, you have to head north! Anywhere above the Arctic Circle

will do, but the farther north you go, the better. Popular viewing destinations include the cities of Tromsø and Alta, which have a great selection of northern lights safaris. The Arctic archipelago of Svalbard is also popular: set at 78° north, it offers the very best chance of seeing a spectacular show—if the weather behaves, that is.

SOME OF YOUR FOOD MIGHT COME FROM A TUBE

Caviar, mayonnaise, liver pâté, and more all come in tubes, which might seem strange to you but which Norwegians love because tube food has one major advantage: convenience! Sandwiches are a vital part of Norwegian culture, with most people bringing packed lunches to work or on weekend hikes and ski trips. Tube food doesn't require utensils to spread it, and if it's not exposed to air, it stays fresh for ages. At your hotel's breakfast buffet, don't be surprised to find an array of tubes containing variations of cream cheese, perhaps bacon or shrimp flavors. So, go ahead and squeeze!

YOU NEED TO KNOW WHEN (AND WHEN NOT) TO TALK TO STRANGERS

Although Norwegians are very nice and polite, they're generally reserved—perhaps even a bit shy. City dwellers in particular prefer to keep to themselves rather than make small talk with strangers. Indeed, you might notice that on public transit, all the window seats tend to be taken, with people preferring to stand instead of sitting next to someone they don't know (until the bus gets crowded and they no longer have a choice). The opposite is true in the mountains, though, where it's common practice to greet strangers and even to make conversation, perhaps while helping fellow hikers to find their way.

DON'T HESITATE TO VISIT IN WINTER

It might seem counter-intuitive, but winter is a great time to visit Norway. Lower temperatures aren't a problem if you layer properly, and it actually doesn't get as cold as you might expect. In addition, prices for airfare and hotels are lower than in the busier summer months. Although it's true that limited daylight can make road trips and outdoor sightseeing tricky, you just have to plan accordingly in places like Stavanger and Bergen, which have only six hours of daylight in December, and Arctic Tromsø, which sees just a handful of daylight hours and no sunlight whatsoever due to the phenomenon of the polar night. Regardless, Norway's vibrant cities are the perfect winter destinations, particularly if you're fond of spending time in cafés and museums. What's more, the blue twilight that illuminates Tromsø between November and January surely makes for a unique experience.

NO, YOU CAN'T SEE IT ALL IN A WEEK

You'll enjoy your time in Norway a lot more if you stick to a certain area rather than trying to cram the highlights of the north, west and south into a single trip. The northern Lofoten Islands alone require about a week to explore, as does the west coast with all its fjords, hiking trails, stave churches, and cities such as Stavanger, Bergen, and Ålesund. What's more, the country's 300,000 square km encompass mountains and fjords that make it hard to get from place to place quickly. (Although domestic flights travel to all the key destinations, they're rather expensive.) A slow travel approach is thus the way to go when visiting Norway. Pick a regional base and explore it and its environs by rental car or bus/train—you'll be surprised by how many hidden gems you'll find!

NORWAY ISN'T THE SAME AS SWEDEN

Obviously, not all Scandinavian countries are the same. Norwegians are proud of their distinct heritage and culture, and they have a friendly rivalry with their neighboring country. So, while in Norway, it's best to avoid praising Swedish companies and artists like IKEA and ABBA. Doing so will result in silence or even eye-rolls.

Getting Here and Around

Norway's government has made a considerable effort to improve public transportation in recent years. Buses, trains, and ferries are perfectly timed to make for seamless travel, meaning your train should arrive a short time before your ferry is set to depart. Hours vary according to the season, so always check with regional tourist offices for up-to-date departure times.

Air Travel

Gardermoen Airport, about 53 km (33 miles) northeast of Oslo, is by far the biggest airport in Norway. This will most likely be your point of entry into the country, but some long-distance flights also touch down at Bergen Airport, about 18 km (11 miles) south of the city. Other international airports are located in Kristiansand, Sandefjord, Stavanger, Tromsø, and Trondheim. Flights into these airport are usually from Norway or from Europe.

A flight from New York to Oslo takes about 8 hours. From London, a nonstop flight takes 1 3/4 hours. American, Delta, and United are among the major carriers with flights into Oslo. Low-cost carriers Norwegian Airlines and Scandinavian Airlines System (SAS) offer regular direct flights to Oslo from New York and Los Angeles, as well as connections through other cities in northern Europe. Budget carriers EasyJet and Ryanair also fly to Oslo from around Europe. If you're flying RyanAir to Oslo, you'll touch down in Torp Airport in Sandefjord, about 110 km (68 miles) south of the city.

Norwegian Airlines and SAS both offer a large selection of domestic flights, as does regional airline Widerøe, which flies to 43 destinations in Norway. Wideroe also does an Explore Norway ticket that lets you fly an unlimited number of times within Norway over a two-week period in July and August. (Some restrictions apply, such as flying more than four times between the same two cities.)

Avinor is the state-owned company that runs most of the country's airports. Its website has information on arrivals and departures, transfers, and parking.

AIRPORT TRANSFERS

Getting to Oslo or Bergen from their respective airports is usually hassle-free. Flybussen buses have frequent departures from the arrivals terminals to downtown destinations. Flytoget express trains have departures every 10 minutes bound for Oslo Central Station, and Bergen Light Rail leaves every 10 minutes for the downtown Byparken Station.

Boat and Ferry Travel

If you love traveling by boat, you won't lack choices in Norway. The jewel in the crown is the coastal steamer Hurtigruten, which has been sailing Norway's coast since 1893 and now calls at 34 ports along the country's western coastline. The full route, which the company calls "the world's most beautiful sea voyage," departs daily from Bergen in the southwest and heads north to Kirkenes, close to the Finnish and Russian borders. It then makes the return trip back to Bergen. The entire trip clocks in at 2,500 nautical miles and takes 12 days. There are cabins, a restaurant, a cafeteria, and shops on board. You can purchase tickets for the entire stretch or individual legs directly from Hurtigruten.

Boats can take you to other destinations as well. The most famous routes are through the many fjords of western Norway. These range from slow-moving ferries that give you time to take in all the scenery to speedboats that let you feel the wind in your hair. Other ferries travel from Oslo to the quaint coastal communities around Oslofjord, the massive waterway that extends all the way to the country's capital.

Don't be surprised if you happen to be driving along a magnificent fjord and the road ends at a ferry port. Taking a ferry isn't only fun, it's often necessary in Norway, as they remain an important means of transportation along the west coast and in the north. Car ferries and smaller passenger ferries connect communities large and small. During the summer, well-used crossings like Lauvvik–Lysebotn even develop queues due to limited car space, so be prepared to arrive early and wait. It's a good idea to book in advance for the tour ferries on scenic stretches like Geiranger–Hellesylt.

Several ferry lines connect Oslo with ports in the United Kingdom, Denmark, Sweden, and Germany. Color Line sails to Kiel, Germany, and to Hirtshals, Denmark. DFDS Scandinavian Seaways sails to Copenhagen via Helsingborg, Sweden.

Bus Travel

Buses can be an effective way to explore smaller regions within Norway. Most destinations are served by a number of local bus routes, many of them operated by the national railway subsidiary Nettbuss. Nor-Way Bussekspress, a chain of 50 Norwegian bus companies serving 500 destinations, can arrange any journey.

There are plenty of long-distance buses that can take you to most destinations around Norway, and most depart from the main bus terminal next to Oslo Central Station. But it's not the best option, because the excellent train system is just slightly more expensive and offers much greater coverage and shorter travel times.

Car Travel

Norway is a country made for drivers, especially those who don't mind long distances. Head for Norway's National Tourist Routes, which are 18 incredibly beautiful drives through the countryside. These routes cover more than 1,850 km (1,150 miles) and are found mostly along the coast. More than half are in and around the western fjords, and a road trip along the edge of these majestic waterways is a great way to experience the region. There are also great drives through the mountains (including the Rondane National Tourist Route) and in the Lofoten Islands (the Lofoten National Tourist Route).

The southern part of Norway is fairly compact—all major cities are about a day's drive from each other. The routes are straightforward, with a gentle curve along the southern coastline. The distances are felt on the way north, where Norway becomes narrower as it inches up to and beyond the Arctic Circle and hooks over Sweden and Finland to touch Russia. In a few remote areas, especially in northern Norway, road conditions can be unpredictable, so plan carefully for safety's sake. Should your road trip take you over the mountains in autumn, winter, or spring, make sure that the mountain pass you're heading to is actually open. Some high mountain roads are closed as early as October due to snow and do not open again until June.

Four-lane highways are the exception and are found only around major cities. Outside main routes, roads tend to be narrow and twisting, with only token

Getting Here and Around

guardrails. In summer, roads are always crowded. Norwegian roads are well marked with directional, distance, and informational signs. Driving is on the right. Yield to vehicles approaching from the right.

Norges Automobil-Forbund and Falck Global Assistance both provide roadside service.

CAR RENTALS

When driving a rental car you are generally responsible for any damage to or loss of the vehicle. Collision policies that car-rental companies sell for European rentals typically do not cover stolen vehicles. Before you rent—and purchase collision or theft coverage—see what coverage you already have under your own auto insurance policy and credit cards. The minimum driving age in Norway is 18, but some car-rental companies require that drivers under 25 pay a surcharge. Before you pick up a car in one city and leave it in another, ask about drop-off charges or one-way service fees, which can be substantial.

RULES OF THE ROAD

You can drive in Norway with your valid U.S., Canadian, U.K., Australian, or New Zealand driver's license. There are toll charges to enter cities like Oslo, Bergen, Trondheim, Stavanger, and Kristiansand. Most roads are monitored by radar and cameras in gray metal boxes. Signs warning of Automatic Traffic Monitoring are posted periodically along many roads. Keep your headlights on at all times and always wear seat belts.

Cruise Ship Travel

There's no better (or more comfortable) way to see Norway's highlights than on coastal cruises that dip into some of the country's famous fjords, the most breathtaking (and famous) of which are along Norway's west coast. Cruises usually include at least one excursion option in every port (usually a walk or a bus tour), so you'll get an overview of every port in which the ship calls and have options to do more extensive exploring or fun activities for a fee.

Most of the major cruise lines—Norwegian, of course, but also Celebrity, Princess, Holland America, and Costa Cruises—offer various trips along the coast. The most luxurious is probably Viking, which has a wide variety of cruises in and around Norway and Scandinavia, calling at ports from Bergen in the south to Honningsvåg in the north.

Train Travel

Norway has some of the most beautiful train rides in the world. Some of them are tourist routes—the Flåmsbana, for example, travels 20 km (12 miles) from Myrdal to Flåm so travelers can take in the view—but many are commercial routes that just happen to pass by stunning scenery. The best known is the Bergensbanen, traveling from Oslo to Bergen. Along the seven-hour journey you'll pass through 180 tunnels and barrel past lakes, streams and pass over the mountains at Finse Station.

Norway's longest rail route runs north to Trondheim, then extends onward as far as Fauske and Bodø. The southern line hugs the coast to Stavanger, while the stunning western line crosses Hardangervidda, the scenic plateau that lies between Oslo and Bergen. If you are traveling from south to north in Norway, flying is often a necessity: The southern city of Stavanger is as close to Rome as it is to the northern tip of Norway

Essentials

Dining

There is a lot to get excited about when it comes to Nordic cuisine. A new focus on local, sustainable ingredients, innovative cooking techniques, and forest produce that can't be found anywhere else make meals memorable. Roast reindeer, fresh-caught salmon and seafood, and a full spectrum of seasonal orchard fruits are just a few of the local delicacies to sample. And we're not just talking about Oslo—Bergen also has fine dining, along with unexpected places like Stavanger in the south and Trondheim in the north. The only problem is that high prices can make it difficult to truly indulge.

That said, Norwegians haven't left behind the food of their grandparents. Dishes people remember from their childhood—such as the mutton stew called *fårikål* or the lye-cured fish called lutefisk—are more popular than ever, especially around the holidays. Any eatery advertising its traditional foods will likely have these or other similar dishes on the menu. Pastries are popular here, so explore the local bakeries.

Kitchens in Norway usually open around noon and close by 10 or 11 pm. Many restaurants are closed on Sundays. The options dwindle when it comes to late-night grub, but there will usually be at least a kebab or pizza shop open even in smaller towns.

Many hotels offer a free breakfast, and it can range from pastries and coffee to a lavish buffet. It's not nearly as common, but a few hotels also offer afternoon tea or a light dinner included in your room rate. Almost all hotels have a restaurant on or near the premises.

DISCOUNTS AND DEALS

Many restaurants offer daily lunch specials, and even the upscale ones tend to offer special menus at bargain prices. You can also save by eating at kiosks or at bakeries rather than sit-down establishments. Ask for tap water—which is excellent in Norway—to avoid paying through the nose for bottled water.

PAYING

Most restaurants these days take credit cards, and often have a credit card machine they bring right to your table to settle up the bill. A 10% tip is the norm in restaurants—the 20% you're used to at home is considered too much. Before tipping, check your bill to make sure an automatic gratuity has not already been added.

RESERVATIONS AND DRESS

Always make a reservation at upscale restaurants, which are often booked weeks in advance. Norwegians are known for not being fussy when it comes to dress, so jeans, a nice shirt, and sneakers will suffice at most establishments. At fancier restaurants, people tend to look chic, so step up your game accordingly.

What It Costs in Norwegian Krone

	$	$$	$$$	$$$$
RESTAURANTS				
	Under NKr 125	NKr 125–NKr 250	NKr 251–NKr 350	over NKr 350

Health & Safety

Norway has one of the world's best health care systems. Pharmacies are everywhere, and you can also buy painkillers and other medications in supermarkets and gas stations. In cities there is usually one pharmacy that is open at night.

Essentials

The cool weather can fool you into thinking you don't need sunscreen, but the sun is often extremely strong. Ticks can be a problem in woodland areas, particularly along the southern coast from Oslo to Trondheim, so wear long pants and bright clothes so you can spot them right away. Ticks should be removed right away, and special tweezers are available at pharmacies.

Lodging

You'll find a wide variety of accommodation in Norway. Most at the upper end of the scale are regional and international chains, but you'll find a few independent and family-owned establishments in the mix. Guesthouses, pensions, and B&Bs tend to be very small and offer much more personal service.

Ice hotels and igloos, many of which are quite luxurious, are more and more popular during the winter months. Along the coast, you'll want to arrange for a stay in a fisherman's cabin. Local tourist offices keep lists of these accommodations and can help make arrangements. Norway also has more than 1,000 campsites where you can pitch a tent. The Norwegian Trekking Association maintains a few huts on hiking trails, both with service and without.

Budget-minded hostels are a mainstay, and not just for backpackers. Many also have rooms reserved for families.

FACILITIES

Most hotels serve continental breakfast, although some offer a better spread than others (if a good morning meal is a must for you, investigate before booking). Some also include a boxed lunch or a light dinner in their rates. Budget lodgings like guesthouses and hostels will usually have a selection of rooms with shared and private bathrooms.

PARKING

Some hotels offer free parking, while others charge an additional fee. Underground parking is your best option in winter, ensuring your car starts and you won't have to clean off ice and snow.

PRICES

Lodging prices fluctuate depending on the season. Accommodations tend to offer deals and discounts during the competitive summer season, and prices often go up in the winter during the northern lights. Prices are also typically higher on the weekends.

RESERVATIONS

Reservations are highly recommended in the summer high season as well as in winter due to the harsh weather conditions. Book well in advance so you can have your pick of rooms with scenic views.

What It Costs in Norwegian Krone

$	$$	$$$	$$$$
HOTELS			
under NKr 750	NKr 750–NKr 1250	NKr 1251–NKr 1900	over NKr 1900

Money

Norway is a non-EU country, and has opted to keep its currency when its neighbors converted to the euro. The Norwegian krone (crown) is written officially as NKr. Price tags are seldom marked this way, but instead read "Kr" followed by the amount, such as Kr 10.

Packing

Packing layers will keep you prepared for weather that can change swiftly. Rain showers can be sudden and unyielding, so a rain jacket or umbrella are handy, while in winter, long underwear, wool socks, and a windproof jacket help you withstand severe chills. If you're hiking, pack long-sleeved shirts and trousers to fend off ticks. The sun can be harsh, so sunscreen and a hat are must-haves. For dinner, bring smart casual attire (such as a button-down shirt).

Passports

All U.S. citizens, even infants, require a valid passport to enter the country for stays of up to three months. Your passport should be valid for at least three months beyond your planned trip or you may be denied entry.

Telephones

The country code for Norway is 47. There are no area codes—you must dial all eight digits of any phone number wherever you are. Telephone numbers that start with a 9 or 4 are usually mobile phones, and are considerably more expensive to call. Telephone numbers starting with the prefix 82 cost extra. Toll-free numbers begin with 800 or 810. Numbers beginning with 815 cost NKr 1 per call.

Tipping

Tipping is not all that common in Norway, since wages are much higher than in other parts of the world. That being said, a 10% tip is ordinary when dining out, especially at nicer establishments. Taxi drivers don't expect a tip, although rounding up by NKr 10 is appreciated.

When to Go

Low Season: Low season is generally from November to December, although northern Norway still gets a fair amount of traffic from aurora borealis–chasers during this period. Be forewarned that chilly winter conditions and darkness-filled days can make travel challenging, and there are roads and mountain passes which shut down from October to the end of May. Some attractions close during this time too.

Shoulder Season: Traveling in spring (April to May) and autumn (September to October) will allow you to beat the crowds and still enjoy milder weather. In the north you might even be able to catch the midnight sun in May or the northern lights in October. Accommodations don't drop their rates, though.

High Season: Throngs of visitors crowd Norway from June to August. Transportation and accommodations tend to be booked well in advance. The weather can be unpredictable, and it's best to pack layers packed for rain or shine. January to March can also be a popular time to visit for skiing, snowmobiling, and even dogsledding.

On the Calendar

January

Polar Night Half-Marathon. Held the first week of January, this half-marathon takes place in the Arctic city of Tromsø on a day when the sun never rises. If you're lucky you'll spot the northern lights. ☎ *77–67–33–63* 🌐 *https://www.msm.no/en/arrangement/morkertidslopet/*

Tromsø International Film Festival. The world's northernmost film festival screens national and international films on an outdoor screen during the third week of January. ☎ *477–70–864* 🌐 *https://tiff.no/en*

Northern Lights Festival. This classical music festival in Tromsø also features jazz, opera, and chamber music. ☎ *77–68–90–70* 🌐 *https://www.nordlys-festivalen.no/en/*

February

Sami People's Day. On February 6, Sami people across northern Norway, Swedish and Finnish Lapland, and parts of Russia celebrate with reindeer races and lasso-throwing championships. ☎ *77–67–33–63* 🌐 *https://www.msm.no/en/arrangement/samisk-uke/*

Holmenkollmarsjen. The so-called Holmenkoll March is a cross-country ski race just north of Oslo. ☎ *22–92–32–00* 🌐 *https://www.skiforeningen.no/kursogarrangement/holmenkollmarsjen/*

Ice Music Festival. All the instruments at this annual celebration are made of ice, including ice cellos and ice drums. 🌐 *https://www.icemusicfestivalnorway.no*

Røros Winter Fair. Held since 1854, this massive outdoor market welcomes 80 horse-drawn sleighs from around the region. ☎ *72–41–00–00* 🌐 *https://www.roros.no/en/roros-winter-fair/*

March

Borealis. Bergen's experimental music festival includes everything from art exhibitions to film screenings. ☎ *416–49–181* 🌐 *https://www.borealisfestival.no/en/*

Finnmarksløpet. This dogsled race travels across Norway's northernmost region. ☎ *900–81–519* 🌐 *https://www.finnmarkslopet.no/home/*

Birkebeinerrennet. This cross-country ski race starts in Rena and ends in Lillehammer. ☎ *41–77–29–00* 🌐 *https://birkebeiner.no/en/ski/birkebeinerrennet-54-km*

April

Sami Easter Festival. A cultural gathering in Karasjok where the Sami people enjoy ice-fishing competitions and reindeer races. 🌐 *http://www.samieasterfestival.com/home.html*

May

Norwegian National Day. On May 17, Norwegians celebrate their country with parades, hot dogs, and ice cream. 🌐 *https://www.visitnorway.com/typically-norwegian/norways-national-day/*

Bergen International Festival. A performing-arts extravaganza, the Bergen International Festival lasts two weeks. ☎ *55–21–06–30* 🌐 *https://www.fib.no/en/*

June

Midnight Sun Marathon. The Arctic city of Tromsø sponsors this run on a night when the sun doesn't set. ☎ *77–67–33–63* 🌐 *https://www.msm.no/en/arrangement/midnight-sun-marathon/*

Sankthansaften. On Saint John's Eve on June 23rd, Norwegians celebrate with bonfires all around the country, but with the most gusto in Ålesund. 🌐 *www.visitnorway.com/media/news-from-norway/sankthans-finds-norway-at-its-brightest-and-most-summery*

Festspillene Nord-Norge. Northern Norway's cultural festival takes place in Harstad. ☎ *77–04–12–30* 🌐 *https://festspillnn.no/en*

July

Moldejazz. The biggest jazz festival in Norway, Moldejazz takes place in the western fjords. ☎ *71–20–31–50* 🌐 *https://www.moldejazz.no/en/*

Riddu Riddu Riddu Riddu is an indigenous culture and music festival hosted in the Lyngen Alps near Tromsø in mid-July. ☎ *971–39–493* 🌐 *https://riddu.no/en*

Glad Mat. Norway's biggest street food festival draws 250,000 visitors to Stavanger. ☎ *51–87–45–78* 🌐 *www.gladmat.no*

August

Parkenfestivalen. Held in Bodø, this festival features national and international performers. ☎ *978–96–486* 🌐 *https://www.parkenfestivalen.no*

Norwegian International Film Festival. Held in Haugesund, this festival gives out the prestigious Amanda Award. 🌐 *https://filmfestivalen.no/en/*

September

NuArt. Norway's only street art festival is held in Stavanger. 🌐 *http://www.nuartfestival.no/home*

SMAK. This salute to northern Norwegian cuisine is held annually in Tromsø. 🌐 *https://www.smakfest.no/en/*

Oslo Marathon. Norway's biggest marathon welcomes 20,000 participants. ☎ *900–47–200* 🌐 *https://oslomaraton.no/en/*

October

Dark Season Blues Festival. The sun doesn't rise in Svalbard for four months, and locals like to say goodbye to the light with a bang. 🌐 *https://www.svalbard-blues.com*

November

Pepperkakebyen Bergen. Norway's biggest gingerbread village opens in Bergen. 🌐 *http://www.pepperkakebyen.org*

December

Christmas Market Røros. This UNESCO World Heritage Site becomes a winter wonderland. ☎ *72–41–00–00* 🌐 *https://julemarkedroros.no*

Helpful Norwegian Phrases

BASICS

Hello	Hei	Hi
Yes/No	Ja/Nei	yah/nay
Please	Vær så snill	vehr soh snihl
Thank you	Takk	tahk
You're welcome	Vær så god	vehr soh goh
I'm sorry (apology)	Unnskyld	ewn-shewl
Sorry (Excuse Me)	Unnskyld meg	ewn-shewl may
Good morning	God morgen	goo mohr-ghen
Good day	God dag	goo dahg
Good evening	God kveld	goo kvehl
Goodbye	Ha det	ha day
Mr. (Sir)	Herr	heh-r
Mrs.	Fru	frooh
Miss	Frøken	freh-kehn
Pleased to meet you	Hyggelig å møte deg	higg-eh-leeg oh mehte day
How are you?	Hvordan går det?	voor-dahn gohr deh

NUMBERS

one-half	halv	hahlv
one	en	ehn
two	to	too
three	tre	treh
four	fire	feer-eh
five	fem	fehm
six	seks	sehks
seven	sju	shew
eight	åtte	oh-teh
nine	ni	nee
ten	ti	tee
eleven	elleve	ehl-veh
twelve	tolv	toll
thirteen	tretten	treh-tehn
fourteen	fjorten	fjor-tehn
fifteen	femten	fehm-tehn
sixteen	seksten	sex-tehn
seventeen	sytten	soh-tehn
eighteen	atten	ah-tehn
nineteen	nitten	nee-tehn
twenty	tjue	sho-eh
twenty-one	tjue-en	sho-eh-ehn
thirty	tretti	treh-tee
fifty	femti	fehm-tee
sixty	seksti	sex-tee
seventy	sytti	soh-tee
eighty	åtti	oh-tee
ninety	nitti	nee-tee
one hundred	hundre	hoon-dreh
one thousand	tusen	too-sehn
one million	en million	ehn million

COLORS

black	svart	svahrt
blue	blå	bloh
brown	brun	broon
green	grønn	groehn
orange	oransje	o-ranch
red	rød	roehd
white	hvit	veet
yellow	gul	ghool

DAYS OF THE WEEK

Sunday	søndag	suhn-dahg
Monday	mandag	mahn-dahg
Tuesday	tirsdag	teesh-dahg
Wednesday	onsdag	ohns-dahg
Thursday	torsdag	toosh-dahg
Friday	fredag	freh-dahg
Saturday	lørdag	loor-dahg

MONTHS

January	januar	jah-noo-ahr
February	februar	feh-broo-ahr
March	mars	mars
April	april	ahp-reel
May	mai	mah-ee
June	juni	joon-ee
July	juli	jool-ee
August	august	auh-goost
September	september	sehpt-ehm-behr
October	oktober	octo-behr
November	november	no-vehm-behr
December	desember	deh-sehm-behr

USEFUL WORDS AND PHRASES

Do you speak English?	Snakker du engelsk?	snahk-kerr doo ehng-ehlsk
I don't speak [Language].	Jeg snakker ikke norsk	yay snahk-kerr ik-keh nohrshk
I don't understand.	Jeg forstår ikke	yay fosh-tawr ik-keh
I don't know.	Jeg vet ikke	yay veht ik-keh
I understand.	Jeg forstår	yay fosh-tawr
I'm American.	Jeg er amerikansk	Yay ahr ah-mehr-ee-kahnsk
I'm British.	Jeg er britisk	yay ahr bree-teesk
What's your name?	Hva heter du	vah heh-tehr doh
My name is ...	Jeg heter ...	yay heh-tehr ...
What time is it?	Hva er klokken?	vah ehr klohk-kehn
How?	Hvordan?	voor-dahn
When?	Når?	nohr
Yesterday	I går	ee gohr
Today	I dag	ee dahg

Tomorrow	I morgen	ee mohr-gehn
This morning	I dag tidlig	ee dahg teed-leeg
Afternoon	I ettermiddag	ee eh-tehr-medd-ahg
Tonight	I kveld	ee kveh-ld
What?	Hva?	vah
What is it?	Hva er det?	vah ehr deht
Why?	Hvorfor?	vor-fohr
Who?	Hvem?	vehm
Where is ...	Hvor er ...	voor ahr
... the train station?	... togstasjonen	toog-sta-shoon-ern
... the subway station?	... t-bane-stasjonen	teh-bahneh-sta-shoon-ern
... the bus stop?	... busstoppet	boos-stahp-eht
... the airport?	... flyplassen	fleeh-plahs-sehn
... the post office?	... postkontoret	pohsst-kohn-tohr-eht
... the bank?	... banken	bahnk-ehn
... the hotel?	... hotellet	ho-tehl-eht
... the museum?	... museet	muse-eht
... the hospital?	... sykehuset	seek-eh-hoos-eht
... the elevator?	... heisen	hi-sehn
Where are the restrooms?	Hvor er toalettet?	voor ahr too-ah-leht-eht
Here/there	Her / Der	hahr / dahr
Left/right	Venstre / Høyre	vehn-strej / hooy-reh
Is it near/far?	Er det langt?	ahr deht lah-nt
I'd like ...	Jeg vil ha ..	yay veel hah
... a room	.. et rom	eht rohm
... the key	.. nøkkelen	nooh-kehl-ehn
... a newspaper	.. en avis	ehn ah-vees
... a stamp	.. et frimerke	eht free-mehr-keh
I'd like to buy ...	Jeg vil kjøpe ..	yay veel chohpe
... a city map	.. et bykart	eht bee-kahrt
... a road map	.. et veikart	eht vay-kahrt
... a magaine	.. et blad	eht blah-d
... envelopes	.. konvolutter	con-voh-loot-ehr
... writing paper	.. papir	pah-peer
... a postcard	.. et postkort	eht post-kohrt
... a ticket	.. en billett	ehn beel-lehtt
How much is it?	Hva koster det?	vah koss-terr deh
It's expensive/ cheap	Er det dyrt/billig?	ahr deht deert / beeh-leeh
A little/a lot	Litt / Mye	leet / mee-eh
More/less	Mer / Mindre	mehr / meen-dreh
Enough/too (much)	Nok / for mye	nohk / fohr mee-eh
I am ill/sick	Jeg er syk	yay ehr seehk
Call a doctor	Ring en lege	ring ehn lay-geh
Help!	Hjelp!	yehlp
Stop!	Stopp!	stop

DINING OUT

A bottle of ...	En flaske med ..	ehn flah-skah meh
A cup of ...	En kopp med ..	ehn cuhp meh
A glass of ...	Et glass med ..	eht glass meh
Beer	Øl	ohl
Bill/check	Regning	rehg-neeng
Bread	Brød	brur
Breakfast	Frokost	frooh-kohst
Butter	Smør	smurr
Cocktail/aperitif	Cocktail	cocktail
Coffee	Kaffe	kah-feh
Dinner	Middag	meed-dahg
Fixed-price menu	Meny med fast pris	meh-new mehd fahst prees
Fork	Gaffel	gahff-erl
I am vegetarian/ I don't eat meat	Jeg er vegetarianer	yay ahr vegh-eh-tahr-ee-ah-nehr
I cannot eat ...	Jeg kan ikke spise ..	yay kahn eeh-keh speeh-seh
I'd like to order...	Jeg vil bestille ..	yay veel beh-steel-leh
Is service included?	Er tips inkludert?	ahr tips ink-loo-dehrt
I'm hungry/ thirsty	Jeg er sulten /tørst	yay ahr sool-tehn / tohrst
It's good/bad	Det er godt / ikke godt	deht ahr goh-t / eek-keh goh-t
It's hot/cold	Det er varmt / kaldt	deht ahr vahr-mt / kahl-t
Knife	Kniv	kneev
Lunch	Lunsj	lunch
Menu	Meny	meh-new
Napkin	Serviett	ssehr-vy-eht
Pepper	Pepper	pehp-pehr
Plate	Tallerken	tahl-ehr-kehn
Please give me ...	Kan jeg få ..	kahn yay foh
Salt	Salt	sahlt
Spoon	Skje	shay
Tea	Te	teh
Water	Vann	cahn
Wine	Vin	veen

Great Itineraries

The Best of the Fjords, 5 days

Western Norway's fjords are what most visitors come to see, and in five days it's more than possible to visit some of the world's most beautiful waterways.

Fly in: Bergen Airport, Flesland (BGO). **Fly out:** Bergen Airport, Flesland (BGO).

DAY 1: BERGEN

Fly into Bergen Airport and pick up the rental car you reserved in advance. On your way to Bergen, stop by the community of Fana to visit the **Fantoft Stave Church,** one of only 28 of its kind that still exist in Norway. It was damaged by fire in 1992, so what you see today is an exact replica of the original. Once in the city, head to the centrally located Hurtigruten Terminal to check in your car before exploring Bergen on foot. Wander around the **Fisketorget** fish market and **Bryggen,** the wharf lined with picture-postcard wooden buildings that evoke the city's maritime past. If you still have time before your evening departure on the Hurtigruten, visit the enormous fortress of **Bergenhus Festing** or take the seven-minute ride on the **Fløibanen** for views of the city from the top of Mt. Fløyen. The Hurtigruten leaves in the evening, but head back to the ship early to have dinner on board.

Logistics: 11 miles (20 minutes by car). Bergen's city center is easily walkable.

DAY 2: ÅLESUND AND GEIRANGER

After a night at sea and a substantial breakfast buffet, you arrive in Ålesund, giving you plenty of time to wander around the city and admire its treasure trove of Art Nouveau buildings. If you're particularly interested in this style of architecture, stop by the **Art Nouveau Center** to learn more about the great fire that destroyed the city in 1904 and how it led to the city's current style. If you're more interested in nature, embark on the hike up nearby **Mt. Aksla,** where you'll have a stunning view of the city and the surrounding fjords and mountains. Depart in the afternoon to make your way to Geiranger, driving along the serpentine road called the **Trollstigen,** one of the most beautiful of the Norwegian Tourist Routes. Along the way you'll pass the **Stigfossen** waterfall, one of many impressive photo ops on your way to Geiranger. Once you arrive, make sure to visit the viewpoint at **Flydalsjuvet** to take in the little village from above.

Logistics: 250-mile Hurtigruten trip from Bergen to Ålesund (12 hours by boat). 65 miles from Ålesund to Geiranger (3 hours by car).

DAY 3: GEIRANGERFJORD, LOEN, AND SOLVORN

Early in the morning, board the car ferry taking you from Geiranger to Hellesylt. The journey really is the destination in this case, as there's no better way to experience the stunning **Geirangerfjord** and its famous Seven Sisters waterfall than from the fjord itself. From Hellesylt, make your way to Loen, where you can find **Loen Skylift,** a cable car that brings you to the top of Mt. Hoven in just five minutes. It's one of the steepest cable cars in the world, and the view from the top certainly makes up for the equally steep ticket price. Overlooking beautiful **Jostedalsbreen National Park**, the top of Mt. Hoven also has some hiking trails you can explore before heading toward the Sognefjord. If you can, spend the night at Walaker Hotel in nearby Solvorn.

Logistics: 50 miles Geiranger to Hellesylt (1 hour by ferry). 38 miles from Hellesylt to Loen (1 hour by car). 91 miles from Loen to Solvorn (2 hours by car).

DAY 4: LÆRDAL, AURLAND, AND EIDFJORD

Take the ferry from Mannheller to Fodnes and begin the short drive to **Lærdal,** a picturesque little village of wooden houses from the 18th and 19th century. A short drive from Lærdal you'll also find **Borgund Stave Church**. Built in 1180, this church was used until 1868 and now serves as a museum where you can learn more about the state of Norway's traditional houses of worship. Afterward, continue your journey to **Aurland** by means of the **Lærdalstunnel,** one of the longest road tunnels in the world. In Aurland, don't miss visiting the viewing platform of **Stegastein,** where you'll have a sky-high view of Aurlandsfjord. Continue your way to the Eidsfjord past the **Skjervsfossen,** an impressive set of waterfalls a two-minute drive from the main road to Eidfjord between the two towns of Voss and Granvin.

Logistics: 2 miles Mannheller to Fodnes (30 minutes by ferry). 23 miles Fodnes to Borgund (30 minutes by car). 29 miles Borgund to Aurland (45 minutes by car). 78 miles Aurland to Eidfjord (2 hours by car).

DAY 5: BERGEN

It's time to head back to Bergen to catch your flight back home. Take the slightly longer Norwegian Tourist Route via **Steinsdalsfossen,** a waterfall about halfway along the way where you'll find a walking path that leads you behind the water.

Logistics: 94 miles from Eidfjord to Bergen Airport (3 hours by car).

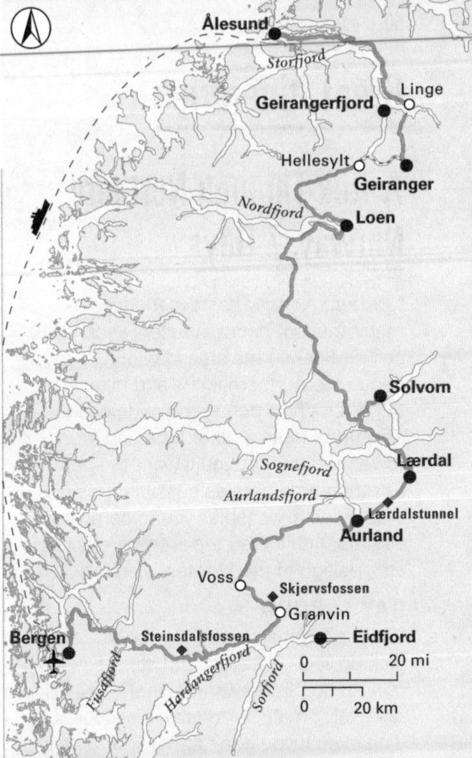

Tips

Due to limited daylight hours and closed roads, this itinerary is best taken between late spring and early autumn.

Especially when traveling during the summer, you should reserve accommodations, car rentals, and, where possible, ferry crossings in advance

The port-to-port option with Hurtigruten can only be prebooked via phone or with a travel agency. Booking this journey online is currently only possible on the Norwegian website.

Great Itineraries

A Trek Through Northern Norway, 7 Days

Northern Norway has experienced a major tourism boom in recent years as people flock to the area in winter to experience the northern lights and in summer to go for a hike during the midnight sun, as it takes quite a bit of time and money to venture this far, you'll want to spend as much time here as possible. This one-week itinerary enables you to combine a city trip with a road trip in the Arctic Circle archipelago of the Lofoten Islands.

DAY 1: BODØ

Catch a flight to Bodø, where you can pick up your rental car and start exploring this Arctic Circle destination. The city is relatively small, so you can discover quite a bit even if you don't arrive first thing in the morning. If you have plenty of time and stamina, go for a hike up the Sherpa Staircase to **Mt. Keiservarden** in order to admire the city and its surroundings from above. Don't want to use all your hiking energy on your first day? Head to the **Norwegian Aviation Museum** to get a glimpse into the country's history in the skies. In the late afternoon or early evening, wander along the pier and around the city center to discover some of Bodø's colorful murals, and make sure to stop by Craig Alibone for the city's finest chocolate pralines.

Logistics: 1 mile from Bodø Airport to the city center (5 minutes by car). The city center is very walkable. Parking is available next to the Norwegian Aviation Museum and at Rønvikfjellet for the hike to Keiservarden.

DAY 2: AROUND BODØ

While Bodø is a picturesque city, on your second day it's time to explore the city's surroundings. Head to **Mjelle**, a sandy beach north of Bodø, which makes for a stunning place to visit regardless of the weather conditions. Farther north and after a short ferry ride, you'll find **Kjerringøy,** a peninsula bordering Sjunkhatten National Park where you can find famous Kjerringøy Trading Post. Fish trading has dominated the area around Bodø since the 19th century, and the old trading post is the perfect place to spend the afternoon.

Logistics: 14 miles from Bodø to Mjelle (30 minutes by car). 15 miles from Mjelle to Kjerringøy (1 hour by car, plus ferry ride).

DAY 3: SALTSTRAUMEN AND SVOLVÆR

Before heading to the Lofoten Islands, make sure to head to **Saltstraumen,** one of the world's strongest tidal currents. Twice a day, whenever the tide goes in or out, this current creates whirlpools in the narrow strait that divides mainland Norway from the island of Straumøya. If you're lucky with the timing, Saltstraumen will put on a show you're unlikely to forget. In the afternoon, it's time to head to the Lofoten Islands. You can either bring your rental car on the Hurtigruten cruise ship to **Svolvær** (journey takes six hours), or you can leave your car and hop on the on the three-hour express boat to Svolvær and rent another car there.

Logistics: 17 miles from Bodø to Saltstraumen (30 minutes by car). 155 miles from Bodø to Svolvær (3 hours by express boat or 6 hours by ferry).

DAY 4: HENNINGSVÆR AND NUSFJORD

After a stroll around the small town of Svolvær, it's time to hit the road and explore the islands of Austvågøy and Vestvågøy on the fourth day of your northern Norway adventure. Make sure to first head to **Henningsvær,** a

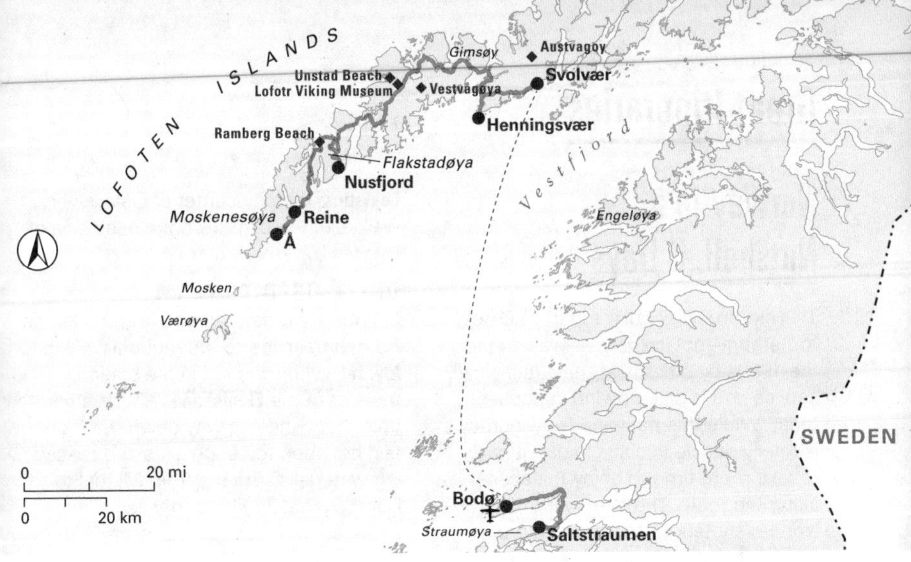

picturesque little village that's most known for its soccer field right next to the ocean, but which also has a contemporary art museum called the Kaviar Factory. Driving south along the E10, stop by **Lofotr Viking Museum** to learn all about the age of the Vikings and why they left for Iceland and Greenland back in the day. Before heading farther south later in the afternoon, head to Unstad Beach to experience the best local spot or surfing. Afterwards, drive to picturesque **Nusfjord,** a little fishing village that couldn't be more Norwegian.

Logistics: 15.5 miles Svolvær to Henningsvær (30 minutes by car). 30 miles Henningsvær to Lofotr Viking Museum (1 hour by car). 7 miles Lofotr Viking Museum to Unstad Beach (15 minutes by car). 19 miles Unstad Beach to Nusfjord (45 minutes by car).

DAY 5: REINE

Your fifth day in the Lofoten Islands will guarantee you scenic views. First off, head over to **Ramberg Beach** for a view of the half-mile-long beach with views for days. Stop by Ramberg Gjestegård for traditional Norwegian cuisine for lunch. In the afternoon, drive on to **Reine,** perhaps the most photographed villages in all of the Lofoten Islands.

Logistics: 9 miles Nusfjord to Ramberg Beach (15 minutes by car). 16 miles Ramberg to Reine (30 minutes by car).

DAY 6: Å

You can't leave the Lofoten Islands without going for at least one hike. While most people hike **Reinebringen** when in Reine, the trail is so popular that it had to be closed for maintenance in 2019. Head to the lesser-known **Trolldalsvatnet** trail, near the briefly mentioned village of **Å.** At a total length of 5 miles, this fairly easy trail will lead you to a lake with stunning views of the mountains on either side. Explore Å before heading back to Svolvær in the afternoon to return your rental car in order to take the express boat early the next morning, or board the Hurtigruten cruise to Bodø.

Logistics: 4 miles Reine to Å (10 minutes by car). 81 miles Å to Svolvær (2 1/2 hours by car).

DAY 7: BODØ

Take the express boat from Svolvær back to Bodø and catch your flight home from Bodø in the afternoon.

Great Itineraries

Norway in a Nutshell, 6 Days

This extremely popular trip from Oslo to Bergen—or vice versa—was created the 1960s by officials at the national rail service and is still growing in popularity today. While this train-and-ferry journey is totally doable in a single day, it pays to take more time to enjoy the scenery along the route. The five-hour trip across Norway's interior is considered one of the most spectacular train rides in the world. You can join an organized tour following this route, but there's no part of the trip that can't easily be done on your own.

DAY 1 & 2: OSLO

Chances are you'll fly into Oslo Airport on an international flight, which makes the city a great starting point for your Norway in a Nutshell adventure. While the city is quite compact and you could, in theory, see all main sights in a day, don't rush but rather take it all in, especially if this is your first time in Norway. Spend your first day in the Sentrum exploring the rooftop of the gleaming white **Opera House,** then stop at some of the newly unveiled museums, including the **Nasjonalmuseet** and the **Munchmuseet.** In the afternoon you can wander along the waterfront to the neighborhoods of Aker Brygge and Tjuvholmen, where you'll find dozens of options for dinner. On your second day, explore the fortress of **Akershus Festning** and the opulent castle of **Slottet** before visiting the peninsula of Bygdøy with its many museums, including the **Norsk Folkemuseum** and the **Viking Ship Museum.** For dinner consider the neighborhood of Grünerlokka, which is a favorite destination for locals.

Logistics: The city center of Oslo is very walkable. You can reach the peninsula of Bygdøy by ferry or bus.

DAY 3: OSLO TO FLÅM

On your third day, start early and take the Bergen train line to the mountain village **Myrdal**. When you reach the station, transfer to the **Flåmsbana** railway, a tiny train that winds its way down the mountain between towering cliffs and cascading waterfalls. The trip from Myrdal to **Flåm** covers 12 miles and takes a little under an hour. You should reach Flåm by late afternoon, giving you enough time to relax in an outdoor café, do a little souvenir shopping, and perhaps visit the **Flåmsbanemuseet,** which gives you a look at how the railway was constructed. Stay overnight in Flåm or one of the nearby villages

Logistics: You can easily explore Flåm on foot.

DAY 4: FLÅM TO VOSS

This leg of your journey begins with a boat trip from Flåm through Aurlandsfjord and into the UNESCO World Heritage Site of Nærøyfjord, the narrowest fjord in Europe. Both inlets are part of the larger Sognefjord, one of Norway's most famous fjords and, at 127 miles from end to end, its longest. The ride lasts two hours and ends at Gudvangen, at which point you board a bus for the one-hour trip to Voss along the old Stalheimskleivane Road with its dramatic hairpin bends. If you can, try to book your stay at the 18th-century Stalheim Hotel, about 22 miles outside Voss.

Logistics: You can easily explore Voss on foot.

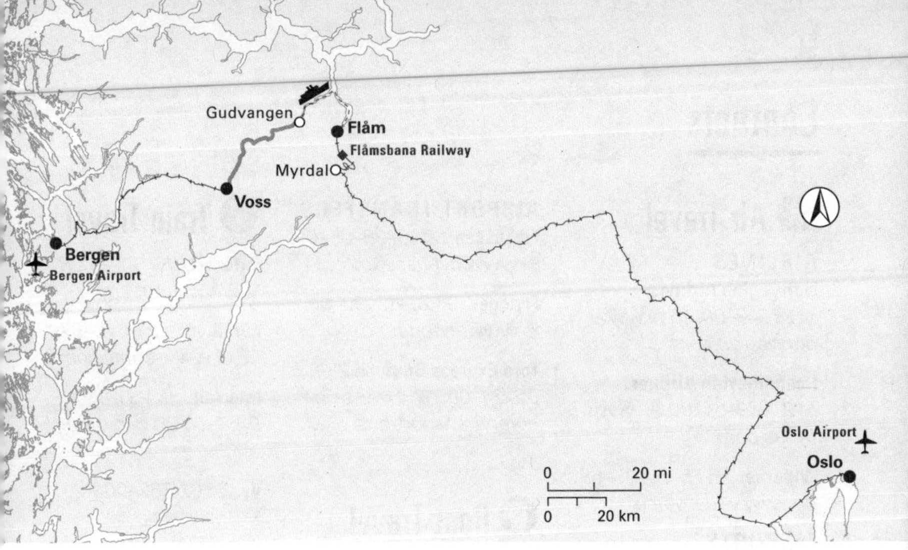

DAY 5 & 6: BERGEN

From Voss, the train to Bergen takes one hour. When you get to Bergen, check into your hotel and head to **Bryggen** to explore the old wharf where some of the city's oldest and best-preserved buildings are found, followed by some souvenir shopping and dinner down by the fish market. Spend your sixth day exploring more of Bergen, starting with a ride on the **Fløibanen** funicular and a walk at the top of **Mt. Fløyen,** where you have a magnificent view of the town from above. If you still have time afterwards, visit the **Edvard Greig Museum** south of the city. Head back to Oslo by train or plane, or see if you can find an outbound flight home that departs from Bergen.

Logistics: The city center of Bergen can easily be explored on foot.

Tips

Especially during peak season in summer, booking your own train and ferry tickets can be significantly cheaper than opting for a tour package.

Train tickets between Oslo and Bergen are usually cheapest about three months in advance.

When traveling in winter, remember that you're only going to get six or seven hours of daylight.

Contacts

Air Travel

AIRLINES

Norwegian Airlines. ☎ *21–49–00–15* 🌐 *www.norwegian.com*

Scandinavian Airlines. ☎ *21–89–64–00* 🌐 *www.flysas.com*

Widerøe. ☎ *75–80–35–68* 🌐 *www.wideroe.no*

AIRPORTS

Avinor. ☎ *06/703–0000* 🌐 *www.avinor.no*

Bergen Airport. ☎ *67–03–15–55* 🌐 *www.airport-bergen.com*

Kristiansand Airport. ☎ *67–03–03–30* 🌐 *avinor.no/en/airport/kristiansand-airport*

Oslo Gardermoen Airport. ☎ *64–81–20–00* 🌐 *www.oslo-airport.com*

Sandefjord Airport. ☎ *33–42–70-00* 🌐 *www.torp.no/en*

Stavanger Airport. ☎ *67–03–10–00* 🌐 *avinor.no/en/airport/stavanger-airport*

Tromsø Airport. ☎ *67–03–46–20* 🌐 *avinor.no/en/airport/tromso-airport*

Trondheim Airport. ☎ *67–03–25–00* 🌐 *avinor.no/en/airport/trondheim-airport*

Kristiansand, Sandefjord, Tromsø, and Trondheim

AIRPORT TRANSFERS

Flybussen. ☎ *48–28–05–00* 🌐 *www.flybussen.no*

Flytoget. ☎ *23–15–90–00* 🌐 *www.flytoget.no*

Torp Express Buss. ☎ *23–00–24–00* 🌐 *www. torp.no/en/transport/bus*

Boat Travel

Colorline. ☎ *99–56–19–00* 🌐 *wwww.colorline.com/denmark-norway*

DFDS Scandinavian Seaways. ☎ *23–10–68–00* 🌐 *wwww.dfds.no*

Hurtigruten. ☎ *810–30–000* 🌐 *www.hurtigruten.com*

Bus Travel

Nettbuss. ☎ *04/070–5070* 🌐 *www.nettbuss.no*

Nor-Way Bussekspress. ☎ *02/231–3150* 🌐 *www.nor-way.no*

Lavprisekspressen. ☎ *06/798–0480* 🌐 *www.lavprisekspressen.no*

Car Travel

Falck Global Assistance. ☎ *21–49–24–15* 🌐 *www.falck.no*

Norges Automobil-Forbund. ☎ *23–32–31–00* 🌐 *www.naf.no*

Train Travel

Entur. ☎ *06/127–9088* 🌐 *www.entur.org*

Eurail. ☎ *+31/640–5793–58* 🌐 *www.eurail.com*

Interrail. ☎ *+31/880–0161–05* 🌐 *www.interrail.eu*

Vy. ☎ *02/362–0000* 🌐 *www.vy.no*

U.S. Embassy/ Consulate

Royal Norwegian Embassy. ✉ *2900 K St N.W, Ste. 500, Washington, D.C.* ☎ *+1202/333–6000* 🌐 *www.norway.no/en/usa*

U.S. Embassy in Norway. ✉ *Morgedalsvegen 36* ☎ *2/130–8540* 🌐 *www.no.usembassy.gov*

Visitor Information

Fjord Norway. 🌐 *www.fjordnorway.com*

Norway National Parks. 🌐 *www.nasjonalparkriket.no/en*

Visit Norway. 🌐 *www.visitnorway.com*

Chapter 3

OSLO

3

Updated by
Alexandra Pereira

Sights	Restaurants	Hotels	Shopping	Nightlife
★★★★★	★★★★☆	★★★☆☆	★★★☆☆	★★★☆☆

WELCOME TO OSLO

TOP REASONS TO GO

★ **Something to scream about:** From Munch to Ibsen, art and literature are deeply entrenched in the culture of Oslo.

★ **From Old Norse to New Nordic:** The dining scene has exploded with chefs rediscovering old recipes and creating new ones.

★ **Take an urban nature walk:** Explore the forests, the fjords, and unparalleled vistas without ever leaving the capital.

★ **Set sail with the Vikings:** Take a look at the impressive ships these early travelers used to explore much of the region.

★ **See what sustainability looks like:** Oslo was crowned Europe's Eco Capital, and its hotels and restaurants are leading the way.

1 **Sentrum.** Oslo is surprisingly compact, with almost all of its most famous sights concentrated in a walkable center. The main street of Karl Johans Gate forms the backbone of downtown Oslo.

2 **Kvadraturen, Aker Brygge, and Tjuvholmen.** Kvadraturen is the oldest part of Oslo still standing. Aker Brygge, a lavishly redeveloped shipyard, has become a summertime destination. Tjuvholmen is popular with locals wanting to stick their toes in the water.

3 **Bygdøy.** Several of Oslo's best-known sights are found on this peninsula. This is where you'll find the royal family's former and current summer residences.

4 **Frogner and Majorstuen.** These stylish neighborhoods combine classic Scandinavian elegance with contemporary European chic.

5 **Holmenkollen.** With what is perhaps the best view of the city, this distant neighborhood has the famous ski jump and miles of ski trails.

6 **Grünerløkka.** This colorful neighborhood draws locals looking for quirky performance spaces, international restaurants, and hidden-away bars.

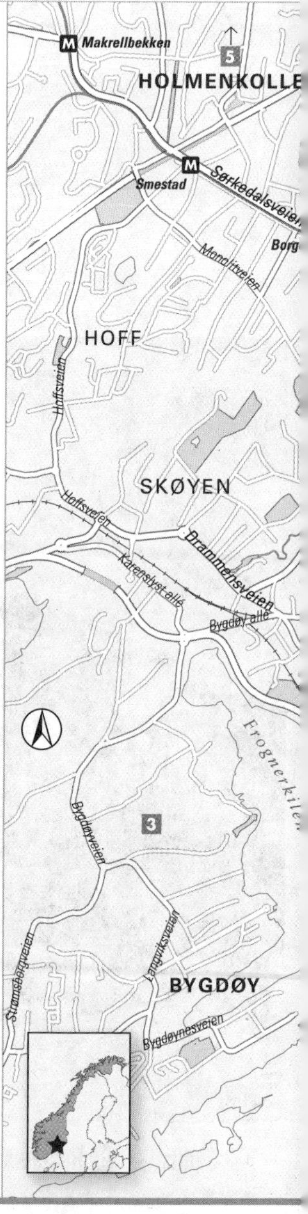

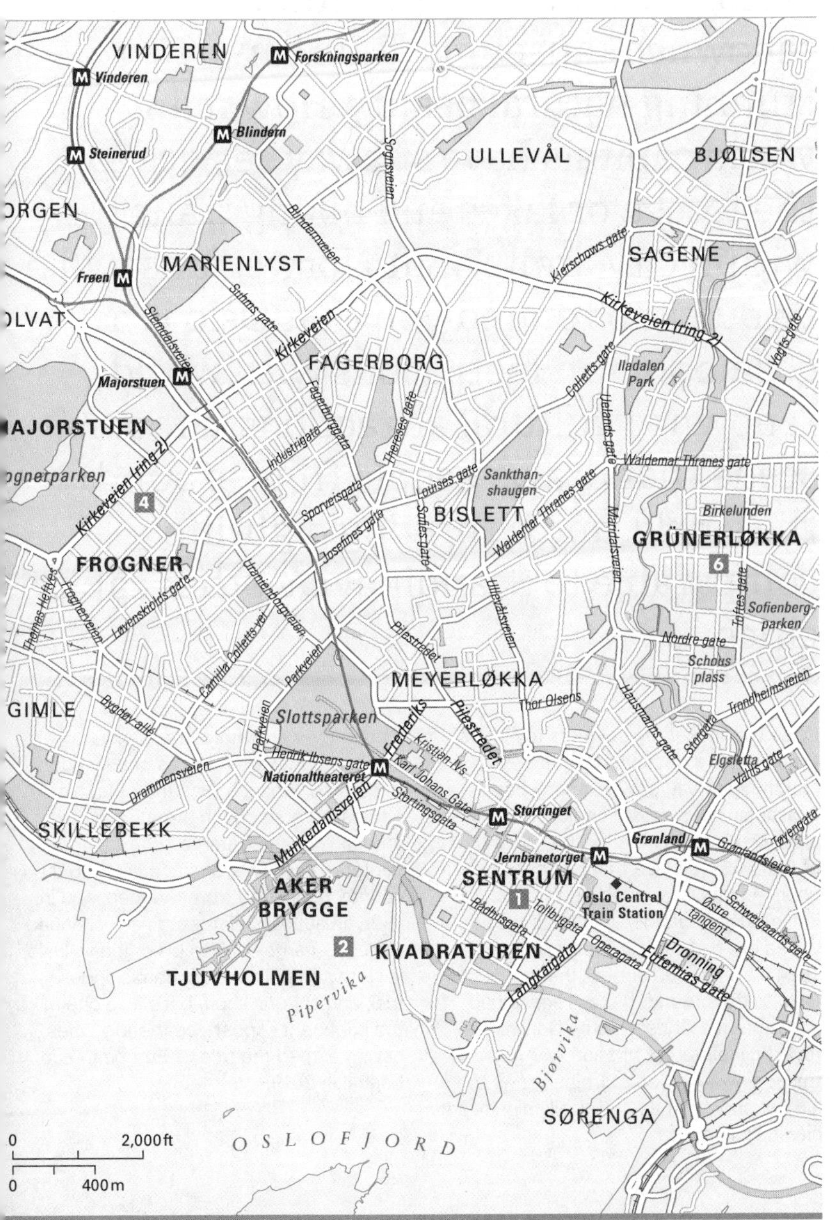

VINDEREN
Vinderen
Forskningsparken
Blindern
Steinerud
ULLEVÅL
BJØLSEN
SAGENE
MARIENLYST
Frøen
Majorstuen
MAJORSTUEN
FAGERBORG
Kirkeveien
Kirkeveien (ring 2)
Iladalen Park
Sankthan-shaugen
BISLETT
FROGNER
GRÜNERLØKKA
Birkelunden
Sofienberg-parken
Schous plass
MEYERLØKKA
GIMLE
Slottsparken
Nationaltheatret
Stortinget
Grønland
Jernbanetorget
SKILLEBEKK
AKER BRYGGE
SENTRUM
Oslo Central Train Station
KVADRATUREN
TJUVHOLMEN
Pipervika
Bjørvika
SØRENGA
OSLOFJORD
0
2,000 ft
0
400 m

What sets Oslo apart from other European cities is not so much its cultural traditions or its internationally renowned museums as its simply stunning natural beauty. How many world capitals have subway service to the forest, or lakes and hiking trails within city limits? But Norwegians will be quick to remind you that Oslo is a cosmopolitan metropolis with world-renowned cultural attractions, a foodie scene that draws people from around the world, and a thriving nightlife comparable to Scandinavia's other capital cities.

Once overlooked by travelers to Norway, Oslo is now a destination in its own right and the gateway to what many believe is Scandinavia's most scenic land. That's just one more change for this town of 670,000—a place that has become good at survival and rebirth throughout its 1,000-year history. In 1348 a plague wiped out half the city's population. In 1624 a fire burned almost the whole of Oslo to the ground. It was redesigned and renamed Christiania by Denmark's royal builder, King Christian IV. After that it slowly gained prominence as the largest and most economically significant city in Norway.

During the mid-19th century, Norway and Sweden were ruled as one kingdom, under Karl Johan. It was then that his namesake grand main street was built, and Karl Johans Gate has been at the center of city life ever since. In 1905 the country separated from Sweden, and in 1925 an act of Parliament finally changed the city's name back to Oslo. Today, Oslo is Norway's political, economic, industrial, and cultural capital. It's also one of the continent's most eco-friendly cities, having earned the title of European Eco Capital in 2019.

Planning

When to Go

You can visit Oslo throughout the year, with locals heading out of doors no matter what the season. Think there's not much to do in a Scandinavian city in the winter? An urban sauna culture has taken the capital by storm, with locals taking dips in the icy waters of the fjord followed by sweats in floating pods. Others take advantage of more traditional winter activities, from ice skating in the city center to tobogganing down the nearby hills. Temperatures can dip to-15°C (5°F), and daylight hours are scarce, so dress warmly and get an early start. And while this most northern of Europe's capitals is geared toward outdoors activities, it caters to indoors types, too.

May through September are the most pleasant months, with the warmest weather coming in a short burst between June and August. Temperatures can sometimes rise to 30°C (86°F), and when this rarity occurs locals embrace it, flocking fjordside to the beaches. Many also escape to their summer houses farther down the fjord or in the mountains. Those who stay take advantage of summertime celebrations like August's five-day music festival Øyafestivalen.

Getting Here and Around

AIR TRAVEL

About 45 km (28 miles) north of the city, Oslo Airport is most likely your first impression of Norway. Luckily it has huge windows with excellent views of the landscape and a state-of-the-art weather system that has drastically decreased the number of delayed flights.

Oslo Airport is a 50-minute drive to the city center along the E6. There is a taxi queue at the front of the airport if you have a lot of luggage or are nervous about negotiating public transport. If you're traveling light, Flybussen buses depart every 30 minutes, one route headed to the center of the city and the other following the ring roads. A quicker way to get downtown is the Flytoget express train, which has departures every 10 minutes to Oslo Central Station. Uber is currently not available in Oslo.

If you're flying RyanAir, you'll touch down in Torp Airport in Sandefjord, about 110 km (68 miles) south of Oslo. Torp Express Buss departs approximately 35 minutes after every arrival. They take almost two hours to reach the city center.

CONTACTS Flybussen. ☎ *21300* 🌐 *www.flybussen.no.* **Flytoget.** ☎ *23–15–90–00* 🌐 *flytoget.no/en.* **Oslo Airport Taxi.** ☎ *23–23–23–23.* **Torp Express Buss.** ☎ *23–00–24–00* 🌐 *www.torp.no/en/transport/bus.*

BOAT TRAVEL

Several ferry lines connect Oslo with ports in the United Kingdom, Denmark, Sweden, and Germany. Color Line sails to Kiel, Germany, and to Hirtshals, Denmark. DFDS Scandinavian Seaways sails to Copenhagen via Helsingborg, Sweden; and Stena Line to Frederikshavn, Denmark.

Small boats and ferries are common in the capital's waters, predominantly as a tourist activity. A ferry to Hovedøya and other islands in the harbor leaves from Aker Brygge. These are great spots for picnics and short hikes. From April through September, ferries run between Aker Brygge and the peninsula of Bygdøy, where many of Oslo's major museums are located.

CONTACTS. Color Line. ☎ *45/99–56–19–00* 🌐 *www.colorline.com/denmark-norway.* **DFDS Scandinavian Seaways.** ☎ *23–10–68–00* 🌐 *www.dfds.no.*

BUS TRAVEL

There are some handy buses, trams, and trains traversing the city. About 50 bus lines, including 16 night buses that run on weekends, serve the city. Most stop at Jernbanetorget opposite Oslo Central Station. The most convenient way to use the system is buying an Oslo Pass (from NKr 445).

CAR TRAVEL

Driving in a city as compact and walkable as Oslo isn't worth the effort, unless you've decided to pick up a car for a longer journey through the countryside. All streets and roads leading into Oslo have tollbooths that form an "electronic ring." The price is NKr 21, or NKr 28 during rush hour. If you have the correct change, drive through one of the lanes marked "Mynt." If you don't, use the "Manuell" lane.

SUBWAY TRAVEL

The Oslo subway system—which you'll see marked with a Blue letter T within a circle and hear referred to as the Oslo Tunnelbane, Oslo T-bane, or just T-banen—has five lines covering 101 stations. In Sentrum, all five lines converge, so you can take any train to downtown stations like Nationaltheatret, Stortinget, Jernbanetorget, and Grønland. All trains also head to Majorstuen, where you can walk to the sculpture garden at Vigeland Park. Line 1 is popular with travelers because it goes to Holmenkollen ski jump. Other than these destinations, the Metro bypasses most neighborhoods popular with tourists. Buses and trams, or your own two feet, are a better option.

TAXI TRAVEL

Taxis tend to be extortionately priced in Oslo, but are easy to call or hail on the street.

CONTACTS OsloTaxi. ☎ *02323* 🌐 *www.oslotaxi.no.*

TRAIN TRAVEL

Norway's state railway, newly rechristened Vy, has two train stations downtown: one at Oslo Sentralstasjon and one at Nationaltheatret. Long-distance domestic and international trains use Sentralstasjon, while commuter trains use Nationaltheatret. Cars reserved for monthly pass holders are marked with a large black "M" on a yellow circle. Trains marked "C," or InterCity, offer such upgraded services as breakfast and business-class seats for an added fee.

CONTACTS Vy. 🌐 *www.vy.no.*

Restaurants

With the rise of ecologically conscious eating habits and an increasingly diverse population, Oslo has a dining scene that's rapidly expanding beyond classic dishes using seafood and game. A few years after New Nordic cuisine emerged on the world stage, the embrace of local meats and cheeses and organic produce remains strong. In fact, there's a good chance that your chef is using ingredients that came from a neighborhood farm or even a greenhouse perched on the roof of the restaurant. But all this doesn't mean that restaurants are limited to regionally focused fare. There's an unusually wide range of European, African, Asian, and Middle Eastern eateries popping up around the city. If you can't decide which sounds the best, try a little bit of everything at one of the city's many multicultural food halls. Vegetarians and vegans find lots of options here, with a significant number of high-end establishments offering meat-free tasting menus. As the city strives to be one of the most proudly sustainable in the world, there are even restaurants serving entire menus made up of food that otherwise would have gone into the waste bin. *Restaurant reviews have been shortened. For full information, visit Fodors.com.*

What It Costs in Norwegian Krone

	$	$$	$$$	$$$$
RESTAURANTS	under NKr 125	NKr 125–NKr 250	NKr 251–NKr 350	over NKr 350

Hotels

An impressive number of boutique and design hotels have given the Oslo hotel scene a much-needed face-lift in recent years. More and more are focusing on sustainability, so they have found ingenious ways to save electricity and reduce waste without impacting your comfort one bit. Many of the city's old favorites are located in the Sentrum, a stone's throw from Oslo Central Station. For a quieter stay, you might choose a hotel in Frogner or Majorstuen, elegant residential neighborhoods, or for views of the city you can head up the mountain to Holmenkollen. Newer neighborhoods like Tjuvholmen have fewer options, but they are likely to be very modern and have the latest amenities like TVs that take your room service order. Most hotels in Oslo include at least a continental breakfast in their rates, and some offer huge buffets that you have to see to believe. *Hotel reviews have been shortened. For full information, visit Fodors.com.*

What It Costs in Norwegian Krone

	$	$$	$$$	$$$$
HOTELS	under NKr 750	NKr 750–NKr 1250	NKr 1251–NKr 1900	over NKr 1900

Nightlife

This is a fun-loving city after dark. Into the early evening, locals often head to Sentrum to the bars on or around the main street of Karl Johans Gate. There's a number of cool wine and cocktails bars tucked among the more rowdy pubs and crowded tourist spots. Aker Brygge and Tjuvholmen, the more glamorous neighborhoods along the old wharf, have many bars and clubs, attracting mostly people willing to spend a little extra for the waterfront location. Grünerløkka has small bars, pubs, cafés, and art spaces catering to a younger clientele. A free-spending crowd also heads to the neighborhoods of Frogner and Bygdøy, where more and more trendy bars are springing up.

Bartending here is a serious profession, which means in cocktail bars ranging from dingy dives to cavernous clubs you're likely to be served creative concoctions with unusual garnishes. Sustainability is a factor here as well, with many bars growing their own botanicals. To find out what's going on around town, pick up a copy of the free monthly paper *Natt og Dag* or Friday's edition of *Avis 1.*

Shopping

Oslo is the best place in the country for buying anything Norwegian. The country is famous for its colorful hand-knitted wool sweaters, and even mass-produced models are of top quality. Prices are regulated, and they are always lower than buying them back home. You'll find designer brands located in Sentrum, where you'll find high-end boutiques and department stores showcasing the very best Norwegian fashion houses like Holzweiler. There's a wide range of antiques in Grünerløkka and Frogner.

Prices in Norway, as in all of Scandinavia, are generally much higher than in other European countries. Prices of handmade articles like knitwear are tightly controlled, making comparison shopping pointless. Otherwise, shops have both sales and specials—look for the words "salg" and "tilbud." Almost all shops are closed Sunday.

Tours

Walking and biking tours are a great way to see Oslo. Various "official" and "unofficial" free walking tours start from Sentrum, but if you want to book ahead, Oslo City and Nature Walks offers hikes along rivers and tours that take you to the city's spookiest haunts. Our Way Tours takes you to spots on and off the beaten path by foot, bike, or Segway. Oslo Guideservice offers very good private group tours focusing on everything from architecture to Vikings. Specialized tours have popped up in recent years, including visits to hipster neighborhood with Our Way Tours.

There are many hop-on/hop-off bus and boat routes run by Stromma, and theme cruises by Båtservice Sightseeing.

CONTACTS Båtservice Sightseeing. 🌐 *nyc.no/boatservice-sightseeing.* **Oslo City and Nature Walks.** 🌐 *oslowalks.no.* **Oslo Guideservice.** 🌐 *guideservice.no.* **Our Way Tours.** 🌐 *ourwaytours.com/our-tours/location/oslo.* **Stromma.** 🌐 *stromma.com/en-no/oslo.*

Visitor Information

CONTACTS Visit Oslo. ✉ *Oslo Central Station, Østbanehallen, Oslo* ☎ *23–10–62–00* 🌐 *www.visitoslo.com* Ⓜ *Jernbanetorget.*

Sentrum

Although the city region is huge (454 square km [175 square miles]), downtown Oslo is compact, with shops, museums, historic buildings, restaurants, and clubs concentrated in a small, walkable center that's brightly illuminated at night. The rapidly diversifying population means some streets maintain a certain quiet charm, while others are a bit more noisy and bustling. Here you'll find the lion's share of historic buildings, such as the Royal Palace and the Parliament Building. This area is also chock-full of museums, including the gleaming new National Museum complex.

GETTING AROUND

Getting from Point A to Point B in Oslo is a breeze—it does have some hills that make walking or biking a bit more of a challenge than, say, Copenhagen, but it's compact and easy to navigate. That said, with an Oslo Pass you can use all of the city's public transportation—buses, trams, trains, and the subway—to travel between neighborhoods. They usually aren't too packed, and the trams even have USB chargers.

SAFETY

Oslo is widely regarded as one of the safest capitals in the world, but don't forget the usual precautions when walking alone late at night. The city has a sleepy reputation, but don't forget you're in an urban metropolis.

Sights

★ **Nasjonalmuseet** (*National Museum*)
MUSEUM | Set to open its doors in 2020, the newly constructed National Museum now stands as the largest art museum in the Nordic region. The eye-catching modern structure not far from the waterfront includes a rooftop hall longer than the Royal Palace and has views of Oslo City Hall, Akershus Fortress, and the Oslofjord. The Edvard Munch section holds such major paintings as *The Dance of Life,* one of two existing oil versions of *The Scream,* and several self-portraits. Classic landscapes by Hans Gude and Adolph Tidemand—including *Bridal Voyage on the Hardangerfjord*—share space with other works by major Norwegian artists. The museum also has works by Monet, Renoir, Van Gogh, and

Downtown Oslo's main thoroughfare, Karl Johans Gate is lined with bars, restaurants, and sidewalk cafés.

Gauguin, as well as contemporary works by 20th-century Nordic artists. Enjoy the landscaped garden seating areas and special events throughout the year. ✉ *Sentrum* ☎ *21–98–20–00* 🌐 *www.nasjonalmuseet.no* Ⓜ *Nationaltheatret.*

Nationaltheatret (*National Theater*)
ARTS VENUE | In front of this neoclassical theater, built in 1899, are statues of Norway's great playwrights, Henrik Ibsen and Bjørnstjerne Bjørnson, who also composed the national anthem. Most performances are in Norwegian, so you may just want to take an English-language guided tour of the interior, which costs NKr 90 and can be arranged in advance. ✉ *Johanne Dybwads pl. 1, Sentrum* ☎ *22–00–14–00* 🌐 *www.nationaltheatret.no.*

Nobels Fredssenter (*Nobel Peace Center*)
MUSEUM | FAMILY | Every year the Nobel Peace Prize is awarded in Oslo—at this high-tech attraction by the harbor, you can learn about past and present laureates and their work through an original installation featuring 1,000 fiber-optic lights; read about Alfred Nobel's inventions and travels in a huge interactive book; and see a documentary on the current laureate in the Passage of Honor room. There are wonderful activities for young would-be peace activists, and changing exhibitions throughout the year. Next to the lobby is a fantastic shop selling unusual designs from around the world. ✉ *Brynjulf Bulls pl. 1, Sentrum* ☎ *483–01–000* 🌐 *www.nobelpeacecenter.org* 🎫 *NKr 120* ⏲ *Closed Mon. Oct.–Apr.* Ⓜ *Nationaltheatret.*

Oslo Domkirke (*Oslo Cathedral*)
RELIGIOUS SITE | Consecrated in 1697 as Oslo's third cathedral, this dark-brown brick structure has since been Oslo's main church. The original pulpit, altarpiece, and organ front with acanthus carvings still stand. Take a look at the ceiling murals painted between 1936 and 1950 by artist Hugo Louis Mohr, and stained-glass windows by Emanuel Vigeland. In the 19th century the fire department operated a lookout from the

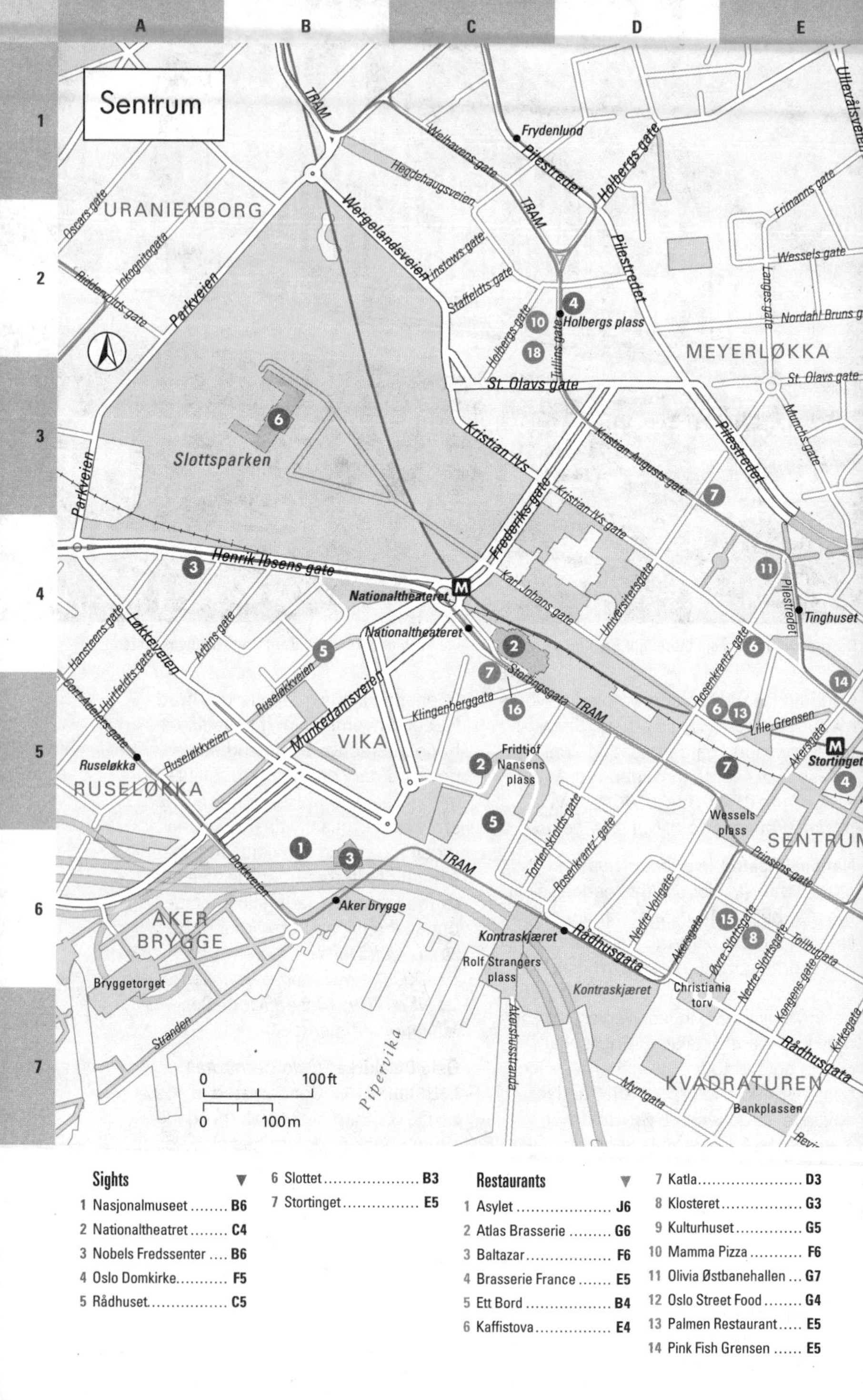

Sights

1 Nasjonalmuseet........ **B6**
2 Nationaltheatret........ **C4**
3 Nobels Fredssenter **B6**
4 Oslo Domkirke........... **F5**
5 Rådhuset................. **C5**
6 Slottet...................... **B3**
7 Stortinget................ **E5**

Restaurants

1 Asylet **J6**
2 Atlas Brasserie **G6**
3 Baltazar..................... **F6**
4 Brasserie France **E5**
5 Ett Bord **B4**
6 Kaffistova.................. **E4**
7 Katla.......................... **D3**
8 Klosteret.................... **G3**
9 Kulturhuset............... **G5**
10 Mamma Pizza **F6**
11 Olivia Østbanehallen ... **G7**
12 Oslo Street Food **G4**
13 Palmen Restaurant..... **E5**
14 Pink Fish Grensen **E5**

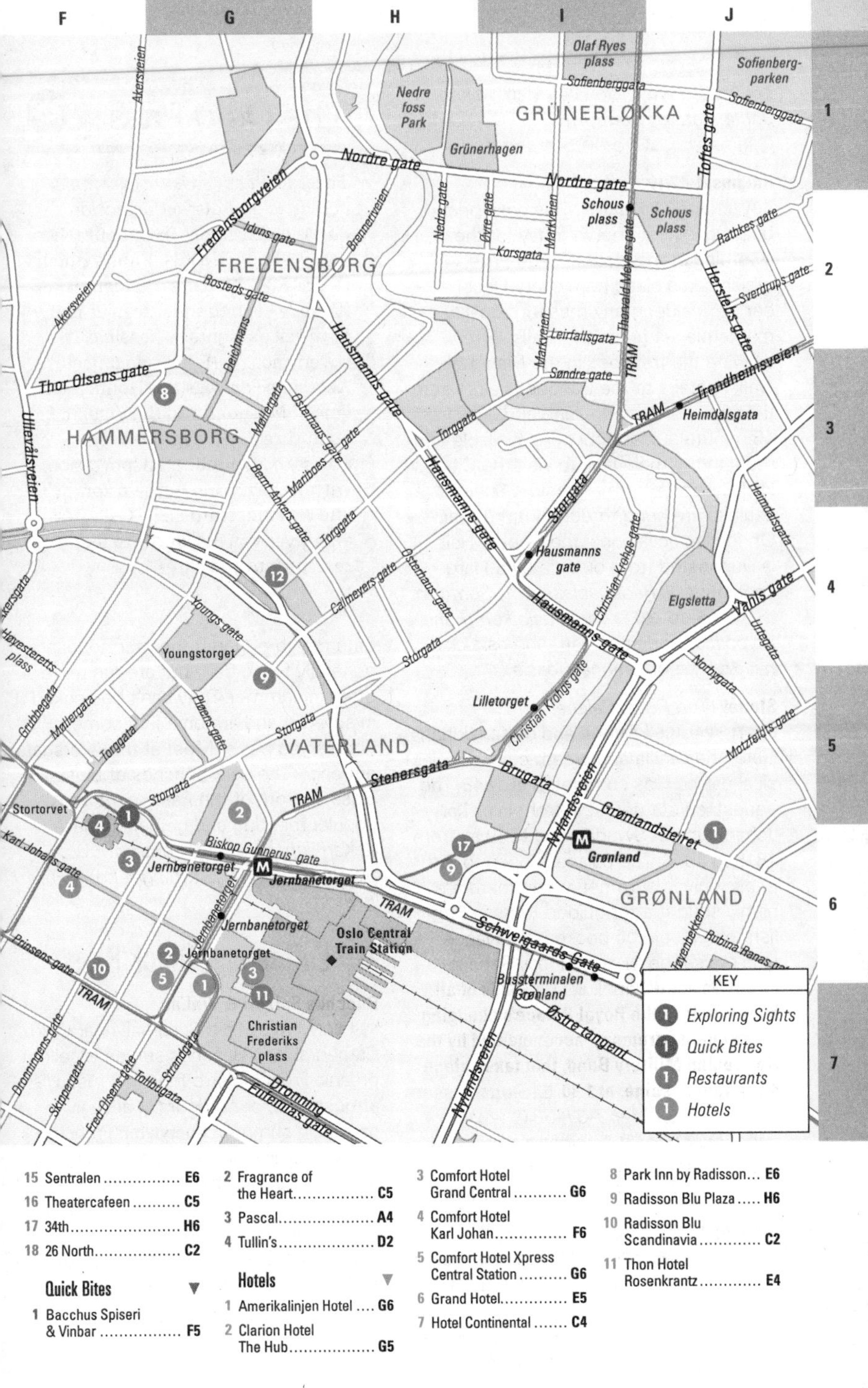

15 Sentralen E6
16 Theatercafeen C5
17 34th....................... H6
18 26 North.................. C2

Quick Bites

1 Bacchus Spiseri & Vinbar F5

2 Fragrance of the Heart................. C5
3 Pascal...................... A4
4 Tullin's.................... D2

Hotels

1 Amerikalinjen Hotel G6
2 Clarion Hotel The Hub.................. G5
3 Comfort Hotel Grand Central G6
4 Comfort Hotel Karl Johan............... F6
5 Comfort Hotel Xpress Central Station G6
6 Grand Hotel............. E5
7 Hotel Continental C4
8 Park Inn by Radisson... E6
9 Radisson Blu Plaza H6
10 Radisson Blu Scandinavia C2
11 Thon Hotel Rosenkrantz............. E4

bell tower, which you can visit. ✉ *Karl Johans gt. 11, Sentrum* ☎ *23–62–90–10* 🌐 *kirken.no* 🎫 *Free* Ⓜ *Stortinget.*

Rådhuset (*City Hall*)
GOVERNMENT BUILDING | This boxy brick building is best known today for the awarding of the Nobel Peace Prize, which takes place here every December 10. Inside, many museum-quality masterpieces grace the walls. After viewing the frescoes in the Main Hall, walk upstairs to the Banquet Hall to see the royal portraits. In June and July, free 45-minute guided tours are available and meet in the main hall. To visit the City Hall Gallery, enter harborside. Special exhibits are hung throughout the year. On festive occasions, the Central Hall is illuminated from outside by 60 large spotlights. ✉ *Rådhusplassen 1, Sentrum* ☎ *23–46–16–30* 🌐 *www.oslo.kommune.no/politics-and-administration/oslo-city-hall* 🎫 *Free* Ⓜ *Nationaltheatret.*

Slottet (*The Royal Palace*)
CASTLE/PALACE | At one end of Karl Johans Gate, the vanilla-and-cream-color neoclassical palace was completed in 1848. The equestrian statue out in front is of Karl Johan, King of Sweden and Norway from 1818 to 1844. The palace is open to the public only in summer, when there are highly sought after guided tours in English that should be booked in advance. Don't miss the 11 am Sunday Service in the Palace Chapel. **■TIP→ Kids of all ages will love the Royal Palace's changing of the guard ceremony, accompanied by the Norwegian Military Band, that takes place daily, rain or shine, at 1:30.** ✉ *Slottsplassen 1, Sentrum* ☎ *81–53–31–33* 🌐 *www.kongehuset.no* 🎫 *Advance tickets NKr 165, any remaining tickets sold at entrance for NKr 125.* Ⓜ *Nationaltheatret.*

Stortinget (*Norwegian Parliament*)
GOVERNMENT BUILDING | Norway's parliament building is a classic dating from 1866. The only way for the public to see it is on an informative one-hour guided tour (in English or Norwegian) every Saturday throughout the year; tours are generally twice-daily but are run more often in summer. They can't be booked in advance and are on a first-come, first-served basis. Meet at the Akersgata entrance. The park benches of Eidsvolls plass, in front of the Parliament, are a popular meeting and gathering place. ✉ *Karl Johans gt. 22, Sentrum* ☎ *23–31–30–50* 🌐 *www.stortinget.no* 🎫 *Free.* Ⓜ *Stortinget.*

The Oslo Pass

The Oslo Pass (🌐 *visitoslo.com/en/activities-and-attractions/oslo-pass*), which comes in 24-hour (NKr 445), 48-hour (NKr 655), and 72-hour (NKr 820) options, is a golden ticket if you're keen to squeeze in as many of the city's sights as possible. It covers most galleries and museums, Akershus Fortress, the Holmenkollen Ski Museum, and the Vigeland Sculpture Park. It grants free access to all public transportation within the two downtown zones and regional trains. The Oslo Pass also gives you discounts to many restaurants and cafés.

Coffee and Quick Bites

Bacchus Spiseri & Vinbar
$$ | **CAFÉ** | In the old Basarhall near Oslo Cathedral, tiny Bacchus serves excellent organic French bistro food in a rustic atmosphere, or outdoors in a lovely garden in summer. **Known for:** French-meets-Nordic cuisine; umbrella-shaded tables in front; all-natural wines. $ *Average main: NKr 250* ✉ *Dronningensgt. 27, Sentrum* ☎ *22–33–34–30* 🌐 *www.bacchusspiseri.no/english* ⏲ *Closed Sun.* Ⓜ *Jernbanetorget.*

Fragrance of the Heart

$$ | **CAFÉ** | This café serves excellent organic coffee and reasonably priced vegetarian and vegan lunch items. There's also a wide range of tempting desserts in a glass display case. **Known for:** desserts are truly a work of art; vegetarian dishes meat eaters will love; live music. *Average main: NKr210 ✉ Fridtjof Nansens pl. 2, Sentrum ☎ 22–33–23–10 🌐 www.fragrance.no Ⓜ Nationaltheatret.*

Pascal

$$ | **CAFÉ** | **FAMILY** | This smart little brasserie serves French-influenced lunchtime fare like croque monsieur or quiche with broccoli or bacon. There's also an impressive array of freshly baked pastries and cakes. **Known for:** array of gluten-free dishes; relaxing atmosphere; respectful staff. *Average main: NKr190 ✉ Henrik Ibsens gt. 36, Sentrum ☎ 22–55–00–20 🌐 pascal.no Ⓜ Nationaltheatret.*

Tullin's

$$ | **CAFÉ** | **FAMILY** | A favorite with students, this eatery has mismatched chairs, artwork of dubious quality in gilt frames, and chandeliers that feel too fancy for the decor. In other words, it has an appealingly laid-back vibe. **Known for:** pizza, burgers, and other comfort food; always filled with young people; speedy service. *Average main: NKr175 ✉ Tullins gt. 2, Sentrum ☎ 22–20–46–16 🌐 tullins.no Ⓜ Nationaltheatret.*

Restaurants

Asylet

$$ | **NORWEGIAN** | A bit east of Sentrum, this popular pub serves homemade traditional Norwegian food in an atmospheric setting under the slightly facetious motto: "nice place, bad service." The building, which dates from the 1730s, was once an orphanage. The big lunch menu features a good selection of *smørbrød* (open-faced sandwiches) as well as smoked-salmon salad and the traditional *karbonade* (a sort of open-faced hamburger, served with fried onions). **Known for:** cozy dining room warmed by a fireplace; sunny beer garden; classic fare. *Average main: NKr 150 ✉ Grønland 28, Grønland ☎ 22–17–09–39 🌐 www.asylet.no Ⓜ Grønland.*

Atlas Brasserie

$$ | **BRASSERIE** | In the former headquarters of the Norwegian America cruise ship, this well-heeled eatery capitalizes on a New York–meets–Oslo vibe. Stop by for an excellent cup of coffee in the plant-filled courtyard, or head to the all-day brasserie for the dazzling seafood platter or steak big enough to share with several friends. **Known for:** blue mussels served in a Roquefort reduction with fries; the tender tomahawk steak can easily serve four; decor is a cheeky take on Scandinavian design. *Average main: NKr 250 ✉ Amerikalinjen Hotel, Jernbanetorget 2, Sentrum ☎ 21–40–59–00 🌐 www.amerikalinjen.com/best-restaurant-i-oslo/the-atlas-restaurant ⏲ No dinner Sun. Ⓜ Jernbanetorget.*

Baltazar

$$ | **ITALIAN** | **FAMILY** | A longtime favorite, this restaurant tucked away under the graceful arcades behind the cathedral does an impressive job of re-creating the sort of trattoria you'd only find in Italy. With wood beams and exposed brick, the casual dining room spreads over three floors. **Known for:** an epic sharing menu for the whole table; classic meat-and-potatoes dishes; reliably good fish soup. *Average main: NKr 250 ✉ Domkirkeparken, Dronningensgt. 27, Sentrum ☎ 23–35–70–60 🌐 www.baltazar.no ⏲ Closed Sun. Ⓜ Jernbanetorget.*

★ Brasserie France

$$$ | **FRENCH** | As its name suggests, this wine bar is straight out of Paris: the long white aprons on the waiters, the Art Nouveau flourishes in the dining room, the old French posters on the walls, and the closely packed tables all add to the illusion. The sumptuous menu includes the classics: steak tartare, entrecôte,

duck confit. **Known for:** an indulgent "bouillabaisse a la maison"; an impressive vegetarian set menu; perfect location near Parliament. *Average main: NKr 300 Øvre Slottsgt. 16, Sentrum 23–10–01–65 www.brasseriefrance.no Closed July and Sun. No lunch weekdays Stortinget.*

Ett Bord

$$ | **SCANDINAVIAN** | Nordic-style tapas are served here with a maximum of style and sustenance, alongside a dedication to sustainability. The usual open-faced shrimp sandwich is done extremely well, as are the steamed mussels, fried peppers, and other small plates. **Known for:** freshest local ingredients; market-like atmosphere; sunny dining room. *Average main: NKr 150 Ruseløkkveien 3, Sentrum 22–83–83–03 www.ettbord.no Closed Sun. Nationaltheatret.*

Kaffistova

$$ | **NORWEGIAN** | Norwegian home cooking is served at this casual eatery on the ground floor of the Hotell Bondeheimen. Classic such as *raspeballer* (potato dumplings), *boknafisk* (dried and salted cod), and *rømmegrøt* (sour cream porridge) are always available. **Known for:** homemade meatballs are famous; open-faced shrimp sandwiches; anything from the dessert display. *Average main: NKr 180 Hotell Bondeheimen, Rosenkrantz gt. 8, Sentrum 23–21–41–00 www.kaffistova.com Stortinget.*

Katla

$$$$ | **ECLECTIC** | An interesting and unusual restaurant, this eatery named for an Icelandic volcano blends Nordic, Asian, Latin American, and other cuisines. The cooking is done over gas grills or—a nod to the name—on hot lava stones. **Known for:** small dishes perfect for sharing; seafood is always the standout; always busy, so book ahead. *Average main: NKr 895 Universitetsgata 12, Sentrum 22–69–50–00 www.katlaoslo.no Closed Sun. and Mon. No lunch weekdays Nationaltheatret.*

Klosteret

$$$ | **SCANDINAVIAN** | Modeled on a church cloister, complete with chanting monks and hundreds of twinkling candles, this underground lair dates back to 1899. (Its real history is more profane: it was a waffle bakery in the early 1900s.) A favorite for more than three decades, this Nordic-Germanic restaurant is a divine experience. Expect a heavy meal, with the seasonal menu focusing on meat and fish options served either à la carte or part of a set menu of three, five, or six courses, along with wine pairings. **Known for:** decadent desserts; great sparkling wines; one-of-a-kind decor. *Average main: NKr 300 Fredensborgveien 13, Sentrum 23–35–49–00 www.klosteret.no Closed Sun., July, and early Aug. Stortinget.*

Kulturhuset

$ | **VEGETARIAN** | Priding itself on a casual "breakfast, brunch, lunch, and munch" menu, the restaurant at this cultural institution always seems to have a crowd. There's a fantastic array of delicious dishes that provide sustenance for the events that take place here day and night. **Known for:** vegan- and vegetarian-friendly menu; quick and tasty meals; cheesy toast. *Average main: NKr 120 Kulturhuset, Youngs gt. 6, Sentrum www.kulturhusetioslo.no/en/food No dinner weekends Jernbanetorget.*

Mamma Pizza

$$ | **ITALIAN** | **FAMILY** | Featuring famous sourdough pizzas, this tiny osteria has the traditional checkered tablecloths and striped awning that call to mind the Emilia-Romagna region of Italy. Serving the city's most authentic pie—head and shoulders above its overpriced competitors—the eatery takes things one step further with refreshing yet strong cocktails or classic aperitifs served while you wait. **Known for:** short stroll from the central train station; don't miss the dessert

of the day; gluten-free dough available. [$] *Average main: NKr 180* ✉ *Dronningens gt. 22, Sentrum* ☎ *915–11–841* 🌐 *www.mammapizza.no* [M] *Jernbanetorget.*

Olivia Østbanehallen

$$ | **ITALIAN** | **FAMILY** | With high ceilings, stained-glass windows, and lots of foliage, the dining room of this long-running Italian eatery is comfortable and cozy—although if the weather cooperates, you'll probably opt for an alfresco meal in the square outside. The food is inexpensive, but very generous in terms of portions. **Known for:** a grand dining room; free focaccia with every meal; central location. [$] *Average main: NKr 200* ✉ *Jernbanetorget 1, Sentrum* ☎ *23–11–54–70* 🌐 *www.oliviarestaurant-er.no* [M] *Jernbanetorget.*

Oslo Street Food

$$ | **ECLECTIC** | **FAMILY** | If you're with a group that can't decide what to have for lunch or dinner, you can sample every cuisine from Nordic to Mexican to Indian to Japanese at this brightly lit, well-designed market a short walk from Central Station. With 16 food stands (Hungarian goulash, anyone?), several bars, and a huge seating area with picnic tables, it's a bustling place where everyone seems to be in great spirits. **Known for:** great place to witness the city's diversity; cheap eats in an expensive destination; seating for large groups. [$] *Average main: NKr 150* ✉ *Torggata 16, Sentrum* ☎ *22–04–00–44* 🌐 *www.oslo-streetfood.no* [M] *Jernbanetorget.*

Palmen Restaurant

$$$ | **BISTRO** | The Grand Cafe gets all the attention, but The Grand Hotel's more casual—but still quite beautiful—lobby restaurant is what Bohemian dreams are made of, with marble, gold, crystal, and velvet adding a luxurious touch. Underneath a spectacular glass ceiling, the dining room is a place where locals come to see and be seen. **Known for:** afternoon tea is a tradition here; dry martinis at the bar; a more relaxed affair. [$] *Average main: NKr 265* ✉ *The Grand Hotel, Karl Johans gt. 31, Sentrum* ☎ *23–21–20–00* 🌐 *www.grand.no* [M] *Stortinget.*

Pink Fish Grensen

$ | **ASIAN FUSION** | **FAMILY** | Sustainability is at the heart of this creative and low-key eatery intent on convincing the world to eat more salmon. Favorites includes poké bowls, hot pots, and even fish-and-chips. **Known for:** menu is a trip around the world; quick stop on a busy day; might convince kids they like fish. [$] *Average main: NKr 120* ✉ *Grensen 17, Sentrum* ☎ *45–85–50–27* 🌐 *www.pinkfish.no* ⏲ *Closed Sun.* [M] *Stortinget.*

Sentralen

$$$$ | **SCANDINAVIAN** | This debonair dining room—a relatively new kid on the block—focuses on organic ingredients prepared with continental flair. Many dishes are presented in unusual new combinations, such as the whole-baked cauliflower in miso and red curry. **Known for:** freshly baked croissants and great coffee in the attached café; the atmosphere is casual; the king crab is amazing. [$] *Average main: NKr 655* ✉ *Upper Slottsgate 3, Sentrum* ☎ *22–33–33–22* 🌐 *www.sentralenrestaurant.no* ⏲ *Closed Sun.* [M] *Stortinget.*

★ Theatercafeen

$$$ | **NORWEGIAN** | An Oslo institution, Theatercafeen has been a meeting place for artists and intellectuals for more than a century. Today it still attracts Oslo's beau monde, and as it's right across the street from the National Theater, it's a good bet for celebrity spotting. **Known for:** traditional dishes like spicy moules frites; desserts like wild strawberry sorbet; sublime fish cakes. [$] *Average main: NKr 300* ✉ *Continental Hotel, Stortingsgt. 24–26, Sentrum* ☎ *22–82–40–50* 🌐 *www.theatercafeen.no* ⏲ *Closed July* [M] *Nationaltheatret.*

34th

$$$ | **NORWEGIAN** | A speedy elevator takes you to the 34th floor of the Radisson Blu

Plaza Hotel, where you'll have panoramic views of the city's unmistakable skyline. (Request a window seat if you can handle heights.) The sleek, modern dining rooms is all about raising Nordic cuisine to it highest level, and you can choose between à la carte offerings and three- or six-course tasting menus. There's no better way to celebrate than with one of the showy cocktails from the bar. **Known for:** keep your eyes peeled for celebrities; some of the best views in Oslo; unusual desserts like licorice macarons. *$ Average main: NKr 330 ✉ Radisson Blu Plaza Hotel, Sonja Henies pl. 3, Sentrum ☎ 22–05–80–34 🌐 www.34th.no ⏲ Closed Sun. and Mon. and most of July. No lunch M Jernbanetorget.*

26 North

$$$ | **NORWEGIAN** | **FAMILY** | Despite being located on the ground floor of a chain hotel, this unexpectedly creative bistro satisfies hungry foodies with its incredible fjord-, farm-, and forest-inspired smorgasbord of dishes ranging from pine-smoked scallops to deer with sweet sausage. "Boards from the Fjords" is what it calls its small plates combining several different dishes meant to share. There are plenty of local cheeses, craft beers, and other happy-making fare. **Known for:** warm welcome from the staff; well-traveled wine list; casual dining room. *$ Average main: NKr 300 ✉ Radisson Blu Scandinavia Hotel, Holbergsplass 30, Sentrum ☎ 23–29–34–25 🌐 www.26north.no ⏲ No dinner Sun. M Nationaltheatret.*

Hotels

★ Amerikalinjen Hotel

$$$$ | **HOTEL** | The handsome headquarters of the Norwegian America Line opened its doors in 1919, and 100 years later it was transformed into this boutique hotel appealing to the design-conscious explorer. **Pros:** sophisticated design throughout; wonderful gym and sauna; room-service cocktails. **Cons:** extremely steep rates; can be a bit of a scene; no space for extra beds. *$ Rooms from: NKr 2092 ✉ Jernbanetorget 2, Oslo ☎ 21–40–59–00 🌐 www.amerikalinjen.com 122 rooms 🍴 No meals M Jernbanetorget.*

Clarion Hotel The Hub

$$ | **HOTEL** | This slick business hotel has all the features of a design hotel: great restaurants and bar, contemporary interiors, and elegantly appointed rooms. **Pros:** location near the central station; sustainability is their mantra; atmosphere. **Cons:** filled with corporate clients; labyrinthine corridors; expensive drinks. *$ Rooms from: NKr 1200 ✉ Biskop Gunnerusgt. 3, Sentrum ☎ 23–10–80–00 🌐 www.nordicchoicehotels.com/hotels/norway/oslo/clarion-hotel-the-hub 810 rooms 🍴 Free breakfast M Jernbanetorget.*

Comfort Hotel Grand Central

$$ | **B&B/INN** | **FAMILY** | Behind the central train station, this modern hotel would be popular for the location alone, but it also scores points for smart, sensible design. **Pros:** some rooms have nice extras like bathtubs; eco-friendly attitude; perfect location. **Cons:** can get very busy; no room service; busy decor. *$ Rooms from: NKr 1200 ✉ Jernbanetorget 1, Sentrum ☎ 22–98–28–00 🌐 www.nordicchoicehotels.no 170 rooms 🍴 Free breakfast M Jernbanetorget.*

Comfort Hotel Karl Johan

$$ | **HOTEL** | **FAMILY** | Along the historic main street of Karl Johan—but tucked away in its own courtyard away from the hustle and bustle—this handy hotel has nicely sized rooms and an eco-friendly vibe. **Pros:** sought-after location; attractive courtyard; delicious bistro. **Cons:** some rooms are extremely small; snacks at the reception area; can be a little noisy. *$ Rooms from: NKr 1200 ✉ Karl Johans gt. 12, Sentrum ☎ 23–01–03–52 🌐 www.nordicchoicehotels.com 181 rooms 🍴 Free breakfast M Jernbanetorget.*

Comfort Hotel Xpress Central Station
$$ | HOTEL | FAMILY | Extremely popular with young travelers, this budget-minded lodging is also a hit with families because of its low-key vibe and unbeatable location. **Pros:** independent check in; gym and roof terrace; welcoming atmosphere. **Cons:** not on an attractive street; no breakfast buffet; few amenities. *$ Rooms from: NKr 900 ✉ Møllergata 26, Sentrum ☎ 22–03–11–00 🌐 www.nordicchoicehotels.no 125 rooms 🍽 No meals Ⓜ Jernbanetorget.*

★ Grand Hotel
$$$$ | HOTEL | Looking like it would be at home on any street in Paris, this grand dame with a mansard roof and Beaux-Arts entrance is the choice of visiting heads of state, rock musicians, and Nobel Peace Prize winners. **Pros:** period touches have been preserved throughout; step-out balconies overlooking the town square; beautiful pool and spa facilities. **Cons:** gets busy during any of the city's festivals; spa and pool are short walk away from hotel; occasionally overrun by conference attendees. *$ Rooms from: NKr 2000 ✉ Karl Johans gt. 31, Sentrum ☎ 23–21–20–00 🌐 www.grand.no 283 rooms 🍽 No meals Ⓜ Stortinget.*

★ Hotel Continental
$$$ | HOTEL | History meets modernity at this landmark—it's a sophisticated stay with stylish guest rooms and posh common areas. **Pros:** exemplary service; eco-friendly ethos; great fitness area. **Cons:** restaurants are often booked in advance; nondescript exterior; business hotel feel. *$ Rooms from: NKr 1800 ✉ Stortingsgt. 24–26, Sentrum ☎ 22–82–40–00 🌐 www.hotelcontinental.no 151 rooms 🍽 Free breakfast Ⓜ Nationaltheatret.*

Park Inn by Radisson
$$ | HOTEL | Just minutes from Akerhus Fortress and other landmarks, this business-minded hotel has surprisingly impressive rooms with gigantic beds, great lighting, and impeccable design. **Pros:** location near the sights; comfortable furnishings; gleaming bathrooms. **Cons:** no restaurant or bar; lobby is a bit chilly; corporate feel. *$ Rooms from: NKr 900 ✉ Øvre Slottsgate 2C, Sentrum ☎ 22–40–01–00 🌐 www.radissonhotels.com/en-us/hotels/park-inn-oslo 118 rooms 🍽 Free breakfast Ⓜ Stortinget.*

Radisson Blu Plaza
$$$ | HOTEL | An elevator isn't usually the top attraction at a hotel, but a ride on the all-glass express elevator to the 34th-floor restaurant and bar makes this shiny tower worth a visit. **Pros:** well-lit pool and fitness area; excellent Nordic restaurant; convenient location. **Cons:** an impersonal feel; staff can get busy; no local charm. *$ Rooms from: NKr 1300 ✉ Sonja Henies pl. 3, Sentrum ☎ 22–05–80–00 🌐 www.radissonblu.com/en/plazahotel-oslo 678 rooms 🍽 Free breakfast Ⓜ Jernbanetorge.*

Radisson Blu Scandinavia
$$ | HOTEL | FAMILY | Rising 22 stories, this modern hotel blends the charm of Nordic design with the amenities of a chain hotel: spacious rooms, light-up wardrobes, cloud-soft beds, and stunning views of the city. **Pros:** basement gym, pool, and spa; fine dining in the hotel; panoramic views. **Cons:** too big for some; windowless gym; long walk to Central Station. *$ Rooms from: NKr 1200 ✉ Holbergsgt. 30, Sentrum ☎ 23–29–30–00 🌐 www.radissonblu.com/en/scandinaviahotel-oslo 499 rooms 🍽 Free breakfast Ⓜ Nationaltheatret.*

Thon Hotel Rosenkrantz
$$$ | HOTEL | An unassuming facade hides one of the most stylish large hotels in Oslo. **Pros:** close to many top attractions; great breakfast buffet; good value. **Cons:** some rooms are a bit noisy; decor is too flashy for some; long walk from train station. *$ Rooms from: NKr 1400 ✉ Rosenkrantz gt. 1, Sentrum ☎ 815–52–440 🌐 www.thonhotels.com 151 rooms 🍽 Free breakfast Ⓜ Stortinget.*

BARS AND LOUNGES

Andre til Høyre

BARS/PUBS | The name means "Second to the Right," and that's basically a roadmap to finding this bar up the stairs at Håndslag. It's a sumptuously decorated space, designed like an elegant, living room fit for entertaining glamorous guests at all hours. Lavish seating and heavy curtains make for a wonderful setting to explore Burgundy and sparkling wines. ✉ *Youngs gt. 19, Sentrum* 🌐 *andretilhoyre.no* ⏲ *Closed Sun.* Ⓜ *Jernbanetorget.*

Angst

BARS/PUBS | Surprisingly cozy yet lively, this bar has brightly colored walls, neon lights, and repurposed wood furniture, as well as a spacious backyard area for weekend parties. The quirky ambience and reliably good music means there's a queue on weekends, so get here early if you're in the mood to party. ✉ *Torggata 11, Sentrum* Ⓜ *Jernbanetorget.*

Bar Robinet

BARS/PUBS | On the edge of Sentrum, this bar is the place for late-night cocktails. (Martinis are a specialty, but if you're feeling brave ask the bartender to mix you something special.) The decor is a mishmash of checkered wallpaper, black-lacquer tables, and moody red lighting. It's around the corner from one of the hippest music venues, and the bands often head here after a set. ✉ *Mariboes gt. 7, Sentrum* Ⓜ *Stortinget.*

★ Bibliotekbaren og Vinterhaven

PIANO BARS/LOUNGES | If you're more partial to lounging than drinking, Hotel Bristol's Library Bar and Winter Garden is a stylish hangout with old-fashioned leather armchairs, huge marble columns, and live piano music. Politicians, musicians, and journalists have come here for nearly 100 years for informal meetings, quiet chats, or just to enjoy the tempting afternoon tea. ✉ *Hotel Bristol, Kristian IVs gt. 7, Sentrum* ☎ *22–82–60–00* 🌐 *www.thonhotels.com* Ⓜ *Stortinget.*

Crowbar and Bryggeri

BREWPUBS/BEER GARDENS | Spread across two floors, Oslo's largest microbrewery offers tasty beers and hearty pub fare like whole suckling pig. The menu changes weekly, and there's always a friendly bearded face to talk you through all the options. ✉ *Torggata 32, Sentrum* ☎ *21–38–67–57* 🌐 *crowbryggeri.com* Ⓜ *Jernbanetorget.*

Dubliner Folk Pub

BARS/PUBS | A fine selection of whiskies and a warm atmosphere give this Irish pub an authentically cheery vibe. There are sports on the telly throughout the week. ✉ *Rådhusgata 28, Sentrum* ☎ *22–33–70–05* 🌐 *www.dubliner.no* Ⓜ *Stortinget.*

Einbar

WINE BARS—NIGHTLIFE | Where Sentrum meets Kvadvraturen, this former potato cellar is the perfect winter hideaway. There's an impressively long list of wines (which complements a small but very good dinner menu) and a Moroccan vibe complete with arched ceilings, squishy seats, and lavish rugs. ✉ *Prinsens gt. 18, Sentrum* ☎ *22–41–55–55* 🌐 *www.restauranteiner.no/einbar* Ⓜ *Stortinget.*

Fredens Bar and Cafe

BARS/PUBS | This neighborhood joint is stripped down, low-key, and very casual—and has low prices to match. It's a breath of fresh air in an area teeming with overpriced watering holes. ✉ *Fredensborgvn 17, Sentrum* ☎ *22–11–42–75* Ⓜ *Stortinget.*

Gunnars Generasjonsbar

BARS/PUBS | Renowned for its hangover cure breakfast, this laid-back spot definitely feels more suited for after hours than the morning after. The tasty pub grub just seems to be more suited to the purple neon lights that come out at night. ✉ *Torggata 13, Oslo*

☎ *23–65–37–20* 🌐 *generasjonsbaren.no* Ⓜ *Jernbanetorget.*

Himkok

BARS/PUBS | Draped in stark white lab coats, the city's most mysterious and skilled mixologists whip up their concoctions in a bar so well hidden that you might miss it if you don't search carefully for the tiny door. The name translates as "Moonshine," and this secretive locale doubles as a distillery. In the summer there's an herb-filled garden with a cider bar. ✉ *Storgata 27, Sentrum* ☎ *22–42–22–02* 🌐 *himkok.squarespace.com* Ⓜ *Jernbanetorget.*

Lardo

WINE BARS—NIGHTLIFE | If natural wines are your thing, slip into this small and low-key bar with a robust selection from around the world. It's a great place to talk grapes with the knowledgeable staff over some salty charcuterie, creamy cheeses, and an ever-changing selection of bar snacks. ✉ *Møllergata 38, Sentrum* ☎ *979–17–477* 🌐 *www.barlardo.no* Ⓜ *Stortinget.*

London Pub

BARS/PUBS | This is the place for proper pints, an unpretentious air, and plenty of camaraderie. Open since 1979, this gay bar welcomes everyone with open arms. ✉ *C. J. Hambros pl. 5, Sentrum* ☎ *22–70–87–00* 🌐 *www.londonpub.no* Ⓜ *Stortinget.*

Lorry

BARS/PUBS | Behind the Royal Palace, this funky spot has stuffed wildlife and century-old sketches of famous Norwegians adorning the walls. It advertises 180 different types of beer, and the mountain trout and other dishes are surprisingly good. It's a local institution that's hugely popular during the *julebord* season (mid-November to Christmas). ✉ *Parkvn. 12, Sentrum* ☎ *22–69–69–04* 🌐 *www.lorry.no* Ⓜ *Storinget.*

★ Pier 42

BARS/PUBS | When early-20th-century Osloites decided to set sail for the United States, they embarked on the Amerikalinjen ships at Oslo Harbor. The cruise line's former HQ is now home to a gorgeous cocktail bar named for their first landing point in New York. This fun locale serves tipples from the boat's heyday, carefully assembled by the shipping line's former bar manager. ✉ *Amerikalinjen Hotel, Jernbanetorget 2, Sentrum* ☎ *21–40–59–00* 🌐 *amerikalinjen.com* Ⓜ *Jernbanetorget.*

★ Torggata Botaniske

BARS/PUBS | Vines and other botanical wonders grow across the ceiling at this bar known for its creative cocktail selection. The nature-centric vibe is a welcome breath of fresh air as you step inside from one of the busiest downtown streets. The ingredients come from the bar's own greenhouse. ✉ *Torggata 17B, Oslo* Ⓜ *Jernbanetorget.*

CAFÉS

Cafe Sor

CAFES—NIGHTLIFE | Rough-hewn tables and exposed brick walls add character to this daytime café with plenty of vegetarian options. At night people turn out for berry-filled cocktails, DJs playing sets, and live music. ✉ *Torggata 11, Sentrum* ☎ *23–65–46–46* 🌐 *www.cafesor.no* Ⓜ *Jernbanetorget.*

Håndslag

CAFES—NIGHTLIFE | A café by day and bar by night, Håndslag has an ever-changing selection of beers and an impressive smorgasbord of bar snacks. It gets pretty crowded, especially when a DJ takes control. ✉ *Youngs gt. 19, Sentrum* ☎ *23–65–31–20* 🌐 *haandslag.no* Ⓜ *Jernbanetorget.*

Uhørt

CAFES—NIGHTLIFE | This quirky, shabby-chic venue is the kind of place where you can happily munch on sandwiches and salads as you enjoy concerts, poetry slams, and standup comedy. Everyone is welcome during the day, but at night it's 23 and older. ✉ *Torggata 11, Sentrum* ☎ *23–65–46–44* 🌐 *uhortistroget.no* Ⓜ *Jernbanetorget.*

MUSIC CLUBS

Cosmopolite

MUSIC CLUBS | Diana Krall has played at this club, as have Angelique Kidjo, Cheb Khaled, Chick Corea, Bo Diddley, Mulatu Astatke, and many other beloved musicians. The calendar usually includes an eclectic mix of world music, jazz, and soul. ✉ *Vogtsgt. 64, Sentrum* ☎ *22–11–33–08* 🌐 *www.cosmopolite.no.*

Gamla

MUSIC CLUBS | With a sophisticated look and a relaxed atmosphere, this intimate nightspot features regular concerts featuring rock and jazz musicians. ✉ *Grensen 1, Sentrum* ☎ *23–35–63–60* 🌐 *www.gamla.no* 🕙 *Closed Sun.* Ⓜ *Stortinget.*

★ Gustav

MUSIC CLUBS | With a free-spirited vibe, this intimate jazz club is named for Gustav Henriksen, founder of the Amerikalinjen cruise ship company. The club in the basement of the Amerikalinjen Hotel boasts an excellent sound system, atmospheric lighting, and a cool crowd that hangs around until the wee hours of the morning. ✉ *Amerikalinjen Hotel, Jernbanetorget 2, Sentrum* ☎ *21–40–59–00* 🌐 *amerikalinjen.com* Ⓜ *Jernbanetorget.*

Herr Nilsen

MUSIC CLUBS | At Herr Nilsen, some of Norway's most celebrated jazz artists perform. There's live music most nights, jam sessions on Tuesday, and jazz on Saturday afternoon. Other than jazz, the focus is New Orleans–style music and bluegrass. ✉ *C. J. Hambros pl. 5, Sentrum* ☎ *22–33–54–05* 🌐 *www.herrnilsen.no* Ⓜ *Storinget.*

Rockefeller Music Hall

MUSIC CLUBS | Commonly referred to as Torggata Bad because the building used to be a public bathing facility, this club has a lineup that includes internationally known hard-rock, alternative, and hip-hop acts—Nick Cave, Blondie, and Fetty Wap have all appeared. Drink prices are steep. ✉ *Torggt. 16, Sentrum* ☎ *22–20–32–32* 🌐 *www.rockefeller.no* Ⓜ *Jernbanetorget.*

Performing Arts

Gamle Logen

ARTS CENTERS | Concerts ranging from solo pianists to jazz trios to string quartets perform at this venue exuding romance and old-time glamour. ✉ *Grev Wedels pl. 2, Sentrum* ☎ *22–33–44–70* 🌐 *www.gamlelogen.no.*

Oslo Konserthus

ARTS CENTERS | Officially the home of the Oslo Philharmonic, Oslo Konserthus is a leading venue for classical musicians, along with jazz and pop performers and ballet dancers. ✉ *Munkedamsveien 14, Sentrum* ☎ *23–11–31–11* 🌐 *www.oslokonserthus.no* Ⓜ *Nationaltheatret.*

Shopping

ANTIQUES

Brocante

ANTIQUES/COLLECTIBLES | Hidden behind a red-and-white awning, this cluttered secondhand store is mostly filled with goods from the late 19th and early 20th centuries. You'll spot plenty of gems here among the stacks of knick-knacks. ✉ *Stensberggata 19, Sentrum* ☎ *958–66–671* 🕙 *Closed Mon. and Fri.*

ART GALLERIES

Kunstnernes Hus (*The Artists' House*)

ART GALLERIES | This gallery exhibits contemporary art and hosts the annual Autumn Exhibition. It also has a bar-restaurant that's a weekend hot spot for artists and local celebrities and the bookstore Nordic Art Press. ✉ *Wergelandsvn. 17, Sentrum* ☎ *22–85–34–10* 🌐 *www.kunstnerneshus.no* 🕙 *Closed Mon.* Ⓜ *Nationaltheatret.*

Oslo's Nonstop Festival

It's an audacious idea, to say the least. Instead of the usual cultural festival taking place every other year, Norway's capital city decided to host a five-year-long celebration that began in 2019 and won't wind up until 2024. Then it plans to start the whole thing all over again in 2025. The Oslo Biennalen (🌐 *www.oslobiennalen.no*) aims to make art more accessible, more dynamic, and, most of all, more out in the open.

"The City of Oslo has a long-standing tradition of supporting art in public space," said Ole G. Slyngstadli, the biennial's executive director. "It is one of our priorities to find new ways of connecting the arts and the general public." So performances are scheduled to take place on the rooftop of the Oslo Opera House, the hallways of City Hall, the waiting area of Oslo Central Station, and dozens of other locations. Buildings will be transformed into huge canvases, and parks will be filled with works of art.

Among the provocative works being presented is "Seven Works for Seven Locations," by Hlynur Hallsson, which will include the words of ordinary residents sprayed on city walls. "Oslo Collected Works," by Jan Freuchen, Jonas Høgli Major, and Sigurd Tenningen, is a sculpture park taking over a empty lot near a subway station. And "Migrant Car" is a three-dimensional photo of a wrecked car reproduced at full size and rolled around the city.

BOOKS

Litteraturhuset

BOOKS/STATIONERY | Behind the Royal Palace and close to Kunstnernes Hus, The House of Literature has a café, a restaurant, a bar, and a good bookstore. You'll likely find young writers diligently working here over coffee. ✉ *Wergelandsveien 29, Sentrum* ☎ *22–95–55–30* 🌐 *www.litteraturhuset.no* Ⓜ *Nationaltheatret.*

Norli

BOOKS/STATIONERY | One of the largest bookstores in Norway, Norli also has a selection of English-language volumes. ✉ *Universitetsgt. 22–24, Sentrum* ☎ *22–00–43–00* 🌐 *www.norli.no* Ⓜ *Nationaltheatret.*

Norlis Antiquarian

BOOKS/STATIONERY | Opening its doors in 1890, this serene emporium's walls are moaning under the sheer weight of classic first editions from Norway and around the world. A second floor is stacked to the rafters with more vintage books, antique maps, and other artifacts. ✉ *Universitetsgata 18, Sentrum* ☎ *22–20–01–40* Ⓜ *Nationaltheatret.*

Tanum

BOOKS/STATIONERY | Strong in the arts, health, and travel, this location of the bookstore chain is a standout. ✉ *Karl Johans gt. 37–41, Sentrum* ☎ *22–47–87–30* 🌐 *www.tanum.no* Ⓜ *Nationaltheatret.*

CLOTHING

Fjong

CLOTHING | Trust the chic and stylish Scandinavians to be at the forefront of a movement that allows a fashion-hungry generation to save money and preserve the planet. The face of sustainable designer fashion, Fjong lets you rent clothing for four days. When you're finished, put them in the protective case they arrived in and send them back. It's a great idea for travelers who want a great look waiting for them. ✉ *Drammensveien 72, Sentrum* ☎ *23–96–10–08* 🌐 *fjong.co.*

FWSS

CLOTHING | This Norwegian brand is characterized by its no-fuss approach to fashion. The chic, natural stone interior of the store in Oslo's Promenaden Fashion District reflects its dedication to simple pieces that build a timeless wardrobe. ✉ *Prinsens gt. 22, Sentrum* ☎ *45–85–10–21* 🌐 *fallwinterspringsummer.com/eu* Ⓜ *Stortinget.*

Indiska

CLOTHING | This popular Swedish chain sells colorful clothing and accessories for women, as well as small pieces of furniture and household items. ✉ *Karl Johans gt. 6, Sentrum* ☎ *22–42–65–00* 🌐 *indiska.com* ⏲ *Closed Sun.* Ⓜ *Jernbanetorget.*

Mette Møller

CLOTHING | This Norwegian women's fashion brand has an ultra-feminine style and an emphasis on sustainable practices. It's designed to be both stylish and durable. ✉ *Prinsens gt. 10, Sentrum* ☎ *942–50–011* 🌐 *www.mettemoller.no* Ⓜ *Jernbanetorget.*

Norway Shop

CLOTHING | Norway Shop has three locations along the square behind City Hall. It stocks a large selection of sweaters and blanket coats. ✉ *Fridtjof Nansens pl. 9, Sentrum* ☎ *22–33–41–97* 🌐 *www.norwayshop.com* Ⓜ *Nationaltheatret.*

Oleana

CLOTHING | Designer Solveig Hisdal, behind Oleana's success, has won many awards for her collections, which she now exports as far as Australia. ✉ *Stortingsgt. 8, Sentrum* ☎ *22–33–31–63* 🌐 *www.oleana.no* Ⓜ *Stortinget.*

Oslo Sweater Shop

CLOTHING | Head here for sweaters and blanket coats—it's a nice place for browsing the various styles. ✉ *Radisson Blu Scandinavia Hotel, Tullinsgt. 5, Sentrum* ☎ *22–11–29–22* 🌐 *www.sweater.no* Ⓜ *Nationaltheatret.*

Tom Wood

CLOTHING | This Norwegian lifestyle brand has a contemporary take on classic jewelry, eyewear, and apparel. It's located close to Promenaden Fashion District. ✉ *Kirkegata 20, Sentrum* ☎ *919–06–226* Ⓜ *Stortinget.*

UFF Vintage

CLOTHING | On one of Oslo's main shopping streets, this shop's gently used clothing for men, women, and children benefit humanitarian causes. ✉ *Prinsens gt. 2B, Sentrum* ☎ *22–42–35–55* 🌐 *www.uffnorge.org* Ⓜ *Jernbanetorget.*

HOUSEHOLD ITEMS

Den Norske Husfliden

HOUSEHOLD ITEMS/FURNITURE | One of the country's finest stores for handmade goods, Den Norske Husfliden—known locally as just Husfliden—has a large selection of beautifully made pewter, ceramics, textiles, and clothing. There's also *bunad*, the national costume. Items like felt boots and slippers make great souvenirs. ✉ *Rosenkrantz' gt. 20, Sentrum* ☎ *22–42–10–75* 🌐 *www.dennorske-husfliden.no* Ⓜ *Stortinget.*

Norway Designs

HOUSEHOLD ITEMS/FURNITURE | If you love Scandinavian design, this venerable retailer stocks art glass, ceramics, silver, and plenty of household items. ✉ *Stortingsgt. 28, Sentrum* ☎ *23–11–45–10* 🌐 *www.norwaydesigns.no* Ⓜ *Nationaltheatret.*

JEWELRY

David-Andersen

JEWELRY/ACCESSORIES | In business since 1876, Norway's best-known goldsmith creates stunning designs in silver as well. ✉ *Karl Johans gt. 20, Sentrum* ☎ *24–14–88–00* 🌐 *www.david-andersen.no* Ⓜ *Stortinget.*

Hasla

JEWELRY/ACCESSORIES | Norway's natural wonders are the inspiration behind these modern yet timeless pieces. A family business since 1980, it creates jewelry in its own studio deep in the Setesdal

Valley. ✉ *Markveien 54, Grünerløkka* ☎ *922–78–777* 🌐 *haslajewelry.com.*

Heyerdahl

JEWELRY/ACCESSORIES | This sleek jeweler and watchmaker has a beautiful location on Karl Johans Gate. ✉ *Karl Johans gt. 37B, Sentrum* ☎ *22–55–25–25* 🌐 *www.heyerdahl.no* Ⓜ *Nationaltheatret.*

Juvelér Langaard

JEWELRY/ACCESSORIES | As chic as they come, this family-run business creates timeless, one-of-a-kind pieces with precious metals and rare gemstones. It also sells brands like Shamballa Jewels and Pomellato. ✉ *Stortingsgaten 22, Sentrum* ☎ *22–00–76–90* 🌐 *langaard.no.*

Sugar Shop Smykkestudio

LOCAL SPECIALTIES | On the edge of Sentrum, this shop, workshop, and gallery focuses on Norwegian design and craftmanship. Many of the pieces in the relaxed showroom are one of a kind. ✉ *Briskebyveien 30, Sentrum* ☎ *22–44–52–79* 🌐 *sugarshop.no.*

SHOPPING CENTERS

GlasMagasinet

DEPARTMENT STORES | Opposite the cathedral, the chic GlasMagasinet is filled with stores selling handcrafted items made of glass, silver, and pewter, as other high-end materials. ✉ *Stortorvet 9, Sentrum* ☎ *22–82–23–00* 🌐 *www.glasmagasinet.no* Ⓜ *Stortinget.*

Oslo City

SHOPPING CENTERS/MALLS | In the center of the city, this sleek shopping center is your last chance for picking up a few items before boarding your train at Oslo Central Station. ✉ *Stenersgaten 1, Sentrum* ☎ *81–54–40–33* 🌐 *oslo-city.steenstrom.no* Ⓜ *Jernbanetorget.*

Paleet

SHOPPING CENTERS/MALLS | Between the Parliament and the Royal Palace, this glittering shopping arcade has the feel of a high-end department store like London's Harrods. ✉ *Karl Johans gt. 37–43, Sentrum* ☎ *23–08–08–11* 🌐 *www.paleet.no* Ⓜ *Nationaltheatret.*

Steen and Strøm

DEPARTMENT STORES | On a gorgeous cobblestone street, the exterior of Steen and Strøm is a line of storefronts featuring high-end Scandinavian retailers. Inside is a more traditional mall with countless well-known brands focusing on clothing for men, women, and children. Downstairs is a sprawling food court with local chains. ✉ *Nedre Slottsgate 8, Sentrum* 🌐 *steenogstromoslo.no* Ⓜ *Stortinget.*

Activities

BIKING

Viking Biking

BICYCLING | This shop rents bikes and equipment, including helmets. The store also offers different sightseeing tours and has maps of the area for those braving it on their own. ✉ *Nedre Slottsgate 4, Sentrum* ☎ *412–66–496* 🌐 *www.vikingbikingoslo.com/en* Ⓜ *Øvre Slottsgate.*

Kvadraturen, Aker Brygge, and Tjuvholmen

Kvadraturen is the oldest part of Oslo. In 1624, after the town burned down for the 14th time, King Christian IV renamed the city Christiania and moved it to the more easily defendable area adjacent to Akershus Fortress. In order to prevent future fires, the king decreed that houses were to be built of stone or brick instead of wood. Kvadraturen translates roughly as "square township," which refers to the area's geometrically ordered streets.

For more than a century this waterfront district was the home of a massive commercial shipyard called Akers Mekaniske Verksted. Postmodern steel-and-glass structures now dominate the skyline. The promenade along the water's edge is crowded with families whenever the weather is sunny. Facing the water are dozens of high-end eateries, upmarket boutiques, and art galleries. Bridges connect it to the quieter Tjuvholmen neighborhood.

GETTING AROUND

This waterfront area isn't right on the subway, although several stations—Nationaltheatret, Stortinget, and Jernbanetorget—are within reasonable walking distance.

Sights

★ **Akershus Festning** (*Akershus Fortress*)
CASTLE/PALACE | Dating to 1299, this stone medieval castle and royal residence was developed into a fortress armed with cannons by 1592. After that time, it withstood a number of sieges and then fell into decay. It was finally restored in 1899. Summer tours take you through its magnificent halls, the castle church, the royal mausoleum, reception rooms, and banquet halls. Explore Akershus Fortress and its resplendent green gardens on your own with the Fortress Trail Map, which you can pick up at the visitor center or download from the website. ⚠ **The castle (or at least selected sections) may be closed to the public on short notice due to functions. Dates are always listed on the website.** ✉ *Akershus festning, Sentrum* ☎ *23–09–39–17* 🌐 *akershusfestning.no* 🎫 *Free, NKr 100 for Akershus Slott.*

★ **Astrup Fearnley Museet** (*Astrup Fearnley Museum of Modern Art*)
MUSEUM | Across the pedestrian bridge from Aker Brygge, the privately funded Astrup Fearnley Museum of Modern Art is one of the city's architectural gems. The waterfront structure was designed by architect Renzo Piano, who placed three separate pavilions under one massive glass roof that—appropriate enough for this former shipbuilding center—resembles a billowing sail. The collection has earned a stellar reputation for its contemporary art from around the world. ✉ *Strandpromenaden 2, Tjuvholmen* ☎ *22–93–60–60* 🌐 *www.afmuseet.no* 🎫 *NKr 130* ⏲ *Closed Mon.*

Munchmuseet (*Munch Museum*)
MUSEUM | Edvard Munch, Norway's most famous artist, bequeathed his enormous collection of works (about 1,100 paintings, 3,000 drawings, and 18,000 graphic works) to the city when he died in 1944. This newly built museum—moved here from a rather dowdy location in a residential neighborhood—is a monument to his artistic genius, housing the largest collection of his works and also mounting changing exhibitions. Munch actually painted four different versions of *The Scream,* the image for which he's best known, and one of them is on display here. While most of the Munch legend focuses on the artist as a troubled, angst-ridden man, he moved away from that pessimistic and dark approach to more optimistic themes later in his career. ✉ *Operagata, Sentrum* ☎ *23–49–35–00* 🌐 *www.munchmuseet.no* 🎫 *NKr 120* Ⓜ *Jernbanetorget.*

Norges Hjemmefront Museum (*Norway's Resistance Museum*)
MUSEUM | Striped prison uniforms, underground news sheets, and homemade weapons tell the history of the resistance movement that arose before and during Norway's occupation by Nazi Germany. A gray, winding path leads to two underground stone vaults in which models, pictures, writings, and recordings trace the times between Germany's first attack in 1940 to Norway's liberation on May 8, 1945. Every year, on the anniversaries of these dates, Norwegian resistance veterans gather here to commemorate Norway's dark days and honor those who lost their lives. The former ammunitions depot and the memorial lie at the exact spot where Norwegian patriots were executed by the Germans. ✉ *Bygning 21, Kvadraturen* ☎ *23–09–31–38* 🌐 *www.forsvaretsmuseer.no/Hjemmefrontmuseet/Information-in-English* 🎫 *NKr 60.*

★ **Operahuset** (*Opera House*)
ARTS VENUE | One of the crown jewels of Scandinavian architecture, the Oslo Opera House is a stunning addition to the city's waterfront. When its first opened its doors, the gala ceremony attracted Denmark's royal family, the leaders of several countries, and a host of celebrities. Designed by the renowned Norwegian architect firm Snøhetta, the white marble and glass building slopes downward toward the water's edge, giving visitors spectacular views of the fjord, the surrounding mountains, and the city skyline. And it doesn't just look good; the acoustics inside the 1,364-seat auditorium are excellent, as are those in the two smaller performance spaces. The space is the permanent home of the Norwegian National Opera and Ballet, and also hosts a full calendar of music, theater, and dance. The Oslo Biennale will be staging performances on the rooftop through 2023. ✉ *Kirsten Flagstads pl. 1, Sentrum* ☎ *21–42–21–21* 🌐 *www.operaen.no* 🎫 *Free; guided tours NKr 120* Ⓜ *Jernbanetorget.*

Tjuvholmen Bystrand
BEACH—SIGHT | **FAMILY** | They call this a "beach," but Tjuvholmen Bystrand is more of a pretty park at the end of a pier with a strip of gravel at the water's edge. Only the bravest toddlers touch their toes to the icy water. ✉ *Boardwalk 2, Tjuvholmen.*

Tjuvholmen Sculpture Park
CITY PARK | Just outside the doors of the Astrup Fearnley Museum of Modern Art is the whimsical Tjuvholmen Sculpture Park, also designed by Renzo Piano. This is a pretty park right on the waterfront where locals picnic on warm summer days. ✉ *Strandpromenaden 2, Tjuvholmen* ☎ *22–93–60–60* 🌐 *www.afmuseet.no* 🕒 *Free.*

Restaurants

BAR Tjuvholmen
$$ | **FUSION** | This waterfront restaurant comes alive on the weekend, when fashion-conscious locals compete for the best seats on the terrace. The hip dining room with long wooden tables emphasizing that meals here are a communal experience is almost as popular. **Known for:** perfectly mixed cocktails; the brunch is legendary; Nordic-style tacos and other treats. [$] *Average main: NKr 145* ✉ *Bryggegangen 6, Tjuvholmen* ☎ *940–02–094* 🌐 *barsocialeating.no* 🕒 *Closed Sun. and Mon. No lunch weekdays.*

★ **Gamle Rådhus**
$$$ | **NORWEGIAN** | If you're in Oslo for just one night and want an authentic dining experience, head to the city's oldest restaurant—housed in Oslo's first town hall, a building that dates from 1641. It is known for its traditional fish and game dishes that take full advantage of the city's access to the best seasonal produce. **Known for:** reliably robust and salty catch prepared to perfection; elegant paneled surroundings lit by candles; the unparalleled delicacy is lutefisk. [$] *Average main: NKr 320* ✉ *Nedre Slottsgt. 1, Sentrum* ☎ *22–42–01–07* 🌐 *www.gamleraadhus.no* 🕒 *Closed Sun.* Ⓜ *Stortinget.*

★ **Hakkaiza**
$$ | **ASIAN FUSION** | Just a 10-minute stroll from the opera house, this Asian eatery on the edge of the Sørenga Marina hits you with the aromatic smells of Peking duck and Korean wings as soon as you walk in the door. The restaurant's dark slate and glass decor is softened a bit with cherry blossoms and twinkling candles. **Known for:** a little bit of every Asian cuisine; lovely location by the waterfront; cutting-edge design. [$] *Average main: NKr 240* ✉ *Sørengkaia 146, Sentrum* ☎ *40–08–91–82* 🌐 *www.hakkaiza.no.*

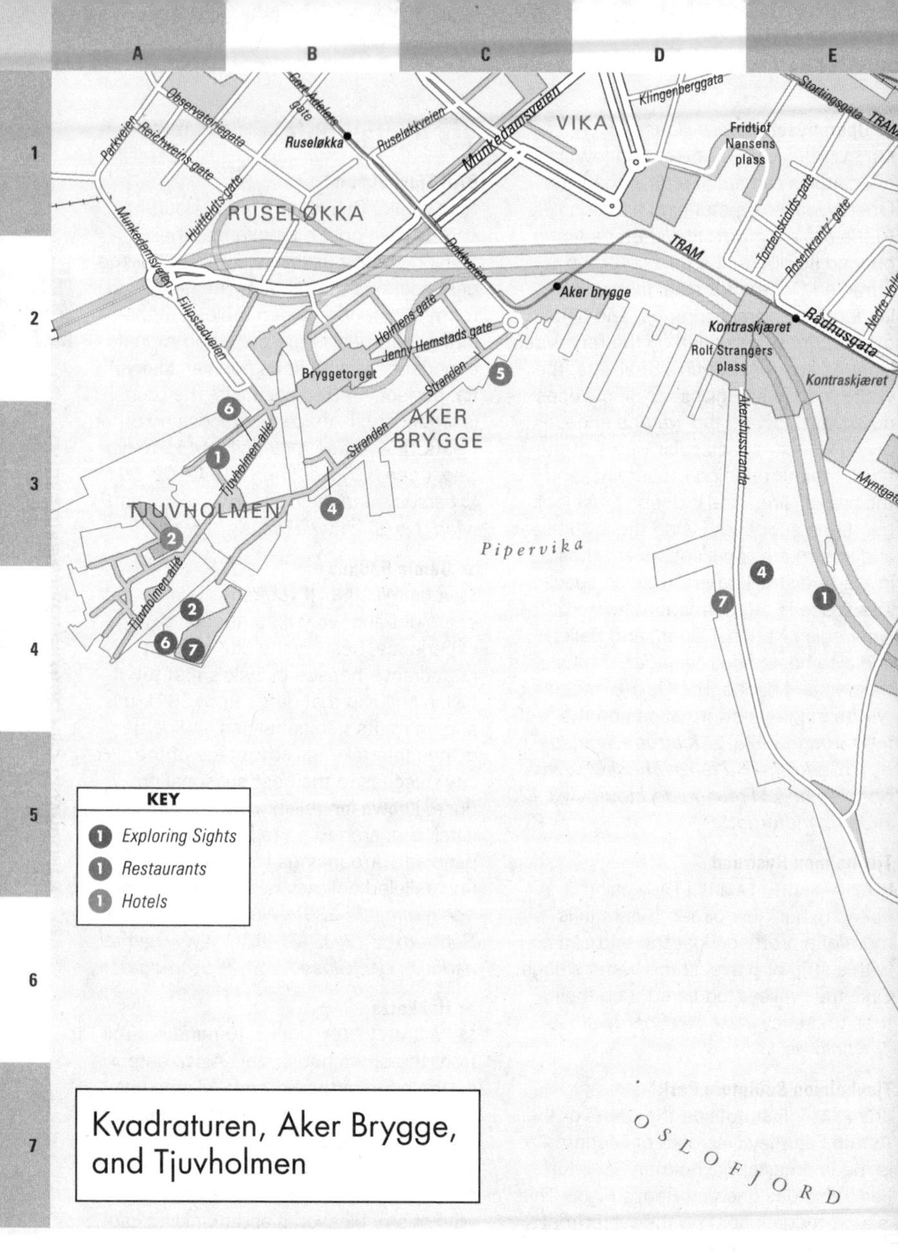

Sights

1 Akershus Festning...... E4
2 Astrup Fearnley Museet.................. A4
3 Munchmuseet I5
4 Norges Hjemmefront Museum E4
5 Operahuset............... I4
6 Tjuvholmen Bystrand... A4
7 Tjuvholmen Sculpture Park A4

Restaurants

1 BAR Tjuvholmen........ A3
2 Gamle Rådhus........... F3
3 Hakkaiza H7
4 Lofoten Fiskerestaurant B3
5 Olivia Aker Brygge...... C2
6 Olivia Tjuvholmen....... B3
7 Solsiden.................. D4
8 Statholdergaarden F3
9 Vippa F7

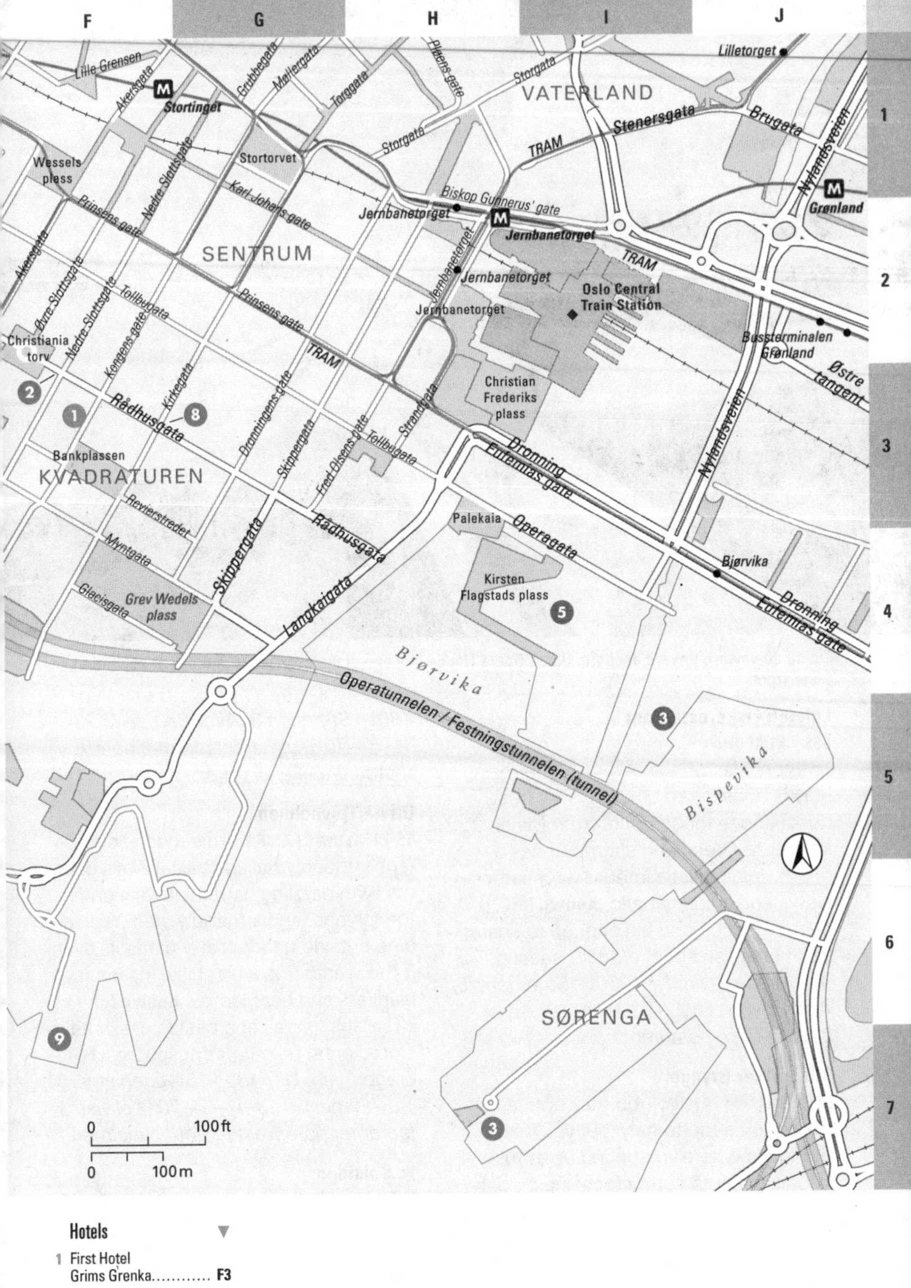

Hotels

1 First Hotel Grims Grenka............ F3

2 The Thief................. A3

Tilting downward toward the fjord, Oslo's Opera House has one of the best views of the ever-expanding waterfront.

Lofoten Fiskerestaurant

$$$ | **SEAFOOD** | Named for the remote Lofoten Islands, this Aker Brygge mainstay is considered one of Oslo's best destinations for seafood, from Maine lobster to Greenland shrimp. It has a bright, minimalistic interior with harbor views and a sunny patio. **Known for:** platters of seafood big enough to share; traditional fish soup; outdoor seating. *Average main: NKr 350 ✉ Stranden 75, Aker Brygge ☎ 22–83–08–08 🌐 www.lofoten-fiskerestaurant.no.*

Olivia Aker Brygge

$$ | **ITALIAN** | **FAMILY** | You may not have set out on a trip to Italy, but you'll feel like that's where you ended up at this Naples-inspired eatery focusing on delicious dishes like fried mozzarella balls, seafood risotto, and wood-fired pizzas topped with imported ingredients. The dining room is elegant, but you'll want to talk your way into a table overlooking the boats in the harbor. **Known for:** individually made pizzas; accommodating staff; waterfront location. *Average main: NKr 180 ✉ Stranden 3, Aker Brygge ☎ 23–11–54–70 🌐 oliviarestauranter.no/#!/restaurant/aker-brygge.*

Olivia Tjuvholmen

$$ | **ITALIAN** | **FAMILY** | This much-adored family-friendly Italian chain always delivers with dazzling harbor views, comfy furnishings, and a friendly staff. You can dine outside under pretty parasols even if the weather is a bit chilly, thanks to blankets and heat lamps. **Known for:** affordable pizzas and pastas; fresh Italian ingredients; buzzing atmosphere. *Average main: NKr 180 ✉ Bryggegangen 4, Tjuvholmen ☎ 23–11–54–70 🌐 oliviarestauranter.no/#!/restaurant/tjuvholmen.*

★ Solsiden

$$$ | **SEAFOOD** | With its high ceiling and huge windows facing the sunny side of the capital, this summer-only seafood restaurant is housed in a former warehouse right by the harbor. Follow the lead of the many locals who call this their favorite spot and indulge yourself with a *plateau de fruits de mer* (seafood platter, the house specialty) or opt for one of the other longtime favorites like the turbot with horseradish puree, the king crab au gratin, or the vegetarian-friendly salt-baked celeriac with walnuts. **Known for:** celebrity sightings are common; good list of wines by the glass; desserts are decadent. *Average main: NKr 330 Akershusstranda 13, Aker Brygge 22–33–36–30 www.solsiden.no Closed Sept.–mid-May.*

Statholdergaarden

$$$$ | **SCANDINAVIAN** | More than 400 years old, the elegant rococo dining room at Statholdergaarden is one of the oldest and most impressive in Norway. Award-winning celebrity chef Bent Stiansen's Asian-inspired French dishes have long been popular with locals. **Known for:** resplendent furnishings; Norwegian delicacies; excellent wine list. *Average main: NKr 470 Rådhusgate 11, Kvadraturen 22–41–88–00 statholdergaarden.no Closed Mon. Stortinget.*

Vippa

$$ | **ECLECTIC** | **FAMILY** | The name refers to its location at the tip of the Vippetangen, the peninsula that juts out into Oslofjord. This lively art, culture, and education center is also a destination for food lovers who want to sample dishes as diverse as poké bowls and halloumi wraps. **Known for:** concerts often accompany dinner; very inclusive environment; lots of local beers. *Average main: NKr 150 Akershusstranda 2, Sentrum 917–28–043 www.vippa.no Closed Mon.*

Hotels

First Hotel Grims Grenka

$$ | **HOTEL** | In a handsome brick building, Oslo's first design hotel has smart lighting, a striking color scheme, and contemporary touches like a clever use of mirrors and glassed-in bathrooms. **Pros:** central location; spacious rooms; comfortable beds. **Cons:** can sometimes feel overdesigned; hallways can be a bit gloomy; can be a bit pricey. *Rooms from: NKr 1196 Kongensgt. 5, Kvadraturen 23–10–72–00 www.firsthotels.com 65 rooms Free breakfast Stortinget.*

★ The Thief

$$$$ | **HOTEL** | Oslo's most tongue-in-cheek boutique hotel is located on Tjuvholmen, meaning Thief Islet, hence the unusual name. **Pros:** free admission to museum next door; a sumptuous breakfast spread; excellent location by the water. **Cons:** expensive rates; small swimming pool; isolated location. *Rooms from: NKr 3000 Landgangen 1, Tjuvholmen 24–00–40–00 thethief.com 118 rooms Free breakfast.*

Nightlife

BARS

BA3

BARS/PUBS | The unusual name refers to the address of this stylish spot with four different bars that cater to your every mood. The Terrassebaren has a light, breezy feel, while the scarlet stools of Inkognito make it feel a bit clandestine. *Bygdøy Allé 3, Frogner 22–55–11–86 www.ba3.no.*

Shopping

SHOPPING CENTERS

Aker Brygge Shopping

SHOPPING CENTERS/MALLS | A waterside pedestrian paradise with more than 30 high-end boutiques and an equal number of upscale bars and restaurants, this renovated shipyard is where Oslo hangs out, especially for after-work beers in summer. *Jenny Hemstads gt., Aker Brygge 22–83–26–80 www.akerbrygge.no.*

Activities

SAILING

Christian Radich

SAILING | Sky-high masts and billowing white sails give the Christian Radich a majestic style. This tall ship offers nine different trips, including several multi-day sails along the coast of Norway. Although you aren't required to have prior sailing experience, you should expect rough seas, high waves, and being asked to participate in crew member tasks. ✉ *Akershusstranda 9, Kvadraturen* ☎ *22–47–82–70* 🌐 *www.radich.no.*

Bygdøy

Southwest of the city center is the Bygdøy Peninsula, where several of the best-known historic sights are concentrated. This is where you'll find the Vikingskipshuset, one of Norway's most popular attractions. The pink castle nestled in the trees is Oscarshall Slott Åd, once a royal summer palace. The royal family's current summer residence—actually just a big white house—is also here.

GETTING AROUND

The subway completely bypasses this sprawling peninsula. The most pleasant way to get to Bygdøy—available from May to September—is to catch the ferry from Pier 3 at the rear of City Hall. Year-round, Bus No. 30 will take you there in 10 to 20 minutes.

Sights

Bygdø Kongsgård (*Bygdøy Royal Estate*)

FARM/RANCH | **FAMILY** | Part of the Norwegian Folk Museum, this manor house and farm of almost 500 acres actually belongs to, and has been occupied by, Norway's royal family. It's a fully operational organic farm offering activities like horseback riding lessons and a chance for kids to pet barnyard animals. The manor house, the king's official summer residence, was built in 1733 by Count Christian Rantzau. Hours are erratic when the royal family is here. ✉ *Dronning Biancas vei, Bygdøy* ☎ *22–12–37–00* 🌐 *bygdokongsgard.no* 🕓 *Closed summer and winter.*

★ **Frammuseet** (*Fram Museum*)

MUSEUM | **FAMILY** | The *Fram* was used by the legendary Polar explorer Roald Amundsen when he became the first man to reach the South Pole in December 1911. Once known as the strongest vessel in the world, this enormous Norwegian polar ship has advanced farther north and south than any other surface vessel. Built in 1892, the *Fram* made three voyages to the Arctic (they were conducted by Fridtjof Nansen and Otto Sverdrup, in addition to Amundsen). Climb on board and peer inside the captain's quarters, which has explorers' sealskin jackets and other relics on display. Surrounding the ship are many artifacts from expeditions. ✉ *Bygdøynesvn. 36, Bygdøy* ☎ *22–13–52–80* 🌐 *www.frammuseum.no* 🎫 *NKr 120.*

Kon-Tiki Museet (*Kon-Tiki Museum*)

MUSEUM | **FAMILY** | The museum celebrates Norway's most famous 20th-century explorer. Thor Heyerdahl made a voyage in 1947 from Peru to Polynesia on the *Kon-Tiki,* a balsa raft, to lend weight to his theory that the first Polynesians came from the Americas. His second craft, the *Ra II,* was used to test his theory that a reed boat could have reached the West Indies before Columbus. The museum also has a film room and artifacts from Peru, Polynesia, and Easter Island. ✉ *Bygdøynesvn. 36, Bygdøy* ☎ *23–08–67–67* 🌐 *www.kon-tiki.no* 🎫 *NKr 120.*

★ **Norsk Folkemuseum** (*Norwegian Museum of Cultural History*)

MUSEUM VILLAGE | **FAMILY** | One of the largest open-air museums in Europe offers the perfect way to see Norway in a day. From the stoic stave church (built in 1200) to farmers' houses made of sod, the old buildings here span Norway's regions and most of its recorded history. Indoors, fascinating displays of richly embroidered, colorful *bunader* (national costumes) from every region includes one set at a Telemark country wedding. The museum also has stunning dragon-style wood carvings from 1550 and some beautiful *rosemaling,* or decorative painted floral patterns. The traditional costumes of the Sami (Lapp) people of northern Norway are exhibited around one of their tents. If you're visiting in summer, ask about Norwegian Evening, a summer program of folk dancing, guided tours, and food tastings. ✉ *Museumsvn. 10, Bygdøy* ☎ *22–12–37–00* 🌐 *www.norskfolkemuseum.no* 🎫 *NKr 160.*

Norsk Maritimt Museum (*Norwegian Maritime Museum*)
MUSEUM | **FAMILY** | Norwegian fishing boats, paintings of fishermen braving rough seas, and intricate ship models are all on display here. The arctic vessel *Gjøa* is docked outside. The breathtaking movie *The Ocean: A Way of Life* delves into Norway's unique coastal and maritime past. Also on display is the model of the Kvaldor boat (AD 600), a 19th-century armed wooden warship, and a modern-day tanker. ✉ *Bygdøynesvn. 37, Bygdøy* ☎ *22–12–37–00* 🌐 *marmuseum.no* 🎫 *NKr 120.*

Oscarshall Slott (*Oscarshall Palace*)
HISTORIC SITE | **FAMILY** | This small country palace was built in eccentric English Gothic style for King Oscar I in the middle of the 19th century. There's a park, pavilion, fountain, and stage on the grounds. The original interior has works by Norwegian artists Adolph Tidemand and Hans Gude. ✉ *Oscarshallveien, Bygdøy* ☎ *91–70–23–61* 🌐 *www.royalcourt.no/* ⏲ *Closed Sun. and Mon. and Oct.–May.*

Senter for Studier av Holocaust og Livssynsminoriteter (*Center for Studies of the Holocaust and Religious Minorities*)
MUSEUM | Located in the beautiful Villa Grande, this museum presents a sobering exhibition on Nazi Germany's murder of 6 million European Jews, including a third of the Jewish population in Norway. ✉ *Villa Grande, Huk Aveny 56, Bygdøy* ☎ *22–84–21–00* 🌐 *www.hlsenteret.no* 🎫 *NKr 70.*

★ **Vikingskipshuset** (*Viking Ship Museum*)
MUSEUM | **FAMILY** | The Viking legacy in all its glory lives on at this classic Oslo museum. Chances are you'll come away fascinated by the *Gokstad, Oseberg,* and *Tune,* three blackened wooden Viking ships that date to AD 800. Discovered in Viking tombs around the Oslo fjords between 1860 and 1904, the boats are the best-preserved Viking ships ever found; they have been on display since the museum's 1957 opening. In Viking times, it was customary to bury the dead with food, drink, useful and decorative objects, and even their horses and dogs. Many of the well-preserved tapestries, household utensils, dragon-style wood carvings, and sledges were found aboard ships. The museum's rounded white walls give the feeling of a burial mound. Avoid summertime crowds by visiting at lunchtime. ✉ *Huk Aveny 35, Bygdøy* ☎ *22–13–52–80* 🌐 *www.khm.uio.no* 🎫 *NKr 100.*

Restaurants

Lanternen
$$ | **SCANDINAVIAN** | Located on a dock extending into the fjord, this eatery is tucked inside a 1920s building that once served as waiting room for ferry passengers. Today it's a popular summertime destination for locals who love the picture-perfect terrace. **Known for:** towering shellfish platters; views of the city; perfect pizzas. 💲 *Average main: NKr 180*

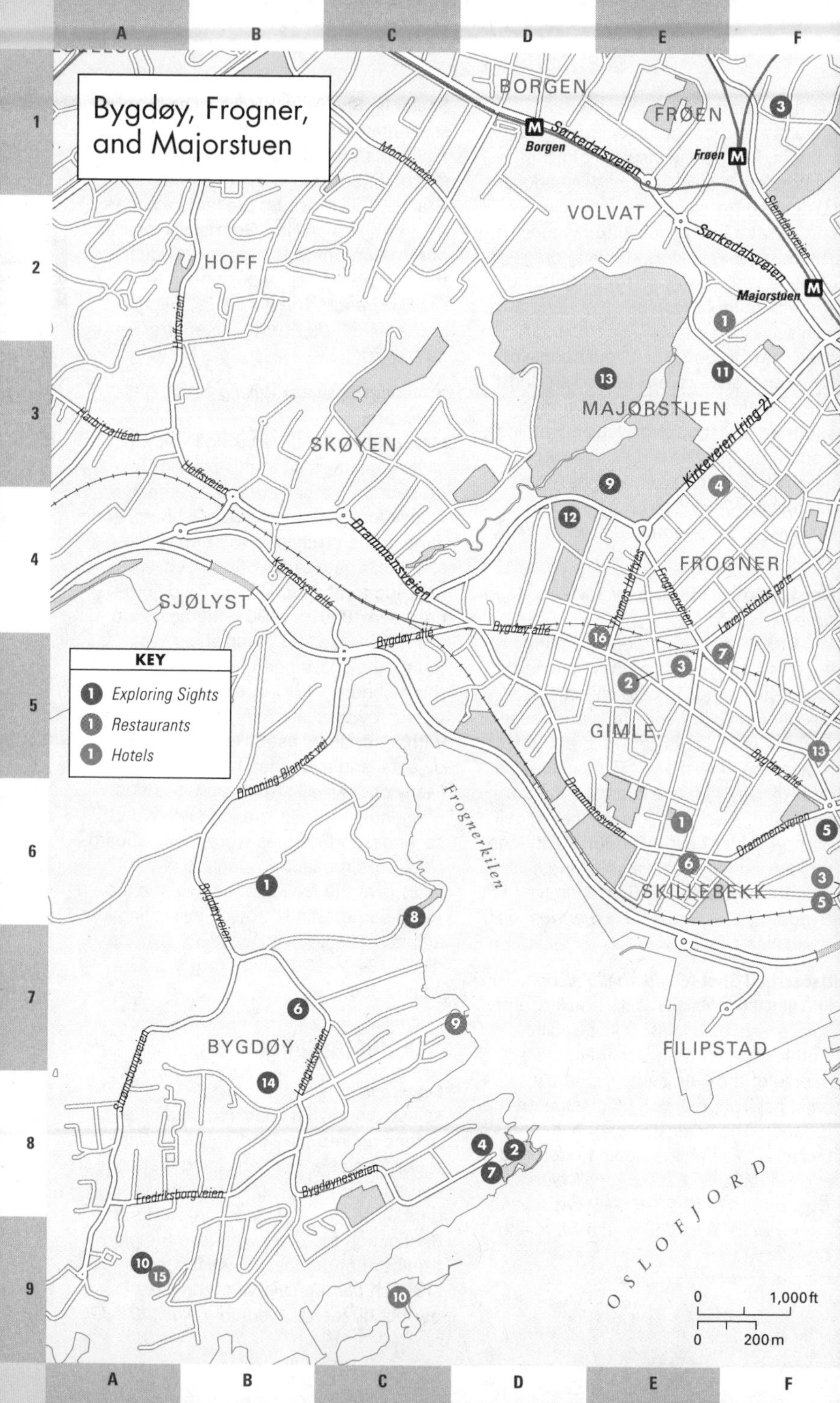

Bygdøy, Frogner, and Majorstuen
A
B
C
D
E
F
1
2
3
4
5
6
7
8
9
BORGEN
FRØEN
Borgen
Frøen
Sørkedalsveien
Monolitveien
VOLVAT
Slemdalsveien
HOFF
Majorstuen
Hoffsveien
MAJORSTUEN
Harbitzalléen
SKØYEN
Kirkeveien (ring 2)
Drammensveien
Kierschows alle
FROGNER
SJØLYST
Thomas Heftyes
Frognerveien
Løvenskiolds gate
Bygdøy allé
KEY
Exploring Sights
Restaurants
Hotels
GIMLE
Dronning Blancas vei
Frognerkilen
Drammensveien
SKILLEBEKK
Bygdøyveien
BYGDØY
FILIPSTAD
Langviksveien
Strømsborgveien
Fredriksborgveien
Bygdøynesveien
OSLOFJORD
0
1,000 ft
200 m

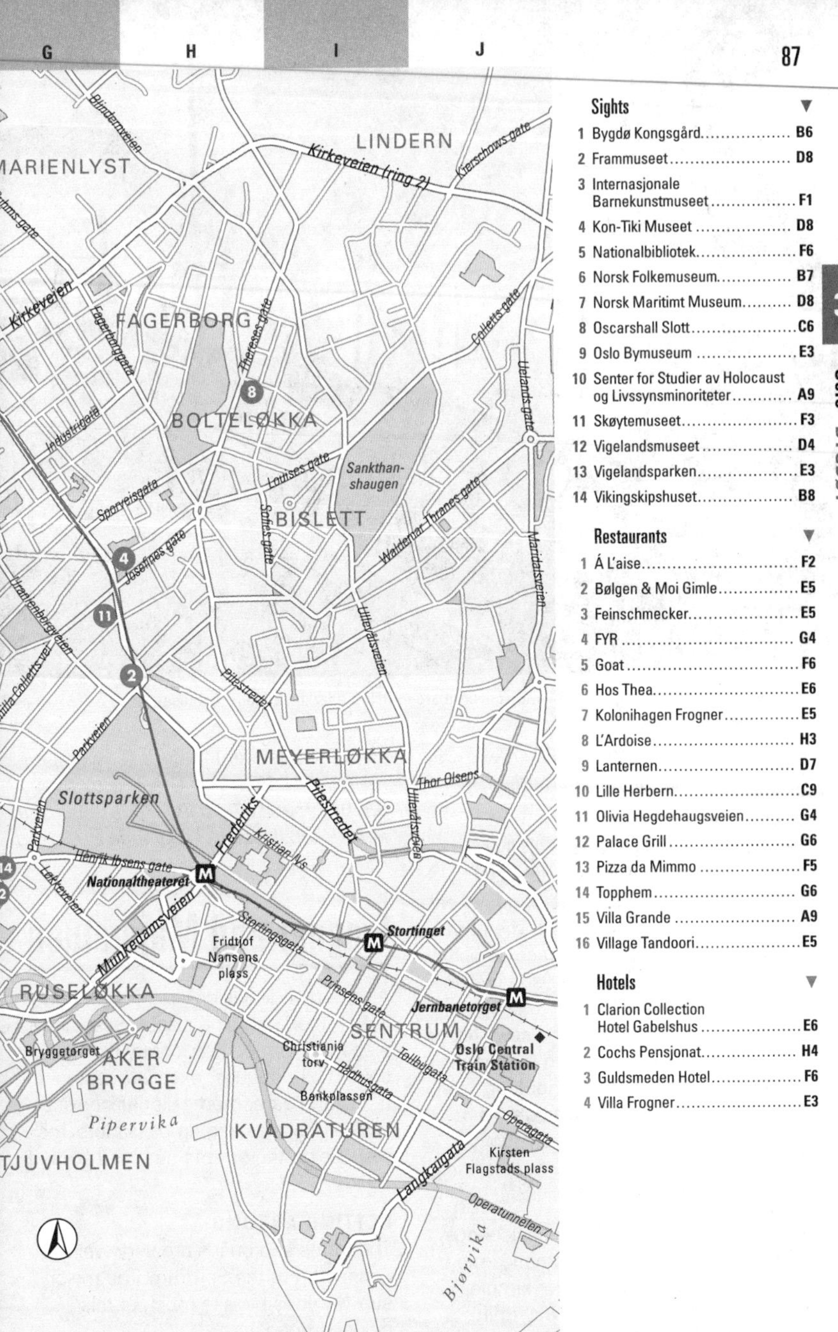

Sights

1 Bygdø Kongsgård B6
2 Frammuseet D8
3 Internasjonale Barnekunstmuseet F1
4 Kon-Tiki Museet D8
5 Nationalbibliotek F6
6 Norsk Folkemuseum B7
7 Norsk Maritimt Museum D8
8 Oscarshall Slott C6
9 Oslo Bymuseum E3
10 Senter for Studier av Holocaust og Livssynsminoriteter A9
11 Skøytemuseet F3
12 Vigelandsmuseet D4
13 Vigelandsparken E3
14 Vikingskipshuset B8

Restaurants

1 Á L'aise F2
2 Bølgen & Moi Gimle E5
3 Feinschmecker E5
4 FYR G4
5 Goat F6
6 Hos Thea E6
7 Kolonihagen Frogner E5
8 L'Ardoise H3
9 Lanternen D7
10 Lille Herbern C9
11 Olivia Hegdehaugsveien G4
12 Palace Grill G6
13 Pizza da Mimmo F5
14 Topphem G6
15 Villa Grande A9
16 Village Tandoori E5

Hotels

1 Clarion Collection Hotel Gabelshus E6
2 Cochs Pensjonat H4
3 Guldsmeden Hotel F6
4 Villa Frogner E3

The best-preserved Viking ships ever discovered are in Oslo's dazzling Vikingskipshuset.

✉ *Huk Aveny 2, Bygdøy* ☎ *22–43–78–38* 🌐 *www.restaurantlanternen.no.*

★ Lille Herbern

$$ | SCANDINAVIAN | FAMILY | Family-run since 1929, this eatery sits on a tiny island of its own just off the Bygdøy Peninsula and is reached by boat. The prime seating is on the breezy terrace, which is shaded from the summer sun by oversized umbrellas and heated to keep out the chill the rest of the year. **Known for:** towering platters of shellfish for sharing; views of the fjord and another leafy islet; historic atmosphere. *$ Average main: NKr 200* ✉ *Herbernveien 1, Bygdøy* ☎ *22–44–97–00* 🌐 *www.lilleherbern.no.*

Villa Grand

$$$$ | SCANDINAVIAN | Hiking aficionados, history lovers, and garden fanatics rub elbows at this palatial villa for simple, traditional simple meals by day (think open-faced sandwiches) and more filling fare by night (whole grilled fish is a favorite). The garden is very pleasant on a warm day. **Known for:** an opulent palace near the water; seasonal meat and game; resplendent buffets. *$ Average main: NKr 565* ✉ *Villa Grand, Huk Aveny 56, Bygdøy* ☎ *67–10–99–70* 🌐 *www.sult.no/selskapslokaler/villa-grande* 🕒 *Closed Mon.*

Frogner and Majorstuen

Also known as Oslo West, Frogner and Majorstuen combine classic Scandinavian elegance with contemporary European chic. Hip boutiques, excellent restaurants, and esteemed galleries coexist with embassies and ambassadors' residences on the streets near and around Bygdøy Allé.

GETTING AROUND

The trams and buses are very well connected to the Sentrum. The major subway lines bypass much of this neighborhood.

Sights

Internasjonale Barnekunstmuseet (*International Museum of Children's Art*)
MUSEUM | The brainchild of Rafael Goldin, a Russian immigrant, this museum showcases an unusual collection of children's drawings from more than 150 countries. You can see the world though the eyes of a child in its exhibitions of textiles, paintings, sculptures, and other works of art. ✉ *Lille Frøens vei 4, Majorstuen* ☎ *22–46–85–73* 🌐 *www.barnekunst.no* 🎟 *NKr 75* 🕘 *Closed Mon. and Fri. Closed mid-Aug.–mid-Sept.*

Nationalbibliotek (*National Library*)
LIBRARY | Complete with elaborate facades, classical statues, and painted dome ceilings, this large, peaceful library has a collection containing the entire cultural and knowledge heritage of Norway. Though mostly in Norwegian, the library regularly hosts exhibits, concerts, lectures, and guided tours (call ahead for English) that detail the vast collections. There's a very good café open all day serving open-faced sandwiches and pastries. ✉ *Henrik Ibsens gt. 110, Frogner* ☎ *81–00–13–00* 🌐 *www.nb.no* 🕘 *Closed Sun.*

Oslo Bymuseum (*Oslo City Museum*)
MUSEUM | FAMILY | One of Scandinavia's largest cities, Oslo has changed and evolved greatly over its thousand years. A two-floor, meandering exhibition covers Oslo's prominence in 1050, the Black Death that came in 1348, the great fire of 1624 and subsequent rebuilding, and the urban development of the 20th century. Among the more interesting relics are the red coats that the first Oslo police officers wore in 1700 and the town's first fire wagon, which appeared in 1765. ✉ *Frognervn. 67, Frogner* ☎ *23–28–41–70* 🌐 *www.oslomuseum.no* 🎟 *NKr 90* 🕘 *Closed Mon.*

Skøytemuseet (*Ice Skating Museum*)
MUSEUM | FAMILY | Tucked away in Frogner Stadium, this is Norway's only museum devoted to ice skates and ice-skaters. Gleaming trophies, Olympic medals, and skates, skates, and more skates serve to celebrate the sport. Photographs of skating legends such as Johann Olav Koss, Hjalmar Andersen, and Oscar Mathisen line the walls. Take a look at ways that skates have evolved—compare the bone skates from 2000 BC to the wooden skates that came later. ✉ *Frogner Park, Middelthunsgt. 26, Frogner* ☎ *22–43–49–20* 🌐 *skoytemuseet.no* 🎟 *NKr 20* 🕘 *Closed Wed.–Sat. and Mon.*

Vigelandsmuseet
MUSEUM | FAMILY | "I am anchored to my work so that I cannot move. If I walk down the street one day a thousand hands from work hold on to me. I am tied to the studio and the road is never long," said Gustav Vigeland in 1912. This museum was the Norwegian sculptor's studio and residence. It houses models of almost all his works, as well as sculptures, drawings, woodcuts, and the original molds and plans for Vigeland Park. Wander through this intense world of enormous, snowy-white plaster, clustered nudes, and busts of such famous Norwegians as Henrik Ibsen and Edvard Grieg. ✉ *Nobelsgt. 32, Frogner* ☎ *23–49–37–00* 🌐 *www.vigeland.museum.no* 🎟 *NKr 120* 🕘 *Closed Mon.* Ⓜ *Majorstuen.*

★ **Vigelandsparken** (*Vigeland Sculpture Park*)
NATIONAL/STATE PARK | FAMILY | A favorite hangout for locals, Vigeland Sculpture Park has 212 bronze, granite, and wrought-iron sculptures by Gustav Vigeland (1869–1943). The 56-foot-high granite *Monolith* is a column of 121 upward-striving nudes surrounded by 36 groups on circular stairs. The *Angry Boy,* a bronze of an enraged cherubic child stamping his foot, draws legions of visitors and has been filmed, parodied, painted red, and even stolen. Kids love to climb on the statues. There's an on-site museum for those wishing to delve deeper into the artist's work.

Hundreds of bronze, granite, and wrought-iron sculptures by Gustav Vigeland are on display at Vigelandsparken.

Frognerparken, Frogner ☎ *23–49–37–00 for museum* *www.vigeland.museum.no* *Free.*

Restaurants

Á L'aise

$$$$ | FRENCH | This is the restaurant to visit on a dark, starry night when you need warming up with a candlelit dining room, five-star service, and fine French cuisine. Draped with heavy curtains, elegant linens, and buttery soft seating, it's a very fancy affair. **Known for:** resplendent sparkling wine trolley; meals finished with a flourish; vast cheese selection. *Average main: NKr 500* *Essendrops gt. 6, Frogner* ☎ *21–05–57–00* *www.alaise.no* *Closed Sun. and Mon.* *Majorstuen.*

Bølgen & Moi Gimle

$$$ | ECLECTIC | FAMILY | Restaurateurs Toralf Bølgen and Trond Moi have a winner in this minimalist restaurant. If you're tired of eating breakfast in your hotel, rise and shine here instead. **Known for:** relaxed atmosphere; award-winning chefs; extensive wine list. *Average main: NKr 255* *Bygdøy Allé 53, Frogner* ☎ *24–11–53–53* *www.bolgenogmoi.no.*

Feinschmecker

$$$$ | FUSION | The name is German, but the food at this warm and stylish eatery spans the globe. Owners Lars Erik Underthun, one of Oslo's foremost chefs, and Bengt Wilson, a leading food stylist, make sure each dish looks as good as it tastes. **Known for:** if you like the food you can buy the cookbook; particularly interesting wine list; elegant dining room. *Average main: NKr 400* *Balchens gt. 5, Frogner* ☎ *22–12–93–80* *www.feinschmecker.no* *Closed Sun.*

FYR

$$$ | NORWEGIAN | A well-heeled arrival on the city's gastronomic scene, this bistro has a candelit dining room with brick walls, an arched ceiling, and a huge terrace shaded with umbrellas. From the platters of fresh shellfish to the grilled-to-perfection steaks, this place is an all-around winner for those who want Nordic fare served with flair. **Known for:** satisfying, generous portions; a cloister-like atmosphere; affordable bar menu. *Average main: NKr 350 ✉ Underhaugsveien 28, Majorstuen ☎ 459–16–392 🌐 www.fyrbistronomi.no.*

Goat

$$$ | **SCANDINAVIAN** | In the stylish Guldsmeden Hotel, this eatery looks like a place you'd come across in a small village, with brick walls, beamed ceilings, and arched windows. The chef here made waves with the signature pulled goat burger, and continues to serve innovative food made with organic ingredients from around the country. **Known for:** creative dishes like black sesame ice cream; wonderful wine pairings; relaxed atmosphere. *Average main: NKr 325 ✉ Guldsmeden Hotel, Parkveien 78, Frogner ☎ 455–03–729 🌐 guldsmedenhotels.com/goat-organic-restaurant.*

Hos Thea

$$$ | **SCANDINAVIAN** | An intimate yet lively dining experience awaits in this longtime favorite with a blue-and-white fleur-de-lis motif. From the open kitchen, Sergio Barcilon and the other chefs often serve the French and Spanish dishes themselves. **Known for:** short walk from the city center; desserts are to die for; elegant surroundings. *Average main: NKr 320 ✉ Gabelsgate 11, Frogner ☎ 22–44–68–74 🌐 www.hosthea.no.*

★ Kolonihagen Frogner

$$$ | **FUSION** | With a resident chef who authored an exquisitely illustrated book on foraging, this leafy courtyard restaurant offers an ever-changing menu of unpretentious comfort food with a Nordic twist. It also has plenty of indoor seating for cozy evenings dining by candlelight. **Known for:** extensive wine list; botanical cocktails; vegan-friendly options. *Average main: NKr 295 ✉ Frognerveien 33, Frogner ☎ 993–16–810 🌐 kolonihagenfrogner.no ⏲ Closed Sun. and Mon.*

★ L'Ardoise

$$$$ | **BRASSERIE** | **FAMILY** | This superb neighborhood brasserie was created by a French pastry chef who's become as revered for his easygoing lunches and elegant dinners as his impressive mille-feuille. The head waiter knows fine wines and pairings extremely well, and the service is warmly attentive. **Known for:** legendary dessert menu; attracts mostly locals; reasonably priced set menu. *Average main: NKr 525 ✉ Thereses gt. 20B, St. Hans Haugen ☎ 22–11–09–65 🌐 www.lardoise.no ⏲ Closed Sun. and Mon.*

Olivia Hegdehaugsveien

$$ | **ITALIAN** | **FAMILY** | The menu at this Italian eatery is inspired by the cuisine of Rome, so the pastas and pizzas are made with fresh ingredients and are always delicious. There's a comfortable two-level dining room, but most people prefer the leafy courtyard where blankets and heaters ward off the chill. **Known for:** Roman-style dishes are amazing; don't miss the excellent biscotti; popular with families. *Average main: NKr 200 ✉ Hegdehaugsveien 34, Majorstuen ☎ 23–11–54–70 🌐 oliviarestauranter.no.*

★ Palace Grill

$$$ | **FRENCH FUSION** | An eight-table restaurant near the Royal Palace, this is one of the most fashionable spots in Oslo. Don't let the "grill" in the name fool you—the atmosphere may be relaxed, but the French-inspired cuisine is taken very seriously. **Known for:** late-night camaraderie; so many wonderful courses; not far from the Sentrum. *Average main: NKr 300 ✉ Solligaten 2, Frogner ☎ 23–13–11–40 🌐 palacegrill.no.*

Pizza da Mimmo

$$ | **ITALIAN** | **FAMILY** | Named for owner Domenico Giardina—known to everyone as Mimmo—this is Oslo's best pizzeria. In 1993, the native of Calabria was the first to bring thin-crust Italian pizza to the city. **Known for:** made-to-order pizzas; laid-back atmosphere; outdoor seating.

$ Average main: NKr 180 ✉ Behrensgt. 2, Frogner ☎ 22–44–40–20 🌐 www.pizzadamimmo.no ⏲ No lunch.

Topphem

$$$$ | **SCANDINAVIAN** | On the edge of Frogner, this eatery not far from the Sentrum proudly names itself an everyday restaurant while maintaining the caliber of a fine-dining establishment. The Mediterranean-meets-Nordic interior design carries through to the food: There's an abundance of freshly caught seafood served with sauces and reductions that avoid any hint of pretentiousness. **Known for:** New Nordic cuisine without all the fuss; cozy leather banquettes; great tasting menus. $ *Average main: NKr 590* ✉ *Henrik ibsens gt. 60c, Frogner* ☎ *930–70–872* 🌐 *www.topphem.no* ⏲ *Closed Sun. and Mon.*

Village Tandoori

$$ | **INDIAN** | **FAMILY** | Walking through this restaurant feels like you're stepping back in time about a hundred years ago. Pakistani owner Mobashar Hussain collected the antique rugs, beaded textiles, and other authentic touches. **Known for:** authentic tandoori chicken; beautiful furnishings; casual atmosphere. $ *Average main: NKr 220* ✉ *Bygdøy Allé 65, Frogner* ☎ *22–56–10–25* 🌐 *villagetandoori.no.*

Hotels

Clarion Collection Hotel Gabelshus

$$ | **HOTEL** | Built as a guesthouse in 1912, this chic boutique hotel hidden behind an ivy-covered facade is one of our favorites in Oslo. **Pros:** charming old-world building; lots of shops and restaurants nearby; complimentary evening meal. **Cons:** rooms aren't as charming as common areas; neighborhood might be too quiet for some; some accommodations are very small. $ *Rooms from: NKr 1200* ✉ *Gabelsgt. 16, Frogner* ☎ *23–27–65–00* 🌐 *www.choicehotels.com* *114 rooms* *Some meals.*

Cochs Pensjonat

$ | **B&B/INN** | A stone's throw from the Royal Palace and near one of Oslo's premier shopping streets, this no-frills family-run guesthouse has reasonably priced, comfortable, and rather spartan rooms. **Pros:** central location; amiable staff; good value. **Cons:** very few amenities; cheaper rooms are tiny; no on-site restaurant. $ *Rooms from: NKr 500* ✉ *Parkvn. 25, Majorstuen* ☎ *23–33–24–00* 🌐 *www.cochspensjonat.no* *90 rooms* *No meals.*

★ Guldsmeden Hotel

$$$ | **HOTEL** | The inviting reception area with soft leather couches, a crackling fireplace, and charm to spare let you know you're in the ultimate Oslo escape. **Pros:** close to the neighborhood's top attractions; on-site hammam big enough for two; rooms are selfie-ready. **Cons:** 20-minute walk to Oslo Central Station; no fitness center; no room service. $ *Rooms from: NKr 1300* ✉ *Parkveien 78, Frogner* ☎ *23–27–40–00* 🌐 *guldsmedenhotels.com* *50 rooms* *No meals.*

Villa Frogner

$ | **B&B/INN** | In a 19th-century villa close to Vigelandparken, this elegant bed-and-breakfast will appeal to anyone who appreciates individually decorated rooms and homemade breakfasts. **Pros:** close to the sculpture park and other attractions; outdoor swimming pool; traditional decor. **Cons:** 15 minute walk to subway; no room service; parking is tricky. $ *Rooms from: NKr 700* ✉ *Nordraaks gt. 26, Frogner* ☎ *22–56–07–42* *14 rooms* *Free breakfast* M *Majorstuen.*

Nightlife

BarOtto

BARS/PUBS | You'll find wines from Burgundy, Bordeaux, Champagne, Tuscany, and Piedmont, many available by the glass, in this slick bar. The mixologists focus on gin concoctions, which you can enjoy along with your grilled ham-and-cheese sandwich. ✉ *Parkveien 80, Frogner* ☎ *909–37–961* 🌐 *www.barotto.no* ⏲ *Closed Sun. and Mon.*

Bygdøy Allé 3

BARS/PUBS | This colorful establishment has a bar on each floor, a comfortable lounge area, and a stage for live performances downstairs. It attracts an older, more sophisticated crowd. ✉ *Bygdøy Allé 3, Frogner* ☎ *22–55–11–86* 🌐 *www.ba3.no* ⏲ *Closed Sun. and Mon.*

Champagneria

BARS/PUBS | Spread over two floors, this classy spot has sidewalk seating and a terrace. Stop by for sparkling wine and some tapas in the heart of Frognerveien's shopping circus. ✉ *Frognerveien 2, Frogner* ☎ *21–08–09–09* 🌐 *www.champagneria.com.*

Josefine Inn

THEMED ENTERTAINMENT | A 19th-century villa hides one of the neighborhood's most pleasant places for aperitifs or digestifs. ✉ *Josefines gt. 16, Majorstuen* ☎ *22–69–34–99* 🌐 *www.josefine.no.*

Shopping

ANTIQUES

Børresen Homannsbyen Antikk og brukt

ANTIQUES/COLLECTIBLES | Let loose in this enormous emporium filled with crystal, china, and other treasures. It ships overseas on request. ✉ *Hegdehaugsveien 36, Frogner* ☎ *22–60–69–69.*

Damms Antikvariat

ANTIQUES/COLLECTIBLES | Antiquarian manuscripts, books, and maps are available from this bookstore, which first opened in 1843. ✉ *Frederik Stangs gt. 41, Frogner* ☎ *22–41–04–02* 🌐 *www.damms.no* ⏲ *Closed Sun.*

Gabel Antikviteter

ANTIQUES/COLLECTIBLES | The name means "fork," and you will find some fascinating tableware at this higgledy-piggledy shop, along with porcelain, tapestries, and more from both country and city households. Call ahead, as there are no fixed hours. ✉ *Gimleveien 21, Frogner* ☎ *918–43–123* 🌐 *www.gabel.no.*

Galleri Gimle

ANTIQUES/COLLECTIBLES | Specializing in 18th-century furniture and chandeliers, this place is worth poking your nose in even if you can't carry it home with you. ✉ *Gimleveien 21, Frogner* ☎ *92–86–35–95.*

Holmenkollen

The hill you see in the distance from many parts of the city, Holmenkollen has the famous ski jump and miles of ski trails. If you're looking for spectacular views of the city, this should be your destination.

GETTING HERE AND AROUND

The Metro's Line 1 is popular with travelers because it travels to Holmenkollen ski jump. Trams and buses also connect this neighborhood to the Sentrum.

Sights

★ Emanuel Vigeland Museum

MUSEUM | Although he never gained the fame of his older brother Gustav, the creator of Vigeland Park, Emanuel is an artist of some notoriety. His alternately saucy, natural, and downright erotic frescoes make even the sexually liberated Norwegians blush. To get here, take the T-bane Line 1 from Nationaltheatret Station toward Frognerseteren and get off at Slemdal, one of Oslo's hillside residential neighborhoods. Slightly off the beaten path near the neighborhood of Slemdal, this museum is a true wonder. **■ TIP→ Plan ahead, as hours are limited.** ✉ *Grimelundsvn. 8, Frogner* ☎ *22–14–57–88* 🌐 *www.emanuelvigeland.museum.no/museum.htm* 🎫 *NKr 80* ⏲ *Closed weekdays mid-May–mid-Sept., Mon.–Sat. mid-Sept.–mid-May* Ⓜ *Slemdal.*

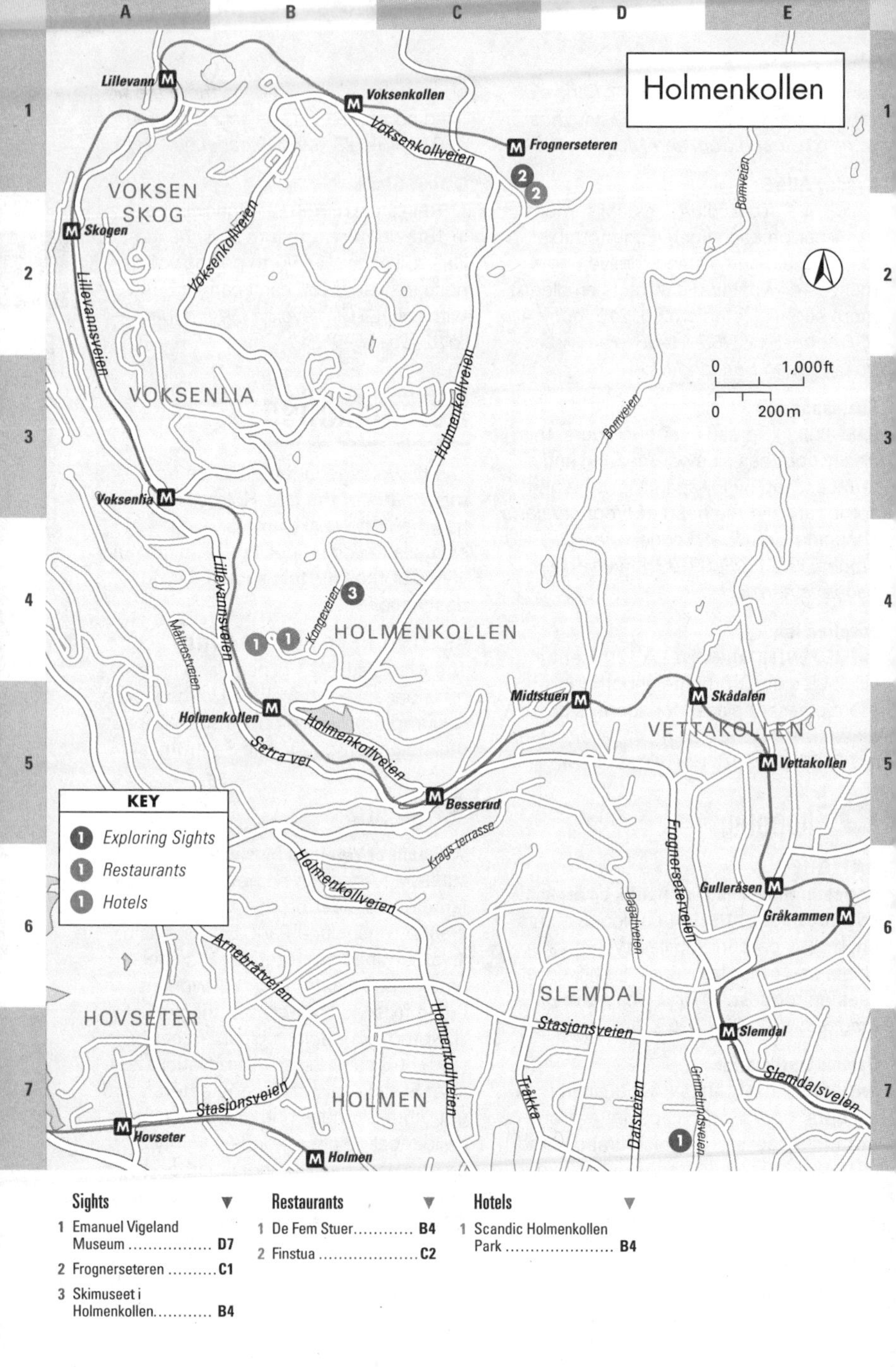

Sights

1 Emanuel Vigeland Museum D7

2 Frognerseteren C1

3 Skimuseet i Holmenkollen............ B4

Restaurants

1 De Fem Stuer............ B4

2 Finstua C2

Hotels

1 Scandic Holmenkollen Park B4

★ Frognerseteren

SCENIC DRIVE | FAMILY | This lookout is the most common place to begin or end a cross-country ski outing or the traditional Sunday hike. It's also the spot where every Oslo host will take his or her guests for a panoramic view of the fjords and city skyline. The lookout area has two restaurants in a building from 1891: the local favorite Kafe Seterstua, a self-service place with sandwiches and waffles, and the sit-down, special-occasion Restaurant Finstua, which specializes in Norwegian smoked and salted foods. Frognerseteren is made of rough-hewn logs and evokes the Norwegian mountain life that exists just minutes from urbane Oslo. ✉ *Holmenkollveien 200, Holmenkollen* ☎ *22–92–40–40* 🌐 *www.frognerseteren.no* Ⓜ *Frognerseteren.*

★ Skimuseet i Holmenkollen (*Holmenkollen Ski Museum*)

MUSEUM | FAMILY | A feat of world-class engineering, this beloved ski jump was first constructed in 1892 and has been rebuilt numerous times, remaining a distinctive part of Oslo's skyline. The cool, futuristic-looking jump you see today still hosts international competitions. The ski-jump simulator puts you in the skis of real jumpers, and the world's oldest ski museum presents 4,000 years of ski history. Guided tours of the museum are available. ✉ *Kongevn. 5, Holmenkollen* ☎ *22–92–32–00* 🌐 *holmenkollen.com* 🎫 *NKr 140.*

Restaurants

★ De Fem Stuer

$$$$ | NORWEGIAN | Near the famous Holmenkollen ski jump, in the historic Scandic Holmenkollen Park Hotel, this highly regarded restaurant serves first-rate food in a grand setting, with stunning views over Oslo. Modern Nordic and international dishes blend classic ingredients with more exotic ones. **Known for:** one of Oslo's most beautiful buildings; exquisite dining room; award-winning chef. $ *Average main: NKr 350* ✉ *Scandic Holmenkollen Park Hotel, Kongevn. 26, Holmenkollen* ☎ *22–92–20–00* 🌐 *www.scandichotels.com/hotels/norway/oslo/scandic-holmenkollen-park/restaurant-and-bar* Ⓜ *Holmenkollen.*

Finstua

$$$$ | NORWEGIAN | Above the Holmenkollen ski jump, Finstua is a great spot to take in sweeping mountain views. With chefs well versed in traditional Norwegian fare, this rustic and elegant spot serves salted and smoked fish, game, and more. **Known for:** luxurious dining room; views from every table; legendary apple cake. $ *Average main: NKr 385* ✉ *Holmenkollvn. 200, Holmenkollen* ☎ *22–92–40–40* 🌐 *www.frognerseteren.no* ⏲ *No lunch weekdays July and Aug.* Ⓜ *Frognerseteren.*

Hotels

★ Scandic Holmenkollen Park

$$ | HOTEL | Dating back to 1894, this stunning and distinguished hotel has a peaceful mountaintop setting with unparalleled views of the city below. **Pros:** some of the best views of the city; among the city's loveliest structures; superb breakfast. **Cons:** far from the city center; no dining options nearby; some rooms are dated. $ *Rooms from: NKr 900* ✉ *Kongevn. 26, Holmenkollen* ☎ *22–92–20–00* 🌐 *holmenkollenparkhotel.no* *336 rooms* *Free breakfast* Ⓜ *Holmenkollen.*

Activities

SKIING

Oslo Vinterpark (*Oslo Winter Park*)

SKIING/SNOWBOARDING | Oslo's most accessible ski center is Oslo Winter Park in Holmenkollen. It has 11 downhill slopes, six lifts, and a terrain park with a half-pipe for snowboarders. On weekends there's night skiing as well.

Art galleries, bars, and cafés line the bustling streets of Grünerløkka.

The season runs from late November to April, depending on snowfall. ✉ *Tryvannsveien 64, Holmenkollen* ☎ *22–14–36–10* 🌐 *www.oslovinterpark.no.*

Grünerløkka

Once a workaday neighborhood north of the center, Grünerløkka now hosts a number of trendy bars, cafés, and eateries. Popular with young people, the area is now known as Oslo's version of New York's Greenwich Village.

Sights

Galleri Heer

MUSEUM | This exhibition space includes an eclectic mix of work: painting, drawing, photography, sculpture, and graphics. Around for four decades, it features a mix of artists of all ages and backgrounds. ✉ *Seilduksgata 4B, Oslo* ☎ *97–62–04–89* 🌐 *www.galleriheer.no* ⏲ *Closed Mon. and Tues.*

Galleri Schaeffers Gate 5

MUSEUM | This performance and exhibition space is known for intimate readings, art installations, and concerts within an elegant 1890s-era tenement building. ✉ *Schaeffers gt. 5, Grünerløkka* ☎ *452–18–078* 🌐 *www.schaeffersgate5.no.*

Coffee and Quick Bites

Kaffebrenneriet

$$ | CAFÉ | Oslo's answer to Starbucks (with much better coffee, locals would say), Kaffebrenneriet has 26 branches throughout the city, including in the trendy Grünerløkka neighborhood. **Known for:** impressive homemade scones; tasty fennel sandwiches; the best local ingredients. 💲 *Average main: NKr160* ✉ *Thorvald Meyers gt. 55, Grünerløkka* ☎ *22–46–13–90* 🌐 *www.kaffebrenneriet.no.*

Restaurants

Bass

$$ | **SCANDINAVIAN** | A tiny green neon sign announces this corner restaurant during the day, while at night it catches your attention with expansive windows that are filled with diners sharing plates of Scandinavian-style tapas. It has a buzzy atmosphere, industrial decor, and a kitchen that isn't afraid of trying something new. **Known for:** the perfect place for groups; interesting wine selection; beautiful presentation. *Average main: NKr 150 Thorvald Meyers gt. 26, Grünerløkka 48–24–14–89 bassoslo.no Closed Mon.*

Fru Hagen

$$ | **BISTRO** | **FAMILY** | The glittering chandeliers and velvet sofas here make it look like a vintage neighborhood hangout. Locals gather here for fresh, well-executed comfort food—especially the spicy chicken salad, a house specialty. *Average main: NKr 190 Thorvald Meyers gt. 40, Grünerløkka 45–49–19–04 www.fruhagen.no.*

Habsak

$$ | **MIDDLE EASTERN** | Two words define the magic and allure of this neighborhood Middle East joint: vegan mezze. Comfortable seating, low lighting, and a laid-back atmosphere make this a budget traveler's dream. (That's no accident—the owners met backpacking in Central America.) Extremely generous servings of hummus, falafel, and other meat-free dishes keep people coming back to this corner café, as do the beers and music. **Known for:** colorful and filling platters; open for breakfast; friendly staff. *Average main: NKr 180 Kingos gt. 1B, Grünerløkka 21–94–90–99 www.habsak.no.*

Kontrast

$$$$ | **SCANDINAVIAN** | Swedish chef Mikael Svensson—recognized as one of the world's finest—is often spotted at this New Nordic restaurant offering two different tasting menus with excellent (and sommelier-curated) wine or juice pairings. Every dish stands up against the next, and all the ingredients are ethically sourced. **Known for:** massive wine selection; dishes are a work of art; chic decor. *Average main: NKr 880 Maridalsveien 15, Grünerløkka 21–60–01–01 www.restaurant-kontrast.no Closed Sun. and Mon.*

Markveien Mat og Vinhus

$$$ | **BISTRO** | Looking for all the world like a Parisian bistro, this restaurant in the heart of Grünerløkka serves French-inspired cuisine to a bohemian crowd. It's a relaxed, artsy place with paintings and prints covering the sunny walls, and candlelit tables. **Known for:** for a treat, try the homemade cheesecake; dining room has a warm glow; continental flair. *Average main: NKr 310 Torvbakkgata 12, Grünerløkka 22–37–22–97 markveien.no Closed Sun.*

Mathallen

$$ | **ECLECTIC** | **FAMILY** | This indoor market is where everyday shoppers, famous chefs, and tourists come to browse the stalls of more than 30 different vendors selling everything from Portuguese desserts to Hungarian wines to Norwegian cheeses and jams. Drop by for a snack or a whole meal. **Known for:** great place for an autumn or winter amble; stock up on brown cheese and other specialties; weekly cooking classes. *Average main: NKr 150 Vulkan 5, Sentrum 22–40–40–00 www.mathallenoslo.no Closed Mon.*

Mucho Mas

$$ | **MEXICAN** | **FAMILY** | The name says it all: massive portions are the order of the day at this tiny taqueria, but a table may be hard to find because the place is so darn popular. Burritos, nachos, and quesadillas are served as spicy as you like in a dining room done up in cool pastel colors. **Known for:** wash everything down with a margarita; surprisingly authentic flavors; a few outdoor tables. *Average main: NKr 200 Thorvald Meyers gt. 36,*

Grünerløkka ☎ 22–37–16–09 🌐 www.muchomas.no.

Munchies

$ | **AMERICAN** | **FAMILY** | This hipster hood's premier burger joint offers 100% organic burgers, served with generous portions of fries and sweet potato fries. The plastic bottles of ketchup and mustard might say fast food, but the local and imported beers insist you slow things down. **Known for:** gluten-free and vegan options; cheerful atmosphere; friendly staff. *$ Average main: NKr 105 ✉ Thorvald Meyers gt. 36A, Grünerløkka 🌐 www.munchies.no.*

New Anarkali

$$ | **INDIAN** | **FAMILY** | Serving mostly Punjabi cuisine, this extremely popular north Indian restaurant is known for its lamb curries and other authentic dishes. In a bright and airy space, there are rich fabrics and ornate furnishings. **Known for:** friendly and attentive staff; big platters of food; intimate feel. *$ Average main: NKr 200 ✉ Markveien 42, Grünerløkka ☎ 22–20–04–21 🌐 newanarkali.no.*

Nighthawk Diner

$$ | **AMERICAN** | This American-style diner is authentic down to the steel counters, upholstered booths, and tall glasses for the ice cream sundaes. (For reference, there's a mural of the eponymous Edward Hopper painting.) It serves excellent hamburgers, fries, shakes, and pies, as well as an all-day breakfast menu. **Known for:** a cure-all for homesick travelers; cheerful atmosphere; old-fashioned jukebox. *$ Average main: NKr 150 ✉ Seilduksgata 15 A, Grünerløkka ☎ 966–27–327 🌐 www.thenighthawk-diner.no.*

Tijuana

$$ | **MEXICAN** | It turns out that tacos and margaritas are the perfect thing to warm up a chilly evening in Oslo. Opened by owners who have spent a lot of time in search of an authentic taqueria, this snug place serves all of Mexico's favorite types of taco—carnitas, barbacoa, al pastor—alongside a long list of punchy tequilas and mezcals. **Known for:** great for a pre- or post-dinner tequila; authentic flavors; outdoor seating. *$ Average main: NKr 200 ✉ Thorvald Meyers gt. 61, Grünerløkka ☎ 900–77–191 🌐 www.tijuana.no.*

Villa Paradiso

$$ | **ITALIAN** | **FAMILY** | Run by a family who found themselves returning from a trip to Italy with a pizza oven, Villa Paradiso makes incredible Neopolitan pies. In an old building with vintage lamps and wood paneling, this trattoria is one of the very best in the neighborhood. **Known for:** outdoor dining under huge umbrellas; huge selection of desserts; wood-fired pizzas. *$ Average main: NKr 180 ✉ Olaf Ryes pl. 8, Grünerløkka ☎ 22–35–40–60 🌐 www.villaparadiso.no.*

Hotels

Scandic Vulkan

$$ | **HOTEL** | **FAMILY** | This contemporary retreat in the heart of Grünerløkka puts you in the middle of restaurants, shopping, nightlife, and the Akerselva River. **Pros:** colorfully decorate rooms; high-flying views; sophisticated feel. **Cons:** long walk to Oslo Central Station; additional cost for parking; dull exterior. *$ Rooms from: NKr 1200 ✉ Maridalsveien 13, Grünerløkka ☎ 21–05–71–00 🌐 www.scandichotels.com/vulkan 149 rooms Free breakfast.*

Nightlife

BARS AND LOUNGES

Aku-Aku

BARS/PUBS | Locals flock to this colorful, noisy, and reasonably authentic tiki bar—the only thing missing is a beach. The decor is eclectic, the music is loud, and the drinks come piled high with slices of fruit or tropical flowers. *✉ Thv. Meyers gt. 32, Grünerløkka ☎ 22–71–75–71 🌐 www.akuaku.no.*

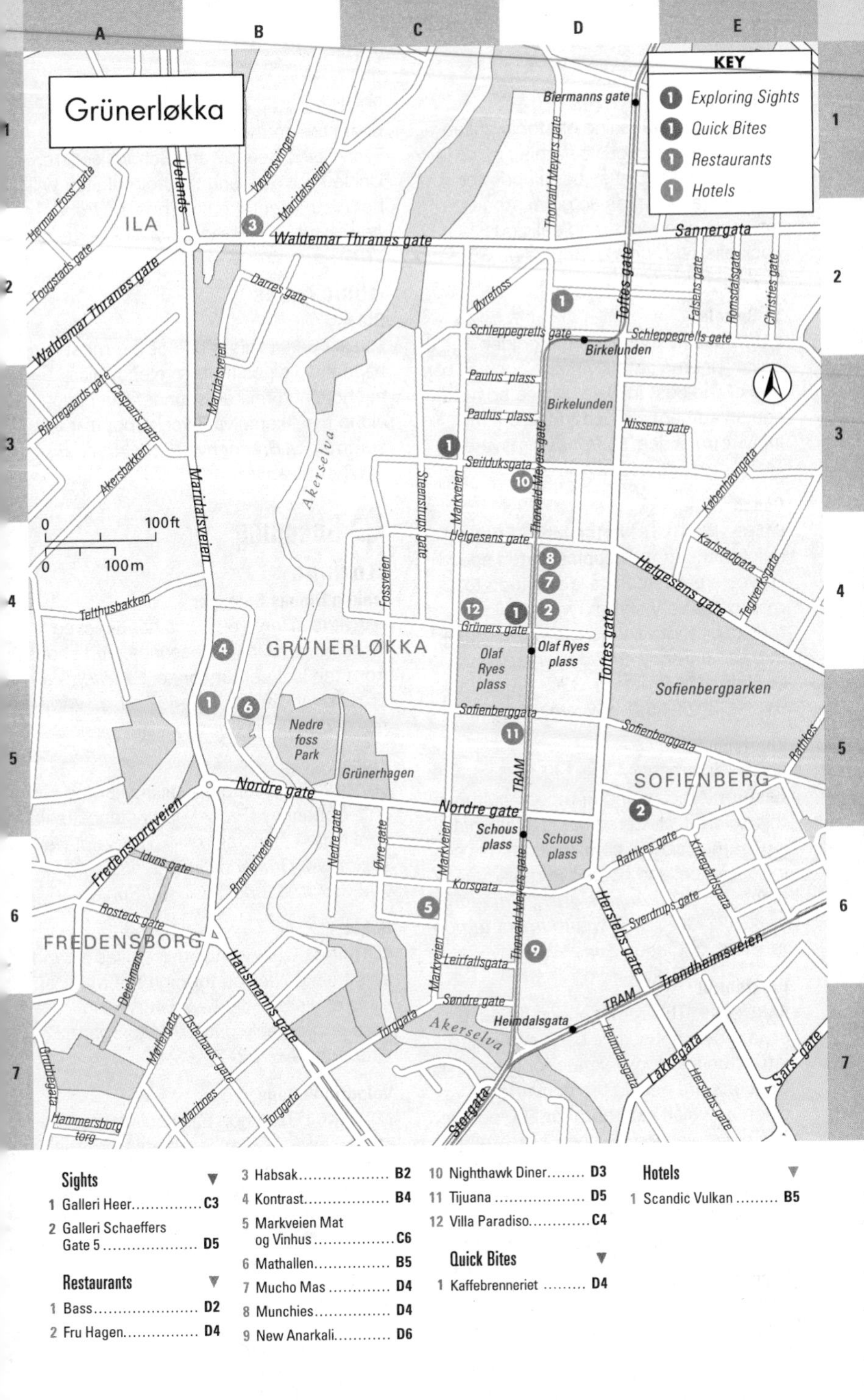

Sights

1 Galleri Heer **C3**

2 Galleri Schaeffers Gate 5 .... **D5**

Restaurants

1 Bass **D2**

2 Fru Hagen **D4**

3 Habsak **B2**

4 Kontrast **B4**

5 Markveien Mat og Vinhus **C6**

6 Mathallen **B5**

7 Mucho Mas **D4**

8 Munchies **D4**

9 New Anarkali **D6**

10 Nighthawk Diner **D3**

11 Tijuana **D5**

12 Villa Paradiso **C4**

Quick Bites

1 Kaffebrenneriet **D4**

Hotels

1 Scandic Vulkan **B5**

Bar Boca
BARS/PUBS | With a line of stools pulled up to the curvaceous bar, this tiny, mysterious space has been open for decades and serves up great stories, interesting regulars, and delicious cocktails. ✉ *Thorvald Meyers gt. 30, Oslo* ☎ *22–04–13–77.*

★ **Bettola**
BARS/PUBS | Experience the golden age of Italian cinema at this vintage cocktail bar, one of the best in Oslo. Movie posters add an authentic touch to the charmingly retro scene. ✉ *Trondheimsveien 2, Grünerløkka* ☎ *465–57–776.*

Couch
CAFES—NIGHTLIFE | In the hip Grünerløkka neighborhood, this sophisticated spot serves creative cocktails and food to match. It's very stylish, with mellow music, picture windows, a wood-topped bar, and a trendy crowd to match. ✉ *Thorvald Meyers gt. 33C, Grünerløkka* ☎ *22–37–07–05* 🌐 *www.tealounge.no.*

Khartoum Bar
CAFES—NIGHTLIFE | A mix of Middle Eastern, African, and European cultures, this colorful, cluttered bar is a fascinating journey across continents. It has an inclusive feel and hosts live music many nights. ✉ *Bernt Ankers gt. 17, Grünerløkka* ☎ *922–32–273* 🌐 *khartoumcontemporary.com* 🕒 *Closed Sun.–Wed.*

Parkteatret
BARS/PUBS | This atmospheric art deco–style movie house has been converted into a fun and funky venue for live music. Concerts are held in the converted cinema, which has room for 500 people. The old projection booth is a recording studio. To get a sense of the laid-back Grünerløkka lifestyle, chill out here with a cocktail. ✉ *Olaf Ryes pl. 11, Grünerløkka* ☎ *22–35–63–00* 🌐 *www.parkteatret.no.*

Schouskjelleren
BREWPUBS/BEER GARDENS | Flickering candles, a massive fireplace, and stained-glass windows make this microbrewery feel like a step back in time. Over 60 beers are on the menu—including Evil Twin Disco Beer 97 and Schouskjelleren Uncle Knut 32—and the helpful staff will help you select the right one. ✉ *Trondheimsveien 2, Grünerløkka* ☎ *21–38–39–30* 🌐 *schouskjelleren.no.*

MUSIC CLUBS

Blå
MUSIC CLUBS | This is one of the most happening clubs for jazz, electronica, hip-hop, and related sounds. The patio, along the Akerselva River, is popular in summer. ✉ *Brennerivn. 9C, Grünerløkka* 🌐 *www.blaaoslo.no.*

Shopping

CLOTHING

Frøken Dianas Salonger
CLOTHING | Here you'll find hand-picked fashions, jewelry, accessories, and shoes from the last century or so. ✉ *Markveien 56, Grünerløkka* ☎ *467–607–11* 🌐 *www.frokendianassalonger.no.*

Probat
CLOTHING | Grünerløkka still has some hip little boutiques. Probat, for instance, sells cool Norwegian T-shirts. ✉ *Thorvald Meyers gt. 54, Grünerløkka* ☎ *22–35–20–70* 🌐 *www.probat.no* 🕒 *Closed Sun.*

Robot
CLOTHING | Quirky and advice-filled attendants help guide you through the magical rows of vintage clothes. Everything here is affordably priced. ✉ *Korsgata 22, Grünerløkka* ☎ *22–71–99–00.*

Velouria Vintage
CLOTHING | This shop has cool clothes, shoes, bags, and accessories from the '60s, '70s, and '80s. ✉ *Thorvald Meyers gt. 34, Grünerløkka* ☎ *909–75–191* 🌐 *velouriavintage.no.*

Chapter 4

OSLOFJORD

Updated by
Alexandra Pereira

Sights	Restaurants	Hotels	Shopping	Nightlife
★★★★☆	★★★☆☆	★★★☆☆	★★☆☆☆	★☆☆☆☆

WELCOME TO OSLOFJORD

TOP REASONS TO GO

★ **Explore massive fortresses:** In towns like Drøbak and Halden you can wander through centuries-old fortresses that defended against invaders by land and sea.

★ **World-class artworks:** An expected surprise in this rather rural region is its impressive array of internationally recognized museums and galleries.

★ **Fjordside dining and drinking:** Alongside abundant shellfish platters and freshly caught salmon and turbot are plenty of locally brewed aquavits and beers.

★ **You sank my battleship:** Explore the fascinating history of the doomed World War II warship *Blücher* at the stunning Oscarsborg Festning.

★ **Stay in a piece of history:** You won't find chain hotels here: Oslofjord's lodgings range from quaint B&Bs to boutique charmers to huge houses on secluded islands.

The lush, green, and hilly communities around Oslo are a pleasure to visit in themselves, but they also contain many historic monuments, interesting museums, and handsome manor houses that give you a glimpse into the daily lives of Norwegians. The eastern fjord is by far the most popular for day-trippers, with towns like Drøbak and Fredrikstad getting the most attention for their lovely waterfronts and well-preserved wooden houses. But the western fjords have their charms as well, drawing people interested in the region's history.

1 **Drøbak.** Popular for day-trips from the capital, Drøbak has all the quaint wooden houses of towns in the south but is convenient enough for a quick visit.

2 **Son.** Popular with a literary crowd, Son has always been a popular resort for Oslo natives, who flock here in the summer to swim and sail.

3 **Fredrikstad.** Norway's oldest fortified city is an easy trip from Oslo, just an hour by train or car.

4 **Halden.** Near the Swedish border, lovely Halden was once a hotly disputed destination, hence its imposing fortress.

5 **Bærum.** While there's not a lot to pull in tourists, this fashionable residential suburb of Oslo does have a couple of impressive museums, as well as Norway's oldest restaurant.

6 **Vollen.** The lovely waterfront town has a good historical museum and is a quick 20-minute train ride from the capital.

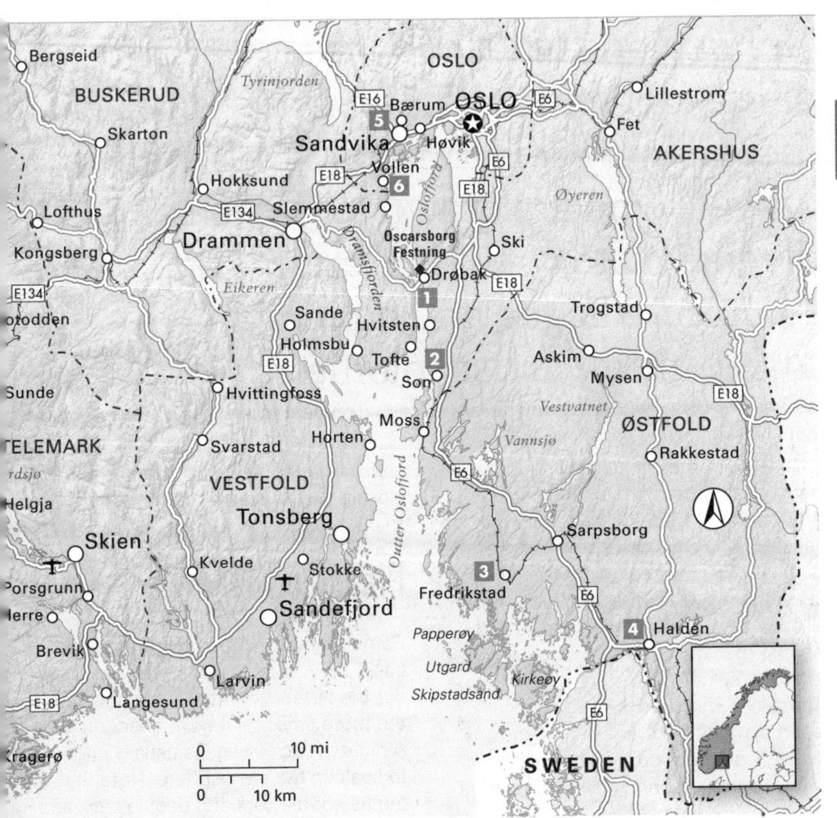

Bergseid
BUSKERUD
Tyrinjorden
OSLO
E16
Bærum
OSLO
E6
Lillestrom
5
Sandvika
Høvik
Fet
Skarton
AKERSHUS
E6
Vollen
Hokksund
E18
6
E18
Øyeren
Slemmestad
E134
Lofthus
Drammen
Oscarsborg Festning
Ski
Kongsberg
Drøbak
E18
Eikeren
E134
Dramsfjorden
1
Trogstad
Sande
Hvitsten
Holmsbu
Tofte
2
Askim
E18
Mysen
Son
Sunde
Hvittingfoss
E18
Vestvatnet
Moss
ØSTFOLD
TELEMARK
Svarstad
Horten
Vannsjø
Rakkestad
VESTFOLD
E6
Helgja
Tonsberg
Outter Oslofjord
Skien
Sarpsborg
Kvelde
Stokke
3
Fredrikstad
E6
Sandefjord
Halden
4
Papperøy
Brevik
Utgard
Kirkeøy
Larvin
Skipstadsand
E18
Langesund
E6
Kragerø
10 mi
SWEDEN
0
10 km

Directly south and west of Norway's capital city, the Oslofjord area is a summer vacation destination for many Norwegians who love the slower pace of life along the tranquil waterway. It's increasingly a destination for travelers as well, who are drawn to its rich and diverse history: Viking landmarks, fortified villages, and bohemian 19th-century artist colonies.

Residents of the capital escape to the east coast of the fjord in the summer, enjoying the idyllic coastal towns that are reachable by car, bus or train—oftentimes by boat or ferry directly from the city's downtown docks. The harbor areas are filled with interesting restaurants and shops. The waterfront towns west of Oslo are seldom explored by travelers. These communities .have traditionally been some of Norway's oldest and wealthiest, their fortunes derived from whaling and lumbering. Museums here recall that proud past.

Planning

When to Go

The weather here is typically Scandinavian, meaning the short summer season (June to August) beckons the capital's masses to their cabins around the fjord. Visiting a month or two earlier or later in the year will be fewer crowds, but will also see some seasonal establishments closing for the season. Always make sure to book ahead.

Planning Your Time

Some of the towns on Oslofjord can easily be visited as day trips from Oslo, but the farther you travel from the capital, the more time you'll want to spend here. A night in each village is usually enough to soak up the atmosphere. Note that ferries shuttle cars and people back and forth between islands and across the fjord, so it is possible to combine this tour with a trip to the west side of the Oslofjord and make a complete circle without backtracking.

Getting Here and Around

There's no need to hit the road, as multiple trains and buses from Oslo Station leave daily bound for coastal communities like Drøbak and Fredrikstad. But the best way to get here is renting an electric car so you can cover more distance and wander a bit off the beaten path. Plenty of charging points pepper the region.

BOAT AND FERRY TRAVEL

In summer, ferries take you from Oslo's Aker Brygge to Drøbak. The journey takes 90 minutes and stops at 12 ports along the way.

BUS TRAVEL

Buses from the main bus terminal in Oslo stop at numerous towns and cities down the coast. Buses take you to Drøbak in an hour, or Fredrikstad in 90 minutes. Flybussen airport shuttles take you directly from Oslo Airport to Frederikstad.

CAR TRAVEL

Driving through this region is a breeze, with the E18 taking you from Oslo to the E6 coastal route, which takes you as far south as Fredrickstad. The signage is in Norwegian, but the names of all the main destinations are the same as the English. If you'd like to explore both sides of the fjord, a tunnel links Drøbak, on the east side of the fjord, with Hurum, on the west side.

TRAIN TRAVEL

Day trips are easy, as hourly trains to Fredrikstad depart from Oslo Central Station.

Restaurants

It's no surprise that many of the most popular restaurants sit on the waterfront and focus primarily on seafood. Keep in mind that many operate only in summer, so call ahead if you're traveling off season.

Hotels

You'll find fewer chain hotels in Oslofjord than most other places around Norway. Scattered around the region are family-run bed-and-breakfasts, luxurious spa hotels, and everything in between. Many are closed during the winter, so call ahead.

Restaurant and hotel reviews have been shortened. For more information, visit Fodors.com.

What It Costs in Norwegian Krone

$	$$	$$$	$$$$
RESTAURANTS			
under NKr 125	NKr 125–NKr 250	NKr 251–NKr 350	over NKr 350
HOTELS			
under NKr 750	NKr 750–NKr 1250	NKr 1251–NKr 1900	over NKr 1900

Visitor Information

CONTACTS Destination Akershus. 🌐 *www.akershus.com/en.* **Visit Østfold.** 🌐 *www.visitoestfold.com/en/.*

Drøbak

35 km (21 miles) south of Oslo.

Drøbak's pretty collection of colorful wooden houses and winding cobblestone streets gives the impression of a typical Sørlander (southern) town, yet it is less than a half-hour's drive from the capital. Oslovians often take day trips to Drøbak to sit by the beach and eat freshly caught shrimp at waterfront restaurants. It has some of the region's most captivating sights, including the island fortress called Oscarbord Festning. If you have kids in tow, take them to see the sea creatures at Drøbak Akvarium.

GETTING HERE AND AROUND

A 20-minutes drive from Oslo—take the E18 or the E6 south, then the E134 for the last few miles to the waterfront–Drøbak is also reachable by bus or train. This is a community that lavishes its

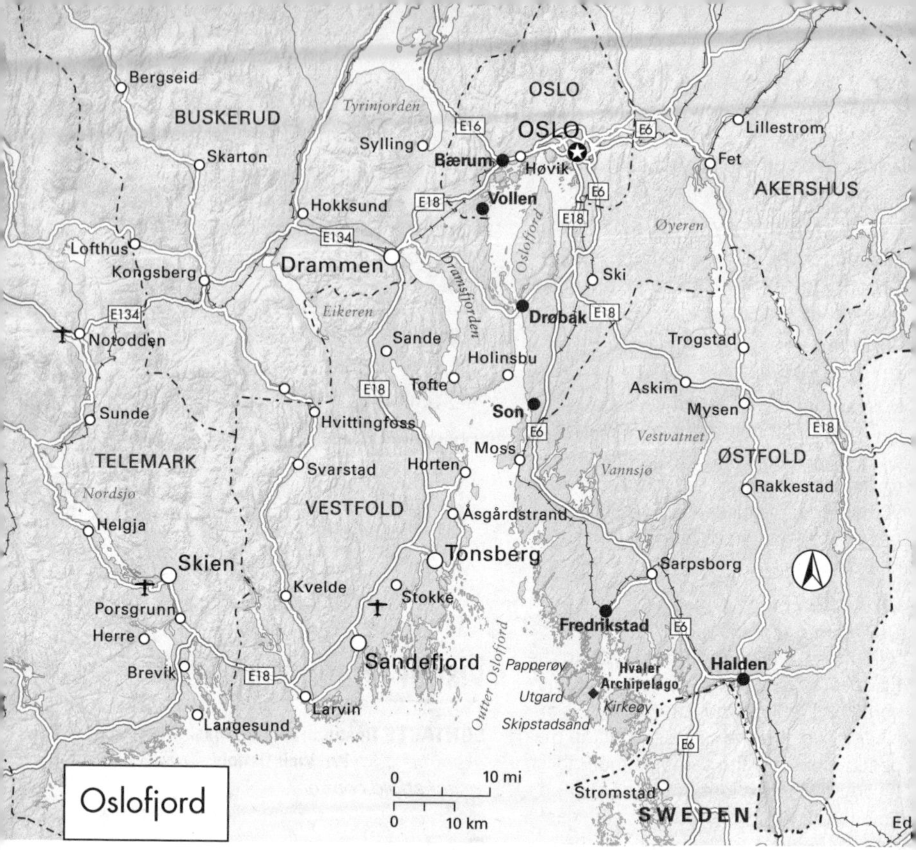

Oslofjord

attention on its waterfront, and getting here by boat shows it off to its best advantage. From May to September you can take the scenic one-hour ferry ride from Oslo's Aker Brygge to Drøbak. If you're driving, the trip takes a little over 30 minutes.

VISITOR INFORMATION

CONTACTS Visit Drøbak. 🌐 *www.visitdrobak.no/en.*

Sights

Drøbak Akvarium (*Drøbak Aquarium*)
ZOO | **FAMILY** | This small but interesting aquarium has 14 tanks filled with creatures from the fjords that will delight youngsters, from a deep-sea eel named Morgan to a catfish called Hugo. In the giant basins kids can touch the colorful starfish collected by manager Klaus Bareksten. ✉ *Havnegata 4, Drøbak* ☎ *91–10–84–20* 🌐 *drobakakvarium.no* 🕑 *NKr 70.*

Drøbak Båthavna (*Drøbak Harbor*)
MARINA | Everyone knows the *Little Mermaid* sculpture in Copenhagen's harbor, but there are three mermaids sitting on the rocks at Drøbak Harbor. The bronze sculpture—a local favorite because of its light, playful look—is by Norwegian artist Reidar Finsrud. They sit beside the harbor not far from the Drøbak Akvarium. ✉ *Havnagata, Drøbak.*

Drøbak Gjestehavn (*Drøbak Marina*)
MARINA | With pretty views of the fjord, Drøbak Marina is the first sight many newcomers see when they arrive in this seaside town. It's the home of Sjøstjernen, one of the region's most popular restaurants. ✉ *Badehusgata, Drøbak* ☎ *64–90–60–00.*

Drøbak Kirke (*Drøbak Church*)
RELIGIOUS SITE | An exquisitely crafted wooden building created in 1764, Drøbak Church sits in the middle of the lush Badeparken. The small but impressive space includes boat sculptures, nautical mobiles, and a special royal balcony over the regular pews. A heavy Gothic crucifix accentuates the altar, contrasting with a dreamy blue-and-white painted ceiling. ✉ *Kirkegata 18, Drøbak* ☎ *64–90–61–70.*

Friluftsmuseet (*Open-Air Museum*)
MUSEUM | **FAMILY** | In the depths of a forest not far from Drøbak you'll find the impressive addition to the Follo Museum. Old houses from around the Oslofjord area have been brought here to create an open-air exhibition that includes displays about the region's history and contemporary arts and handicrafts. ✉ *Belsjøveien 17, Drøbak* ☎ *66–93–66–36* 🌐 *mia.no/follomuseum/friluftsmuseet* ⏲ *Closed Mon.*

★ **Oscarsborg Festning** (*Oscarsborg Fortress*)
MILITARY SITE | Reached by ferry from Drøbak or Oslo, the imposing Oscarsborg Fortress with huge cannons on its battlements is a must-see for any first-time visitor to the region. The east side of the fortress has lovely views of the fjord and the waterfront of Drøbak. Enter the fortress through its dark, hidden corridors and you'll be transported back to 1845, when the island was named for King Oscar and transformed into a stronghold to repel attacks by sea. By 1905, it was regarded as the strongest fortress in Europe. It continued to be an important military base until World War II, when it launched the torpedoes that sank the German battleship *Blücher* in 1940. It was officially decommissioned in 2002, when it became primarily a site for summertime opera and other performances. Guided tours of the on-site museum are given by enthusiastic guides. Enjoy a light lunch at the fjordside cafeteria, or a magical meal at the Oscarsborg Hotel's restaurant. ✉ *Oscarsborg* ☎ *81–55–19–00* 🌐 *www.visitnorway.com/listings/oscarsborg-fortress-museum/2634.*

Tusenfryd Amusement Park
AMUSEMENT PARK/WATER PARK | **FAMILY** | Norway's oldest amusement park still offers plenty of thrills with its more than 30 rides and attractions. ThunderCoaster, a huge wooden roller-coaster with the steepest drop in Europe, is a real adrenalin rush. The park is in Vinterbro, on the way from Oslo. A daily shuttle bus departs from Oslo Bussterminalen Galleriet, near Oslo Central Station. Hours vary, but it's usually open daily in summer and weekends in spring and fall. ✉ *Fryds Vei 25, Vinterbro* 🌐 *www.tusenfryd.no/en/park-info* 🎫 *NKr 329.*

Coffee and Quick Bites

Guri Malla
$ | **NORWEGIAN** | **FAMILY** | This charming ice cream parlor feels a bit like an Italian gelateria. Homemade varieties like pistachio and caramel are churned out and transformed into cones, cups, or sundaes. **Known for:** good selection of homemade pastries; quick lunchtime sandwiches; tempting display cases. [$] *Average main: NKr 25* ✉ *Torget 3, Drøbak* ☎ *901–98–700.*

Restaurants

Det Gamle Bageri Ost & Vinstue
$$ | **NORWEGIAN** | Even the name—which translates as the Old Bakery, Wine, and Cheese Room—has plenty of charm at this eatery in an 18th-century wooden house painted an earthy red. Drop by early for salads and sandwiches, or later in the day for such hearty fare as salmon in a mouthwatering sweet-mustard sauce. **Known for:** outdoor tables are in high demand; music-loving crowd; small but robust menu. [$] *Average main: NKr 220* ✉ *Havnebakken 1, Drøbak* ☎ *64–93–21–05.*

Kumlegården

$$ | **NORWEGIAN** | A vast and exciting menu of delicacies from the sea, forest, and farm distinguish this low-ceilinged restaurant and lounge. A smart à la carte lunch and dinner menu draws locals and tourists alike, and the lovely interior is well kept and full of character. **Known for:** old-fashioned, friendly service; creative seafood starters; reindeer main dishes. *Average main: NKr 240 Niels Carlsens gt. 11, Drøbak 64–93–89–90.*

Sjøstjernen

$$ | **NORWEGIAN** | Located at Drøbak Gjestehavn, this local favorite has a name that means "Starfish" in Norwegian. The concrete-and-glass facade is a chic standout in this traditional town, and from your table you'll have fjord views for miles. **Known for:** no better place to take in the fjord; buzzy atmosphere; live music. *Average main: NKr 180 Badehusgata 27, Drøbak 90–75–61–15.*

Skipperstuen

$$ | **NORWEGIAN** | Overlooking the harbor, this charming waterside gem has a gleaming white dining room inside and an expansive terrace outside with tables shaded by a huge tree. Seafood is the specialty here, ranging from salmon carpaccio prepared with smoked black tea to steamed mussels with white wine and cream. **Known for:** casual but elegant ambience; fresh shellfish and bread; beautiful views. *Average main: NKr 220 Havnebakken 11, Drøbak 64–93–07–03 www.skipperstuen.no Closed Mon. and Tues.*

Telegrafen

$$ | **NORWEGIAN** | The original building was destroyed by a fire, but it was carefully restored using old-fashioned carpentry techniques. It's the spitting image of the original, down to the types of wood trim and the patterns of the wallpaper. **Known for:** exquisite architectural design; fjord views from terrace; tasty desserts. *Average main: NKr 250 Storgata 10, Drøbak 64–90–82–00.*

Hotels

Oscarsborg Hotel

$$$ | **HOTEL** | It's housed in an old army barracks, but don't let that fool you into thinking that this historic hotel on the island of Oscarsbord doesn't have charming surroundings, chic furnishings, and amenities to rival any other lodging in the area. **Pros:** handsome brick building with lots of character; wonderful restaurant with sweeping views; fitness area. **Cons:** reachable only by boat; no pool or spa area; not all rooms have views. *Rooms from: NKr 1300 Oscarsborg Festning, Oscarsborg 64–90–40–00 www.festningshotellene.no 89 rooms Free breakfast.*

★ Ramme Fjordhotell

$$$$ | **HOTEL** | Surrounded by manicured gardens, flower-filled greenhouses, earthy stables, and dense forests, Ramme Fjordhotell is a very special place. **Pros:** exquisitely designed property; delicious farm-to-table cuisine; easy to reach from Oslo. **Cons:** all this opulence comes at a high price; not close to other dining options; near, but not on, the fjord. *Rooms from: NKr 2250 Rammeveien 100, Hvitsten 12 km (8 miles) south of Drøbak 64–98–32–00 www.ramme.no/no/Hotell 42 rooms Free breakfast.*

★ Reenskaug Hotel

$$ | **HOTEL** | For more than a century, this has been Drobak's most prized place for an overnight stay. **Pros:** well-regarded restaurant and bar; central location; historic charm. **Cons:** simple continental breakfast; easy to get lost in corridors; weak Wi-Fi in some areas. *Rooms from: NKr 1039 Storgata 32, Drøbak 64–98–92–00 www.reenskaug.no 28 rooms Free breakfast.*

On an island in the middle of the Oslofjord, Oscarsborg Festning has protected the waterway since 1845.

Shopping

Drøbak is a community that feels like it was made for shopping. Strogata, one of the main streets, has shops and cafés and a gorgeous art deco cinema. Anchored by a huge blue-and-white library, the market area of Torget is surrounded by pretty old buildings. If you're looking for fashion boutiques, try Niels Carlsens Gate.

★ Galleri Finsrud

ART GALLERIES | With a shock of white hair and paint-covered dungarees, artist Reidar Finsrud is often found at his studio and gallery displaying works ranging in style from neoclassical to contemporary. There's also a manicured garden full of ponds and fountains. But the pièce de résistance is Finsrud City, a scale model of a community constantly in motion. The details is amazing, down to boats in the harbor, buses whizzing through tunnels, and tourists taking snapshots from a bridge. ✉ *Badeveien 12, Drøbak* ☎ *64–93–23–99* 🌐 *galleri-finsrud.no* ⏲ *Closed Sun.*

★ Tregaarden's Julehus (*Tregaarden's Christmas House*)

GIFTS/SOUVENIRS | **FAMILY** | Christmas never ends in Drobak, thanks to shop owner Eva Johansen, who bubbles over with enthusiastic stories about her connection to Santa Claus. Kids send him thousands of letters in care of Johansen, a testament to how convincing she can be. She drew and designed many of the beautifully made cards, toys, and ornaments on sale here. The glittering shop, which dominates the town's central square, was originally built in 1876 to house seafarers unable to reach Oslo when the fjord was frozen over. ✉ *Havnebakken 6, Drøbak* ☎ *64–93–41–78* 🌐 *julehus.no.*

Son

25 km (15 miles) south of Droøbak.

You can swim, sail, or sun on the banks of Son (pronounced soon), just south of Drnbak. An old fishing and boating village, this resort town has traditionally attracted artists and writers. Artists still flock here—if you're lucky you'll see author Jo Nesbo performing with his band—as do city folk in summer.

GETTING HERE AND AROUND

Directly south of Drøbak, the coastal village of Son is an easy side trip. There are also buses here from Oslo that take about 40 minutes.

Sights

Son Kystkultursenter (*Son Coastal Culture Center*)
MUSEUM | On the harbor in Son, the diminutive Son Coastal Culture Center has a museum on the dock, some handsome old boats in the water, and a small shop. ✉ *Storggata 19, Son* ☎ *66–93–66–36* 🌐 *www.follomuseum.com* ⏲ *Closed Mon. and mid-Aug.–mid-May.*

Restaurants

Restaurant Sjoeboden Son
$$ | **NORWEGIAN** | In a rusty red building on the waterfront, Restaurant Sjoeboden Son has a cozy dining room with walls made from rough-hewn logs and an outdoor terrace extending out over the water. There are plenty of seafood dishes, such as steamed mussels with perfectly done fries. **Known for:** beautiful older building on the waterfront; exceptional service start to finish; small menu of local favorites. $ *Average main: NKr 220* ✉ *Storgata 27, Son* ☎ *465–44–811* ⏲ *Closed Mon.*

Hotels

Hotell Refsnes Gods
$$$ | **HOTEL** | This historic hotel has one of Norway's best kitchens and a fine wine cellar. **Pros:** opulence of a grand country house; haven for art and history lovers; natural setting. **Cons:** prices on the high side; may feel a bit formal; far from major sights. $ *Rooms from: NKr 1300* ✉ *Godset 5, Son* ☎ *69–27–83–00* 🌐 *www.clasicnorway.no/hotell/hotell-refsnes-gods* *57 rooms* 🍽 *Free breakfast.*

★ **Son Spa**
$$$$ | **HOTEL** | In the idyllic artists' colony of Son, this much-loved property is much more than a spa (although many people do come for the indoor and outdoor pools, hot tubs, and saunas, along with a range of indulgent treatments). **Pros:** well-equipped spa area and fitness room; great restaurant and evening entertainment; spacious and bright guest rooms. **Cons:** you have to love ultra-modern design; restaurant is loud when there's live music; pool area can get crowded. $ *Rooms from: NKr 2000* ✉ *Hollandveien 30, Son* ☎ *64–98–48–00* 🌐 *www.sonspa.no* *148 rooms* 🍽 *Free breakfast.*

Fredrikstad

61 km (38 miles) south of Son.

Norway's oldest fortified city lies peacefully at the mouth of the Glomma, the country's longest river. Its bastions and moat date from the 1600s. Don't miss the atmospheric Gamlebyen, or Old Town, with half-timbered houses, moats, and drawbridges.

GETTING HERE AND AROUND

Getting to Fredrikstad is easy, whether you're coming from Drøbak or Son farther up the coast (driving is the best option for the short trip) or all the way from Oslo (driving down the E6 takes about an hour, and a train from Oslo Central Station takes just a few minutes longer).

Fredrikstad's atmospheric Gamlebyen, or Old Town, draws visitors all summer.

The fun and free ferry linking old and new towns is a must.

VISITOR INFORMATION

CONTACTS Visit Fredrikstad and Hvaler. *www.visitoestfold.com/en/fredrikstad-and-hvaler.*

Sights

Fredrikstad Domkirke (*Fredrikstad Cathedral*)

RELIGIOUS SITE | In the center of town is the massive Fredrikstad Cathedral, built in 1860 in a flamboyant neogothic style. It contains stained-glass decorations by Emanuel Vigeland, whose work also adorns Oslo Cathedral. *Riddervoldsgate 5, Fredrikstad* *69–95–98-00.*

Fredrikstad Museum

MUSEUM | **FAMILY** | This small museum not far from the waterfront details the development of the town from the 16th century to the present day. It's especially fun for kids, who get to whittle toys that kids from bygone days would have enjoyed. Hours vary, so call ahead. *Tøihusgaten 41, Fredrikstad* *69–11–56–50* *ostfoldmuseene.no/fredrikstad* *NKr 80.*

Restaurants

Big Fish Cafe

$$ | **NORWEGIAN** | This family-run bistro and brewery is beloved by locals, summer seasoners, and first-timers alike. It serves the usual fish-and-chips and seafood platters, but nothing is greasy, slapdash, or standard. **Known for:** massive outdoor terrace; killer cocktails; cool staff. *Average main: NKr 220* *Torvet 6, Fredrikstad* *69–37–88–00* *bigfishcafe.no* *Closed Mon.–Thurs.*

Første Reis

$$ | **NORWEGIAN** | This restaurant may look unassumingly traditional, but is in fact incredibly innovative when it comes to fresh takes on old favorites. The wine selection is extensive, so enjoy a chilled glass of Chablis with a simple shrimp sandwich for lunch or something heartier along with a decadent grilled turbot in

a chocolate sauce for dinner. **Known for:** quirky takes on Norwegian classics; catch of the day from the fjord; elaborate desserts. *Average main: NKr 208 Under Kollen 2, Fredrikstad 919–17–733 www.forste-reis.no.*

Majoren

$$$ | **NORWEGIAN** | Fit for the explorer in need of a hearty lunch or dinner, this much-loved seafood and game restaurant is run by a dedicated Austrian hunter, angler, and forager named Markus Nagele. Order catch of the day, or take advantage of its famous game buffet. **Known for:** heavy game banquets; hunting and fishing crowd; near the major sights. *Average main: NKr 250 Voldportgaten 73, Fredrikstad 69–32–15–55 www.majoren.no.*

Hotels

★ Gamlebyen Hotell

$$$ | **HOTEL** | With each room named after a Norwegian national treasure, the Gamlebyen Hotell is a true gem in the center of Fredrikstad. **Pros:** organic toiletries and heart-shaped chocolates on your pillow; light and airy decor; superb breakfast. **Cons:** no reception at night; some rooms are small; books up fast. *Rooms from: NKr 1258 Voldportgaten 72, Fredrikstad 400–539–09 gamlebyenhotell.no 15 rooms No meals.*

Shopping

Glashütte

CRAFTS | A well-known glass-blowing studio and shop, Glashütte's work is exhibited and sold in galleries throughout Norway. You can watch glassblowers perform their magic, creating everything from squat schnapps glasses to delicate vases. The staff will even create a one-of-a-kind souvenir you can pick up after it cools. *Torsnesvn. 1, Fredrikstad 69–32–28–12 www.glasshytta-gamlebyen.no.*

Halden

30 km (18 miles) south of Fredrikstad.

This idyllic little town has several historic attractions well worth a visit. Since it's close to the Swedish border, it once needed fortifications in order to fend off attacks—Norwegians and Swedes had ongoing border disputes. The most famous skirmish at Fredriksten fortress resulted in the death of King Karl XII in 1718.

GETTING HERE AND AROUND

Trains and buses travel here from Oslo, Fredrikstad, and other communities along the waterfront. The E6 is a straight shot from Fredrikstad, and the drive takes about 40 minutes.

VISITOR INFORMATION

CONTACTS Visit Halden. *69–19–09–80 www.visithalden.com.*

Sights

★ Fredriksten Festning (*Fredriksten Fortress*)

MILITARY SITE | **FAMILY** | Built in the late 1600s to keep out Swedish invaders, this star-shaped fortress sits at the city's highest point. The exhibit in the former prison describes its involvements in international conflicts from the 17th century to World War II. An old pharmacy illustrates the history of pharmacology, including the use of bird claws in folk medicine. At the far end of the inner courtyard, the bakery could once bake enough bread to feed 5,000 men, while the brewery could easily keep their thirsts quenched with 3,000 liters of beer. If all this makes you feel hungry, stop by Fredriksten Kro, an old-fashioned pub with outdoor seating. *Generalveien 27, Halden 69–11–56–50 www.visithalden.com.*

★ **Rød Herregård**

HOUSE | Rød Herregård is one of the finest and best-preserved 18th-century manors in Norway. A restored building houses period furniture, artwork, and an amazing display of stuffed-animal hunting trophies. An impressive baroque garden and an English garden surround the manor on the edge of the fjord. The house has a unique weapons collection, as well as a café and a gallery that are only open in the summer. Guided tours are offered three times a day May to September. ✉ *Herregårdsveien 10, Halden* ☎ *69–11–56–50* 🌐 *www.visitoestfold.com/no/halden/artikler/Rod-Herregard* ⏲ *Closed Oct.–Apr.*

Restaurants

Rekekaféen

$$ | **NORWEGIAN** | **FAMILY** | Near dockside sheds on a floating pier in the marina, Rekekaféen has a reputation for fresh fish and seafood. Enjoying the sea breezes and the views of the waterfront, the fishing boats are so close you can reach out and touch them. **Known for:** tasty smoked fish and shrimp; enormous seafood platters; fish soup is a favorite. [$] *Average main: NKr 250* ✉ *Strandstredet 4, Halden* 🌐 *www.rekekafeen.no* ⏲ *Closed Mon. and Tues.*

Bærum

13 km (8 miles) west of Oslo.

One of Oslo's fashionable suburbs, Bærum is about 20 minutes from the city. The area is mostly residential, but along the banks of the Lomma River is the charming Bærums Verk. In the 1960s the owners of the Bærums Verk iron foundry fixed up their old industrial town and made it into a historical site. Today the stores, workshops, and exhibitions among the idyllic surroundings attract many visitors to its grounds. As you explore the beautifully restored village, notice the cramped wooden cottages lining Verksgata, where the workers once lived. Notice that the doors arc in the back of the buildings; this was in case a fire from the works spread through the main street.

GETTING HERE AND AROUN

Bærum itself is a suburb of Oslo, so you have many ways to get here: buses, trains, or car. To get to Bærums Verk, take the subway to Lysaker Station, then transfer to bus 150.

Sights

Henie Onstad Kunstsenter (*Henie Onstad Art Center*)

MUSEUM | This impressive contemporary museum houses Norway's largest collection of international modern art. After skater Sonja Henie married shipping magnate Niels Onstad, they began to put together a collection of early-20th-century art, including important works by Munch, Picasso, Bonnard, and Matisse. The ultramodern, minimalist building, designed by Norwegian architects Jon Eikvar and Sven Erik Engebretsen, stands out impressively beside the scenic Oslofjord. There's also a sculpture park, a children's play area, and a well-regarded restaurant on-site. ✉ *Sonia Henies Vei 31, about 12 km (7 miles) southwest of Oslo, Bærum* ☎ *67–80–48–80* 🌐 *hok.no* 🎫 *NKr 120* ⏲ *Closed Mon.*

Museum of Bærums Verk

HISTORIC SITE | This museum has an extensive collection of cast-iron ovens that were produced at Bærums Verk, ranging from the 18th century to the mid-20th century when the plant closed its doors. Tours are available in English. ✉ *Verksgata 15, Bærums Verk* ☎ *67–13–00–18* 🌐 *www.baerumsverk.no* 🎫 *Free.*

Restaurants

Værtshuset Bærums Verk
$$$$ | NORWEGIAN | Norway's oldest restaurant, Værtshuset (literally "The Inn") is a must on any itinerary including the neighboring ironworks. The inn opened its doors in 1640 and was a frequent stop on the King's Road from Oslo to Bergen. **Known for:** wild game like venison; charming dining room; excellent staff. *Average main: NKr 665* *Vertshusveien 10, Bærums Verk* *67–80–02–00* *www.vaertshusetbaerum.no.*

Vollen

14 km (9 miles) southwest Bærum.

This waterfront community has a gorgeous harbor overlooking the fjord. It's a great place to stop as you're exploring the coast.

GETTING HERE AND AROUND

A train is the fastest way to get to Vollen from Oslo, taking just 20 minutes. Driving, either on your own or in a bus, takes about 10 minutes longer.

VISITOR INFORMATION

CONTACTS Destinasjon Vollen. *destinasjonvollen.no.*

Sights

Oslofjordmuseet (*Oslofjord Museum*)
MUSEUM | It started with a sprawling collection of wooden boats, but the Oslofjord Museum has become so much more than that. Here you can learn everything about the country's maritime past, its ever-growing beach culture, the history of boatbuilding—you name it, they have it. *Chr. Jensens Vei 8, Vollen* *406–06–635* *mia.no/oslofjordmuseet* *NKr 50* *Closed Mon.*

Restaurants

Vito's Restaurant
$$ | NORWEGIAN | This friendly, family-run restaurant on the waterfront offers everything from lasagna with a hearty meat sauce to fresh mussels with fries (a classic, and done very well here). The Sicilian chef prides himself on a varied menu that prioritizes Sicilian influences and fresh produce. **Known for:** waterfront location with plenty of outdoor seating; sophisticated decor; superb bar. *Average main: NKr 250* *Slemmestadveien 416, Vollen* *66–79–89–95* *vitosrestaurant.no.*

Chapter 5

SOUTHERN NORWAY

Updated by
Lisa Stentvedt

Sights ★★★★★ | Restaurants ★★★★★ | Hotels ★★★★☆ | Shopping ★★★☆☆ | Nightlife ★★☆☆☆

WELCOME TO SOUTHERN NORWAY

TOP REASONS TO GO

★ **Hike Preikestolen:** Towering Pulpit Rock is one of Norway's most famous hikes, and you're rewarded at the end with breathtaking views.

★ **Explore Kristiansand:** Wander the beautiful streets of the "capital of southern Norway," where you'll never run out of interesting historical sights.

★ **Relax in coastal towns:** You'll rub elbows with vacationing Norwegians in lovely waterfront communities like Kragerø and Sandefjord.

★ **Dig deep in Stavanger:** With an interesting history, this colorful city is home to northern Europe's largest and best-preserved collection of wooden houses.

★ **Cruise the Lysefjord:** One of Norway's most popular destinations, this majestic waterway reveals wonders like the gravity-defying Kjerag Boulder.

Southern Norway is comprised of beautiful coastal towns scattered along the southern coastline of Norway. Expect an archipelago of small, stone islands, and lots of sailing history and culture. Kristiansand and Stavanger are the best-known towns, but there are dozens of smaller waterfront communities well worth exploring.

1 Sandefjord. This beautiful coastal town is deeply rooted in fishing culture.

2 Kragerø. A popular holiday destination for Norwegians, Kragerø has lots of activity in high season.

3 Risør. This town has one of the best-preserved collection of wooden houses in Europe.

4 Arendal. This charming town has a little of the French Riviera's sophistication.

5 Grimstad. The perfect getaway, this idyllic summer town is famous as a shipbuilding center.

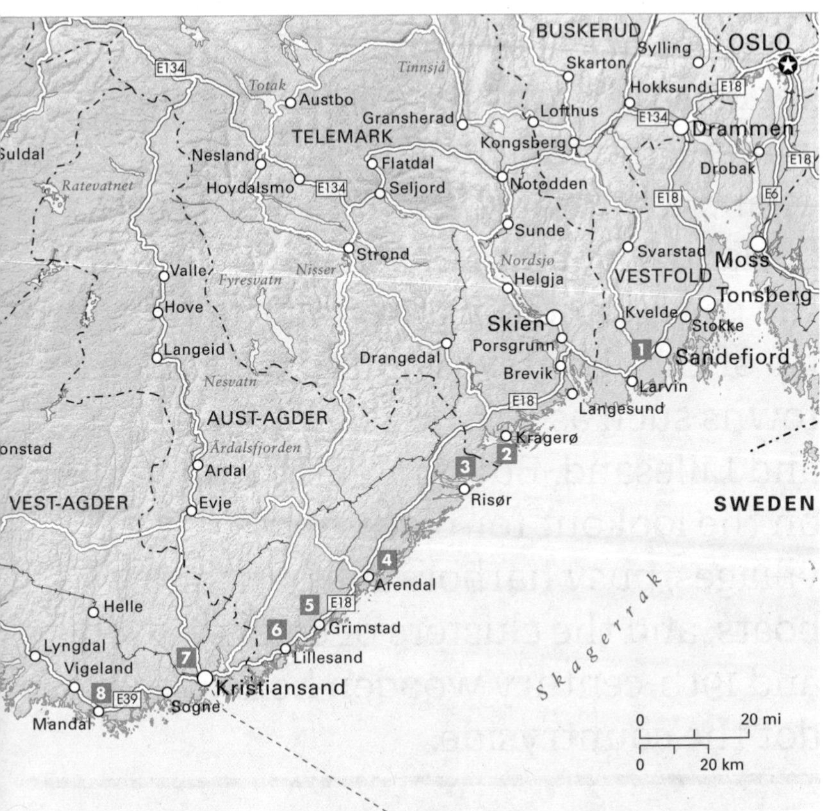

6 Lillesand. White wooden houses make this one of the region's most charming villages.

7 Kristiansand. Nicknamed "Summer City," this is definitely the destination for sun-soaked beaches.

8 Mandal. The southernmost town in Norway, this place has a gorgeous sandy beach.

9 Stavanger. The perfect starting point for exploring Pulpit Rock and the Kjerag Boulder.

10 Haugesund. Fun festivals throughout the year mean this community is always hopping.

In summer, many of Oslo's residents migrate to the beautiful and sunny southern coast. Southern Norway is an ideal getaway for those who want to get close to nature, with a mild summer climate and terrain varying from inland mountains and forests to coastal flatland. Nicknamed Norway's Riviera, the coast stretching around the southern tip of the country is dotted with resort towns such as Kristiansand, Sandefjord, and Lillesand. But you'll also want to be on the lookout for picturesque coastal villages, busy harbors full of fishing boats, and the clusters of colorful, 18th- and 19th-century wooden houses that dot the countryside.

The drive along the North Sea Road is a real pleasure. Wide, sun-kissed beaches have their blue waters warmed by the Gulf Stream. Sandy terrain turns to coastal flatlands, inland mountain peaks and green forests ideal for cycling, hiking, and mountaineering. Freshwater lakes and rivers, and this section of the ocean, are some of the best places for canoeing, kayaking, and rafting. The region is the perfect habitat for such wildlife as beavers, deer, foxes, and many birds. Southern Norway offers many unique experiences, whether you want to hike the famous Pulpit Rock or gaze out over the archipelago in Kragerø.

Planning

Visiting the area is not difficult, especially if you have a car. The communities are strung along the North Sea Road starting from Sandefjord in the east, passing Kristiansand in the south, then heading west to Stavanger. You can easily spend a day exploring the smaller towns, and that much or more in towns like Kristiansand

and Stavanger. Determine the length of your trip according to the number of towns you want to visit.

When to Go

The area is at its best in the summer season, from May to August. It gets quite warm during these months, and you will be surprised that you are still in Norway. The water in the ocean is cold no matter what the season, but that doesn't stop Norwegians. Traveling in the shoulder season in April and September is also pleasant, with warm weather and fewer people competing for the perfect spot on the sand.

Getting Here and Around

Getting to this region couldn't be easier. If you're pressed for time, you can fly into several of the coastal airports. There are also plenty of buses and trains speeding you here from Oslo and Bergen. The most picturesque way, of course, is by boat. Driving here is a snap, whether you make your way down from the larger cities or pick up a rental car once you're on the coast.

AIR TRAVEL

Stavanger is the major airport in the region, with SAS Scandinavian Airlines offering nonstop flights from Oslo, Bergen, Trondheim, and some European cities like Copenhagen. Norwegian offers flights from Oslo, Bergen, and some European cities. Loganair flies here from Newcastle, and Wizzair flies here from Gdansk and Kaunas.

Widerøe Airline specializes in flights within Norway, and serves both Kristiansand and Stavanger. Kristiansand Airport is served by SAS and Widerøe, with flights from Oslo, Bergen, and other Norwegian cities. Norwegian flies from Oslo, and KLM flies from Amsterdam.

BOAT TRAVEL

Fjord Line offers car ferries shuttling you between Stavanger and Bergen, Oslo, and Hirtshals, Denmark daily. It also runs between Kristiansand and Hirtshals.

CONTACTS Fjord Line. ☎ *51–46–40–99* 🌐 *fjordline.com/nb.*

BUS TRAVEL

Nor-Way Bussekspress runs between Oslo and Stavanger, about a 10-hour trip, and between Kristiansand and Stavanger, a 4 1/2-hour trip. Vy offers several daily departures for the 5-hour journey between Oslo and Kristiansand. Agder Kollektivtrafikk operates all public bus transport in the area.

CONTACTS Agder Kollektivtrafikk. ☎ *38–03–83–00* 🌐 *akt.no.* **Nor-Way Bussekspress.** ☎ *22–31–31–50* 🌐 *nor-way.no.* **Vy.** ☎ *40–70–50–70* 🌐 *vy.no.*

CAR TRAVEL

From Oslo it's 330 km (205 miles) to Kristiansand and 455 km (281 miles) to Stavanger. E18 mostly follows the coastline to Kristiansand, while E39 stays a little farther inland as it heads to Stavanger. Although seldom wider than two lanes, it is easy driving because it is so flat. Driving from Bergen to Stavanger is more challenging, requiring some detours and one or two ferry crossings.

TRAIN TRAVEL

The Sørlandsbanen leaves Oslo Central Station eight times daily for the five-hour journey to Kristiansand and seven times daily for the eight- to nine-hour journey to Stavanger. Eight more trains travel the three-hour Kristiansand–Stavanger route.

CONTACTS Vy. ☎ *61–05–19–10* 🌐 *vy.no.*

Restaurants

The restaurants in southern Norway are often heavily focused on seafood, and you can find some of the best (and freshest) fish at these establishments. All the major towns in the region are located on or very near to the ocean, so you'll find plenty of waterfront tables with spectacular views. The restaurants in the region tend to be casual, so there's no need to change before dinner. Norwegians do enjoy dressing up a little when dining out, however.

Hotels

Expect some charming hotels in the region, ranging from guesthouses to classic Norwegian chains such as Nordic Choice Hotels and Thon Hotels. The chains are always a safe choice, as they deliver the same great service regardless of which location you visit. The guesthouses and boutique hotels, however, provide you with a charming, rustic experience, and can make you feel at home in a way that no chain can.

Restaurant and hotel reviews have been shortened. For full information, visit Fodors.com.

What It Costs in Norwegian Krone

	$	$$	$$$	$$$$
RESTAURANTS	under NKr 125	NKr 125–NKr 250	NKr251–NKr350	over NKr 350
HOTELS	under NKr 750	NKr 750–NKr 1250	NKr 1251–NKr 1900	over NKr 1900

Visitor Information

CONTACTS Visit Sørlandet. *visitsorlandet.com.* **Region Stavanger.** *51–85–92–00* *no.regionstavanger-ryfylke.com.*

Sandefjord

124 km (77 miles) south of Oslo.

Sandefjord has been a popular destination for Norwegians (particularly those from Oslo) since the 1800s, when it was discovered as a spa destination. For a long time, trading and whaling were the major livelihoods of the city, and you still see traces of this today. It can be crowded, especially in the summer, but the tradeoff is great restaurants (with local seafood, of course) and boat excursions that take you along the beautiful coastline.

GETTING HERE AND AROUND

Sandefjord has easy connections with Oslo by bus, and Vestfoldbanen trains travel in each direction several times a day. E18 goes through the municipality as it continues farther down the coast, getting you here from Oslo in 90 minutes.

Sights

Bryggekapellet
RELIGIOUS SITE | Europe's only floating church, the little chapel of Bryggekapellet invites you in to light a candle or just contemplate the sound of the waves below. *Brygga 1, Sandefjord* *33–47–62–52* *sandefjord.kirken.no* *Closed Mon. Closed Sept.–May.*

Hvalfangstmonumentet (*Whaling Monument*)
MEMORIAL | Surrounded by graceful plumes of water, this handsome sculpture by Knut Steen has become a symbol of Sandefjord. The monument itself rotates continuously, which is quite impressive. *Hvalfangstmonumentet, Sandefjord.*

Hvalfangstmuseet (*Whaling Museum*)
MUSEUM | The only museum of its kind in Europe, this gem specializes in the history of whaling and whales. The main attraction—one that the kids will find

Southern Norway
OSLO
Drammen
Moss
Tonsberg
Skien
SWEDEN
Skagerrak
TELEMARK
VESTFOLD
AUST-AGDER
VEST-AGDER
ROGALAND
Stavanger
see detail
map
Kristiansand
see detail
map
Haugesund
Kopervik
Skudeneshavn
Forde
Bomlafjord
Vindafjord
Boknafjord
Josenfjord
Sand
Suldal
Saebo
Fister
Store
Auravatnet
Ratevatnet
Lysebotn
Roskrep-
fjorden
Sandnes
Kleppe
Bryne
Egersund
Sogndal
Tonstad
Vidrak
Helle
Lyngdal
Vestbygda
Spangereid
Vigeland
Mandal
Sogne
Valle
Hove
Langeid
Ardal
Årdalsfjorden
Evje
Nesvatn
Fyresvatn
Nisser
Totak
Austbo
Nesland
Hoydalsmo
Strond
Tinnsjå
Gransherad
Flatdal
Seljord
Notodden
Sunde
Nordsjø
Helgja
Tordal
Drangedal
Neslandsvatn
Porsgrunn
Brevik
Langesund
Kragerø
Jomfruland
Nasjonalpark
Risør
Arendal
Grimstad
Lillesand
Lofthus
Kongsberg
Skarton
Sylling
Hokksund
Komnes
Hvittingfoss
Svarstad
Kvelde
Stokke
Sandefjord
Larvin
Dramsfjord
Drobak
Sande
Tofte
Holen
Ski
Oslofjord
E134
E39
E18
E6
0
20 mi
0
20 km

fascinating—is a life-size model of a blue whale. The building itself has a long history, dating back to 1917. ✉ *Museumsgt. 39, Sandefjord* ☎ *94–79–33–41 vestfoldmuseene.no/hvalfangstmuseet* 🎫 *NKr 25* ⊗ *Closed Mon. Oct.–Apr.*

Restaurants

★ La Scala

$$ | **INTERNATIONAL** | This eatery doesn't just put you close to the water—it's actually floating just off the dock, providing views in nearly every directions. Decorated in maritime style, it has windows that can be rolled up to let you enjoy the summer breezes. **Known for:** perfect location; fireplace warms up cool nights; cozy atmosphere all year. $ *Average main: NKr 250* ✉ *Brygga 5, Sandefjord* ☎ *33–46–15–90* 🌐 *la-scala.no* ⊗ *Closed Sun.*

Kragerø

203 km (126 miles) southwest of Oslo, 89 km (55 miles) southwest of Sandefjord.

For many Norwegians, having a *hytte* (cabin) here is a longtime dream. Boats are the most popular mode of transportation in Kragerø, and the main street is a channel where people tie up at the dock and go ashore to dine at one of the many great restaurants.

GETTING HERE AND AROUND

From Oslo or Kristiansand, travel along E18 until you get to Gjerdemyra. From there, follow local Route 38 to the center of Kragerø. From Kragerø there are several boat connections out to the bigger islands in the archipelago. The nearest buses drop you off at Neslandsvatn Station in the nearby community of Drangedal.

Sights

Berg – Kragerø Museum

MUSEUM | This charming manor house in Louis XVI style was built by the Homann family in 1803, and it was used by them until 1943. Here you can learn about the history of the family and the "cabin life" that has become so popular in Norway. It also has an interesting exhibit on artist Edvard Munch, who spent time in Kragerø. ✉ *Barthebrygga 12, Kragerø* ☎ *35–54–45–00* 🌐 *telemarkmuseum.no/en/other-museums/berg-kragero-museum* ⊗ *Closed Sept.–May.*

★ Jomfruland Nasjonalpark (*Jomfruland National Park*)

NATIONAL/STATE PARK | Easily reached by ferry from Kragerø, Jomfruland National Park is a great way to see the archipelago and the animals that inhabit the area. Established in 2016, the 117-square-km (45-square-mile) protected area includes the islands of Jomfruland and Stråholmen. About 98% of the park area is ocean. Watch where you step, as tiny creatures inhabit the sand dunes. ✉ *Kragerø* 🌐 *jomfrulandnasjonalpark.no.*

Kittelsenhuset (*Kittelsen House*)

MUSEUM | Norwegian artist Theodor Kittelsen grew up in Kragerø, and his childhood home is now a museum. He is most famous for illustrating many children's stories and fairy tales, and most Norwegians have fond memories of his art. ✉ *Th. Kittelsens Vei 5, Kragerø* ☎ *35–54–45–00* 🌐 *telemarkmuseum.no/kittelsenhuset* 🎫 *NKr 80* ⊗ *Closed Mon. Closed Sept.–May.*

Restaurants

★ Skåtøy Kafe

$$ | **INTERNATIONAL** | Just 10 minutes by boat from Kragerø, charming Skåtøy Kafe has a perfect location on Skåtøy Island. There's inviting outdoor seating, a friendly staff, and a warm atmosphere. **Known for:** tasty fish soup; large selection of

The waterfront community of Risør is one of the best preserved wooden towns in Europe.

wine; open all summer. $ *Average main: NKr 200* ✉ *Stoppedalveien 2, Skåtøy Island* ☎ *92-04-33-14* 🌐 *skatoykafe.no* ⏲ *Closed Sept.–May.*

Risør

234 km (145 miles) southwest of Oslo, 51 km (32 miles) southwest of Kragerø.

One of the best preserved wooden towns in Europe, Risør is a charming coastal community with a long history of boatbuilding.

GETTING HERE AND AROUND

Risør is accessible by car, and is just under a three-hour drive from Oslo. The nearest train station is Gjerstad, which is served by Sørlandsbanen between Oslo and Kristiansand. If you're headed here by train, Gjerstad Station is 35 km (22 miles) from Risør.

Sights

Risør Akvarium

ZOO | FAMILY | The only saltwater aquarium in southern Norway, Risør Akvarium has more than 500 fish and marine animals that you can watch through massive glass windows. Kids love feeding the fish and checking out Norway's largest lobster. ✉ *Strandgate 14, Risør* ☎ *41-64-87-59* 🌐 *risorakvarium.no* 🎟 *NKr 100* ⏲ *Closed weekdays mid.-Aug.–mid.-June.*

Risør Fiskemottak

STORE/MALL | A stone's throw from the fishing trawlers and store warehouses, this market is where fishermen bring their fresh catch every day. *Fiskemottak* means "fish landing," and the name says it all. You're likely to see types of fish you've never laid eyes on before. ✉ *Solsiden 3, Risør* ☎ *37-15-23-50* 🌐 *fiskemottaket.no.*

Restaurants

★ Stangholmen Fyr (*Stangholmen Lighthouse Restaurant*)
$$$ | **NORWEGIAN** | This unique dining experience, open only in the summer months, allows you to sample the freshest local fish and seafood at a real lighthouse. Built right on the rock, the small building is made of white clapboard and has shutters that can close during inclement weather. **Known for:** the journey here is half the fun; seafood doesn't get any fresher; well-prepared steaks, too. *Average main: NKr 350* ✉ *Stangholmen Fyr, Risør* ☎ *900–93–400* 🌐 *stangholmen.no* 🕓 *Closed mid-Aug.–mid-June.*

Arendal

259 km (161 miles) southwest of Oslo, 49 km (30 miles) southwest of Risør.

In Arendal's *Tyholmen* (Old Town), pink and red flowers tumble from the flower boxes on the windows of the wooden houses. This is a charming town where you'll enjoy strolling through the narrow streets leading off the waterfront. Don't miss the town hall, built in 1815. It's Norway's tallest timber structure and has more than 300 portraits, most of them painted in the 19th century by local artists.

GETTING HERE AND AROUND

Arendal is 260 km (418 miles) south of Oslo. The drive along E18 takes about 3 hours and 20 minutes. There's also frequent bus service from Oslo operated by Vy.

Sights

Bomuldsfabriken
MUSEUM | An unusual gallery space, the restored Bomuldsfabriken (Cotton Factory) operated from 1898 to 1960, producing cotton flannel clothing. Today it has frequently changing art exhibits and a permanent collection of 35 works by some of Norway's foremost painters. ✉ *Oddenveien 5, Arendal* 🌐 *bomuldsfabriken.no* 🕓 *Closed Mon.*

★ Kuben Arendal
MUSEUM | Established in 1832, this museum displays a fascinating array of artifacts pertaining to coastal life, from toys to farm tools. Find out about the 1767 slave ship *Fredensborg* and learn more about the region's folk art traditions. ✉ *Parkveien 16, Arendal* ☎ *37–01–79–00* 🌐 *kubenarendal.no* 🎫 *NKr 90* 🕓 *Closed Mon.*

Merdøgaard Skjærgårdsmuseum
MUSEUM | A little off the beaten path, this museum is a 30-minute boat ride from Arendal. The early-18th-century sea captain's home now has exhibits exploring life in the region. After visiting, enjoy a swim on the beach or a walk around the island. ✉ *Merdøy, Arendal* 🌐 *kubenarendal.no/opplev-paa-kuben/merdoegaard* 🎫 *Guided tour NKr 90* 🕓 *Closed Sept.–mid-June.*

Restaurants

Egon Arendal
$$ | **INTERNATIONAL** | Norwegian classics made with high-quality ingredients are the staple at this eatery with a cozy dining room and a small terrace on the street. The atmosphere is casual, and orders are usually placed at the bar before you find a table. **Known for:** family-friendly vibe; outdoor seating; great appetizers. *Average main: NKr 240* ✉ *Thon Hotel Arendal, Friergangen 1, Arendal* ☎ *37–05–21–72* 🌐 *egon.no/restauranter/arendal.*

Hotels

Clarion Hotel Tyholmen
$$$ | **HOTEL** | This maritime hotel has the sea at close quarters and a magnificent view of the fjord. **Pros:** central location; excellent restaurant; breakfast included.

Cons: cash not accepted; parking is extra; books up in high season. *Rooms from: NKr 1500* *Teaterplassen 2, Arendal* *37–07–68–00* *nordicchoicehotels.no/hotell/norge/arendal/clarion-hotel-tyholmen* *96 rooms* *Free breakfast.*

Grimstad

277 km (172 miles) southwest of Oslo, 22 km (14 miles) southwest of Arendal.

Grimstad is a pretty coastal town with a charming wharf. In the mid-19th century, the town became famous as a shipbuilding center, and from 1844 to 1850 the teenage Henrik Ibsen worked as an apprentice at the local apothecary shop. Grimstad has attracted so many other writers over the years that it's called the "Town of Poets." A popular Norwegian short-film festival is held here in early summer.

GETTING HERE AND AROUND

E18 runs through the municipality, linking Grimstad to Kristiansand and other towns along the coast. Several daily buses operate between Grimstad and Oslo. Grimstad is a 3 1/2-hour drive from Oslo.

Sights

Ibsenhuset (*Ibsen House*)
MUSEUM | Restored to the way it looked in 1837, this museum is where playwright Herik Ibsen wrote his first play, *Catilina*. The museum also has a maritime exhibition and a section honoring Terje Vigen, a folk hero who was the subject of a poem by Ibsen. He is credited with riding to Denmark to bring back food for the starving Norwegians. *Henrik Ibsens gt. 14, Grimstad* *37–04–04–90* *gbm.no/ibsenmuseet* *NKr 90* *Closed Sept.–mid-June.*

Restaurants

★ Apotekergaarden
$$ | **INTERNATIONAL** | In the center of town, Apotekergaarden offers seating in a charmingly old-fashioned dining room or outside on a terrace. The varied menu offers something for everyone, including pizza topped with fresh mozzarella and baked in a stone oven. **Known for:** fish direct from the fishermen; great selection of small plates; large array of burgers. *Average main: NKr 225* *Skolegaten 3, Grimstad* *37–04–50–25* *apotekergaarden.no.*

Lillesand

294 km (183 miles) southwest of Oslo, 21 km (13 miles) southwest of Grimstad.

An idyllic coastal town, Lillesand has one of Norway's best harbors, which is usually bustling with locals taking their boats out for a spin. In town you will see many of the white wooden houses typical of the region.

GETTING HERE AND AROUND

Lillesand can be reached by car via E18, which goes through the municipality. In the summer, it is possible to travel between Lillesand and Kristiansand by boat, with several stops in between. Lillesand is a 3 1/2-hour drive from Oslo, and a half-hour drive from Kristiansand.

Sights

Høvåg Kirke (*Høvåg Church*)
RELIGIOUS SITE | Dating from AD 1000, the 33-foot-long Høvåg Church was expanded in 1768 and again in 1828. Construction wasn't completed until 1966, when the beautiful stone structure finally looked as it does today. *Bliksundveien 64, Høvåg, Lillesand* *489–55–788* *hovag.org.*

Lillesand By og Sjøfartsmuseum (*Lillesand Town and Maritime Museum*)
MUSEUM | In an Empire-style building from 1827, the Lillesand Town and Maritime Museum is a window into the region's seafaring past. You can see how sailmakers worked and the city's first fire pump. ✉ *Nygårdsgata 1, Lillesand* ☎ *46–81–75–10* 🌐 *lillesandmuseet.com* ⏲ *Closed Mon. and mid-Aug.–mid-June.*

 Restaurants

Hos Oss på Fiskebrygga Lillesand
$$ | **NORWEGIAN** | Fiskebrygga literally means "the fishing dock", and the name sets the tone for this restaurant on the waterfront in Lillesand. The menu consists mostly of (fresh) seafood, and throughout the summer they host live concerts on the dock. **Known for:** great location; most dishes can be prepared as a child portion; friendly staff. $ *Average main: NKr 190* ✉ *Strandgata 18, Lillesand* ☎ *32–27–02–03.*

 Hotels

★ **Hotel Norge**
$$$$ | **HOTEL** | Right on the harbor, this classic with a red-tile roof and white clapboard exterior has some of the best views in Lillesand. **Pros:** great location; gorgeous exterior; lots of atmosphere. **Cons:** slightly dated in some areas; no fitness area; books up fast. $ *Rooms from: NKr 1900* ✉ *Strandgaten 3, Lillesand* ☎ *37–27–01–44* 🌐 *hotelnorge.no* *25 rooms* *Free breakfast.*

Kristiansand

319 km (198 miles) southwest of Oslo, 28 km (17 miles) southwest of Lillesand.

Nicknamed *Sommerbyen* ("Summer City"), Norway's fifth-largest city draws visitors for its sun-soaked beaches and beautiful harbor. According to legend, in 1641 King Christian IV marked the four corners of Kristiansand with his walking stick, and within that framework the grid of wide streets was laid down. The center of town, called Kvadraturen ("The Quad"), still retains the grid, even after numerous fires. In the northeast corner is Posebyen, one of northern Europe's largest collections of low, connected wooden houses. There's a market here every Saturday in summer. The fish market is near the south corner of the town's grid, right on the sea.

GETTING HERE AND AROUND

From Oslo take the E18, from Stavanger the E39.

AIR TRAVEL
Kristiansand is served by Scandinavian Airlines, with nonstop flights from Oslo, Bergen, and Trondheim. Widerøe and Norwegian also link Kristiansand with other cities within Norway. Kjevik Airport is about 16 km (10 miles) northeast of the town center. The Flybussen airport bus heads downtown, stopping at several hotels along the way. The journey takes 25 minutes.

CONTACTS Flybussen. ☎ *51–59–90–60* 🌐 *flybussen.no.*

BUS TRAVEL
Several bus companies have daily departures for the five-hour journey to Oslo and the four-hour trip to Stavanger. All leave from Kristiansand Bus Terminal. Buses are much slower than trains, taking roughly an hour longer to reach their destination.

CAR TRAVEL
From Oslo it's a 326-km (202-mile) drive to Kristiansand along E18.

CRUISE TRAVEL
Cruise ships dock directly at Kristiansand's cruise-ship terminal. The town's main sights are a 1/3-mile or 10-minute walk from the terminal.

TAXI TRAVEL
Taxis to the airport start at NKr 340, depending on the time of day.

CONTACTS Agder Taxi. ☎ *38–00–20–00* 🌐 *agdertaxi.no.*

TRAIN TRAVEL

There are regular train departures for Kristiansand from Oslo (4 1/2–5 hours) and Stavanger (3 hours). Kristiansand's train station is at Vestre Strandgata.

CONTACTS Vy. ☎ *61–05–19–10* 🌐 *www.vy.no.*

TOURS

The City Train is a 25- to 30-minute tour of the city center.

CONTACTS City Train. ☎ *41–78–88–88* 🌐 *citytrain.no.*

VISITOR INFORMATION

CONTACTS Kristiansand Turistinformasjon. (*Kristiansand Tourist Information*) ✉ *Rådhusgt. 18, Kristiansand* ☎ *38–07–50–00* 🌐 *visitnorway.com/places-to-go/southern-norway/kristiansand.*

Sights

Agder Naturmuseum og Botanisk Hage (*Agder Natural History Museum and Botanical Garden*)
MUSEUM | The area's natural history from the Ice Age to the present is on display at this museum, starting with the coast and moving on to the mountains. There's a rainbow of minerals on display, as well as a rose garden with varieties from 1850. There's even the country's largest collection of cacti. ✉ *Gimle gård, Gimleveien 23, Kristiansand* ☎ *38–05–86–20* 🌐 *naturmuseum.no* 🎫 *NKr 80* ⏲ *Closed Mon. and Sat. in mid-Aug.–mid-June.*

Christiansholm Festning (*Christiansholm Fortress*)
HISTORIC SITE | This circular fortress with 16-foot-thick walls, on a promontory opposite Festningsgata, was completed in 1672. Its role has been much more decorative than defensive; it was used once, in 1807, during the Napoleonic Wars, to defend the city against British invasion. Now it contains art exhibits. However, the best part is walking around the grounds. ✉ *Kristiansand* ☎ *38–00–74–60* ⏲ *Closed Jan. and Feb.*

★ **Dyreparken i Kristiansand** (*Kristiansand Zoo and Amusement Park*)
ZOO | **FAMILY** | One of Norway's most popular attractions, Dyreparken Kristiansand is actually five separate parks, including a water park (bring bathing suits and towels), a forested park, an entertainment park, a theme park, and a zoo, which contains an enclosure for Scandinavian animals such as wolves, snow foxes, lynxes, and elks. The theme park, Kardemomme By (Cardamom Town), is named for a book by the Norwegian illustrator and writer Thorbjørn Egner. In the zoo, the "My Africa" exhibition allows you to move along a bridge observing native savanna animals such as giraffes and zebras. The park is 11 km (6 miles) east of town. ✉ *Kristiansand Dyrepark, Kristiansand* ☎ *97–05–97–00* 🌐 *dyreparken.no* 🎫 *NKr 479.*

★ **Gimle Gård** (*Gimle Manor*)
MUSEUM | A wealthy merchant-shipowner built handsome Gimle Manor around 1800 in the Empire style. Inside are furnishings from that period, along with moody portraits, glittering chandeliers, and hand-printed wallpaper. It is said to be the most beautiful manor house in the region, and if you enjoy picturesque buildings with a history, you'll enjoy visiting Gimle. ✉ *Gimleveien 23, Lillesand* ☎ *38–12–03–50* 🌐 *vestagdermuseet.no/gimlegard* ⏲ *Closed Sept.–May.*

Kristiansand Kanonmuseum (*Kristiansand Cannon Museum*)
MUSEUM | **FAMILY** | At the Kristiansand Cannon Museum you can see the cannon that the occupying Germans rigged up during World War II. With a caliber of 15 inches, the cannon was said to be capable of shooting a projectile halfway to Denmark. In the bunkers, related military materials are on display. Kids love running around the grounds, but keep an eye on them, since there aren't railings

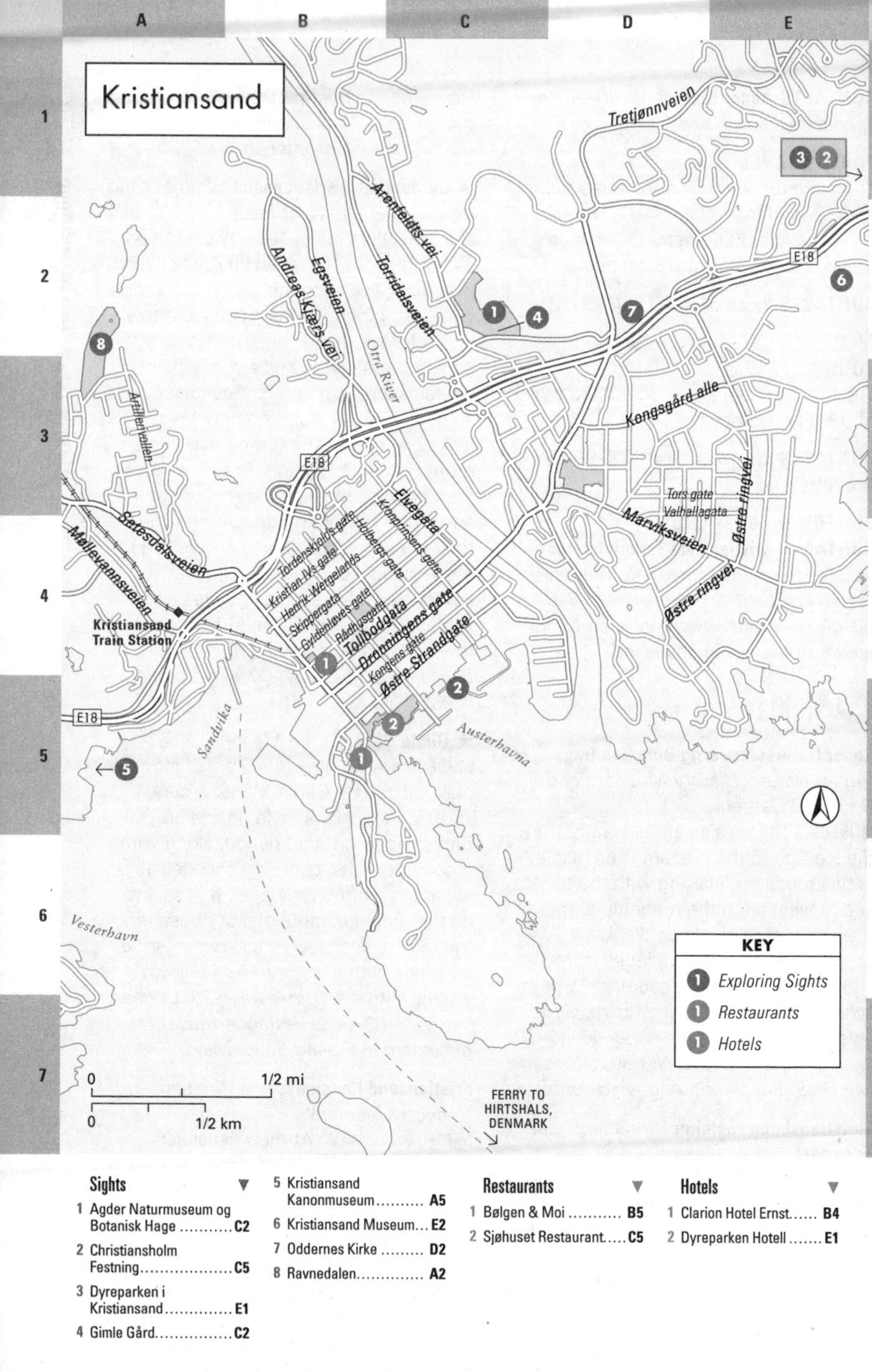

Sights

1 Agder Naturmuseum og Botanisk Hage C2

2 Christiansholm Festning.................... C5

3 Dyreparken i Kristiansand.............. E1

4 Gimle Gård................ C2

5 Kristiansand Kanonmuseum.......... A5

6 Kristiansand Museum... E2

7 Oddernes Kirke D2

8 Ravnedalen.............. A2

Restaurants

1 Bølgen & Moi B5

2 Sjøhuset Restaurant..... C5

Hotels

1 Clarion Hotel Ernst...... B4

2 Dyreparken Hotell E1

everywhere. ✉ *Kroodden, Kristiansand* ☎ *38–08–50–90* 🌐 *vestagdermuseet.no/kanonmuseum/* ⏲ *Closed Mon.–Sat. Sept.–Nov and Feb.–May. Closed Dec. and Jan.*

Kristiansand Museum (*Vest-Agder County Museum Kristiansand*)
MUSEUM VILLAGE | **FAMILY** | The region's largest cultural museum has more than 40 old buildings on display. The structures, transported from other locations in the area, include two *tun* farm buildings traditionally set in clusters around a common area which were intended for extended families. If you have children with you, check out the old-fashioned toys, which can still be played with. The museum is 4 km (2½ miles) east of Kristiansand on E18. ✉ *Vigeveien 22B, Kongsgård, Kristiansand* ☎ *38–12–03–50* 🌐 *vestagdermuseet.no/kristiansand* 🎟 *NKr 100* ⏲ *Closed Sept.–May (except Sun. in Sept.).*

Oddernes Kirke (*Oddernes Church*)
RELIGIOUS SITE | The striking rune stone in the cemetery of Oddernes kirke says that Øyvind, godson of Saint Olav, built this church in 1040 on property he inherited from his father. One of the oldest churches in Norway, it has a baroque pulpit from 1704 and is dedicated to Saint Olav. ✉ *Jegersbergvn. 6, Kristiansand* 🌐 *oddernes.no* 🎟 *Free.*

Ravnedalen (*Ravnedalen Valley Nature Park*)
NATIONAL/STATE PARK | A favorite with hikers and strolling nannies, Ravnedalen is a lush park that's filled with flowers in springtime. Wear comfortable shoes to hike the narrow, winding paths up the hills and climb the 200 steps up to a 304-foot lookout. There is a café on-site, and open-air concerts in summer. ✉ *Kristiansand.*

Restaurants

Bølgen & Moi
$$$ | **NORWEGIAN** | Toralf Bølgen and Trond Moi, two of Norway's most celebrated restaurateurs, run what's the southernmost addition to their chain of high-profile restaurants. Near the old fishing pier, the scene is more chic than rustic, with artwork and dinnerware designed by local artist Kjell Nupen. **Known for:** great seafood; refined atmosphere; smooth service. $ *Average main: NKr 335* ✉ *Nodeviga 2, Kristiansand* ☎ *38–17–83–00* 🌐 *bolgenogmoi.no/restauranter/kristiansand* ⏲ *No lunch weekdays.*

Sjøhuset Restaurant
$$$ | **SEAFOOD** | Considered one of the city's best restaurants, this white-trimmed red building was built in 1892 as a salt warehouse. The specialty is seafood. **Known for:** fresh seafood; local ingredients; traditional dishes. $ *Average main: NKr 345* ✉ *Østre Strandgt. 12A, Kristiansand* ☎ *38–02–62–60* 🌐 *sjohuset.no* ⏲ *Closed Sun. No lunch except summer.*

Hotels

Clarion Hotel Ernst
$$$ | **HOTEL** | This traditional city hotel opened in 1858 and is still considered among Kristiansand's best. **Pros:** lots of contemporary artworks; breakfast gets rave reviews; pleasant and helpful staff. **Cons:** some rooms get noise from nearby nightlife; parking in the city center is often difficult; standard rooms are on the small side. $ *Rooms from: NKr 1400* ✉ *Rådhusgt. 2, Kristiansand* ☎ *38–12–86–00* 🌐 *nordicchoicehotels.no/hotell/norge/kristiansand/clarion-hotel-ernst* 🛏 *200 rooms* 🍽 *Free breakfast.*

Dyreparken Hotell
$$$ | **HOTEL** | **FAMILY** | Built like Noah's Ark, this modern hotel is designed to appeal to children of all ages: inspired by the nearby zoo, many of the rooms go a little

wild, with tiger-stripe chairs and paw prints on walls. **Pros:** fun design; next to the zoo; easy parking. **Cons:** children everywhere, especially holidays and weekends; some rooms are a bit small; so-so breakfast. *Rooms from: NKr 1300* *Dyreparkveien 2, Kristiansand* *97–05–97–00* *dyreparken.no/overnatting/dyreparken-hotell* *160 rooms* *Free breakfast.*

Activities

TrollAktiv

TOUR—SPORTS | **FAMILY** | About an hour's drive from Kristiansand, TrollAktiv organizes activities ranging from mountain climbing and biking to sailing and rafting to unusual options like beaver or deer safaris. This is definitely the place for outdoorsy types. *Syrtveit 4, Evje* *37–93–11–77* *trollaktiv.no.*

Mandal

363 km (226 miles) southwest of Oslo, 46 km (29 miles) southwest of Kristiansand.

Norway's southernmost town, this former Dutch port is now famous for its historic center made up of well-preserved wooden houses. Summer visitors also come for its long, sandy beach.

GETTING HERE AND AROUND

E39 goes through Mandal, and Route 455 takes you north to Marnardal Station to catch the Sørlandsbanen train. There is also a bus terminal in Mandal with several connections to the surrounding area.

Sights

★ Lindesnes Fyr

LIGHTHOUSE | Norway's first lighthouse was illuminated in 1656 on this spot near the country's southernmost point. It was closed the same year by the Danish king because its light was not considered strong enough, and it didn't reopen for 69 years. Many lighting methods have been used since, including coal in the early 1800s. An exhibition in the museum traces the changing methods. *Lindesnesveien 1139, Mandal* *38–25–54–20* *lindesnesfyr.no* *NKr 80* *Closed weekdays Oct.–Mar.*

Mandal Kirke (*Mandal Church*)

RELIGIOUS SITE | Built in 1821, this is Norway's largest Empire-style wooden church. *Kirkebakken 2, Mandal* *38–27–28–70* *kirken.no/mandal.*

Restaurants

★ Restaurant Under

$$$$ | **NORWEGIAN** | Europe's first underwater restaurant, Under sits well below sea level, with a massive wall of glass that gives you a look into the icy waters of the North Sea. It's an architectural and engineering marvel, looking like a modern building tipping gently into the ocean and connected to onshore rocks by a bridge. **Known for:** panoramic views; fresh seafood; Norwegian classics. *Average main: NKr 2250* *Bålyveien 48, Mandal* *under.no* *Closed Sun.–Tues. in low season.*

Stavanger

206 km (128 miles) northwest of Mandal, 211 km (131 miles) south of Bergen via car and ferry, 540 km (336 miles) west of Oslo.

Stavanger has always prospered from the riches of the sea. During the 19th century, huge harvests of brisling (also called sprat) and herring helped put it on the map as the sardine capital of the world. Some people claim the locals are called Siddis, from S(tavanger) plus iddis, which means "sardine label," although some linguists argue it's actually a mispronunciation of the English word "citizen."

During the past three decades a different product from the sea has been Stavanger's lifeblood—oil. Since its discovery in the late 1960s, North Sea oil hasn't just transformed the economy; Stavanger has emerged as cosmopolitan and vibrant, more bustling than other cities with a population of only 130,000. Norway's most international city, it has attracted residents from more than 90 nations. Roam its cobblestone streets or wander the harbor front and you're likely to see many cafés, fine restaurants, and lively pubs, as well as many museums, galleries, and other venues that are part of its rich, dynamic art scene.

Stavanger has earned the title "Festivalbyen" (festival city) for its year-round celebrations. More than 20 official festivals are held throughout the year—comedy, food, chamber music, jazz, organ, literature, beach volleyball, biathlon, wine, and more. There are probably just as many unofficial events, since locals love any reason to have a party.

GETTING HERE AND AROUND

AIR TRAVEL

Stavanger's Sola Airport, 14 km (11 miles) south of downtown, is served by SAS, with nonstop flights from Oslo, Bergen, and Kristiansand, as well as some European cities. The low-cost airline Norwegian also has flights from Oslo to Stavanger.

The Flybussen (airport bus) leaves the airport every 15 minutes. It stops at hotels and outside the train station in Stavanger before heading back to the airport.

NOR-WAY Bussekspress and Vy runs regularly between Stavanger and Oslo (nine hours), Bergen (five hours), and Kristiansand (four hours).

BUS TRAVEL

Public transport within Stavanger is operated by the bus company Kolumbus. It's more than adequate for getting you to the major sites and then some. There's reason to consider not bothering with the bus, though; the center of town is pedestrians-only in places, and if you're of average fitness you could easily rely on your own two feet all day.

CONTACTS Kolumbus. ☎ *51–92–52–00* 🌐 *www.kolumbus.no.*

CAR TRAVEL

Driving from Bergen to Stavanger along the jagged western coastline is difficult and requires a detour of 150 km (93 miles), or many ferry crossings. Some areas in Stavanger's city center are closed to car traffic, and one-way traffic is the norm in the rest of the downtown area.

TAXI TRAVEL

Stavanger taxis are connected with a central dispatching office. Journeys within Stavanger are charged by meters that accept credit cards.

CONTACTS Stavanger Taxi. ☎ *51–90–90–90* 🌐 *stavanger-taxi.no.*

TRAIN TRAVEL

Sørlandsbanen leaves Oslo Central Station several times daily for the eight-hour journey to Stavanger. Trains travel the three-hour Kristiansand–Stavanger route throughout the day.

TOURS

Two-hour bus tours leave for Lysefjord and the iconic Preikestolen (Pulpit Rock) and Kjeragbolten (Kjerag Boulder) from Vågen daily at 1 between June and August. Rødne Fjord Cruise, Fjord Tours, and Norled offer a variety of sightseeing tours by boat. A one-hour hop on, hop off bus tour takes you through the city in the summer season.

Passenger-only Norled Flaggruten boats link Bergen and Stavanger in 4 1/2 hours. There are no car ferries between the two cities.

CONTACTS Fjord Tours. ☎ *55–55–76–60* 🌐 *fjordtours.no.* **Norled Flaggruten.** ☎ *51–86–87–00* 🌐 *norled.no.* **Rødne Fjord Cruise.** ☎ *51–89–52–70* ✉ *mail@rodne.no* 🌐 *rodne.no.* **Stavanger City Tour.** 🌐 *city-sightseeing.com/en/70/stavanger.*

Did You Know?

Norway's southernmost town is Mandal, know for the old clapboard houses that tumble down to its harbor.

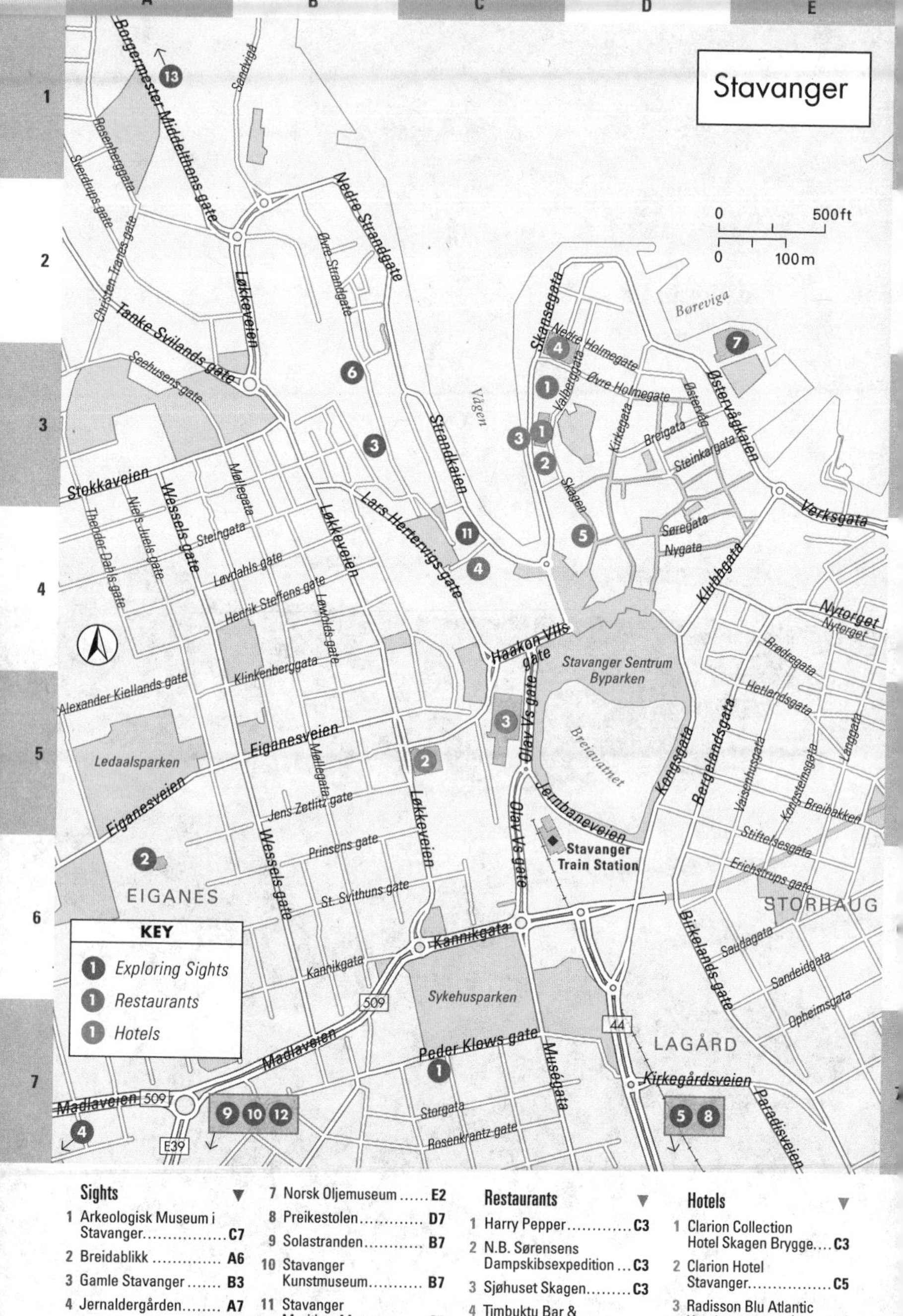

Sights

1 Arkeologisk Museum i Stavanger................ **C7**
2 Breidablikk **A6**
3 Gamle Stavanger **B3**
4 Jernaldergården........ **A7**
5 Lysefjord................. **D7**
6 Norsk Hermetikkmuseum **B3**
7 Norsk Oljemuseum **E2**
8 Preikestolen............ **D7**
9 Solastranden............ **B7**
10 Stavanger Kunstmuseum........... **B7**
11 Stavanger Maritime Museum....... **C4**
12 Sverd i Fjell **B7**
13 Utstein Kloster **A1**

Restaurants

1 Harry Pepper............ **C3**
2 N.B. Sørensens Dampskibsexpedition ... **C3**
3 Sjøhuset Skagen......... **C3**
4 Timbuktu Bar & Restaurant................ **C4**
5 XO Steakhouse.......... **D4**

Hotels

1 Clarion Collection Hotel Skagen Brygge.... **C3**
2 Clarion Hotel Stavanger................. **C5**
3 Radisson Blu Atlantic Hotel.................... **C5**
4 Victoria Hotel............ **C2**

VISITOR INFORMATION

CONTACTS Region Stavanger og Ryfylke. (*Stavanger tourist information*) ☎ *51–85–92–00* 🌐 *regionstavanger-ryfylke.com.*

Sights

Arkeologisk Museum i Stavanger (*Museum of Archaeology*)
MUSEUM | FAMILY | Designed to help children understand the prehistoric past, the Museum of Archaeology has changing exhibits, instructive models, and movies designed to make learning history fun. Children can research their ancestors with computer games, go on treasure hunts, and look through stones in search of fossils and other signs of life. There are also old-fashioned games and toys, which have become popular attractions. ✉ *Peder Klows gt. 30A, Stavanger* ☎ *51–83–26–00* 🌐 *am.uis.no* 🎫 *NKr 100* ⏲ *Closed Mon. Sept.–Apr.*

Breidablikk
HISTORIC SITE | FAMILY | With a perfectly preserved interior, this 19th-century manor house feels as if the owner has only momentarily slipped away. The building is an outstanding example of what the Norwegians call "Swiss-style" architecture, and also has some elements of the Norwegian National Romantic style. It was built in 1882 by the Norwegian merchant and shipowner Lars Berentsen. ✉ *Eiganesveien 40A, Stavanger* ☎ *51–84–27–00* 🌐 *breidablikkmuseum.no* 🎫 *NKr 95* ⏲ *Closed Sept.–May.*

★ **Gamle Stavanger** (*Old Stavanger*)
HISTORIC SITE | The charm of the city's past is on view in Old Stavanger, northern Europe's largest and best-preserved wooden house settlement. The 150 houses here were built in the late 1700s and early 1800s. Wind down the narrow cobblestone streets past small white houses and craft shops with many-paned windows and terra-cotta roof tiles. ✉ *Stavanger.*

Jernaldergården
MUSEUM | Although it's a reconstruction of an Iron Age farm, Jernaldergården feels like the real thing because the newly built structures have been positioned on the original foundations. Relics such as a Bronze Age gravestone have been discovered here, and more research is underway. Taste some mead, the Vikings' favorite drink, or have breakfast or lunch on wooden benches in front of roaring fireplaces. ✉ *Madlamarkveien 152, Stavanger* ☎ *51–83–26–00* 🌐 *am.uis.no/jernaldergarden* 🎫 *NKr 100* ⏲ *Closed Mon.–Sat. Sept.–May.*

★ **Lysefjord**
SCENIC DRIVE | A very popular attraction in Stavanger, the breathtaking Lysefjord is best seen by boat. Along the way you can take in famous sights, like the sheer cliffs of Pulpit's Rock and the balancing act of the Kjerag Boulder. Most travelers drive to Lauvvik and take a round-trip cruise from there.

Norsk Hermetikkmuseum (*Norwegian Canning Museum*)
MUSEUM | From the 1890s to the 1960s, canning sardines and other fish products was Stavanger's main industry. This fascinating museum, in a former canning factory, recounts what it was like to live here during that period. Occasionally the public can take part in the production process, sometimes tasting newly smoked brisling. The museum was slated to reopen in late 2020 after extensive renovations. ✉ *Øvre Strandgate 88, Stavanger* ☎ *51–84–27–00* 🌐 *norskhermetikkmuseum.no* 🎫 *NKr 95* ⏲ *Closed mid-Aug.–mid-May.*

★ **Norsk Oljemuseum** (*Norwegian Petroleum Museum*)
MUSEUM | FAMILY | Resembling a shiny offshore oil platform, the dynamic Norsk Oljemuseum is an absolute must-see. In 1969 oil was discovered off the coast of Norway. The museum explains how oil forms, how it's found and produced, its many uses, and its impact on Norway.

Interactive multimedia exhibits accompany original artifacts, models, and films. A reconstructed offshore platform includes oil workers' living quarters—as well as the sound of drilling and the smell of oil. The highly recommended museum café, by restaurateurs Bølgen og Moi, serves dinners as well as lighter fare. ✉ *Kjeringholmen, Stavanger Havn, Stavanger* ☎ *51–93–93–00* 🌐 *norskolje.museum.no* 🎫 *NKr 120.*

★ **Preikestolen** (*Pulpit Rock*)
VIEWPOINT | A huge cube with a vertical drop of 2,000 feet, Pulpit Rock is not a good destination if you suffer from vertigo—it has a heart-stopping view. The clifflike rock sits on the banks of the finger-shape Lysefjord. You can join a boat tour from Stavanger to see the rock from below, or you can hike two hours to the top on a marked trail. The track goes from Preikestolhytta, where there is a big parking lot.

Solastranden
BEACH—SIGHT | Sola's beach has 2⅓ km (1½ mile) of sandy beach ideal for windsurfing and beach volleyball. Other prime beach spots are Vaulen badeplass, Godalen badeplass, Viste Stranden, and Sande Stranden. The World Tour Beach Volleyball tournament is held downtown on a temporary beach volleyball court at the end of June. ✉ *Axel Lunds Veg 23, Stavanger.*

Stavanger Kunstmuseum (*Stavanger Art Museum*)
MUSEUM | This art museum sits by the lovely Lake Mosvannet, about 3 km (2 miles) from the city center. Its holdings, which cover the early 19th century to the present, include an extensive collection of works by Lars Hertervig (1830–1902), a great romantic painter of Norwegian landscapes. The Halvdan Hafsten Collection has paintings and drawings created between the world wars. ✉ *Henrik Ibsens gt. 55, Stavanger* ☎ *93–21–37–15* 🌐 *stavangerkunstmuseum.no* 🎫 *NKr 95* 🕒 *Closed Mon.*

Stavanger Maritime Museum
MUSEUM | Housed in the only two shipping merchants' houses that remain completely intact is Stavanger Maritime Museum. Built between 1770 and 1840, the restored buildings trace the past 200 years of trade, sea traffic, and shipbuilding. Visit a turn-of-the-20th-century general store, merchant's apartment, and a sailmaker's loft. A reconstruction of a shipowner's office and a memorial are also here, as are two 19th-century ships, the sloop *Anna af Sand*, and the Colin Archer yacht *Wyvern*, moored at the pier. ✉ *Strandkaien 22, Stavanger* ☎ *51–84–27–00* 🌐 *stavangermaritimemuseum.no* 🎫 *NKr 95* 🕒 *Closed Mon. mid-Sept.–mid-May.*

Sverd i Fjell (*Swords in Rock*)
MEMORIAL | The site where Norway was founded has been memorialized by these three huge bronze swords, designed by artist Fritz Røed and unveiled by King Olav in 1983. The memorial is dedicated to King Harald Hårfagre (Harald the Fairhaired), who through an 872 battle at Hafrsfjord managed to unite Norway into one kingdom. The Viking swords' sheaths were modeled on ones found throughout the country; the crowns atop the swords represent the different Norwegian districts that took part in the battle. ✉ *Møllebukta, Hafrsfjord, Stavanger.*

Utstein Kloster (*Utstein Abbey*)
HISTORIC SITE | Founded in the late 1200s, Utstein is the best preserved medieval monastery in Norway. Public transport to the abbey isn't that good, so it's best to hire a car. By bus or car it's about a half-hour trip north of Stavanger on a coastal highway. If you rent a car to get to Utstein, you can also take in the medieval ruins and Stone Age rock carvings on nearby Åmøy Island as well as Fjøløy Fyr, a lighthouse. ✉ *Mosterøyveien 801, Stavanger* ☎ *51–84–27–00* 🌐 *utsteinkloster.no* 🎫 *NKr 95* 🕒 *Closed Nov.–Feb. Closed Mon.–Sat. in Sept., Oct., Mar., and Apr.*

Restaurants

Harry Pepper

$$$ | **SOUTHWESTERN** | You woldn't know it from the Scandinavian facade, but Harry Pepper combines Tex-Mex cuisine with Norwegian tastes. Prickly cacti and tacky souvenirs make for a lighthearted and fun interior. **Known for:** lively atmosphere; tasty food; many brands of tequila. *Average main: NKr 300 Skagenkaien 33, Stavanger 51–89–39–59 harry-pepper.no No lunch Sun.*

★ N. B. Sørensens Dampskibsexpedition

$$$ | **NORWEGIAN** | Norwegian emigrants waited here before boarding steamships crossing the ocean to North America 150 years ago. The historic wharf house is now a popular waterfront restaurant and bar. **Known for:** creative cocktails at the bar; a well-thought-out theme; sizzling steaks. *Average main: NKr 275 Skagen 26, Stavanger 81–55–28–81 nbsorensen.no.*

Sjøhuset Skagen

$$ | **NORWEGIAN** | A sort of museum, this former boathouse from 1770 is filled with wooden beams, ship models, lobster traps, and other sea relics. The Norwegian and international menu may offer such fare as baked lime- and chili–marinated halibut, trout, whale steak, and reindeer and baked fennel, or, in fall and winter, turkey served with cabbage, prunes, Waldorf salad, and boiled potatoes. **Known for:** the best ingredients from the countryside; authentic atmosphere; lots of history. *Average main: NKr 250 Skagenkaien 13, Stavanger 90–41–73–27 skagenrestaurant.no.*

Timbuktu Bar & Restaurant

$$$ | **ECLECTIC** | This is one of Stavanger's trendiest restaurants. The main focus here is Asian-inspired street food served as small plates so that you can taste a greater variety of dishes and ingredients than you would otherwise. **Known for:** popular destination for after-work drinks; tapas-style dishes perfect for sharing; visiting celebrity chefs. *Average main: NKr 255 Nedre Strandgt. 15, Stavanger 815–52–884 www.herlige-restauranter.no/timbuktu Closed Sun. and Mon. No lunch.*

XO Steakhouse

$$$ | **NORWEGIAN** | This pub-style restaurant's interior is in keeping with the traditional Norwegian dishes that emerge from the kitchen. Enjoy local favorites such as lutefisk and *pinnekjøtt* (lamb cooked on birch twigs) during the months leading up to Christmas, or the grilled steaks and other meats that are available the rest of the year. **Known for:** a longtime favorite; live music on weekends; casual atmosphere. *Average main: NKr 300 Skagen 10, Stavanger 91–00–03–07 xosteakhouse.no Closed Sun.*

Hotels

Clarion Collection Hotel Skagen Brygge

$$ | **HOTEL** | A symbol of Stavanger, this classic hotel's white wooden wharf houses are common subjects for city postcards and photographs, and it has a well-deserved reputation for superb service. **Pros:** central location; good views of the harbor; complimentary afternoon tea and evening meal. **Cons:** some rooms are small; noise from nearby nightlife; added charge for pets. *Rooms from: NKr 1100 Skagenkaien 28–30, Stavanger 51–85–00–00 nordicchoicehotels.no/hotell/norge/stavanger/clarion-collection-hotel-skagen-brygge 118 rooms Some meals.*

Clarion Hotel Stavanger

$$$ | **HOTEL** | This downtown business hotel has an up-to-the-minute design, and many visitors have named this their favorite hotel in town. **Pros:** comfortable rooms; sauna and hot tub on the top floor; 24-hour room service. **Cons:** books up in advance; no fitness facilities; no pool. *Rooms from: NKr 1300 Arne Rettedals gt. 14, Stavanger*

☎ 51–50–25–00 ⊕ nordicchoicehotels.no/hotell/norge/stavanger/clarion-hotel-stavanger ⇌ 249 rooms 🍽 No meals.*

Radisson Blu Atlantic Hotel

$$ | HOTEL | In the heart of downtown, the Radisson Blu Atlantic—one of Stavanger's largest hotels—overlooks Breiavatnet Pond. **Pros:** generous-size rooms; sauna with great views; huge buffet breakfast. **Cons:** slightly impersonal feel; books up early; rooms lack character. *[$] Rooms from: NKr 995 ✉ Olav Vs gt. 3, Stavanger ☎ 51–76–10–00 ⊕ radissonhotels.com/en-us/hotels/radisson-blu-stavanger-atlantic ⇌ 365 rooms 🍽 No meals.*

Victoria Hotel

$$$ | HOTEL | Built in 1900, Stavanger's oldest hotel retains a clubby Victorian style, with elegant carved furniture and floral patterns. **Pros:** great location; stylish restaurant; good breakfast. **Cons:** some rooms are small; can be a bit noisy on weekends; old-fashioned wallpaper. *[$] Rooms from: NKr 1300 ✉ Skansegt. 1, Stavanger ☎ 51–86–70–00 ⊕ victoria-hotel.no ⇌ 107 rooms 🍽 Free breakfast.*

Nightlife

Café Sting

CAFES—NIGHTLIFE | A restaurant, nightclub, art gallery, and performance venue, Café Sting is also an institution. *✉ Valberget 3, Stavanger ☎ 948–46–789 ⊕ cafesting.no.*

Hansenhjørnet

BARS/PUBS | Sun-kissed Hansenhjørnet is a large outdoor bar and restaurant that always attracts a crowd. *✉ Skagen 18, Stavanger ☎ 51–89–52–80 ⊕ hansenhjornet.com.*

Nåløyet

BARS/PUBS | Appropriately named Needle's Eye, Stavanger's answer to a London pub is close and cozy. *✉ Nedre Strandgt. 13, Stavanger ☎ 918–69–951.*

Shopping

Bøker og Børst

BOOKS/STATIONERY | At this independent bookstore, café, and pub, there's funky artwork on the walls and a cozy garden in back. *✉ Øvre Holmegate 32, Stavanger ☎ 51–86–04–76 ⊕ bokerogborst.no.*

Sølvsmeden på Sølvberget

JEWELRY/ACCESSORIES | If jewelry's your passion, head to the city's best shop. *✉ Sølvberggt. 5, Stavanger ☎ 51–89–42–24 ⊕ solvsmeden.no ⊙ Closed Sun.*

Syvende Himmel

CLOTHING | For something different, head for Øvre Holmegate, Stavanger's most colorful street. It's full of small boutiques. Syvende Himmel, for instance, specializes in retro and alternative clothes and accessories in bright colors and funky designs. *✉ Øvre Holmegt. 21, Stavanger ☎ 51–01–29–61 ⊙ Closed Sun.*

Activities

HIKING

Stavanger Turistforening (*Stavanger Trekking Association*)

HIKING/WALKING | Specialized books and maps are available through Stavanger Turistforening, the local trekking association. The office can help you plan a hike through the area, particularly in the rolling Setesdalsveiene Hills and the thousands of islands and skerries of the Ryfylke Archipelago. The association has 44 cabins for members (you can join on the spot) for sleeping along the way. *✉ Olav Vs gt. 18, Stavanger ☎ 51–84–02–00 ⊕ stf.no.*

Haugesund

82 km (51 miles) north of Stavanger, 138 km (86 miles) south of Bergen via car and ferry, 443 km (275 miles) west of Oslo.

The small port town of Haugesund prides itself on its historical importance as the seat of the Viking kings and birthplace of Norway (the country was unified in the 9th century by King Harald the Fairhaired, who ruled from Avaldsnes, a short distance from Haugesund). The town's origins lie in its position near an important straight, where ships could avoid stormy open seas. It was also a major source of herring. Nowadays Haugesund is best known as one of Norway's principal cultural centers. The city hosts the Norwegian International Film Festival and an important citywide jazz festival held every August.

GETTING HERE AND AROUND

The Haugesund Airport, located on the island of Karmøy, connects the city with Oslo, Bergen, London, Copenhagen, and other major international cities, serviced by SAS, Ryanair, Norway, and Widerøe airlines. Haugesund connects by bus to Bergen and Oslo.

Car and passenger ferries link Haugesund with Utsira, and passenger ferries connect to Røvaer and Feøy.

Sights

★ Nordvegen Historiesenter (*Nordvegen History Center*)
MUSEUM VILLAGE | FAMILY | Outside of Haugesund, Avaldnes is the seat of Norway's first kings and thus considered the "birthplace of Norway," an important status for the city. For a rich overview—from the Bronze Age to the Middle Ages—of this historically significant region, the Norwegian History Center is a must. In the center, Norway's story is laid out through timelines, life-size costumed figures, and multimedia exhibits. The grounds include a fascinating outdoor Viking farm re-creating life in the 7th and 8th centuries, and 13th-century St. Olav's church, the last vestige of the kings' royal manor. *✉ Kong Augvalds veg 103, Avaldsnes ☎ 52–81–24–00 🌐 vikinggarden.no 🎫 NKr 110 ⏲ Closed Mon., Tues., and Thurs.–Sat. Oct.–Apr.*

Restaurants

Brovingen Mat & Vin
$$$$ | MODERN EUROPEAN | In the Scandic Maritim Hotel on the edge of the harbor, Brovingen Mat & Vin is Haugesund's only upscale restaurant. Both elegant and laid back, the dining room attracts a lively, sophisticated crowd of locals and visitors who appreciate fine dining. **Known for:** multiple-course tasting menus; creative cuisine; lovely location. *$ Average main: NKr 765 ✉ Scandic Maritim Hotel, Åsbygaten 3, Haugesund ☎ 52–86–32–70 🌐 hotelmaritim.no/restaurant/brovingen.*

Il Forno
$$ | ITALIAN | FAMILY | Italy meets Norway at this cozy dockside eatery, a standout among the other casual restaurants on this popular restaurant row, specializing in a large selection of fresh pasta (many dishes capitalize on the local seafood), crostini, and a superb oven-fired pizza. The restaurant takes reservations, but walk-ins are welcome and food can be taken out. **Known for:** stone-oven pizzas; friendly atmosphere; quick service. *$ Average main: NKr 170 ✉ Smedasundet 91, Haugesund ☎ 47–77–92–77 🌐 inventum.no/il-forno.*

★ Lothes Restaurant
$$$$ | EUROPEAN | This waterfront restaurant, café, and bar in a pretty white clapboard house is a good bet for consistently well-prepared, high-quality dining. The cozy restaurant focuses on a more sophisticated cuisine, and the offerings may include crayfish gazpacho and veal entrecôte on its prix-fixe menu. **Known for:** views of Smedasundet; interesting set menu; two different dining rooms. *$ Average main: NKr 585 ✉ Skippergt 4, Haugesund ☎ 52–71–22–01 🌐 lothesmat.no ⏲ Closed Sun. and Mon.*

Hotels

★ Clarion Collection Hotel Amanda

$$$ | **HOTEL** | Scenic views over the waterfront and marina are just one advantage of this centrally located hotel, named for the Norwegian International Film Festival (held in Haugesund), hence the film-named rooms. **Pros:** free Wi-Fi and other amenities; casual atmosphere; meals included in rates. **Cons:** rooms facing harbor can be noisy; not all rooms have views; slightly expensive rates. *Rooms from: NKr 1500 ✉ Smedasundet 93, Haugesund ☎ 52–80–82–00 🌐 nordicchoicehotels.no/hotell/norge/haugesund/clarion-collection-hotel-amanda/ 133 rooms Some meals.*

Scandic Haugesund

$$ | **HOTEL** | The modern, centrally located Scandic Haugesund—on the town's picturesque harbor near shopping, restaurants, and nightlife—meets all the criteria for a pleasant stay. **Pros:** good buffet breakfast; free Wi-Fi; eye-catching views. **Cons:** no in-room minibars; difficult to adjust heating; impersonal feel. *Rooms from: NKr 1100 ✉ Kirkegt. 166, Haugesund ☎ 21–61–41–00 🌐 scandichotels.no/hotell/norge/haugesund/scandic-haugesund 157 rooms Free breakfast.*

Thon Hotel Saga

$$ | **HOTEL** | The centrally located Thon Hotel Saga Haugesund isn't the most compelling hotel to look at, but the friendly service adds a personal touch that can be lacking in chain hotels. **Pros:** close to restaurants and shopping; complimentary coffee in the lobby; breakfast and weekday dinner included. **Cons:** some areas quite dated; simple interior in the rooms; no fitness center. *Rooms from: NKr 900 ✉ Skippergaten 11, Haugesund ☎ 52–86–28–00 🌐 thonhotels.no/hoteller/norge/haugesund/thon-hotel-saga 109 rooms Some meals.*

Nightlife

Kompasset Bar

PIANO BARS/LOUNGES | A sleek, cozy piano bar and lounge with plenty of atmosphere and views over the harbor, Kompasset's list of well-crafted cocktails, wines by the glass, and a bevvy of local beers insure a pleasant evening to the strains of live piano music. ✉ *Scandic Maritim Hotel, Åsbygaten 3, Haugesund* ☎ *52–86–30–30* 🌐 *hotelmaritim.no/restaurant/kompasset-bar* *Closed Sun.*

Samson Bar & Cafe

BARS/PUBS | This "New York–inspired" cocktail bar features an extensive tapas menu and plenty of wines by the glass. ✉ *Strandgt. 130, Haugesund* ☎ *52–72–22–15* 🌐 *samsonbar.no.*

Performing Arts

★ Sildajazz (*Haugesund International Jazz Festival*)

FESTIVALS | A major event in Norway, the Haugesund Jazz Festival, held every year in August, features an extensive roster of Norwegian and international jazz artists performing in more than 25 venues throughout the city and beyond. The festival's other attractions include an international art exhibition, a market, a children's parade, and a program of free outdoor concerts. ✉ *Haugesund* ☎ *52–74–33–80* 🌐 *sildajazz.no.*

Shopping

Haraldsgata (*Haraldsgata street*)

SHOPPING NEIGHBORHOODS | This street, just a block from the harbor, is Norway's longest pedestrian street. Here you'll find luxury fashion boutiques, jewelry, bookstores, gifts, and souvenirs. It's also a nice spot to stop for a coffee, snack, or teatime at one of the many cafés or bakeries. ✉ *Haraldsgata, Haugesund.*

Chapter 6

CENTRAL NORWAY

Updated by
Cecilie Hauge Eggen

Sights	Restaurants	Hotels	Shopping	Nightlife
★★★★★	★★★★☆	★★★★☆	★★☆☆☆	★★☆☆☆

WELCOME TO CENTRAL NORWAY

TOP REASONS TO GO

★ **Climb Galdhøpiggen and Glittertind:** Head to the top of the highest peaks in Norway, where you can take in stunning views of spectacular Jotunheimen National Park.

★ **Ride the Sjoa River:** Feel the adrenaline rushing through your veins on a white-water rafting trip down the rapids of this iconic waterway.

★ **Track the musk ox.** In Dovrefjell-Sunndalsfjella National Park you can set off on the trail of these majestic creatures and may others.

★ **Explore stave churches:** These elaborately carved wooden churches, many of them built in the early 1200s, are a national treasure.

★ **See nature in a new way:** Stay high above the trees, in the middle of a dense forest, or on a mountainside where you can see roaming herds of reindeer.

Central Norway is dominated by the valleys of Gudbrandsdalen and Valdres, both of which run roughly northwest from Oslo. The high point of any journey here is a visit to the three national parks: Rondane, Jotunheimen, and Dovrefjell-Sunndalsfjella. All three are accessible from more than one town, making the region easy to explore. The lovely town of Lillehammer is the winter sports capital of Norway.

1 **Hamar.** On the eastern shore of Mjøsa Lake. Hamar is the home to the famous Domkirkeodden and the ruins of the 950 year old Hamar Cathedral.

2 **Lillehammer.** The regional capital holds a special place in the hearts of many sports fans, as it hosted the 1994 Winter Olympics. It's still a favorite for cross-country and alpine skiing.

3 **Ringebu.** The tiny town is known for its impressive stave church, as well as hikes through the surrounding mountain peaks.

4 **Otta.** Sitting near the confluence of two mighty rivers, the Otta and the Gudbrandsdalslågen, Otta is known for white-water rafting and as a major gateway for Rondane National Park.

5 **Lom.** With a breathtaking view, Lom sits among the region's highest and most dramatic mountain peaks.

6 **Dombås.** This is the best place to access spectacular Dovrefjell-Sunndalsfjella National Park, an ecosystem that is home to reindeer, wolverines, Arctic foxes, and golden eagles.

7 **Røros.** Founded in 1644, Røros is one of the oldest wooden towns in Europe. Its status as an early mining town made it a UNESCO World Heritage Site.

8 **Beitostølen.** This small mountain village is situated at the foot of Jotunheimen Nasjonalpark, making it a good starting point for climbing the peaks of Besseggen, Bitihorn, and Rasletind.

9 **Fagernes.** The Valdres Folk Museum is one of the draws of this mountain community, which puts you within striking distance of several national parks.

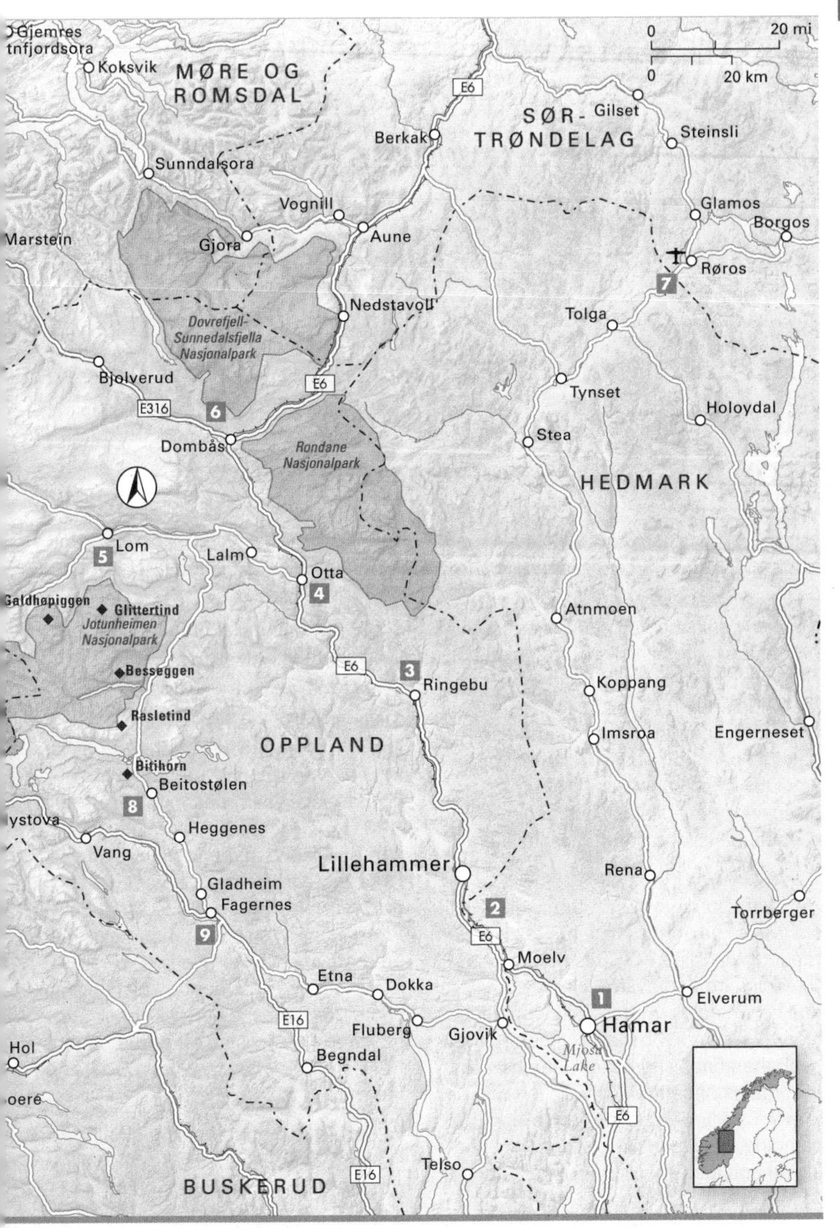
Gjemres
tnfjordsora
Koksvik
MØRE OG ROMSDAL
SØR-TRØNDELAG
Gilset
Steinsli
Berkak
E6
Sunndalsora
Vognill
Aune
Glamos
Borgos
Marstein
Gjora
Røros
7
Nedstavoll
Tolga
Dovrefjell-Sunnedalsfjella Nasjonalpark
Bjolverud
E6
Tynset
E316
6
Holoydal
Dombås
Rondane Nasjonalpark
Stea
HEDMARK
Lom
5
Lalm
Otta
4
Galdhøpiggen
Glittertind
Jotunheimen Nasjonalpark
Atnmoen
Besseggen
E6
3
Ringebu
Koppang
Rasletind
Imsroa
Engerneset
OPPLAND
Bitihorn
Beitostølen
8
ystova
Heggenes
Vang
Lillehammer
Rena
Gladheim
Fagernes
2
Torrberger
9
E6
Moelv
Etna
Dokka
1
Elverum
E16
Fluberg
Gjovik
Hamar
Hol
Begndal
Mjøsa Lake
oere
E6
Telso
E16
BUSKERUD
0 20 mi
0 20 km

Have no doubt, central Norway boasts some of the country's finest scenery. Yes, the fjords are fantastic, but there are good reasons why the Norwegians call this area the heart of Norway; Nature is a big one. Northwards from Oslo, the landscape turns to rolling hills that become steeper and sharper the farther you go. The lush valleys of Valdres and Gudbrandsdalen charm you with picturesque farming villages huddled around impressive wooden stave churches.

Maybe you'll stop and pause here, breathing in the history and traditions of Norway, or maybe you'll head towards the pride and joy of most Norwegians, the vast wilderness of three impressive national parks: Rondane, Jotunheimen, and Dovrefjell-Sunndalsfjella. You'll discover emerald lakes, gushing rivers, vast plateaus, and steep massifs literally reaching sky high.

Being situated on the eastern side of Norway's major mountain ranges keeps most of the rain away. This results in a drier climate with warm, sunny summers and cold, snowy winters. No wonder Norwegians don't bat an eye before they pack their bags and head to the hills and mountains of central Norway, many of them every weekend. Hiking, biking, rock climbing, glacier walking, canoeing, and alpine and cross-country skiing are but some of the popular outdoor activities in this beautiful region.

MAJOR REGIONS

Gudbrandsdalen Valley. This valley runs in a northwesterly direction from Lake Mjøsa, where you'll find the towns of Hamar of Lillehammer, extending 230 km (140 miles) along the Gudbrandsdalslågen River toward the town of Dombås. Here you can explore the very best of the Norwegian countryside, from heavily forested hills to soaring mountains with breathtaking views. This scenic valley is more or less surrounded by national parks like Rondane and Dovrefjell-Sunndalsfjella. Branching off to the north is the Østerdalen Valley, where you'll find the mining town of Røros.

Valdres. This mountainous region is situated between the two grand valleys, Gudbrandsdalen and Hallingdal. The crown jewel here is Jotunheimen National Park, known for its string of awe-inspiring peaks. The summer-only Route 51 runs through the plateau, reaching 1,389 meters (4,557 feet) above sea level. The town of Fagernes is here, as is the ski resort of Beitostølen.

Planning

When to Go

With a temperate inland climate, the hills and valleys of central Norway are excellent for travel year-round. In the summer months, the temperatures are perfect for hikes through the mountains, and if you wait until early fall, the forests are practically bursting with colour. High season is mid-June to August, but many mountain lodges open for summer in May and don't say good-bye to the last guest until September. Shoulder season, spring and fall, often has beautiful weather and fewer tourists. If you're looking for winter sports, you can ski here from November to April.

Getting Here and Around

AIR TRAVEL

The airport closest to the region is in Oslo.

CONTACTS Air Leap. ☎ *86–39–85–38* 🌐 *www.airleap.no.*

BOAT TRAVEL

The boat *Mjøscharter* sails the waters of Lake Mjøsa. During the summer the boat carries tourists around the lake, saving you some travel time. For instance, the trip from Hamar to Helgøya is a 50-minute drive, but only 10 minutes by boat.

CONTACTS Mjøscharter. ✉ *Storhamargata 55, Hamar* ☎ *48–39–54–49* 🌐 *www.mjoscharter.no.*

BUS TRAVEL

Nor-Way Bussekspress offers buses to Lillehammer (Øst-Vestekspressen) and the Valdres region (Valdresekspressen). Opplandstrafikk and Trønderbilene run local through the county of the county of Oppland, which includes most of central Norway. Hedmark Trafikk services the county of Hedmark, Hamar included.

In winter, ski buses from Lillehammer head to the region's alpine and cross-country ski resorts. During the summer months, buses run to mountain resorts along Rondane National Tourist Route.

CONTACTS Hedmark Trafikk. ☎ *91–50–20–40* 🌐 *www.hedmark-trafikk.no.* **Nor-Way Bussekspress.** ☎ *23–31–31–50* 🌐 *www.nor-way.no.* **Opplandstrafikk Bus Service.** ☎ *91–50–71–77* 🌐 *www.opplandstrafikk.no.*

CAR TRAVEL

The easiest way to get around central Norway is by car. You'll find many little villages hidden along the narrow, winding roads spread across region. The main road from Oslo to Hamar, Lillehammer, and other towns in the Gudbrandsdalen Valley is E6. From Ringebu you can take a detour onto Route 27 heading toward Venabygdsfjellet for the Rondane National Tourist Route. It's open to traffic throughout the year, but some sections may be closed for short periods in winter when the weather is bad.

The main road through Valdres is E16 from Oslo to Fagernes, continuing on Route 51 to Beitostølen, passing through the summer-only Valdresflya National Tourist Route.

From Oslo to Røros, the shortest way is starting on E6, and continuing on Route 3. In winter, a four-wheel drive might prove worth the extra cost because the smaller roads can get icy.

TRAIN TRAVEL

The regional train service between Oslo and Lillehammer offers at least a dozen daily departures, and up to half a dozen daily departures northbound towards Trondheim. The train is a convenient and comfortable way of travelling, and on the route through Gudbrandsdalen you can marvel at the beautiful views of Lake Mjøsa. The Rauma line between Dombås and Åndalsnes is even more scenic.

CONTACTS Vy. ✉ *Vy* ☎ *61–05–19–10* 🌐 *www.vy.no.*

Restaurants

The restaurants of central Norway tend to concentrate on the region's fish and game, typically served with sauces made with berries and mushrooms. Lamb is always delicious, as is reindeer. Arctic char, perch, and especially trout from the waters high above sea level are also frequently on the menu.

Hotels

Central Norway offers the most wonderful array of lodgings, and most places you can choose between the classic chain hotels and the old and charming guesthouses. In the valleys and up on the mountains you will find a fine selection of historic lodges with marvelous views. If you seek a once-in-a-lifetime experience, try the glamorous igloo-shaped tents at Arctic Dome Sjusjøen or the moose observation tower of Elgtårnet. In the national parks and the surrounding areas, the Norwegian Trekking Association has a number of lodges, staffed and unstaffed.

CONTACTS Norwegian Trekking Association. 🌐 *www.ut.no.*

Restaurant and hotel reviews have been shortened. For full information, visit Fodors.com.

What It Costs in Norwegian Krone

	$	$$	$$$	$$$$
RESTAURANTS				
	under NKr 125	NKr 125–NKr 250	NKr 251–NKr 350	over NKr 350
HOTELS				
	under NKr 750	NKr 750–NKr 1250	NKr 1251–NKr 1900	over NKr 1900

Visitor Information

Located in Otta, Nasjonalparkriket offers information on the national parks of Rondane, Dovre, Dovre-Sunndalsfjella, Reinheimen, Breheimen, and Jotunheimen. In Dombås, the cozy café Heime doubles as the tourism office.

CONTACTS Heime Otta Tourism Office. ✉ *Kyrkjevegen 2D, Dombås* ☎ *918–87–716* 🌐 *www.facebook.com/heimekoseleg.* **Nasjonalparkriket.** (*National Park System*) ✉ *Ola Dahls gt. 1, Otta* ☎ *61–24–14–44* 🌐 *www.nasjonalparkriket.no.*

Hamar

127 km (79 miles) north of Oslo.

On a northeast fork of Lake Mjøsa, Hamar was the seat of a bishopric during the Middle Ages. Four Romanesque arches, which are part of the cathedral wall, remain; they are today the symbol of the city. Ruins of the 13th-century monastery now form the backbone of a glassed-in exhibition of regional artifacts, some of which are from the Iron Age. This lively city—the largest in the country's interior—has a wide array of attractions and serves as a gateway to central Norway.

GETTING HERE AND AROUND

Travelers headed to Hamar usually fly through Oslo. Traveling here by train takes about an hour, and there are hourly

A glittering glass superstructure protects a quartet of delicate Romanesque arches at Domkirkeodden.

departures from Oslo Airport. From Oslo Central Station, the trip takes 90 minutes. There are also several daily buses from Oslo to Hamar. By car, follow E6.

TOURS

The world's oldest paddle steamer still in operation, the *Skibladner*, also called the *White Swan of the Mjøsa*, was first launched in 1856. It departs daily from Hamar, connecting towns along the lake. The steamer creeps up to Lillehammer three days a week, and other days stops at Eidsvoll. The period-perfect saloons for gentlemen and ladies have been lovingly restored.

CONTACTS Skibladner. ✉ *Brygga 31, Hamar* ☎ *61–14–40–80* 🌐 *www.skiblader.no.*

VISITOR INFORMATION

CONTACTS Hamar Tourism Office. ✉ *Hamarregionen Turistkontor, Grønnegata 52, Hamar* ☎ *40–03–60–36* 🌐 *www.hamarregionen.no.*

Sights

Domkirkeodden (*Cathedral Point*)
MUSEUM | FAMILY | The four Romanesque arches that formed part of the wall of the medieval cathedral that once stood on this spot now form the centerpiece of Cathedral Point. The impressive glass superstructure constructed over and around the ruins make this one of the most unusual museum buildings in Europe. Also on the grounds sit 50 or so idyllic grass-roof houses from around the region that show what life was like when Hamar was a flourishing town. An organic garden that has 350 different types of herbs. ✉ *Strandveien 100, Hamar* ☎ *62–54–27–00* 🌐 *www.domkirkeodden.no* 🎫 *Nkr 110* ⏲ *Closed mid-Sept.–mid-May.*

Eidsvollsbygningen (*Eidsvoll House*)
MUSEUM | FAMILY | A 50-minute drive south along Lake Mjøsa, Eidsvoll House is one of Norway's most important national symbols because this was the place where the Norwegian Constitution

was drawn up and signed in 1814. It is a beautiful example of neoclassical architecture. Today the museum is made up of the house itself, several ancillary buildings, and the surrounding park. There's a souvenir and shop and a café with outdoor seating. ✉ *Carsten Ankers veg 19, Eidsvoll Verk* ☎ *63–92–22–10* 🌐 *www.eidsvoll1814.no* 🎫 *Nkr 140* ⏲ *Closed Mon. Sept.–Apr.*

Hamar Olympiahall (*Hamar Olympic Hall*)
ARTS VENUE | FAMILY | This impressive stadium hosted the speed-skating and figure-skating events of the Lillehammer Winter Olympics in 1994. Shaped like an upside-down Viking ship, the massive space was voted the most magnificent structure of the 20th century by the national Norwegian newspaper *Dagbladet*. The best way to see the interior is to watch a sporting event inside. ✉ *Åkersvikvegen 1, Hamar* ☎ *62–51–75–00* 🌐 *www.vikingskipet.com.*

Norsk Jernbanemuseum (*Norwegian Railway Museum*)
MUSEUM | FAMILY | One of Europe's first railway museums, opened in 1896, the Jernbanemuseet documents the development of Norway's railways. There is plenty of train memorabilia inside, while locomotives and carriages are on narrow-gauge tracks just out the doors. You can take a short ride on Tertittoget, the last steam locomotive built by Norway's state railway, from mid-May to mid-August. The museum enjoys a beautiful location by Lake Mjøsa, north of Hamar. ✉ *Strandveien 161, Hamar* ☎ *40–44–88–80* 🌐 *www.jernbanemuseet.no* 🎫 *Nkr 120* ⏲ *Closed Mon. Jan.–May and Sept.–Dec.*

Beaches

Koigen Beach
BEACH—SIGHT | FAMILY | Hamar's new beach area by the lake of Mjøsa is located a few steps away from the city center. Here you will find the talk of the town—the most expensive diving tower in Norway, as well as a sandy beach with an artificial island, basketball courts, volleyball courts, skate facilities, a barbecue area, and a well-equipped playground. The beach walk is serene and scenic year round. **Amenities:** food and drink; toilets. **Best for:** sunset; surfing; swimming; walking. ✉ *Koigen, Hamar* ✣ *From the city center, walk towards the lake till you find the road named Brygga. Koigen is located about 500 meters from city center.* ☎ *400–36–036* 🌐 *www.visit-hedmark.no.*

Restaurants

Heim Gastropub Hamar
$$ | BURGER | If you are seeking creamed mussel soup or a range of other tasty local specialties paired with the perfect beer, Heim Gastropub is the place to be. It's also the right place for a burger and other pub grub. **Known for:** friendly and courteous staff; over 100 types of beers; casual and cozy interior. 💲 *Average main: NKr 200* ✉ *Torggata 41, Hamar* ☎ *62–80–94–20* 🌐 *heim.no/hamar* ⏲ *No lunch weekdays.*

Kai and Mattis' Café
$$ | ECLECTIC | FAMILY | The first thing that catches your eye in Kai & Mattis Café is the bright red interior, the opposite of sedate Scandinavian design. The second thing most likely will be the sweet scent of delicious cakes. **Known for:** tasty homemade lunches; warm and friendly service; extraordinary soft serve. 💲 *Average main: NKr 200* ✉ *Torggata 53, Hamar* ☎ *62–53–01–45* 🌐 *www.facebook.com/kaiogmattis* ⏲ *Closed Sun. and Mon.*

Hotels

First Hotel Victoria
$$ | HOTEL | With panoramic views of Lake Mjøsa, Hamar's oldest hotel ensures that loyal guests return again and again by making sure it keeps up with the times. **Pros:** walking distance to almost

everything; sleeping kit including sleep mask and earplugs; nice breakfast included. **Cons:** not all rooms have lake view; some rooms are a bit noisy; no minibar or fridge in rooms. *Rooms from: NKr 1165* *Strandgt. 21, Hamar* *62–02–55–00* *www.firsthotels.com/hotels/norway/hamar/first-hotel-victoria/* *200 rooms* *Free breakfast.*

Scandic Hamar

$$ | HOTEL | A 10-minute walk from downtown, the Scandic Hamar offers quiet, spacious rooms with a sleek, business-minded feel. **Pros:** quiet location; small shop selling snacks; close to nearby park. **Cons:** large and impersonal; no air-conditioning; only a few rooms have a fridge. *Rooms from: NKr 989* *Vangsvegen 121* *21–61–40–00* *www.scandichotels.com/hotels/norway/hamar/scandic-hamar* *239 rooms* *Free breakfast.*

Festiviteten Bar og Scene

BARS/PUBS | Originally a movie theater—they preserved a row or two of red-velvet seats—Festiviteten is now a bar, club, and concert venue. The wood paneling and furnishings give the bar a warm and authentic atmosphere. *Vangsvegen, Hamar* *92–83–39–99* *www.festivitetenhamar.no.*

Løiten Brænderi

CRAFTS | FAMILY | The Norwegian candle maker Løiten Lys is a great reason to visit Løiten Brænderi. Spread over four stories, the old distillery buildings are filled with an impressive assortment of handmade candles, as well as other crafts. *Brennerivegen 10, Løten* *901–98–805* *www.lbr.no.*

Activities

There's plenty to do around Hamar, from hiking and biking in the surrounding hills to kayaking and boating on Norway's largest lake, Lake Mjøsa.

BOATING

Infoteket

BOATING | A 50-minute drive from Hamar, Infoteket rents boats and kayaks and offers some courses and guided tours. It's among the best that rent boats on Lake Mjosa. *Tingnesveien 796* *47–16–59–13* *www.infoteket.no.*

DOGSLEDDING

Hedmarksvidda Husky

SNOW SPORTS | This outfitter offers dogsledding and other outdoor activities throughout the year. *Ellevsætervegen 637, Brumunddal* *92–86–04–10* *www.hedmarksviddahusky.no.*

Lillehammer

168 km (104 miles) north of Oslo, 62 km (39 miles) northwst of Hamar.

Overlooking Lake Mjøsa, Lillehammer enjoys an idyllic location and is the main gateway to the Gudbrandsdalen Valley. The city is not very large, but is rich in museums and features some of the most beautifully preserved late-19th-century wooden houses, many of them along the main pedestrian street of Storgata. Many Norwegians have great affection for Lillehammer, the winter sports resort town that hosted the 1994 Winter Olympics. Many of the Olympic venues are still in use and open to visitors, making the region a popular destination for winter sports enthusiasts. In winter, several ski resorts offer a vast network of groomed cross-country trails. The same mountains make the region excellent for hikes and bicycling during the summer months.

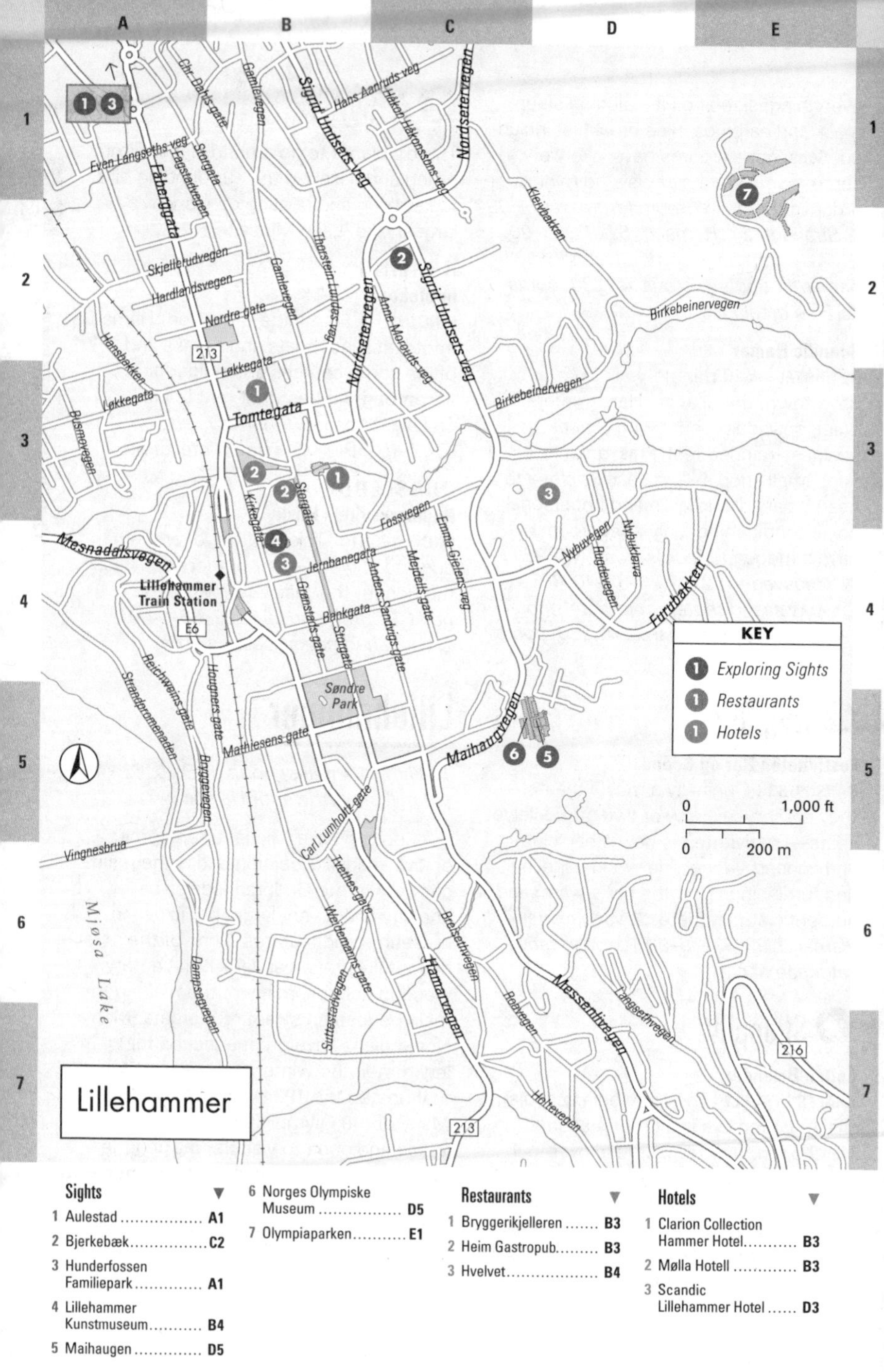

Sights

1 Aulestad A1
2 Bjerkebæk................ C2
3 Hunderfossen Familiepark.............. A1
4 Lillehammer Kunstmuseum........... B4
5 Maihaugen.............. D5
6 Norges Olympiske Museum D5
7 Olympiaparken........... E1

Restaurants

1 Bryggerikjelleren B3
2 Heim Gastropub......... B3
3 Hvelvet................... B4

Hotels

1 Clarion Collection Hammer Hotel........... B3
2 Mølla Hotell B3
3 Scandic Lillehammer Hotel D3

GETTING HERE AND AROUND

Travelling from Oslo Airport to Lillehammer takes less than two hours by car (via E6), bus, or train. From there you can get to most resorts in the area in less than 90 minutes.

TOURS

Lillehammer Guide Union leads free 60- to 90-minute walks through Lillehammer to help you get to know the city and the people who live there.

CONTACTS Lillehammer Guide Union. ✉ *Jernbanetorget 2, Lillehammer* ☎ *90–86–45–53* 🌐 *www.facebook.com/LillehammerGuideforening.*

VISITOR INFORMATION

CONTACTS Lillehammer and Gudbrandsdalen Tourism Office. ✉ *Jernbanetorget 2, Lillehammer* ☎ *61–28–98–00* 🌐 *www.lillehammer.com.* **Lillehammer Taxi.** ✉ *Oskar Skoglys vei 2* ☎ *06565* 🌐 *www.06565.no.*

Sights

Aulestad

MUSEUM | Get up close and personal with Bjørnstjerne Bjørnson, the writer, politician, and theater director whose home was a 20-minute drive from Lillehammer. He lived at Aulestad with his wife Karoline for more than a quarter of a century until his death in 1910, and visitors get to travel back in time to see the whole house as it looked when he lived there, including the smoking room that was nicknamed "the pigsty." Karoline was greatly inspired by their travels, and the country house is filled with art she collected from near and far. ✉ *Aulestadvegen 6-14* ☎ *61–28–89–00* 🌐 *www.aulestad.no* 🎫 *Nkr 135* ⏲ *Closed Oct.–May. Closed weekdays in Sept.*

Bjerkebæk

MUSEUM | Within walking distance of downtown Lillehammer sits Bjerkebæk, the home and studio of Norwegian artist Sigrid Undset, who was awarded the Nobel Prize for literature in 1928. The charming old log houses were moved here from two different farms in Gudbrandsdalen. The interior remains as it was furnished in the 1930s by Undset herself, and is filled with artifacts and books reflecting her personal taste. ✉ *Bjerkebæk, Sigdri Undsets veg 16E, Lillehammer* ☎ *61–28–89–00* 🌐 *www.bjerkebek.no* 🎫 *135 Nkr* ⏲ *Closed Oct.–May. Closed weekdays in Sept.*

Hunderfossen Familiepark (*Hunderfossen Family Park*)

AMUSEMENT PARK/WATER PARK | FAMILY | The world's biggest troll sits atop a cave in this tiny amusement park. The glittering gold *eventyrslottet*, or fairy-tale castle, is a must-see. There's a petting zoo for small children, plenty of rides for their older siblings, and an Epcot-like exhibits about oil and gas. ✉ *Fossekrovegen 22, Fåberg* ✣ *13 km (8 miles) north of Lillehammer* ☎ *61–27–55–30* 🌐 *www.hunderfossen.no* 🎫 *NKr 385* ⏲ *Closed Sept.–June.*

Lillehammer Kunstmuseum (*Lillehammer Museum of Art*)

MUSEUM | One of the most important art collections in Norway is housed at the Lillehammer Kunstmuseum, a venerable institution that first opened its doors in 1927. The 1,400 works include pieces by Edvard Munch and Adolph Tidemand. The original building has been remodeled and joined by a newer building designed by Snøhetta. Sculptor Bård Breivik created a sculpture garden that sits between the two buildings. ✉ *Stortorget 2, Lillehammer* ☎ *61–05–44–60* 🌐 *www.lillehammerartmuseum.com* 🎫 *Nkr 135* ⏲ *Closed Mon. Sept.–May.*

Maihaugen

MUSEUM | Europe's largest open-air museum, Maihaugen was founded in 1887 by Anders Sandvig, an itinerant dentist who accepted odds and ends—and eventually entire buildings—from the people of Gudbrandsdalen in exchange for his services. Eventually he turned the collection over to the city of Lillehammer, which provided land for the museum. The exhibit "We Won the Land" is an inventive meander through Norway's history. During high season craftspeople show off their skills, and there's a popular Christmas market at the end of the year. ✉ *Maihaugvegen 1, Lillehammer* ☎ *61–28–89–00* 🌐 *www.maihaugen.no* 🎫 *From NKr 135* ⏲ *Closed Mon. Sept.–May.*

Norges Olympiske Museum (*Norwegian Olympic Museum*)
MUSEUM | This popular museum is a tribute to the Olympic ideal and covers the history of the games from their start in ancient Greece in 776 BC to the present day. Multimedia presentations, interactive installations, and artifacts like sailboats and skis illustrate Norwegian sporting history in the Gallery of Honor. Some of the captions are in English. ✉ *Maihaugvegen 1, Lillehammer* ☎ *61–28–89–00* 🌐 *ol.museum.no* 🎫 *Nkr 135* ⏲ *Closed Mon. Sept.–Apr.*

Olympiaparken (*Olympic Park*)
SPORTS—SIGHT | **FAMILY** | This park might be the closest thing to actually competing in the Olympics. You can visit the ski-jump tower, ride the chairlift, or step inside the bobsled simulator at the Lysgårdsbakkene Ski Jump Arena, where the 1994 Winter Olympics opening and closing ceremonies were held. You can go tobogganing at the Kanthaugen Freestyle Arena or bobsled—or "wheelbob" in the summer—at the Olympic Bobsleigh and Luge Track. ✉ *Birkebeinervegen 122, Lillehammer* ☎ *61–05–42–00* 🌐 *www.olympiaparken.no.*

Restaurants

Bryggerikjelleren
$$$$ | **NORWEGIAN** | Located in the cellar of an old brewery dating from 1855, Bryggerikjelleren has been serving Lillehammer's best steaks for at least three decades. The interiors are dark, intimate, and cozy, consisting of three rooms with vaulted ceilings centered around a stylish bar. **Known for:** bartenders pour a perfect gin and tonic; excellent wine list; attentive staff. 💲 *Average main: NKr 400* ✉ *Elvegata 19, Lillehammer* ☎ *61–27–06–60* 🌐 *www.bblillehammer.no* ⏲ *No lunch.*

Heim Gastropub
$$ | **BURGER** | A cozy, rustic restaurant with a casual atmosphere focusing on home-made burgers and fish-and-chips, but also offering some Norwegian specialties such as cured meat salad and local cheeses in addition to an impressive range of beers. Gets extra lively on the weekends. **Known for:** great chili fries; self-tap system gives you the opportunity to tap the beer yourself; charming interiors. 💲 *Average main: NKr 200* ✉ *Storgata 84, Lillehammer* ☎ *61–10–00–82* 🌐 *www.heim.no* ⏲ *No lunch weekdays.*

Hvelvet
$$$ | **SCANDINAVIAN** | **FAMILY** | Considered by locals to be one of Lillehammer's best restaurants, Hvelvet—Norwegian for "The Vault"—offers fine wining and dining inside the former location of the Norwegian Bank. The interiors are decorated in a modern yet classic style with handsome wood floors and crisp white tablecloths. **Known for:** warm atmosphere; good children's menu; excellent value. 💲 *Average main: NKr 345* ✉ *Stortorget 1, Lillehammer* ☎ *907–29–100* 🌐 *www.hvelvet.no* ⏲ *Closed Sun.*

Hotels

Arctic Dome Sjusjøen
$$$$ | **RENTAL** | **FAMILY** | If the idea of glamping—glamorous camping—in the middle of the Norwegian wilderness sounds appealing, head to this spacious, luxurious tent shaped like an igloo, idyllically located in Sjusjøen (roughly 30 minutes east of Lillehammer). **Pros:** food delivered right to the tent; rent include use of two canoes; helpful and friendly staff. **Cons:** not accessible by public transportation; dogsledding not always available; outside toilet. 💲 *Rooms*

from: NKr 3750 ✉ Sjusjøvegen, Sjusjøen ☎ 94–84–62–70 🌐 no.sjusjoenhusky-tours.no 🛏 1 room 🍽 No meals.

Clarion Collection Hammer Hotel
$$ | HOTEL | FAMILY | A cozy atmosphere, courteous staff, and fresh rooms with a contemporary design and comfortable beds—these would be enough to make this one of Lillehammer's finest lodgings, but the biggest perk might be a delicious evening meal featuring soup, salad, and a main course that's included in the price. **Pros:** afternoon sweets; well-equipped gym; sauna and relaxation room. **Cons:** underground parking is extra; superior rooms have coffee and tea; no air-conditioning. *$ Rooms from: NKr 1240 ✉ Storgata 108, Lillehammer ☎ 61–26–73–73 🌐 www.nordicchoicehotels.com/hotels/norway/lillehammer/clarion-collection-hotel-hammer/ 🛏 142 rooms 🍽 Free breakfast.*

Mølla Hotell
$$$ | HOTEL | FAMILY | This bright yellow former mill has been transformed into a charming hotel with a reception area that feels like a private home and rooms designed in a pleasant, contemporary fashion. **Pros:** central location; cozy atmosphere; friendly staff. **Cons:** small showers; some rooms can be a bit noisy; not the largest rooms. *$ Rooms from: NKr 1425 ✉ Elvegt. 12, Lillehammer ☎ 61–05–70–80 🌐 www.mollahotell.no 🛏 58 rooms 🍽 Free breakfast.*

Scandic Lillehammer Hotel
$$$ | HOTEL | FAMILY | With a luxurious spa and wellness area, fitness center with a dedicated yoga room, indoor and outdoor pool, two well-regarded restaurants, and plenty of family-friendly activities, this spacious hotel offers a little bit for everyone. **Pros:** lovely garden and outdoor terrace; affordable children's menu; free parking. **Cons:** 20-minute walk from the railway station; some rooms are a bit outdated; business hotel vibe. *$ Rooms from: NKr 1400 ✉ Turisthotellvegen 6, Lillehammer ☎ 61–28–60–00 🌐 www.scandichotels.com 🛏 303 rooms 🍽 Free breakfast.*

Nightlife

Toppen Bar
BARS/PUBS | Enjoy the gorgeous view at this historic bar on the top floor of the Mølla Hotel. It overlooks the Olympic ski jump arena, and there are vintage photographs and other memorabilia about the sport. *✉ Mølla Hotel, Elvegata 12, Lillehammer ☎ 61–05–70–80 🌐 www.mollahotell.no.*

Shopping

Fabrikken
CERAMICS/GLASSWARE | At this creative hub you'll find different kinds of local artists in their studios making jewelry, ceramics, and other works of art. *✉ Løkkegata 9, Lillehammer ☎ 40–00–19–89 🌐 www.fabrikken.org ⏲ Closed Sun.*

Galleri Zink
ART GALLERIES | This gallery specializing in contemporary art shows some of Norway's best-known artists. *✉ Sigrid Undsets pl. Storgata 49, Lillehammer ☎ 48–19–23–03 🌐 www.gallerizink.no ⏲ Closed Mon.*

Activities

BIKING

Hafjell Bike Park
BICYCLING | About 20 minutes from Lillehammer, Hafjell Bike Park offers downhill riding with 18 trails for beginners and experts. The gondola and chair lift take you and your bike to the trail head. The on-site shop has bike rentals and protective gear. *✉ Hundervegen 122 ☎ 40–40–15–00 🌐 www.hafjell.no.*

Nordseter Fjellpark
BICYCLING | This outfitter offers mountain bike, canoe, and kayak rentals during the summer and cross-country skiing lessons

in the winter. ✉ *Nordsetervegen 1361, Lillehammer* ☎ *994–37–000* 🌐 *www.nordseter.no.*

BOATING

Gålå Event

BOATING | Enjoy a day of kayaking and canoeing in three different mountain lakes in Gålå, about 90 minutes from Lillehammer. The outfitter also has bikes, kayaks, and canoes for rent and offers guided moose safaris and dogsledding. ✉ *Gålåvegen, Gålå* ☎ *46–64–79–27* 🌐 *www.visitgala.no.*

Strand Fjellstue

BOATING | Close to Lake Espedalsvatnet, this outfitter is an hour's drive from Lillehammer. They offer boats, canoes, and kayaks for rent. ✉ *Strandsetervegen 7, Espedalen* ☎ *61–28–57–20* 🌐 *www.strand-fjellstue.no.*

DOGSLEDDING

Sjusjøen Husky Tours

SNOW SPORTS | This outfitter offers dogsledding in Sjusjøen, a 30-minute drive from Lillehammer. During the summer months the tours are on wheels. ✉ *Sjusjøvegen, Mesnali* ☎ *94–84–62–70* 🌐 *www.sjusjoenhuskytours.no.*

SKIING

Some of the country's best ski resorts are to be found in the Gudbrandsdalen region, and a ski pass gets you into all of them. With both high-mountain and forest terrain, Hafjell Alpine Resort, 10 km (6 miles) north of Lillehammer, is the region's largest alpine facility. Gålå Alpin, 89 km (40 miles) north of Lillehammer, is an all-around ski facility, with spectacular terrain and views of Jotunheimen and Rondane national parks. It has cross-country trails and organized activities like ice fishing, snow rafting, and sleigh riding.

★ Gålå Alpin

SKIING/SNOWBOARDING | One of the smaller ski resorts in the region, Gålå Alpin is a great venue for families who enjoy both alpine skiing and cross-country skiing. There are eight lifts leading up to 14 slopes, and several cross-country skiing trails in wonderfully scenic surroundings. ✉ *Børkdalsvegen 1, Gålå* ☎ *48–10–02–40* 🌐 *www.gala-alpin.no.*

Hafjell Alpine Resort

SKIING/SNOWBOARDING | A 15-minute drive from Lillehammer, Hafjell Alpine Resort offers both family-friendly slopes and more challenging runs for thrill-seekers. There are 18 lifts, including a gondola, leading up to 33 slopes. ✉ *Hafjell Alpine Resort, Hundervegen 122, Øyer* ☎ *40–40–15–00* 🌐 *www.hafjell.no.*

Ringebu

56 km (miles) north of Lillehammer.

Nicknamed Norway's smallest city, Ringebu is worth a stop for its lovely stave church and its charming shops selling local art and regional delicacies. It's surrounded by the hills and mountains of Gudbrandsdalen, and the Gudbrandsdalslågen flows nearby. From Ringebu it is not far to the beautiful Venabygdsfjellet in Rondane National Park, or to the mountain villages of Gålå, Skåbu, and Espedalen on the southern side of Gudbrandsdalslågen. Ringebu is home to Kvitfjell ski arena, which served as a downhill venue in the 1994 Winter Olympics in Lillehammer.

GETTING HERE AND AROUND

From Oslo Airport, travel time to Ringebu is about 2 1/2 hours either by train, bus or by car. You follow E6 all the way.

Ringebu Prestegar (*Ringebu Rectory*)

MUSEUM | A five-minute walk north of the Ringebu Stave Church, the 1743 Ringebu Rectory has a beautiful view towards the Gudbrandsdalslågen River and the surrounding mountains. Today the rectory consists of six buildings, and the main one is used as a gallery for the works of famous Norwegian artist Jakob Weidemann. There is also a large, lush garden with perennials and more than 150 rosebushes. ✉ *Ringebu Prestegard, Ringebu* ☎ *976–87–950* 🌐 *www.ringebustavkirke.no/prestegarden* 🎟 *Nkr 60* ⏲ *Closed Sept.–May.*

★ **Ringebu Stavkyrkje** (*Ringebu Stave Church*)

RELIGIOUS SITE | The spectacular Ringebu Stave Church is one of the largest of the remaining 28 stave churches in Norway. The church dates back to the 1220s, and was rebuilt in 1630 after the Lutheran Reformation. The eye-catching red tower was completed in 1631. In 1717 the church was painted for the first time, and at one point it was completely white. In 1921 the church was renovated and the original colors were brought back. Inside there is a statue of St. Laurentius dating from around 1250. ✉ *Ringebu stavkyrkje, Ringebu* ✥ *2 km (1 mile) south of town* ☎ *61–28–08–74* 🌐 *www.stavechurch.no* 🎟 *NKr 70* ⏲ *Closed late Aug.–May.*

Restaurants

Venabu Mountain Hotel Restaurant

$$ | **NORWEGIAN** | At the top of Ringebufjellet, this scenically situated hotel is well known for its restaurant, offering a wide selection of Norwegian specialties such as mountain trout and moose burgers. The Norwegian buffet, served every Wednesday, provides an amazing range of dishes found in the region. **Known for:** tasty local fish and game; wide assortment of cheeses; amazing views. $ *Average main: NKr 250* ✉ *Venabu Mountain Hotel, Rondevegen 860, Venabygd* ☎ *61–29–32–00* 🌐 *www.venabu.no.*

Hotels

Elgtårnet i Espedalen

$$$$ | **RENTAL** | Strongly resembling a giant game of Jenga, this slender tower soaring 40 feet above the ground is a one-of-a kind experience and not for the faint-hearted. **Pros:** an isolated location far from civilization; unparalleled views of the pristine forest; woolen slippers to keep your feet warm. **Cons:** requires a 30-minute walk from the parking lot; no electricity or running water; bring your own sleeping bag. $ *Rooms from: NKr 3500* ✉ *Espedalsvegen 2346, Espedalen* ☎ *908–37–773* 🌐 *www.elgtarn.no* 🛏 *1 room* 🍽 *No meals.*

Skåbu Mountain Hotel

$$$ | **HOTEL** | **FAMILY** | This family-run mountain hotel offers rooms and apartments with a luxurious feel and expert service. **Pros:** quiet and serene location; exquisite restaurant; breakfast included. **Cons:** few other restaurants nearby; isolated location; no air-conditioning. $ *Rooms from: NKr 1400* ✉ *Skåbuvegen 23-207, Skåbu* ☎ *61–29–55–00* 🌐 *www.skabufjellhotell.no* 🛏 *17 rooms* 🍽 *Free breakfast.*

Venabu Mountain Hotel

$$$ | **HOTEL** | **FAMILY** | In the center of the scenic Venabygdsfjellet Plateau, this lodging takes full advantage of its location at the southern edge of Rondane National Park. **Pros:** some rooms have nice touches like heated bathroom floors; restaurant is known for its delicious local cuisine; beautiful sunny terrace. **Cons:** airport transfers only in winter; isolated location; no air-conditioning. $ *Rooms from: NKr 1500* ✉ *Rondevegen 860, Venabygd* ☎ *61–29–32–00* 🌐 *www.venabu.no* ⏲ *Closed May. Closed weekdays Oct.–Dec.* 🛏 *56 rooms* 🍽 *Free breakfast.*

Performing Arts

★ **The Peer Gynt Festival**

CONCERTS | Every August, Henrik Ibsen's drama *Peer Gynt* is performed as part of one of Norway's largest cultural festivals in the small mountain village of Gålå, about a 30-minute drive from Ringebu. The nine-day celebration also includes concerts, exhibits, and lectures.

✉ *Valsetervegen 10, Gålå* ☎ *959–00–770* 🌐 *www.peergynt.no* 💳 *NKr 800.*

Shopping

Annis Pølsemakeri
LOCAL SPECIALTIES | The word *pølse* is Norwegian for sausage. The traditional meats from Annis are well known around the country and sold to many of the best restaurants. You can also buy locally made jams, cheeses, and beers in the rustic shop. ✉ *Tomtegata 10, Ringebu* ☎ *61–28–03–54* 🌐 *www.polsemakeri.no* ⏲ *Closed Sun.*

Activities

BOATING

Dalseter Mountain Lodge Canoe Rental
BOATING | Not far from Lake Breidsjøen in Espedalen, Dalseter Mountain Lodge rents canoes and small rowboats. ✉ *Espedalsvegen 2346, Espedalen* ☎ *61–29–99–10* 🌐 *www.dalseter.no.*

HIKING

Venabu Mountain Hotel Guided Walks
HIKING/WALKING | Experience the beauty of Rondane National Park with a guided walk customized for your level of experience, from a morning stroll around the plateau to a challenging hike to the summit. Venabu can also be of help if you want to try cross-country skiing, dogsledding, and sleigh riding. ✉ *Venabu Mountain Hotel, Rondeveien 860, Venabygd* ☎ *61–29–32–00* 🌐 *www.venabu.no.*

SKIING

★ **Kvitfjell Alpine Resort**
SKIING/SNOWBOARDING | From November until May you can hit the slopes at Kvitfjell Alpine Resort, one of the region's best ski areas. About 45 minutes from Lillehammer, you will find more than 20 miles of slopes covering all skill levels, two family areas, two terrains parks, and 14 lifts. One extraordinary perk is that you can ski on two sides of the same mountain: the Østsiden (Eastern Side), which features the slope used in the 1994 Winter Olympics, and the Vestsiden (Western Side). You can even take the lift up a second mountain, Varden, for absolutely stunning views. The resort offers several eateries and a fun after-ski scene. ✉ *Kvitfjellvegen 47, Fåvang* ☎ *61–24–90–00* 🌐 *www.kvitfjell.no.*

Otta

51 km (32 miles) northwst of Ringebu.

In northern Gudbrandsdalen Valley, where the emerald-green glacier river Otta meets the Gudbrandsalslågen River, lies the small city of Otta. The convenient location—between the national parks of Rondane and Jotunheimen and a short drive to the famous white-water rafting river Sjoa—is perfect for exploring the surrounding area.

GETTING HERE AND AROUND

The closest airport is Røros Airport, a three-hour drive or a seven-hour train ride to the northeast. Otta is situated along E6 and is a four-hour drive from either Oslo or Trondheim. The Dovre Railway will take you to Otta from Oslo in 3 1/2 hours, while the bus ride take approximately 5 hours.

From Otta it is a 30-minute drive into the mountains to the two main entry points of Rondale National Park, Mysuseter and Høvringen. If you're staying nearby, hotels often offer shuttle service to Otta.

CONTACTS Otta Tourism Office. ✉ *Ola Dahls gt. 1, Otta* ☎ *61–24–14–44* 🌐 *www.nasjonalparkriket.no.*

Sights

Kvitskriuprestein
NATURE SITE | A natural phenomenon of earth and stone, these pillars called Kvitskriuprestein—the White Priests—stand

guard in the Uladalen Valley not far from Otta. The only examples of this geological wonder in northern Europe, the highest pillars reach nearly 20 feet high and are more than 200 years old. ✉ *Off E6, Otta* ✥ *about 4 km (2 miles) north of Otta.*

★ **Rondane Nasjonalpark** (*Rondane National Park*)
MOUNTAIN—SIGHT | The country's first official national park, Rondane remains an essential destination for outdoors enthusiasts for its 10 summits towering more than 2,000 meters (6,561 feet) in the north and open moors and rolling hills in the southeast. Rondeslottet and Storronden are two of the most popular peaks in the sprawling park covering much of two counties, but there are countless trails suitable for every level of experience and fitness. Brudesløret, a waterfall known in English as the Bridal Veil, is a particularly beautiful trail running 4 km (2 1/2 miles) from the park's Mysusæter Entrance. Also starting here is an easy trail to a viewpoint atop Ranglarhøe, a peak that rises 1,130 meters (3,707 feet). ✉ *Mysusæter Entrance, Fv 444, Rondane Nasjonalpark* ☎ *61–24–14–44* 🌐 *www.nasjonalparkriket.no.*

Restaurants

Pillarguri Café
$$ | **NORWEGIAN** | **FAMILY** | A century old, this charming café sits in the middle of downtown Otta. Popular among locals, it's known for use of local produce, especially in regional specialties like trout and moose (as well as for toppings for American-style pizzas). **Known for:** terrace is perfect for sunny days; lots of atmosphere; friendly service. $ *Average main: NKr 150* ✉ *Storgata 7, Otta* ☎ *61–23–01–04* 🌐 *www.pillarguri.no.*

Spiseriet Rondane
$$$ | **NORWEGIAN** | **FAMILY** | Using local produce as much as possible in its carefully curated menu, the mountainside Spiseriet Rondane lets you choose among such local delicacies as mouth-watering reindeer fillet with a red wine glaze or crispy fried mountain trout with a horseradish-sour cream sauce. Whatever you do, don't miss the selection of award-winning Norwegian cheeses. **Known for:** gorgeous views; wide variety of local beers; tasty coffee with juniper syrup. $ *Average main: NKr 300* ✉ *Rondane Høyfjellshotell, Rondanevegen 1264, Mysusæter* ☎ *61–20–90–90* 🌐 *www.rondane.no.*

Hotels

Øigardseter Mountain Lodge
$$$ | **HOTEL** | **FAMILY** | Welcoming guests for over 100 years, this charming lodge offers exceptional views of the surrounding mountains. **Pros:** family-friendly vibe; pool table and other games; helpful hosts and staff. **Cons:** slim selection of nearby restaurants; no à la carte menu in restaurant; no room TVs. $ *Rooms from: NKr 1590* ✉ *Høvringenvegen 914, Høvringen* ☎ *61–23–37–13* 🌐 *www.oigardseter.com* *40 rooms* *Free breakfast.*

Rondane Haukliseter Mountain Hotel
$$$ | **HOTEL** | **FAMILY** | Close to the Høvringen entrance of beautiful Rondane National Park, this family-run lodging offers everything from comfortably furnished traditional rooms to rustic cabins. **Pros:** friendly staff; relaxed atmosphere; great for outdoors lovers. **Cons:** no TV in rooms; no nearby restaurants; no telephones in rooms. $ *Rooms from: NKr 1800* ✉ *Hauklisetervegen 31, Høvringen* ☎ *61–23–37–17* 🌐 *www.rondane.com* *24 rooms* *Free breakfast.*

Thon Hotel Otta
$$$ | **HOTEL** | **FAMILY** | If you prefer cosmopolitan hotels over mountain lodges, the strikingly modern Thon Hotel Otta will do nicely. **Pros:** complimentary tea and coffee; family rooms available; light and spacious. **Cons:** business on its mind;

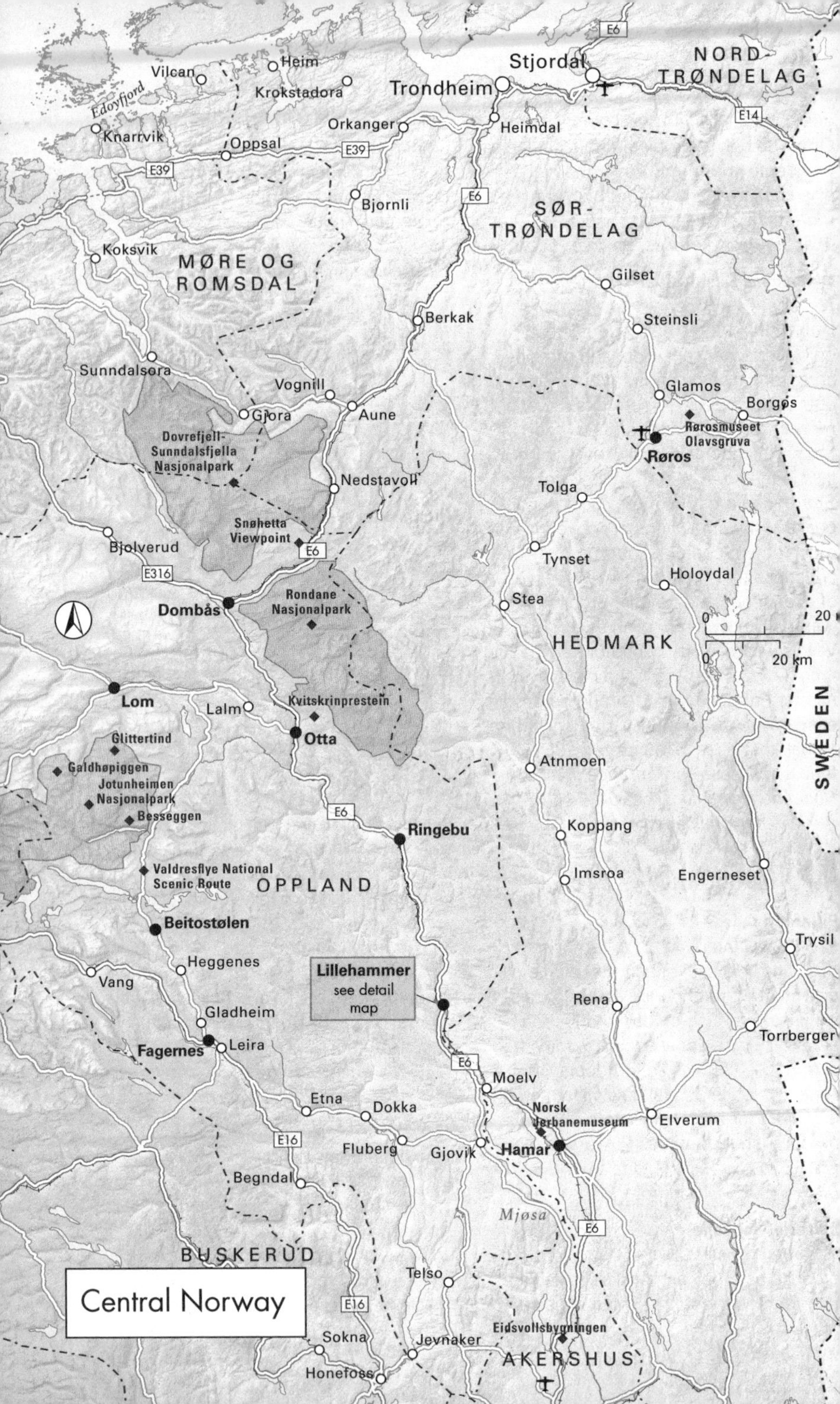

Central Norway
Vilcan
Heim
Krokstadora
Edoyfjord
Knarrvik
Oppsal
Orkanger
Trondheim
Stjordal
Heimdal
NORD-TRØNDELAG
E6
E14
E39
Bjornli
SØR-TRØNDELAG
Koksvik
MØRE OG ROMSDAL
Gilset
Berkak
Steinsli
Sunndalsora
Vognill
Aune
Gjora
Glamos
Borgos
Rørosmuseet Olavsgruva
Røros
Dovrefjell-Sunndalsfjella Nasjonalpark
Nedstavoll
Tolga
Snøhetta Viewpoint
Tynset
Bjolverud
E316
Holoydal
Stea
Dombås
Rondane Nasjonalpark
HEDMARK
0
20
20 km
Lom
Lalm
Kvitskrinprestein
Otta
SWEDEN
Glittertind
Galdhøpiggen
Jotunheimen Nasjonalpark
Besseggen
Atnmoen
Ringebu
Koppang
Valdresflye National Scenic Route
OPPLAND
Imsroa
Engerneset
Beitostølen
Trysil
Heggenes
Lillehammer see detail map
Vang
Rena
Gladheim
Torrberger
Fagernes
Leira
Moelv
Etna
Dokka
Norsk Jerbanemuseum
Elverum
Fluberg
Gjovik
Hamar
E16
Begndal
Mjøsa
BUSKERUD
Telso
Eidsvollsbygningen
Sokna
Jevnaker
AKERSHUS
Honefoss

no fridges in rooms; can be a bit noisy. *Rooms from: NKr 1300* ✉ *Ola Dahls gt. 7, Otta* ☎ *61–21–08–00* 🌐 *www.thonhotels.no/hoteller/norge/otta* *85 rooms* *Free breakfast.*

Activities

HIKING

Rondane National Park's 10 summits towering over 2,000 meters (6,561 feet) attract hikers all year round. Rondeslottet, the highest and most popular peak in Rondane, reaches a spectacular 2,178 meters (7,146 feet), and, if weather permits, treats you to a 360-degree view of the entire region. From Rondvassbu, the most popular route, the hike takes approximately five hours and passes another 2,000-meter summit, the peak of Vinjeronden.

The second highest summit in Rondane is the 2,138-meter (7,014-foot) peak of Storronden. Although it's a colossus of a mountain, it's shorter and easier than Rondeslottet. Storronden is the park's southernmost peak and gives you stunning views of the taller peaks to the north as well as the plains to the south. Remember to bring your binoculars, as you might be able to spot one of the wild reindeer herds roaming the area.

Rondane is known for its marvelous colors in almost all seasons, due to the vast vegetation above the tree line, and for its accessibility for all kinds of hikers, not just the peak hunters. A wonderful hike suitable for children is the peak of Veslesmeden—known to be one of the easiest 2,000-meter (6,561-foot) hikes in the country. Veslesmeden towers an airy 2,013 meters (6,604 feet) and the views to the Rondeslottet, Vinjeronden, and Storronden are nothing but spectacular. In clear weather, you might even see all the way to Jotunheimen.

The national park is the main destination for hikers, but it's not the only one. Pillarguri, the 825-meter (2,795-foot) peak of Thokampen Mountain, sits on the west side of the Gudbrandsdalslågen River. There are signposted trails, and you'll pass by Sameti, the cabin of the famous local psychic and mystic Marcello Haugen. When you reach the top, you are awarded with a beautiful view towards Jotunheimen in the north.

Rondaneguiden

TOUR—SPORTS | Offering custom-designed guided tours on foot, by ski, or on snowshoes, Rondaneguiden is a good outfitter for trips to Rondane National Park. Electric bicycles are for rent in summer. ✉ *Rondaneguiden, Ola Dahls gt. 1, Otta* ☎ *94–09–40–04* 🌐 *www.rondaneguiden.no.*

WHITE-WATER RAFTING

The Sjoa River, a 20-minute drive from Otta, is the most famous white-water rafting river in the country. Trips here are not for the faint of heart, as they rush through narrow canyons and over gushing rapids, leaving you a lot wetter than you might expect. There are guided trips for all levels of expertise. There are rafting expeditions on the Otta River as well.

★ Sjoa Rafting

WHITE-WATER RAFTING | FAMILY | By the shores of the Sjoa River, family-friendly Sjoa Rafting offers expeditions ranging from a few hours to a full day. In addition, you can explore the region even further with activities like canyoning, riverboarding, and bridge swinging. The season lasts from May to October. ✉ *Rte. 257, Nedre Heidal* ✢ *off E6* ☎ *90–07–10–00* 🌐 *www.sjoarafting.no.*

Lom

61 km (38 miles) west of Otta.

Nestled between Norway's highest and most dramatic mountain peaks, Lom attracts outdoor enthusiasts from all over the world. Three scenic drives traverse the area, making this a great place to have your own car.

GETTING HERE AND AROUND

By car, Lom can be reached via Route 15 and Route 55. Express buses run to Lom from Oslo, Bergen, and Trondheim.

Sights

Galdhøpiggen

MOUNTAIN—SIGHT | The highest mountain in Norway, Galdhøpiggen is a 2,469-meter behemoth that you can hike round-trip in just five to seven hours. The popular 5-km (3-mile) trail starts from Juvasshytta, already 1,850 meters above sea level. Guided hikes depart daily in the summer from Juvasshytta. ✉ *Juvasshytta, Raubergstulvegen, Lom* ☎ *61–21–29–90* 🌐 *visitjotunheimen.no.*

Galdhøpiggen Klatrepark

AMUSEMENT PARK/WATER PARK | **FAMILY** | With ziplines, slacklines, and climbing webs, this park has eight courses of varying difficulty. This is definitely a great day out for the whole family. ✉ *Galdhøpiggvegen 453, Lom* ☎ *61–21–27–99* 🌐 *aktivilom.no* 🎫 *NKr 340* ⏲ *Closed Sept.–May.*

Prestfosstraversen

BODY OF WATER | **FAMILY** | This is a unique way to see the waterfall and river in Lom. A short zipline takes you soaring along the river, under the bridge, and over the Prestfoss Waterfall (hence the name). You'll see nature in a new way as Prestfossen splashes you as you zoom past. ✉ *Prestfosstraversen, Brubakken 2, Lom* 🌐 *aktivilom.no* 🎫 *NKr 195* ⏲ *Closed Sept.–May.*

Restaurants

★ Bakeriet i Lom

$ | **CAFÉ** | The Lom Bakery is a popular place to stop for Norwegians driving through the area. Whether it's for a loaf of fresh bread to bring home or a Norwegian Skolebolle for the road, the bakery doesn't disappoint. **Known for:** stone oven; baking classes throughout the year; cookbook for sale in the bakery. $ *Average main: NKr 50* ✉ *Sognefjellsvegen 7* ☎ *61–21–18–60* 🌐 *bakerietilom.no.*

Activities

HIKING

Aktiv i Lom

HIKING/WALKING | This company offers guided hikes to Galdhøpiggen, as well as other activities including glacier walks and kayaking. ☎ *61–21–27–99* 🌐 *aktivilom.no.*

Dombås

46 km (29 miles) northwest of Otta.

In the far northern part of the Gudbrandsdalen Valley, the tiny village of Dombås is the ideal starting point for visits to Dovrefjell-Sunndalsfjella Nasjonalpark. From here you can hop aboard the scenic train to Åndalsnes.

GETTING HERE AND AROUND

At the junction of E6 and E136, Dombås is a 4 1/2-hour drive north from Oslo and a 3-hour drive south from Trondheim. The Dovre Railway runs from Oslo to Trondheim, stopping at Dombås several times a day. The ride from Oslo takes about 4 hours.

VISITOR INFORMATION

To protect the wild reindeer herds roaming Dovrefjell, the only transportation allowed to Snøheim, a starting point for hikes in Dovrefjell, is the Snøheim Shuttle Bus. Five daily departures from late June to early October.

CONTACTS Dombås Tourist Information. ✉ *Kyrkjevegen 2D, Dombås* ☎ *918–87–716* 🌐 *www.facebook.com/dombasturistinformasjon.* **Snøheim Shuttle Bus.** ✉ *Hjerkinnhusveien 33, Hjerkinn* ☎ *47–86–22–86* 🌐 *www.snoheim.dnt.no.*

A Ride on the Rauma

One of the most unforgettable journeys through Norway is a spectacular train ride through the Romsdalen Valley. The 114 km-long Rauma Railway (www.vy.no/en), traveling between Dombås and Åndalsnes, crosses 32 bridges, including the mighty Kylling Bridge that took 10 years to build. Constructed of solid granite, it spans the Rauma River and looks postcard-perfect from the train windows. You will also get to experience the spectacular Trollveggen, the tallest vertical rock wall in Europe, and the remote and beautiful wilderness around Reinheimen National Park.

In the summer, the comfortably appointed trains slow down to give travelers the best possible photo ops. An English-language commentary informs you about what you are seeing. The sightseeing trains run from April to August. The trip from Dombås to Åndalsnes take about 90 minutes, or a little more in summer.

Sights

Dombås Kyrkje (*Dombås Church*)
MUSEUM | In the center of Dombås you'll find this small, beautiful church built in 1939. Designed by architect Magnus Poulsson, the cruciform church has a striking wooden altarpiece with 10 elaborate paintings depicting the life of Jesus. *Kyrkjevegen 6, Dombås 61–24–14–44 visitdovrefjell.no/dombs-kirke Closed early Aug.–late June.*

★ Dovrefjell-Sunndalsfjella Nasjonalpark
MOUNTAIN—SIGHT | Known for its dramatic contrasts, Dovrefjell-Sunndalsfjella National Park ranges from the almost alpine scenery in the northwest to the rounded mountains and drier climate in the east. Snøhetta, towering a stunning 2,286 meters (7,500 feet) from the plateau below, was for a long time thought to be the highest peak in Norway. (It's now the twenty-fourth, falling behind Jotunheimen in Rondane Nasjonalpark.) Both Kongsvold/Reinheim and Hjerkinn are good starting points for the daylong trek up this mountain. Dovrefjell is home to herds of wild reindeer, musk oxen, and Arctic foxes, among other fascinating creatures. *Dovrefjell-Sunnedalsfjella Nasjonalpark 61–24–14–44 www.nasjonalparkriket.no.*

★ Snøhetta Viewpoint
VIEWPOINT | The large Norwegian Wild Reindeer Centre Pavilion, more commonly known as Snøhetta Viewpoint, offers panoramas of Mt. Snøhetta and Dovrefjell-Sunndalsfjella National Park. The building was designed by the Norwegian architectural agency Snøhetta and functions as a warm, dry place to sit down, take a break, and enjoy the views. With a bit of luck, you might spot musk ox and wild reindeer. The building is open from June until mid-October and can be reached via the hiking trail from the Snøhetta parking lot or the train station at Hjerkinn. *Viewpoint Snøhetta, Hjerkinn www.villrein.no Free Closed Oct.–May.*

Restaurants

Moskusgrillen
$$ | **NORWEGIAN** | **FAMILY** | In the middle of Dombås, Moskusgrillen serves traditional Norwegian dishes ranging from *potetball* (potato dumplings often served with meat) to *elgkarbonader* (elk in a cream

You can spot a majestic musk ox in Dovrefjell-Sunndalsfjella National Park.

sauce). If you're looking for something more familiar for the kids, there are a dozen or more kinds of pizza that you can enjoy on the outside terrace. **Known for:** friendly staff; large outdoor terrace; accessible children's menu. *Average main: NKr 200* *Kyrkjevegen 1, Dombås* *61–24–01–00* *www.moskusgrillen.no.*

Hotels

Dombås Hotel

$$$ | **HOTEL** | **FAMILY** | At the foot of the Dovrefjell Mountains, the Dombås Hotel has a central location close to the restaurants and shops in the village. **Pros:** great views of the mountains; relaxing sauna area; outdoor terrace for the sunny days. **Cons:** some rooms need renovations; can be a bit noisy; windows don't open. *Rooms from: NKr 1300* *Domaasgrendi 1, Dombås* *61–24–10–01* *www.dombas-hotell.no* *99 rooms* *Free breakfast.*

Furuhaugli Turisthytter

$$ | **B&B/INN** | **FAMILY** | Set among the birch trees of Dovrefjell-Sunndalsfjella National Park, the mountainside Furuhaugli Turisthytter takes full advantage of the region's peace and quiet. **Pros:** offers a popular musk ox safari; rooms have their own kitchenettes; children's play area. **Cons:** rooms are pretty basic; few nearby restaurants; books up quickly. *Rooms from: NKr 1250* *Furuhauglie 80, Dombås* *61–24–00–00* *www.furuhaugli.no* *6 rooms* *Free breakfast.*

Hjerkinn Mountain Lodge

$$$ | **HOTEL** | **FAMILY** | An historic mountain lodge with an active farm on the premises, Hjerkinn Mountain Lodge is currently being run by the 12th and 13th generations of the same family and is one of the country's oldest businesses. **Pros:** outdoor hot tub; serene atmosphere; friendly staff. **Cons:** meals at fixed times; few restaurants in area; not all rooms have double beds. *Rooms from: NKr 1550* *Kvitdalsvegen 12, Hjerkinn*

☎ *61–21–51–00* 🌐 *www.hjerkinn.no* *26 rooms* 🍽 *Free breakfast.*

Shopping

Dovre Handverkstugu

LOCAL SPECIALTIES | This charming shop and gallery in an old schoolhouse in the center of Dombås sells traditional crafts like knitted sweaters and painted porcelain. ✉ *Bondegardsvegen 1, Dombås* ☎ *48–17–38–43* 🕐 *Closed Sun.*

Activities

BIKING

A bike trail named the Tour de Dovre makes it possible to experience not only Dovrefjell-Sunndalsfjella Nasjonalpark, but also Rondane Nasjonalpark. The starting point is Dombås, where you bicycle on a gravel road 32 km (20 miles) to Hjerkinn.

Dovrefjell Adventures

BICYCLING | Bike rentals are available at Dovrefjell Adventures, as are canoe rentals and guided excursions like moose safaris. ✉ *Dovrefjell Adventures, Nordre Stasjonsveg 26, Dombås* ☎ *45–45–66–33* 🌐 *www.dovrefjelladventures.no.*

HIKING

Dovrefjell-Sunndalsfjella National Park and the surrounding areas cover approximately 4.367 square kilometers (1,686 square miles), making this one of the largest continuous protected areas in mainland Norway. The varied landscape, from the more rounded hills in the east to the sharp peaks and deep valleys in the west, makes Dovrefjell a hiker's haven. The majestic Snøhetta, the highest peak in Dovrefjell, is a popular destination.

WILDLIFE-WATCHING

Furuhaugli Musk Ox Safari

WILDLIFE-WATCHING | Dovrefjell is well known for its herd of musk ox, and watching the majestic animals in their natural habitat is a unique experience. Although you might get lucky and spot them on your own on a hiking trip, a guided trip with Furuhaugli Musk Ox Safari will increase your chances drastically. If you are lucky, you might also stumble upon a herd of reindeer ✉ *Furuhaugli 80, Dovrefjell-Sunnedalsfjella Nasjonalpark* ☎ *61–24–00–00* 🌐 *www.furuhaugli.no.*

Røros

178 km (110 miles) northeast of Dombås, 154 km (96 miles) southeast of Trondheim, 392 km (243 miles) north of Oslo.

This colorful timber town was founded in 1646 when copper ore was first found in the area, and over the years Røros became one of the country's most important mining hubs. Due to its authentic wooden buildings, narrow streets, and unique character, the town was included on the list of UNESCO World Heritage Sites in 1980. Røros is a charming, lively little town, especially during the summer and in December, when the twinkling decorations and lively market turns Røros into a fairy tale. There are plenty of cozy cafés and shops selling traditional arts and crafts.

GETTING HERE AND AROUND

Røros Airport has daily flights from Trondheim and Oslo. The drive from Trondheim takes two hours on Route RV30, while Oslo is a five-hour drive on the E6 and RV3. There are several train departures from Oslo and Trondheim. Most local sights are easily accessible by foot, but taxis and buses are available.

CONTACTS Røros Taxi. ✉ *Johan Falkbergets vei 2, Røros* ☎ *72–41–12–58.*

VISITOR INFORMATION

CONTACTS Røros Tourism Office. ✉ *Peder Hiortgata 2, Røros* 🌐 *www.roros.no.*

Sights

Røros Kirke (*Røros Church*)
BUILDING | Built in the golden age of the Røros Copper Company, this 1,600-seat church was completed in 1784 and remains one of the largest in Norway. The white-and-green tower hovering above the rooftops of Røros is an impressive sight. It went through an extensive restoration in 2010. ✉ *Kjerkgata 39, Røros* ☎ *72–41–95–31* 🌐 *www.roroskirke.no* 🎫 *NKr 50* ⏲ *Closed weekdays Sept. 12–May 1.*

Rørosmuseet Olavsgruva (*Olav's Mine*)
FACTORY | Røros Copper Works was open from 1937 to 1972, and Olav's Mine was the last to be worked in this area. It has remained more or less untouched since it was shut down, and provides a vivid picture of the mining industry in Røros. Tours travel 50 meters (164 feet) underground into the main mine, lit by the occasional lightbulb and traversed by wooden walkways. Bring good shoes and warm clothes, as the temperatures remain a few degrees above freezing throughout the year. There are stairs, so the mine is not wheelchair accessible. ✉ *Gruveveien 612, Glåmos* ✣ *13 km (8 miles) east of Røros* ☎ *72–40–61–70* 🌐 *www.rorosmuseet.no* 🎫 *NKr 130* ⏲ *Closed Sun.–Wed., Fri., and Sun. only mid-Sept.–May.*

Rørosmuseet Smelthytta (*Røros Museum Smelthytta*)
MUSEUM | **FAMILY** | Covering the history of the Røros Copper Works, Smelthytta was built on the ruins of the smelter that burned down in 1975. The exhibitions are brought to life by models of mines and mining equipment. There are scheduled guided tours, as well as audio guides in English. ✉ *Malmplassen, Røros* ☎ *72–40–61–70* 🌐 *www.rorosmuseet.no* 🎫 *NKr 110* ⏲ *Closed early to mid-May.*

Restaurants

Vertshuset Røros
$$ | **NORWEGIAN** | **FAMILY** | In an historic wooden building, this restaurant lets you choose between a more formal dining room in the main building with elegant decor and crisp linens, and a casual pub in the old servants' quarters and coach house. The Vertshuset, to the left as you enter from the street, offers three- and six-course set menus focusing on local fish and game, while the pub to the right has an array of burgers and Norwegian cured meat and cheeses. **Known for:** outdoor terrace; authentic atmosphere; wide variety of beers. 💲 *Average main: NKr 250* ✉ *Kjerkgata 34, Røros* ☎ *72–41–93–50* 🌐 *www.vertshusetroros.no.*

Hotels

ErzscheiderGården
$$$ | **HOTEL** | **FAMILY** | With Røros Kirke as a next-door neighbor, this family-run hotel has charm to spare and is known for its friendly and authentic atmosphere. **Pros:** delicious breakfast buffet; outdoor furniture for summer days; welcoming staff. **Cons:** no air-conditioning; up a steep hill; rooms are on the small side. 💲 *Rooms from: NKr 1695* ✉ *Spell Ola veien 6, Røros* ☎ *72–41–11–94* 🌐 *www.erzscheidergaarden.no* *24 rooms* *Free breakfast.*

Røros Hotel Bath and Wellness
$$$ | **HOTEL** | **FAMILY** | A short walk from the center of Røros, this homey hotel is renowned for its heated swimming pool and its abundant breakfast buffet. **Pros:** friendly staff; cozy atmosphere; two restaurants. **Cons:** some rooms need renovation; no tea or coffee in room; no air-conditioning. 💲 *Rooms from: NKr 1350* ✉ *An-Magrittveien 48* ☎ *72–40–80–00* 🌐 *www.roroshotell.no* *80 rooms* *Free breakfast.*

Nightlife

Skanckebua Bar

BARS/PUBS | This bar overlooking Kjerkgata, the main street in Røros, has an old-fashioned feel thanks to the handsome dark-wood paneling. Besides drinks, it also offers a menu of small plates. ✉ *Kjerkgata 28, Røros* ☎ *72–41–05–67* 🌐 *www.bergstaden.no.*

Shopping

Per Lysgaard Ceramics

CERAMICS/GLASSWARE | A store and gallery in one, this shop presents a wide range of creative, colorful, and more or less functional ceramics and sculptures made by artist Per Lysgaard. The backyard is filled to the brim and is a must-see. ✉ *Kjerkgata 5, Røros* ☎ *72–41–27–34* 🌐 *www.lysgaard.no* ⏲ *Closed Sun.*

Røros Tweed Outlet

CRAFTS | Weaving high-quality woolen blankets since 1940, Røros Tweed is still one of the most important textile brands in the country. Made in Norway, these goods are made with the softest local wool. ✉ *Tollef Bredalsvei 8, Røros* ☎ *72–40–67–20* 🌐 ⏲ *Closed Sun.*

Activities

Situated 630 meters (2,066 feet) above sea level, Røros has plenty of hiking, biking, and cross-country skiing opportunities.

BIKING

Røros Guide

TOUR—SPORTS | This outfitter offer guided biking and hiking tours of the area for all levels of experience and fitness. If you want to strike out on your own, it also rents bikes. ✉ *Tollef Bredals vei 11, Røros* ☎ *977–61–521* 🌐 *www.rorosguide.no.*

DOGSLEDDING

Røros Husky Tours

TOUR—SPORTS | Mush your own team of dogs or ride along as a passenger wrapped in warm reindeer skins on a dogsledding trip in the mountains surrounding Røros. ✉ *Ormhaugen Gård, Røros* ☎ *915–15–228* 🌐 *www.roroshusky.no.*

SKIING

Enjoy the beautiful and friendly skiing terrain in the Røros region with over 300 miles of groomed ski trails, or make your own trails on the vast mountain plateau. The season usually starts in November and lasts until May.

Røros Sport AS

SKIING/SNOWBOARDING | Rent your perfect pair of skis from this centrally located sports shop, one of the best in the area. ✉ *Bergmannsgata 13, Røros* ☎ *72–41–12–18* 🌐 *www.facebook.com/rorossport/.*

SNOWMOBILING

Røros Hotell

TOUR—SPORTS | Join a guided snowmobiling tour through the nearby national parks with this well-regarded outfitter. Choose between half-day or full-day trips, enjoying a hot beverage and a snack along the way. ✉ *Røros Hotell, An-Magrittveien 48, Røros* ☎ *72–40–80–00* 🌐 *www.roroshotell.no.*

Fagernes

190 km (118 miles) northwest from Oslo.

Fagernes's name comes from two Norwegian words: *fager*, meaning "fair" or "beautiful," and *nes*, meaning "headland." On the glittering Strondefjorden, the town lives up to its name because of its location in the middle of one of Norway's most beautiful regions. It's a perfect starting point for hikes in Jotunheimen National Park. The town itself is home to several interesting sights, including the beautiful open-air Valdres Folkemuseum.

GETTING HERE AND AROUND

If you are driving, E16 runs from Oslo and Bergen, and Route 250 and Route 33 run from Lillehammer. The Valdresekspressen express bus runs up to eight times daily between Oslo and Fagernes. There are also daily departures from Bergen and Lillehammer.

CONTACTS Fagernes Taxi. ✉ *Fagernes Taxisentral, Jernbanevegen 13, Fagernes* ☎ *61–36–18–00* 🌐 *www.fagernestaxi.no.* **Fagernes Tourism Office.** ✉ *Fagernes-Turistkontor, Jernbanevegen 7, Fagernes* ☎ *61–35–94–10* 🌐 *www.valdres.no.*

Sights

Hedalen Stavkyrkje (*Hedalen Stave Church*)

RELIGIOUS SITE | Dating back to around 1163, the Hedalen Stave Church looks like it comes straight from a fairy tale. Inside is a wooden reliquary (an ornate container for relics) in the shape of a miniature church, one of just a few of this style that can still be found in Norway. The Hedal Madonna sculpture, dating back to the mid-1200s, is one of the most stunning pieces of medieval ecclesiastical art in Norway. ✉ *Hedalsvegen, Hedalen* ☎ *61–35–94–10* 🌐 *www.hedalen.no/stavkirka* 🎫 *NKr 60* ⏲ *Closed mid-Aug.–late June.*

Valdres Folkemuseum (*Valdres Folk Museum*)

MUSEUM | **FAMILY** | On a beautiful peninsula jutting out into the Strondefjord, the open-air Valdres Folkemuseum covers 30 acres and includes more than 100 historic structures, many of them dating back centuries. One of the most interesting is a wooden warehouse that was originally built in the 1300s, and medieval ornaments decorate the doorposts. Inside a striking modern building, the permanent exhibition takes a fascinating look at *bunader*, Norwegian traditional costumes. Kids will also love the displays of folk instruments and vintage toys. It's a good idea to book the guided tours offered in July and August well in advance. ✉ *Tyinvegen 27, Fagernes* ☎ *61–35–99–00* 🌐 *www.valdresmusea.no/valdres-folkemuseum* 🎫 *NKr 100* ⏲ *Closed weekends Oct.–June.*

Restaurants

Munkekroen

$$$ | **NORWEGIAN** | **FAMILY** | At the Valdres Folk Museum, this restaurant uses fresh local ingredients in such dishes as reindeer, trout, and *rakfisk* (fish that has been salted and fermented for months). It has a modern Scandinavian feel thanks to the sleek furnishings and the wall of windows overlooking the fjord, but the wood beams and peaked ceiling evoke the more traditional structures nearby. **Known for:** Norwegian delicacies; friendly and helpful staff; overlooking the Strondafjorden. 💲 *Average main: NKr 265* ✉ *Valdres Folkmuseum, Tyinvegen 27, Fagernes* ☎ *61–36–01–77* 🌐 *www.munkekroen.com* ⏲ *Closed Mon. and Tues.*

Hotels

★ Herangtunet Boutique Hotel

$$$$ | **HOTEL** | Close to the Heggefjorden, this gem of a hotel is surrounded by picturesque forests and lakes. **Pros:** attractive terrace and garden; outdoor whirlpool tub; lots of amenities. **Cons:** isolated location; no nearby restaurants; no air-conditioning. 💲 *Rooms from: NKr 2000* ✉ *Herangtunet, Heggenes* ☎ *976–33–310* 🌐 *www.herangtunet.com* 🛏 *9 rooms* 🍽 *Free breakfast.*

★ Nythun Mountain Lodge

$$$$ | **HOTEL** | **FAMILY** | A charming husband-and-wife team—they'll introduce themselves as Jørn and Marit when you arrive—run this alpine-style hotel in the mountains about 14 km (9 miles) from Fagernes. **Pros:** serene location; friendly hosts; beautiful views. **Cons:** some rooms are small; no air-conditioning; books up fast. $ *Rooms from: NKr 3000* ✉ *Nythun Fjellstue, Steinsetbygdvegen 2233, Etnedal* ☎ *906–67–304* 🌐 *www.nythun.no* 🛏 *17 rooms* 🍴 *Free breakfast.*

Scandic Valdres
$$$ | HOTEL | FAMILY | Enjoying an idyllic location on the shores of Strandefjorden, this massive hotel offers gorgeous views from many of the brightly decorated rooms. **Pros:** award-winning breakfast; playground for the kids; amenities abound. **Cons:** has a business hotel feel; not all rooms have minibars; no air-conditioning. $ *Rooms from: NKr 1650* ✉ *Jernbaneveien 26, Fagernes* ☎ *61–35–80–00* 🌐 *www.scandichotels.com/hotels/norway/fagernes/scandic-valdres* 🛏 *138 rooms* 🍴 *Free breakfast.*

Nightlife

Nabo Bar
BARS/PUBS | Rough-hewn walls, a glowing fireplace, and flickering lights create a cozy atmosphere at one of the area's most popular bars. ✉ *Jernbanevegen 278, Fagernes* ☎ *472–77–747* 🌐 *www.barcraft.no.*

Shopping

Valdres Vilt og Tradisjonsmat (*Valdres Traditional Foods*)
LOCAL SPECIALTIES | This traditional farmhouse has been transformed into a charming shop selling different kinds of local game (including grouse and beaver, in season) and an assortment of traditional cured meats. There's also honey, jams, and juices. ✉ *Tyinvegen 960* ☎ *908–56–808.*

Activities

BIKING

Intersport Fagernes
BICYCLING | With a wide variety of sports gear for sale, this shop also has bicycles for rent. It's very popular, so reserve in advance. ✉ *Gullsmedvegen 2, Fagernes* ☎ *61–36–29–40* 🌐 *www.intersport.no/butikker/fagernes-sportsforretning.*

HIKING

Jotunheimen Travel
TOUR—SPORTS | This company offers guided tours and sends you on self-guided tours where you can discover some of the most popular hiking routes in Jotunheimen. ✉ *Fagernes Skysstasjon Jernbanevegen 7, Fagernes* ☎ *61–36–59–00* 🌐 *www.jotunheimentravel.com.*

HORSEBACK RIDING

Myhre Gård
HORSEBACK RIDING | This farm offers horseback riding excursions for people of all skill levels. Choose between two-hour trips, daylong rides, or treks lasting several nights. ✉ *Myhre Gård, Nordheimveien 12, Skammestein* ☎ *915–20–232* 🌐 *www.myhregard.com.*

Beitostølen

38 km (24 miles) northwest of Fagernes, 224 km (139 miles) northwest from Oslo.

At the entrance of Jotunheimen National Park, Beitostølen is known as a great winter destination that practically guarantees snow from November to May. During the summer months, the small mountain village is a great starting point for hikes in the mountains.

GETTING HERE AND AROUND

From Oslo Central Station you can take the Valdresekspressen bus service to Beitostølen. You'll be traveling through the beautiful Begnadalen Valley during the journey of barely four hours. By car, it's a three-hour drive along E16 and Route 51.

Jotunheimen National Park covers a huge area, and is accessible from Beitostølen in the Valdrees Valley or Otta in the Gudbrandsdalen Valley. Local buses serve the most popular hiking areas during the summer months.

Running between two crystal-clear alpine lakes, Besseggen Ridge is the country's most popular day hike.

TOURS

Over 100 years old, the Bitihorn takes you on a trip on Lake Bygdin where you will see more than 10 of Jotunheimen's peaks topping out at over 2,000 meters (6,651 feet). If you are lucky, you might even spot reindeer. The Gjendebåten is a passenger ferry that takes you from Gjendesheim in the west to Gjendebu in the east.

CONTACTS Beitostølen Tourism Office. ✉ *Bygdinvegen 3780, Beitostølen* ☎ *61–35–94–20* 🌐 *www.valdres.no.* **Bitihorn** . ✉ *Jernbanevegen 7, Fagernes* ☎ *61–36–16–00* 🌐 *www.jvb.no.* **Gjendebåten.** ✉ *Øygardsvegen 187, Vågå* ☎ *913–06–744* 🌐 *www.gjende.no.*

Sights

Beitostølen Lyskapellet (*Beitostølen Light Chapel*)
BUILDING | The late Norwegian artist Ferdinand Finne created unique painted glass in this beautiful chapel. ✉ *Sentervegen 2, Beitostølen* 🌐 *www.lyskapellet.no.*

★ **Besseggen Ridge**
VIEWPOINT | About 60,000 people walk the Besseggen Ridge every year, making this Norway's most popular day hike. In Jotunheimen Nasjonalpark, the mountain ridge is between Gjende and Bessvatnet, two clear alpine lakes, and the trail offers beautiful views of the landscape. The best time to visit is when the Gjendebåten boat is running from mid-June to mid-October. Park at Reinsvangen where the shuttle bus takes you to Gjendeosen and the Gjendebåten boat. ✉ *Tessanden* ✥ *Reinsvangen* ☎ *61–24–14–44* 🌐 *www.nasjonalparkriket.no.*

★ **Jotunheimen Nasjonalpark** (*Jotunheimen National Park*)
NATIONAL/STATE PARK | Since the 19th century, Jotunheimen Nasjonalpark has been one of most popular areas in the country for hiking and mountain climbing. It earns its name (Jotunheimen is Norwegian for "Home of the Giants") by having the largest concentration of peaks higher than 2,000 meters (6,561 feet) in northern Europe. This includes

the country's two highest mountains, Galdhøpiggen and Glittertind. Jotunheimen also features several lakes, the largest being Gjende. The national park has an extensive network of tracks and trails, and you will find hikes and treks suitable for everybody. ✉ *Jotunheimen Nasjonalpark* ☎ *61–24–14–44* 🌐 *www.nasjonalparkriket.no.*

Valdresflye National Tourist Route

SCENIC DRIVE | During this scenic drive over the mountain plateau of Valdresflye you can stop almost wherever you like, either to photograph the beautiful landscape or go for a hike in the mountains. During the summer, several local farms sell traditional foods. 🌐 *www.nasjonaleturistveger.no/en/routes/valdresflye* ⏲ *Closed Dec.–Mar.*

Restaurants

Bessheim Restaurant

$$ | **NORWEGIAN** | Traditional dishes such as reindeer and moose from local hunters and mountain trout from a nearby lake are among the signature dishes at the renowned Bessheim Restaurant. The restaurant is light and airy, adding to the relaxed atmosphere. **Known for:** local delicacies; cozy dining room; scenic location. $ *Average main: NKr 220* ✉ *Bessheim Fjellstue og Hytter, Sjodalsvegen 2977, Tessanden* ☎ *61–23–89–13* 🌐 *www.bessheim.no.*

Hytta Mat and Vinhus

$$$ | **NORWEGIAN** | A hidden gem in Beitostølen, Hytta Food and Winehouse is renowned for its fine local cuisine. The restaurant is set in a traditional Norwegian cowshed, and the wooden walls and floors and reindeer skins slung across the chairs give it a rustic feel. **Known for:** amazing deer fillet; friendly hosts and staff; authentic ambience. $ *Average main: NKr 300* ✉ *Finntøppveien 2, Beitostølen* ☎ *904–00–288* 🌐 *www.beitstolen-restaurant.com* ⏲ *Closed Mon. and Tues.*

Hotels

Bergo Hotel

$$$ | **HOTEL** | **FAMILY** | Centrally located in downtown Beitostølen, the Bergo Hotel has a distinctive character and a pleasant atmosphere, with interiors—especially the dining rooms, the reception area, and the lounges—echoing longtime traditions and decorated by local artists. **Pros:** this is the place to go after hitting the slopes; close to the ski lift; friendly staff. **Cons:** small rooms; no air-conditioning; busy during high season. $ *Rooms from: NKr 1670* ✉ *Bygdinvegen 3782, Beitostølen* ☎ *61–35–10–00* 🌐 *www.beitstolen.com* *30 rooms* 🍽 *Free breakfast.*

★ **Hindsæter Mountain Hotel**

$$$ | **HOTEL** | **FAMILY** | This historic hotel has stunning views of the Sjodalen Valley and Jotunheimen National Park. **Pros:** wellness room with whirlpool and saunas; family rooms available; ski- and snowshoe rentals. **Cons:** no à la carte dinner options; rooms on the small size; books up fast. $ *Rooms from: NKr 1640* ✉ *Sjodalsveien 1549, Tessanden* ☎ *61–23–89–16* 🌐 *www.hindseter.no* *26 rooms* 🍽 *Free breakfast.*

Jotunheimen Mountain Lodge

$$$ | **HOTEL** | **FAMILY** | Appreciated by outdoors enthusiasts for its proximity to Jotunheimen National Park, by nature lovers for its jaw-dropping views, and by foodies for its well-regarded restaurant, Jotunheimen Mountain Lodge has much to recommend it. **Pros:** kayaks for rent; courteous staff; comfy common area. **Cons:** few nearby dining options; not many room amenities; books up fast. $ *Rooms from: NKr 1700* ✉ *Sognefjellsvegen, Bøverdalen* ☎ *61–21–29–18* 🌐 *www.jotunheimen-fjellstue.com* ⏲ *Closed Oct.–May.* *18 rooms* 🍽 *Free breakfast.*

Nordre Ekre Farm Hotel

$$$ | **HOTEL** | **FAMILY** | In the heart of the mountain village of Heidal, close to both

Rondane and Jotunheimen national parks, you'll find this small, charming hotel full of Norwegian history. **Pros:** fantastic food in the restaurant; great views of the mountains; serene and quiet location. **Cons:** books up quickly; few nearby restaurants; no air-conditioning. *Rooms from: NKr 1595* *Heidalsvegen 1265* *481–20–866* *www.nordre-ekre.no* *7 rooms* *Free breakfast.*

Radisson Blu Mountain Resort Beitostølen
$$$ | **HOTEL** | **FAMILY** | You can enjoy panoramic views of the surrounding mountains and valleys and feel serenely secluded at this bustling hotel, but still be a stone's throw from cross-country and downhill ski trails. **Pros:** spa has a swimming pool and sauna; attentive and friendly staff; outdoor terrace for sunny days. **Cons:** some rooms lack Wi-Fi; no air-conditioning; noisy during high season. *Rooms from: NKr 1790* *Bygdinvegen 3812, Beitostølen* *61–35–30–00* *www.radissonblu.com/en/resort-beitostolen* *124 rooms* *Free breakfast.*

Nightlife

Svingen Pub
BARS/PUBS | Despite its modest size, Svingen Pub is known for having Beitostølen's hottest aprés-ski scene. The generous outdoor terrace dotted with heat lamps is the perfect spot to enjoy a beer or an evening concert. *Bergo Hotel, Bygdinvegen 3784, Beitostølen* *906–50–390* *www.barcraft.no.*

Activities

BIKING

The Valdres Valley has hundreds of miles of signposted cycling routes, among them is the popular Mjølkevegen (Milky Way) through some of the region's prettiest scenery. And Jotunheimen Nasjonalpark is also a great place to ride.

Bike and Hike
BICYCLING | This outfitter rents bikes and offers guided tours throughout the region. *Gjendesvegen 200, Tessanden* *941–77–712* *www.bikeandhike.no.*

DOGSLEDDING

Beito Husky Tours
TOUR—SPORTS | Offers dogsledding day trips and overnight trips throughout the year, this outfitter is extremely popular. Make sure to book in advance. *Beitovegen 350, Beito* *41–76–06–16* *www.beitohuskytours.com.*

Chapter 7

BERGEN

Updated by
Janicke Hansen

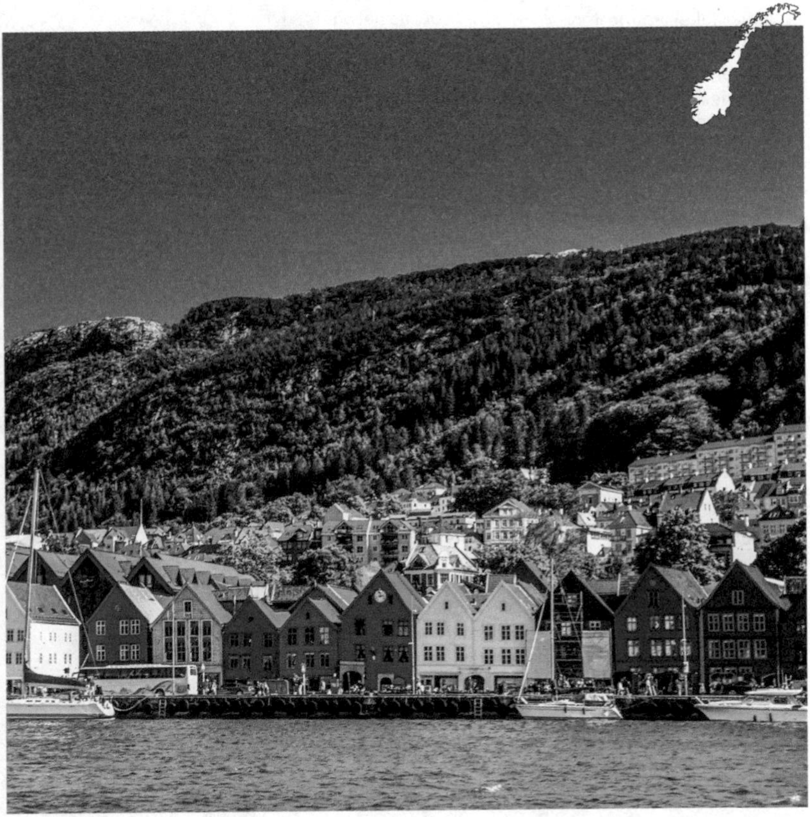

Sights	Restaurants	Hotels	Shopping	Nightlife
★★★★★	★★★★☆	★★★★☆	★★★☆☆	★★★★☆

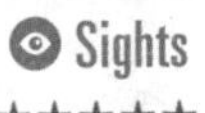

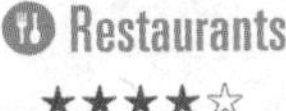

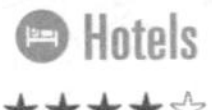

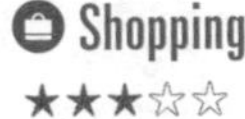

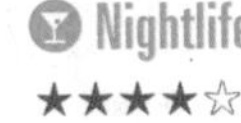

WELCOME TO BERGEN

TOP REASONS TO GO

★ **Walk along the waterfront:** The string of colorful wooden buildings along Bergen's wharf are an unforgettable UNESCO World Heritage Site.

★ **Fly up the Fløibanen:** In just seven minutes, this funicular takes you from the city streets to the top of a mountain with spectacular views of the fjord.

★ **Something fishy at the Fisketorget:** In business since the 1200s, the always bustling Bergen Fish Market is one of Norway's most popular outdoor markets.

★ **Trek to Troldhaugen:** Learn about composer Edvard Grieg, Bergen's favorite son, at the ornate mansion where he wrote many of his most famous pieces.

★ **Unlock the KODE:** Scattered along the shore of Lake Lille Lungegårdsvann you'll find a string of wonderful museums with collections spanning the centuries.

1 Bryggen. Located on the northeast side of Bergen's harbor, Bryggen is a picture-perfect row of reconstructed wooden houses. Head here for a visit to the city's ancient fortress or its modern fish market.

2 Nordnes. Beginning near the fish market, this peninsula on the northwest side of the harbor is home to the city's much-loved aquarium and has eye-popping views of Bryggen.

3 Sentrum. The heart of Bergen is the long, narrow central square of Torgallmenningen, a pedestrian-only thoroughfare that runs through the modern neighborhood of Sentrum.

4 Sandviken. A residential area north of Bergen's hulking fortress, Sandviken is home to the beautifully restored 19th-century homes of the Old Bergen Museum.

5 Greater Bergen. Just outside the borders of the city you'll find some of its best-known attractions, including the gorgeous homes of composers Edvard Greig and Ole Bull.

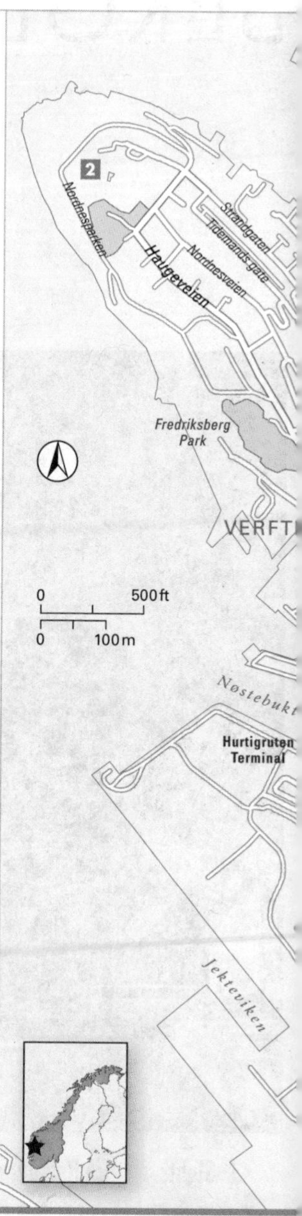

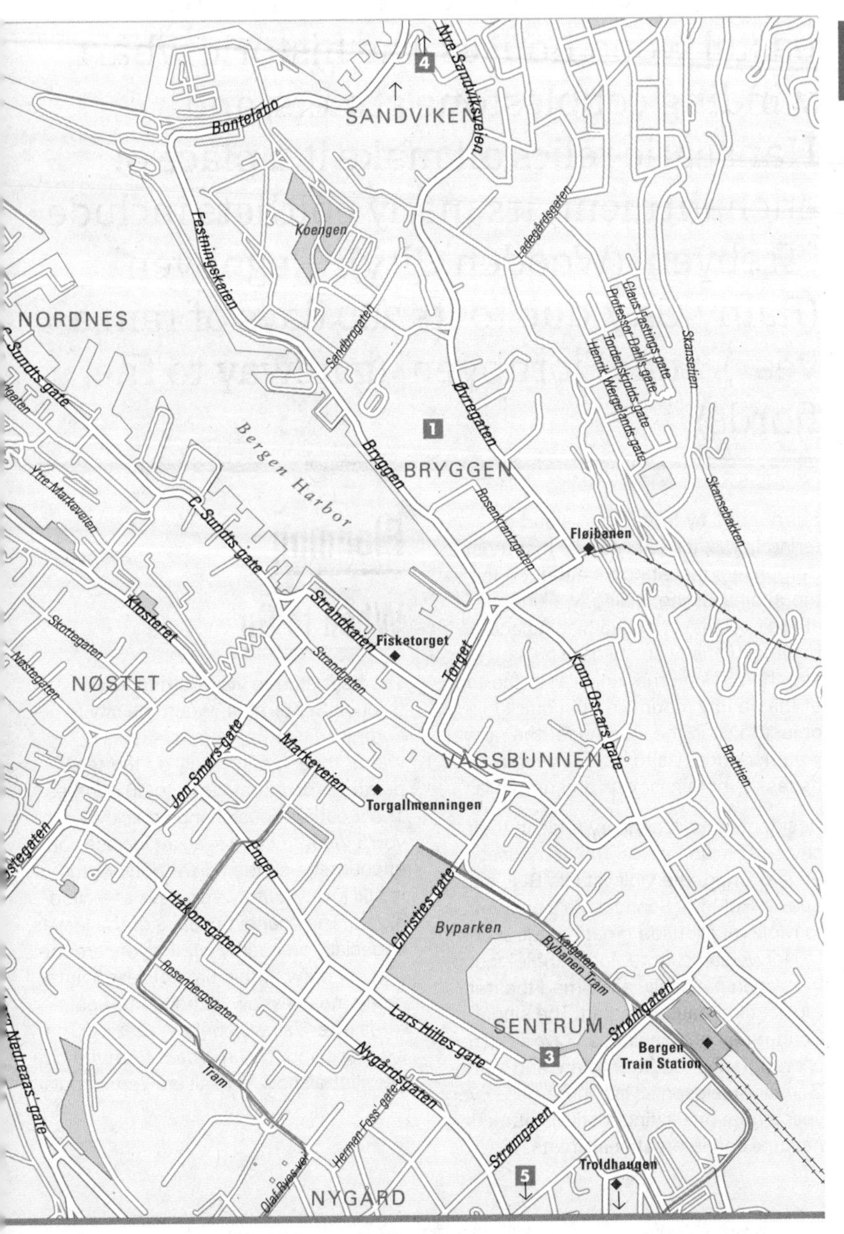

SANDVIKEN
Bontelabo
Nyre Sandviksveien
Koengen
Festningskaien
Ladegårdsgaten
Claus Fastings gate
Professor Dahls gate
Tordenskjolds gate
Henrik Wergelands gate
Skanseien
NORDNES
C. Sundts gate
Sandbrogaten
Øvregaten
Bergen Harbor
Bryggen
BRYGGEN
Rosenkrantzgaten
Skansebakken
Fløibanen
Ytre Markeveien
C. Sundts gate
Klosteret
Strandkaien
Fisketorget
Strandgaten
Torget
Kong Oscars gate
Skottegaten
Nøstegaten
NØSTET
Jon Smørs gate
Markeveien
VÅGSBUNNEN
Torgallmenningen
Brattlien
Engen
Christies gate
Byparken
Håkonsgaten
Kaigaten
Bybanen Tram
Rosenbergsgaten
Lars Hilles gate
SENTRUM
Strømgaten
Bergen Train Station
Nygårdsgaten
Tram
Nedreaas' gate
Herman Foss' gate
Strømgaten
Olaf Ryes vei
Troldhaugen
NYGÅRD

Many visitors fall in love with Bergen, Norway's second-largest city, at first sight. Seven rounded lush mountains, pastel wood houses, the historic wharf, winding cobblestone streets, and Hanseatic relics all make it a place of enchantment. Its many epithets include "Trebyen" (Wooden City), "Regnbyen" (Rainy City, due to its 260 days of rain a year), and "Fjordbyen" (gateway to the fjords).

Surrounded by forested hills and glittering fjords, it's only natural that most Bergensers feel at home either on the mountains (skiing, biking, walking, or at their cabins) or at sea (fishing and boating). On any sunny day you'll often see them taking the funicular to the top of the nearby mountain for a quick hike or just to sit in the sun. As for the rainy weather, most visitors quickly learn the necessity of rain jackets and umbrellas.

Residents take legendary pride in their city and its luminaries. The composer Edvard Grieg, the violinist Ole Bull, and Ludvig Holberg, Scandinavia's answer to Molière, all made great contributions to Norwegian culture. Today their legacy lives on in nationally acclaimed theater, music, film, dance, and art. The singer Sondre Lerche, pianist Leif Ove Andsnes, choreographer Jo Strømgren, and author Gunnar Staalesen all live in Bergen. Every year a host of exciting festivals attracts national and international artists.

Planning

When to Go

The best time to visit Bergen is May through September, when the city is surprisingly temperate. It is usually warm, though only rarely do the temperature top out at close to 80 degrees. The weather does change quickly, so you'll want to carry a jacket in case you encounter a sudden downpour. Autumn is still lovely, with warm days and crisp nights. The changing colors of the leaves, especially on nearby Mt. Fløyen, are the biggest draw at this time of year. Winter rarely means snow, although temperatures often fall well below freezing. The ski areas about 90 minutes from the city get all the snow, and all are very popular.

Planning Your Time

Although it's a very compact city, you'll want several days to explore Bergen. Plan a day for exploring Bryggen and its hulking fortress, and another for Sentrum and its string of museums. The sights outside the city, such as the museum houses of Edvard Greig and Ole Bull, take at least half a day to get there and back.

If you're visiting outside of summer, remember that daylight hours are limited. Museums also have shorter hours, so get to the sights you most want to see early in the day. Even popular sights like Bergenhus Festning close earlier in winter.

Getting Here and Around

AIR TRAVEL

SAS, Norwegian, and Widerøe have the most flights into Bergen, but Air Baltic, Air France, British Airways, Finnair, Icelandair, KLM, Lufthansa, Swiss, Vueling, and Wizz Air also fly here. Flesland Airport is a 30-minute bus ride from Bergen. Flybussen, the airport bus, departs every 15 minutes and drops passengers off at the bus station in downtown Bergen. The cost is about NKr 115. A taxi stand is conveniently located outside the arrivals gate. Trips downtown cost about NKr 450 to NKr 500. You can also take light rail trains from the airport to the city center. The trip takes about 45 minutes and costs Nkr 38.

CONTACTS Flybussen Bergen. 🌐 *www.flybussen.no/billett/#/reise/til/bergen-flyplass/bgo.*

BOAT AND FERRY TRAVEL

Boats have always been Bergen's lifeline to the world. The jewel in the crown is the Hurtigruten coastal express, which departs daily for the 11-day round-trip to Kirkenes in northern Norway. Norled has several routes, including one to the popular tourist destination of Flåm and the Nordfjord area in the western fjords. Fjord Line sails to Denmark.

Cruise ships dock at Skoltegrunnskaien and Jekteviken/Dokkeskjærskaien. Both are within a 15-minute walk of the city center. Free shuttle buses are available from Jekteviken/Dokkeskjærskaien. From Skoltegrunnskaien, buses stop near the docks.

CONTACTS Fjord Line. ☎ *51–46–40–99* 🌐 *www.fjordline.com.* **Hurtigruten.** ☎ *77–59–72–04* 🌐 *www.hurtigruten.no.* **Norled.** ☎ *51–86–87–00 press 9 for English* 🌐 *www.norled.no.*

BUS TRAVEL

Nor-Way Bussekspress operates several daily buses between Oslo and Bergen. The journey takes 9 to 10 hours. Buses also connect Bergen with Stavanger and Ålesund.

Tide is the main bus operator in Bergen, with buses throughout the day and at night on weekends (Friday and Saturday until 4 am).

CONTACTS Nor-Way Bussekspress. 🌐 *www.nor-way.no.* **Tide.** 🌐 *www.tide.no/en.*

CAR TRAVEL

Bergen is 462 km (287 miles) from Oslo. There are three main routes between Oslo and Bergen, with Route 7 across the Hardangervidda Plateau the most scenic. The 67-km (42-miles) stretch between Haugastøl and Eidfjord is part of the designated National Tourist Route. If you choose Route 52 over Hemsedalsfjellet or E16 over Filefjell you will pass through the world's longest road tunnel.

From Granvin, Route 7 hugs the fjord part of the way, making for spectacular scenery, but the road is very narrow. A quicker but less scenic drive is to follow Route 13 from Granvin to Voss, then take E16 from Voss to Bergen. Be aware that there are lots of tunnels on that road. In winter, several mountain passes are prone to closing at short notice. The Public Roads Administration's road information line can give you the status of most roads.

Driving from Stavanger to Bergen involves two ferries and a long journey packed with stunning scenery. Downtown Bergen is enclosed by an inner ring road. It's best to leave your car at a parking garage (the cheapest and most accessible is ByGarasjen, near the train station, and Klostergarasjen, near Nordnes) and walk.

CONTACTS Statens vegvesen. (*Public Roads Administration*) ☎ *22–07–30–00* 🌐 *www.vegvesen.no.*

TAXI TRAVEL

Taxi stands are in strategic locations downtown. Taxis are dispatched by the Bergen Taxi central office and can be booked in advance. Bergen Taxi runs the largest and most reliable service.

CONTACTS Bergen Taxi. ☎ *07000* 🌐 *www.bergentaxi.no.*

TRAIN TRAVEL

There are several departures daily along the Oslo–Bergen route, one of the most beautiful train rides in the world. The trip takes a little less than seven hours and costs about NKr 579. The main train station in Bergen is in Sentrum, within easy walking distance of several of the most popular hotels.

CONTACTS VY. (*Norwegian State Railways*) ☎ *815–00–888* 🌐 *www.vy.no.*

Restaurants

Bergen has a world-class dining scene, with a dozen or so restaurants winning international awards. The city sits on the waterfront, so seafood features prominently on most menus. Traditional dishes are popular here, although the city's sophisticated palettes are attracted more and more to New Nordic cuisine. Most kitchens tout their use of local ingredients—often with links to specific farmers or ranchers—and change their dishes with the seasons.

Hotels

There's a huge variety of hotels in and near the city center, ranging from smaller guesthouses to grand hotels. Boutique hotels are very popular, so this is a great city if you're into great design. If you want to be walking distance to the major sights, look for an address in Bryggen or Sentrum.

Restaurant and hotel reviews have been shortened. For full information, visit Fodors.com

What It Costs in Norwegian Krone

$	$$	$$$	$$$$
RESTAURANTS			
under NKr 125	NKr 125–NKr 250	NKr 251–NKr 350	over NKr 350
HOTELS			
under NKr 750	NKr 750–NKr 1250	NKr 1251–NKr 1900	over NKr 1900

Nightlife

Bergen is a university town, and the many thousands of students who live and study here make the city's nightlife much more exciting than you might expect for a town of its size. Many of the most popular bars and clubs are in Sentrum, but Vågsbunnen has become more and more popular.

Shopping

Bergen has several cobblestoned pedestrian shopping streets, including Gamle Strandgaten, Torgallmenningen,

Hollendergaten, and Marken. Stores selling Norwegian handicrafts are concentrated along the wharf in Bryggen. Near the cathedral, the tiny Skostredet has become popular with young shoppers. The small, independent specialty stores here sell everything from army surplus gear to tailored suits and designer trinkets. Most Bergen shops are open Monday to Wednesday and Friday from 9 to 5, Thursday from 9 to 7, and Saturday from 10 to 3.

Festivals and Events

Festspillene (*Bergen International Festival*)
MUSIC | Held the last week of May and first week of June, this very popular festival brings famous names in classical music, jazz, ballet, the arts, and theater to town. ☎ *55–21–06–30* 🌐 *www.fib.no.*

Visitor Information

CONTACTS Visit Bergen. (*tourist information*) ☎ *55–55–20–00* 🌐 *www.visitbergen.com.*

Bryggen

Bergen was founded in 1070 by Olav Kyrre as a commercial center. In the 14th century, Hanseatic merchants settled in Bergen and made it one of their four major overseas trading centers. The surviving Hanseatic wooden buildings on Bryggen (the quay) are topped with triangular cookie-cutter roofs and painted in red, blue, yellow, and green. Monuments in themselves (they are on the UNESCO World Heritage List), the buildings tempt travelers and locals to the shops, restaurants, and museums inside. In the evening, when the Bryggen is illuminated, these modest buildings, together with the stocky Rosenkrantz Tower, the Fløyen, and the yachts lining the pier, are reflected in the waters of the harbor—and provide one of the loveliest cityscapes in northern Europe.

Vågsbunnen, just to the south, is one of the city's most vibrant and eclectic neighborhoods. Here you'll find many of the area's cutting-edge bars and clubs and daring designer boutiques.

Sights

Bergenhus Festning (*Bergenhus Fortress*)
BUILDING | The major buildings at the medieval Bergenhus are Håkonshallen (Håkon's Hall) and Rosenkrantztårnet (Rosenkrantz Tower). Both are open to visitors. **Håkonshallen** is a royal ceremonial hall erected during the reign of Håkon Håkonsson in the mid-1200s; it sometimes closes for public holidays or special events. It was badly damaged by the explosion of a German ammunition ship in 1944 but was restored by 1961. Erected in the 1560s by the governor of Bergenhus, Erik Rosenkrantz, **Rosenkrantztårnet** served as a combined residence and fortified tower. ✉ *Bergenhus, Bryggen* ☎ *55–30–80–30* 🌐 *www.bymuseet.no/en/* 🎫 *NKr 100* 🕒 *Rosenkrantztårnet closed Mon.–Sat. mid-Sept.–mid-May.*

★ **Bryggen** (*Bryggen Hanseatic Wharf*)
HISTORIC SITE | A trip to this merchant city is incomplete without a trip to the historic Hanseatic harborside, Bryggen. A row of mostly reconstructed 14th-century wooden buildings that face the harbor makes this one of the most charming walkways in Europe, especially on a sunny day. Several fires, the latest in 1955, destroyed some of the original structures, but you'd never know it now. Today the old houses hold boutiques and restaurants, and wandering through the wooden alleys here will be a highlight of your trip. Bryggen has been a UNESCO World Heritage Site since 1979. ✉ *Bryggen, Bryggen.*

Sparkling Lake Lille Lungegårdsvann is fronted by a series of world-class museums.

Bryggens Museum

MUSEUM | This museum contains archaeological finds from the Middle Ages. An exhibit on Bergen circa 1300 shows the town at the zenith of its importance, and has reconstructed living quarters as well as artifacts such as old tools and shoes. Back then, Bergen was the largest town in Norway, a cosmopolitan trading center and the national capital. ✉ *Dreggsallmenningen 3, Bryggen* ☎ *55–30–80–30* 🌐 *www.bymuseet.no/en* 🎫 *NKr 100.*

Det Hanseatiske Museum og Schøtstuene (*The Hanseatic Museum and Schøtstuene*)

MUSEUM | One of the best-preserved buildings in Bergen, the Hanseatic Museum was the 16th-century office and home of an affluent German merchant. The apprentices lived upstairs, in boxed-in beds with windows cut into the wall. Although claustrophobic, the snug rooms had the benefit of being relatively warm—a blessing in the unheated building. In summer, there are daily guided tours in Norwegian, German, French, and English. ✉ *Finnegården 1A, Bryggen* ☎ *53–00–61–10* 🌐 *www.museumvest.no/english* 🎫 *NKr 160.*

Domkirke (*Bergen Cathedral*)

RELIGIOUS SITE | The cathedral's long, turbulent history has shaped the eclectic architecture of the current structure. The Gothic-style choir and the lower towers are the oldest, dating from the 13th century. Note the cannonball lodged in the tower wall—it dates from a battle between English and Dutch ships in Bergen harbor in 1665. One of the nicest ways to enjoy the cathedral is attending one of the frequent organ concerts held here. ✉ *Domkirke gt., Bryggen* ☎ *55–59–32–73.*

Fisketorget (*Bergen Fish Market*)

MARKET | In a strikingly modern building on the waterfront, the busy fish market is one of Bergen's most popular attractions. Turn-of-the-20th-century photographs of this pungent square show fishermen in Wellington boots and raincoats and women in long aprons. Now the fishmongers wear bright-orange rubber overalls as they look over the day's catch. You'll want to come at lunchtime, when you can enjoy the catch of the day while watching the boats in the harbor. Try a classic Bergen lunch of shrimp or salmon on a baguette with mayonnaise and cucumber. Fruits, vegetables, and flowers are also on offer, as are handicrafts. ✉ *Torget 5, Bryggen* ☎ *55–55–20–00 tourist information.*

★ **Fløibanen** (*Mount Fløyen Funicular*)
TRANSPORTATION SITE (AIRPORT/BUS/FERRY/TRAIN) | A magnificent view of Bergen and its suburbs can be taken in from the top of Mt. Fløyen, the most accessible of the city's seven mountains. The eight-minute ride on the funicular takes you to the top, 320 meters (1,050 feet) above the sea. A car departs at least every half hour. On the top is a restaurant and café, a shop, and a playground. Stroll along the path that goes back to downtown or explore the mountains that lead to Ulriken, the highest of the mountains surrounding Bergen. ✉ *Vetrlidsalmenningen 21, Bryggen* ☎ *55–33–68–00* 🌐 *floyen.no/en/* 🎫 *NKr 65 each way.*

Lille Øvregaten
HISTORIC SITE | The name means "Little Upper Street," and this charming thoroughfare is one of the oldest in the city. Along a bumpy cobblestone lane, these 19th-century clapboard houses are a glimpse of Bergen 100 years ago. ✉ *Lille Øvregaten, Bryggen.*

Mariakirken (*St. Mary's Church*)
RELIGIOUS SITE | In continuous use since the early Middle Ages, Bergen's oldest existing building dates from around 1170. The twin-spired church's oldest treasures include the altarpiece from the end of 15th century, the incredibly ornate pulpit, and the remaining wall paintings depicting biblical scenes. ✉ *Dreggen 15, Bryggen* ☎ *55–59–71–75* 🌐 *kirken.no/nb-NO/fellesrad/Bergen/menigheter/bergen-domkirke-menighet/turisme/turistinformasjon* 🎫 *Free mid-May–mid-Sept.; NKr 75 mid-Sept.–mid-May.* ⏲ *Closed weekends late May–mid-Sept. Closed Sat.–Mon., Wed., and Thurs. mid-Sept.–late May.*

 Coffee and Quick Bites

Godt Brød
$$ | **CAFÉ** | This popular organic bakery makes scrumptious cinnamon rolls (several different kinds) and delicious open-faced sandwiches to order. **Known for:** uses only organic ingredients; vegan-friendly recipes; good on-the-fly lunches. $ *Average main: NKr150* ✉ *Nedre Korskirkeallmenningen 12, Vågsbunnen* ☎ *55–32–80–00* 🌐 *www.godtbrod.no.*

Pygmalion
$$ | **CAFÉ** | A couple of café tables on the sidewalk draw you to this storefront eatery, which is just as appealing on the inside, thanks to exposed brick walls and wide-plank wood floors. The menu is casual fare, including sandwiches and salads. **Known for:** vegetarian and vegan options; delicious baked goods; central location. $ *Average main: NKr150* ✉ *Nedre Korskirkeallmenningen 4, Vågsbunnen* ☎ *55–32–33–60* 🌐 *www.pygmalion.no.*

 Restaurants

Bare
$$$$ | **NORWEGIAN** | The elegant but spare mirrored dining room at this local favorite puts all the emphasis where it should be: on the creative dishes coming out of the kitchen. And you'll get to sample quite a few of them, depending on whether you opt for the "half menu" consisting of 7 courses or go all the way with an 11-course extravaganza. **Known for:** fine dining at its best in Bergen; wine pairings couldn't be better; attentive service. $ *Average main: NKr 1250* ✉ *Torgallmenningen 2, Vågsbunnen* ☎ *400–02–455* 🌐 *www.barerestaurant.no* ⏲ *Closed Sun. and Mon.*

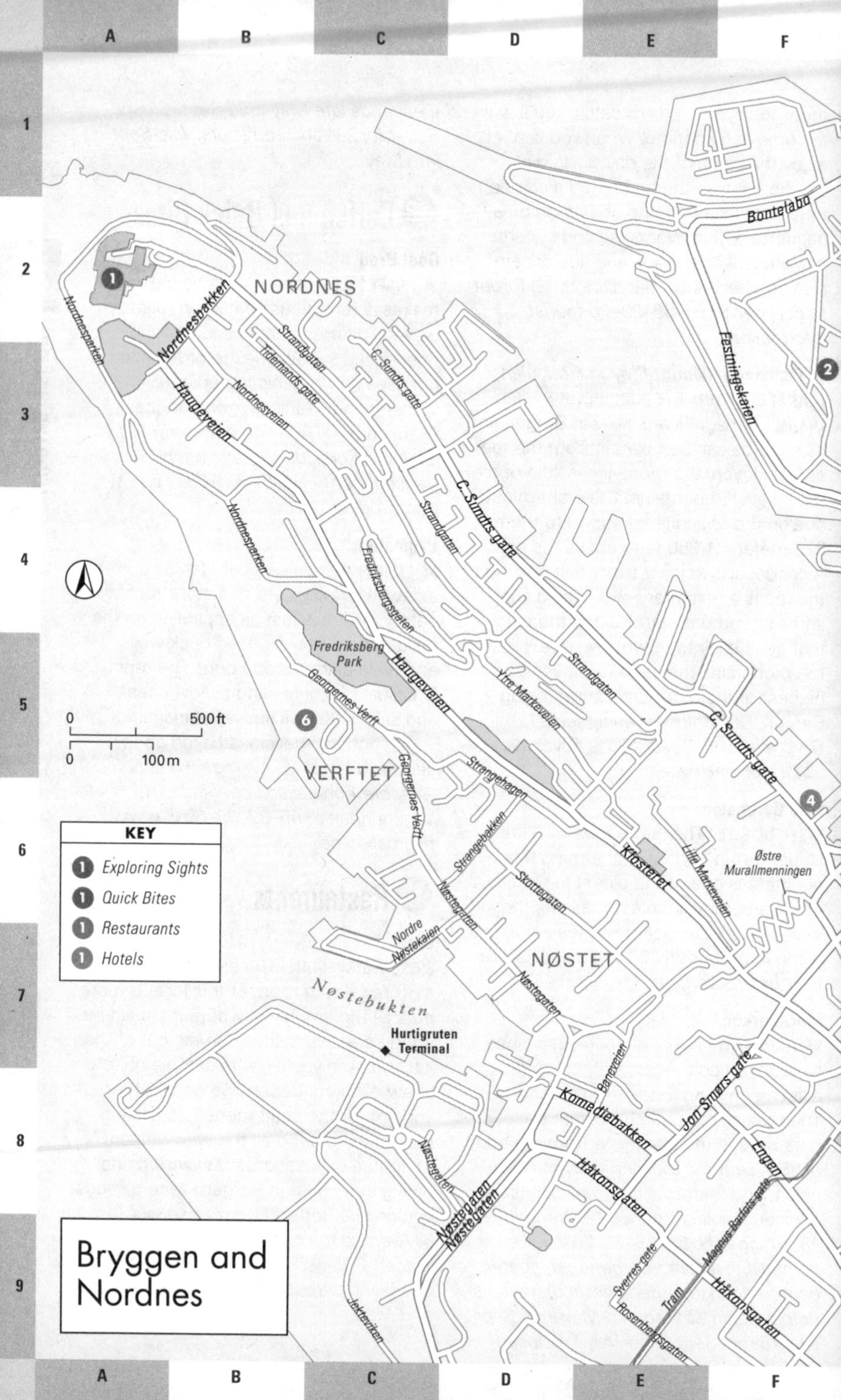

Bryggen and Nordnes
KEY
Exploring Sights
Quick Bites
Restaurants
Hotels
NORDNES
VERFTET
NØSTET
Nøstebukten
Hurtigruten Terminal
Fredriksberg Park
Østre Murallmenningen
Nordnesbakken
Nordnesparken
Haugeveien
Strandgaten
Tidemands gate
C. Sundts gate
Nordnesveien
Fredriksbergsgaten
Georgernes Verft
Ytre Markeveien
Strangehagen
Strangebakken
Nøstegaten
Nordre Nøstekaien
Skottegaten
Klosteret
Lille Markeveien
Bontelabo
Festningskaien
Baneveien
Komediebakken
Jon Smørs gate
Engen
Håkonsgaten
Magnus Barfots gate
Sverres gate
Rosenbergsgaten
Tram
Jekteviken
0 500ft
0 100m

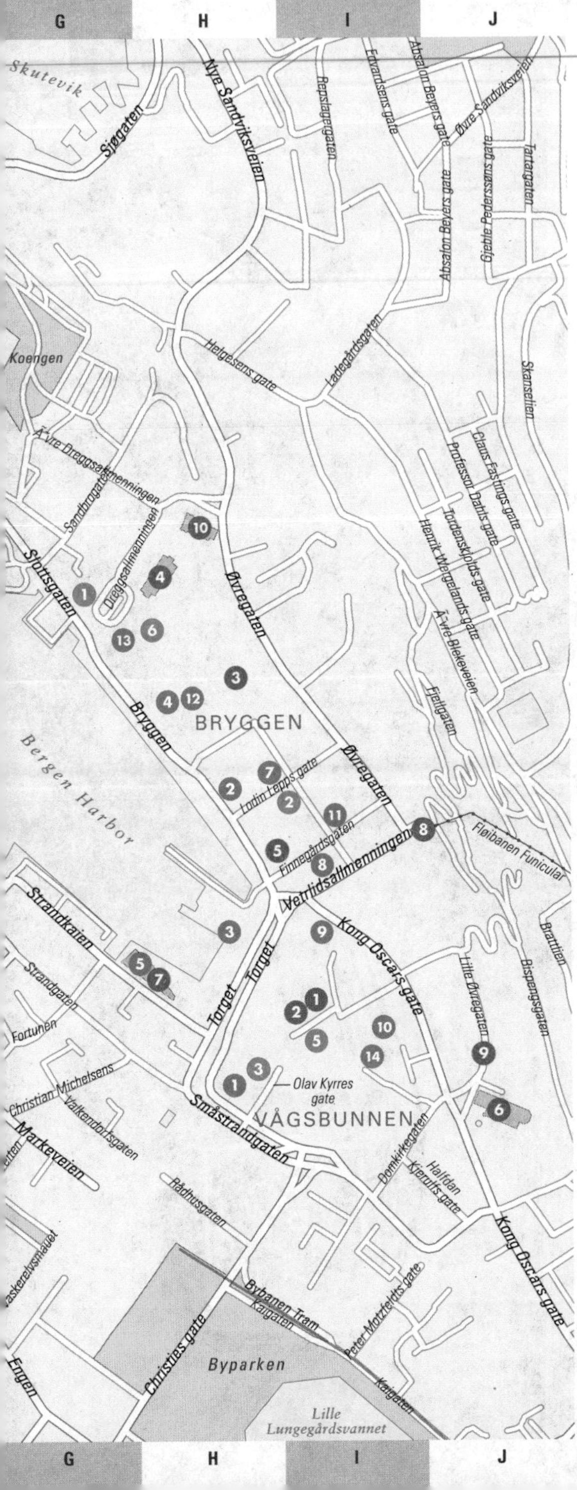

Sights

1 Akvariet i Bergen A2
2 Bergenhus Festning................ F3
3 Bryggen.............................. H5
4 Bryggens Museum H4
5 Det Hanseatiske Museum og Schøtstuene H6
6 Domkirke.............................. J7
7 Fisketorget........................... H7
8 Fløibanen I6
9 Lille Øvregaten...................... J7
10 Mariakirken H4

Restaurants

1 Bare H7
2 Bryggeloftet & Stuene H5
3 Bryggeriet H6
4 Enhjørningen H5
5 Fish Me H6
6 Kafe Kippers......................... B5
7 Nama.................................... H5
8 Restaurant 1877..................... I6
9 Ridderen I6
10 Roll & Rock American Diner....... I7
11 Soya Restaurant.................... I6
12 To Kokker H5
13 26 North.............................. G4
14 Villani.................................. I7

Quick Bites

1 Godt Brød.............................. I7
2 Pygmalion I7

Hotels

1 Clarion Collection Hotel Havnekontoret G4
2 First Hotel Marin.................... I5
3 Hotel Bergen Børs.................. H7
4 Hotel Clarion Admiral F6
5 Magic Hotel Korskirken............ I7
6 Radisson Blu Royal Bergen H4

Did You Know?

The Fløibanen transports passengers to the top of Mt. Floyen in just eight minutes.

Bryggeloftet & Stuene
$$$ | **NORWEGIAN** | Hearty Norwegian country fare suits the cozy dining room, which has a handsome fireplace, oil paintings depicting the city's maritime past, and wooden display cases filled with model ships and other artifacts. A reindeer fillet in a cream sauce comes highly recommended, as do the monkfish and the venison. **Known for:** great location in the center of Bryggen; the best place to try traditional fish soup; generous portions. *Average main: NKr 350 Bryggen 11, Bryggen 55–30–20–70 www.bryggeloftet.no.*

Bryggeriet
$$ | **NORWEGIAN** | The beer couldn't be any better than at the waterfront Bryggeriet, which brews its own at its restaurant on the pier at Zachariasbryggen. The gleaming copper vats, tucked away behind a pane of glass, give the place a warm and welcoming atmosphere. **Known for:** views of the fjord are spectacular; fish comes from the nearby market; try a flight of beers. *Average main: NKr 250 Torget 2, Bryggen 55–55–31–55 bryggeriet.biz Closed Mon. and Tues.*

★ **Enhjørningen**
$$$$ | **NORWEGIAN** | This restaurant, one of the best seafood restaurants in town, is named after the unicorn that adorns the doorway of the old wooden building in which it is housed. It may look old-fashioned, but there's nothing medieval about Enhjørningen's menu—it's contemporary Norwegian and it changes according to the day's catch. **Known for:** steamed halibut and other local seafood; traditional dishes with a modern twist; waterfront location. *Average main: NKr 360 Enhjørningsgården 29, Bryggen 55–30–69–50 www.enhjorningen.no Closed Sun. Sept.–mid-May. No lunch.*

Fish Me
$$ | **NORWEGIAN** | Located in Bergen's bustling fish market, this eatery takes advantage of the fresh seafood in icy display cases not far from your table. In warm weather, the umbrella-shaded terrace is the place to be, especially those tables with unobstructed views across to Bryggen. **Known for:** great location with a view across the fjord; the best fish from local suppliers; the sushi is a big draw. *Average main: NKr 250 Fisketorget, Strandkaien 3, Bryggen 450–23–000 www.fishme.no/fish-me-restaurant.*

Nama
$$$ | **JAPANESE** | The city's most popular Japanese restaurant—the name means "fresh and raw" in Japanese—has garnered enthusiastic good reviews for its *izakaya* (traditional pub) atmosphere, its *robatayaki* (barbecue) dishes, and, of course, its wide array of sushi. On one of the smaller streets just behind Bryggen, it's stylish decorated and has huge windows that let in lots of light. **Known for:** led the small plates craze in Bergen; delicious roasted meats; fine wine selection. *Average main: NKr 275 Lodin Lepps gt. 2B, Bryggen 55–32–20–10 www.namasushi.no.*

Restaurant 1877
$$$$ | **NORWEGIAN** | Travel through time at this nostalgic venue full of traces of Bergen's proud past—from the well-used copper pots hanging on the wall down to the vintage dishes that arrive at your table with a flourish. With a great love of Norway's traditional food, the restaurant focuses on what it gets from local farmers and fishermen. **Known for:** location in the historical Kjøttbasaren; pleasant dining on the veranda; seasonal tasting menu. *Average main: NKr 795 Vetrlidsallmenningen 2, Bryggen 928–71–877 www.restaurant1877.no Closed Sun.*

Ridderen
$$$ | **CONTEMPORARY** | This restaurant has plenty of history: its two main dining rooms are whitewashed storage rooms that once served as potato cellars. The surroundings date back to the Middle Ages, but the food's as upscale and modern-feeling as could be, using

traditional German recipes and giving them a modern twist—think mussels in a light cream sauce or pork knuckles with sauerkraut. **Known for:** perfect destination for a romantic dinner for two; located in one of the oldest parts of Bergen; near the fish market, so the seafood is fresh. *Average main: NKr 300 Kong Oscars gt. 1A, Vågsbunnen 55–32–00–70 ridderen.no Closed Mon. No lunch Tues.–Thurs. and Sun.*

Roll & Rock American Diner

$$ | **AMERICAN** | Burgers, fries, and shakes—the menu couldn't be any more authentic than at this diner right out of the movie American Graffiti. There's a black-and-white checkerboard floor, red vinyl booths, and a a bright yellow jukebox with all your favorite hits from yesteryear. **Known for:** as American as apple pie (which also happens to be on the menu); gets all the little details right, like the tall sundae glasses; affordable children's menu. *Average main: NKr 169 Skostredet 14, Vågsbunnen 55–31–55–55 rollogrock.no.*

Soya Restaurant

$$$ | **CHINESE FUSION** | **FAMILY** | Serving authentic Chinese fare, this restaurant encoarges guests to dine family-style and enjoy a wide range of dishes. Asian architectural flourishes mix well with the modern Scandinavian design. **Known for:** contemporary takes on Chinese cookery; you can make a meal on the dim sum; great location in Finnegård. *Average main: NKr 279 Finnegårdsgaten 6, Bryggen 56–90–12–55 soyarestaurant.no.*

★ To Kokker

$$$$ | **NORWEGIAN** | In a 300-year-old building on the wharf, it's no surprise that the charming To Kokker has crooked floors and off-kilter molding. Ranked among Bergen's best restaurants, it serves excellent seafood and game prepared the traditional way with a contemporary twist. **Known for:** tucked away on one of Bryggen's side streets; one of the city's most tradition dining rooms; an update of old recipes. *Average main: NKr 595 Enhjørningsgården 29, Bryggen 55–30–69–55 www.tokokker.no Closed Sun. No lunch.*

26 North

$$$ | **NORWEGIAN** | A gorgeous glass ceiling covers the main dining room at this restaurant, one of the best in Bryggen. There's also a terrace if you're here on a warm evening. **Known for:** the best of New Nordic cooking; great location in Bryggen; pleasant outdoor terrace. *Average main: NKr 325 Radisson Blu Hotel Bryggen, Bryggen 47 477–10–467 26north.no/bergen/ Closed Sun. No lunch.*

Villani

$$$ | **ITALIAN** | The moment you step inside this authentic trattoria, the sweet and smoky smell of wood-fired pizza fills your nostrils. The homemade pasta dishes are also a speciality. **Known for:** corner location along the bustling Skostredet; a huge selection of hand-picked italian wines; cozy dining room. *Average main: NKr 259 Skostredet 9a, Vågsbunnen 55–31–55–55 www.villani.no.*

Hotels

Clarion Collection Hotel Havnekontoret

$$$$ | **HOTEL** | This neoclassical hotel dating from the 1920s has an unbeatable location in the middle of Bryggen. **Pros:** a true feeling of luxury throughout; pleasing design throughout; free afternoon tea and dinner. **Cons:** low ceilings on the upper floor; some rooms are quite small; front rooms can be noisy. *Rooms from: NKr 2000 Slottsgt. 1, Bryggen 55–60–11–00 www.nordicchoice-hotels.com/clarion/clarion-collection-hotel-havnekontoret 116 rooms Some meals.*

First Hotel Marin

$$$ | **HOTEL** | Along the harbor stands an elegant brick building that once housed one of Bergen's largest print shops; now

it's a business hotel within walking distance of the city's top sights. **Pros:** suites are among the city's most stylish; gym room and sauna available; good deals in off season. **Cons:** some rooms can be noisy in summer; service get mixed reviews; some rooms need renovation. *Rooms from: NKr 1350 ✉ Rosenkrantzgt. 5–8, Bryggen ☎ 53–05–15–00 ⊕ www.firsthotels.com/Our-hotels/Hotels-in-Norway/Bergen/First-Hotel-Marin 151 rooms Free breakfast.*

Hotel Bergen Børs

$$$ | HOTEL | This fashionable hotel is located on the upper floors in one of Bergen's most historic buildings, the former stock exchange. **Pros:** central location between Bryggen and Sentrum; home to one of the best restaurants in Bergen; luxurious rooms with a view. **Cons:** easy to get lost in the corridors; small seating area in the lobby; some noise from the city. *Rooms from: NKr 1525 ✉ Vågsalmenningen 1, Vågsbunnen ☎ 55–33–64–00 ⊕ www.bergenbors.no 127 rooms Free breakfast.*

Magic Hotel Korskirken

$$ | HOTEL | In one of the city's most happening neighborhoods, this centrally located lodging works its magic on the guest rooms, which compensate for their small size with smart and stylish design. **Pros:** within a stone's throw of a dozen restaurants and cafés; rooms are out of a shelter magazine; beautifully restored buildings. **Cons:** can be noisy, especially on weekends; entrance is a bit underwhelming; some rooms small for two people. *Rooms from: NKr 1159 ✉ Nedre Korskirkeallmenning 1, Bryggen ☎ 55–90–01–00 ⊕ magichotels.no/utforsk-vare-hoteller/korskirken 90 rooms Free breakfast.*

Radisson Blu Royal Bergen

$$$ | HOTEL | If you're here to see the sights, the Radisson Blu Royal Bergen puts you close to the wooden houses of old Bryggen and the medieval fortress Bergenhus Festning. **Pros:** location in the heart of the historic quarter; walking distance to famous attractions; great food on room service menu. **Cons:** bar gets overcrowded during events; popular with tour groups; lots of day-trippers. *Rooms from: NKr 1250 ✉ Dreggsallmenningen 1, Bryggen ☎ 55–54–30–00 ⊕ www.radissonhotels.com/en-us/destination/norway/bergen 342 rooms No meals.*

Nightlife

Baklommen Bar

BARS/PUBS | With Y-shaped beams holding the ceiling aloft, this intimate cocktail bar is located in one of the crooked old buildings on the wharf. *✉ Enhjørningsgården 29, Bryggen ☎ 55–30–69–55 ⊕ www.tokokker.no/baklommen-bar Closed Sun. and Mon.*

Bar 3

GATHERING PLACES | This is the place for fun and games—shuffleboard, Ping-Pong, and pinball are among those on offer at the laid-back Bar 3. There's also an interesting selection of beers and lots of space for you and your friends to spread out. *✉ Rosenkrantzgt. 3, Bryggen ☎ 488–89–200 ⊕ bar3.no.*

Biblioteket Bar

BARS/PUBS | Enjoy a creative cocktail in this elegant lounge overlooking the busy harbor. Biblioteket has DJs and live music, but never set the volume to a level where a conversation is no longer possible. *✉ Vetrlidsallmenningen 2, Bryggen ☎ 55–01–18–85 ⊕ www.biblioteketbar.no.*

Folk & Røvere

BARS/PUBS | The specialty here is craft beers, as you'll know from the broad blackboard over the bar listing the wide range of stouts, porter, ales, and other brews. Belly up to the bar, grab a table on the sidewalk, or head across the street to the covered patio. *✉ Sparebanksgaten 4, Vågsbunnen ☎ 57–00–14–99 ⊕ folkogrovere.net.*

No Stress

BARS/PUBS | The name is something of an in joke: this artisan cocktail bar is located in the former location of a clothing shop called Stress. It has a nostalgic and homey interior, blending furnishings from the '60s, '70s, and '80s. ✉ *Hollendergaten 11, Vågsbunnen* 🌐 *www.nostressbar.no.*

Performing Arts

Litteraturhuset

READINGS/LECTURES | You'll feel well read just walking in the door of the Litteraturhuset, which hosts book readings, intellectual debates, and spirited discussions about art, literature, and other hot topics in Bergen. There's also a bookstore with both new and classic works in English and a tasty café and brasserie. ✉ *Østre Skostredet 5-7, Vågsbunnen* 🌐 *www.litthusbergen.no* ⏲ *Closed Sun.*

Shopping

Berle Bryggen

CLOTHING | Here you'l find the complete Dale of Norway collection of sweaters and cardigans, as well as trolls, pewter, down duvets, and other traditional knitwear and souvenir items. ✉ *Bryggen 5, Bryggen* ☎ *55–10–95–00* 🌐 *www.sns.no.*

Oleana

CLOTHING | The flagship store of this famous Norwegian design shop is full of gorgeous clothes and textiles with traditional and contemporary patterns, all made in Norway. ✉ *Strandkaien 2A, Bryggen* ☎ *55–31–05–20* 🌐 *www.oleana.no.*

Råvarene

SPECIALTY STORES | Sustainable and reusable products are on offer at this cutting-edge shop, which promotes a waste-free lifestyle. ✉ *Skostredet 5, Vågsbunnen* ☎ *930–64–960* 🌐 *raavarene.com* ⏲ *Closed Sun.*

Ting Bergen

HOUSEHOLD ITEMS/FURNITURE | Here you'll find a variety of useful and affordable designer items for your home, your kids, and yourself. It's the perfect place to pick up a smart gift. ✉ *Bryggen 13, Bryggen* ☎ *55–21–54–80* 🌐 *www.ting.no/ting-i-bergen-1.*

Nordnes

On the opposite, southern side of the harbor, Nordnes is mainly a residential area but features a great aquarium within walking distance of the fish market.

GETTING HERE AND AROUND

When you're standing on the dock in Bryggen, you're gazing across the water to the peninsula of Nordnes. The main destination for travelers is Akvariet i Bergen, a 20-minute walk from the fish market. You can also take a bus or the ferry from the fish market.

Sights

Akvariet i Bergen (*Bergen Aquarium*)

ZOO | **FAMILY** | Focusing on fish found in the North Sea, the Bergen Aquarium is one of the largest in Europe. It has 60 tanks filled with dozen of species from massive salmon to sinewy eels (which tend to wrap around each other), and two outdoor pools that are the home of playful seals, otters, and penguins. There is also a section displaying alligators from different parts of the world on display. Kids can hold starfish and other creatures in the touch tanks, or watch as trainers feed their charges. ✉ *Nordnesbakken 4, Nordnes* ☎ *55–55–71–71* 🌐 *akvariet.no* 🎟 *NKr 285.*

Restaurants

Kafe Kippers

$$ | **NORWEGIAN** | In a former sardine factory, Kafe Kippers specializes in seafood dishes like Arctic char with artichoke, radish, and dill or steamed mussels with herbs and garlic. This large outdoor café on the waterfront is a pleasant stop for lunch or at sunset when you can warm up with a cozy wool blanket and enjoy a spectacular view of the North Sea. **Known for:** spectacular views; trendy location; off the tourist trail. *Average main: NKr220 Georgernes Verft 12, Nordnes 55–30–40–80 www.kafekippers.no.*

Hotels

Hotel Clarion Admiral

$$$ | **HOTEL** | If you're looking for stunning views, you won't do better than the Hotel Clarion Admiral, which looks across the water to the colorful facades of Bryggen. **Pros:** unbeatable views across to Bryggen; lavish dining room on the waterfront; walking distance to the aquarium. **Cons:** can be booked up with conferences; a bit far from the action; chain hotel feel. *Rooms from: NKr 1500 C. Sundts gt. 9, Bergen 55–23–64–00 www.nordicchoicehotels.com/hotels/norway/bergen/clarion-hotel-admiral 210 rooms Free breakfast.*

Nightlife

Altona Vinbar

BARS/PUBS | For a quiet glass of wine in an intimate and historic setting, try award-winning Altona and its 400-year-old wine cellar. The vaulted ceilings and exposed brick add a lot of atmosphere. The food is good, too. *Augustin Hotel, Strandgaten 81, Nordnes 55–30–40–72 Closed Sun.*

Sentrum

Although most newcomers head directly to Bryggen, Sentrum is the real heart of the city. A cluster of the city's best museums—known under the collective name KODE—ring the sparkling Lake Lille Lungegårdsvann. Peaceful Byparken is a popular place for a stroll in summer, or for a spot of sunbathing in between gallery visits. The Norwegian Theater is located at the end of Ole Bulls plass, a tree-lined avenue with many cafés and restaurants—the place to be in the evening.

GETTING HERE AND AROUND

Bergen's city center is fairly small, so the best way to get around is by foot. From the train station and bus station it's only a short walk to the Sentrum.

Sights

Grieghallen

ARTS VENUE | Home of the Bergen Philharmonic Orchestra and stage for the Bergen International Festival, this music hall is a conspicuous slab of glass and concrete that's used throughout the year for cultural events. The acoustics are marvelous. Built in 1978, the hall was named for the city's famous son, composer Edvard Grieg (1843–1907). *Edvard Griegs pl. 1, Sentrum 55–21–61–00 www.grieghallen.no.*

KODE 1

MUSEUM | Looking out over the pretty Byparken, this neoclassical edifice was called the Permanenten when it first opened in doors in 1896. The centerpiece of the collection is the Sølvskatten—the Silver Treasure–a glittering display of items of gold, silver, and other precious metals created in Bergen. It also holds an eclectic collection of antiques and artworks from Europe and Asia. The Italian eatery Bien Centro is located

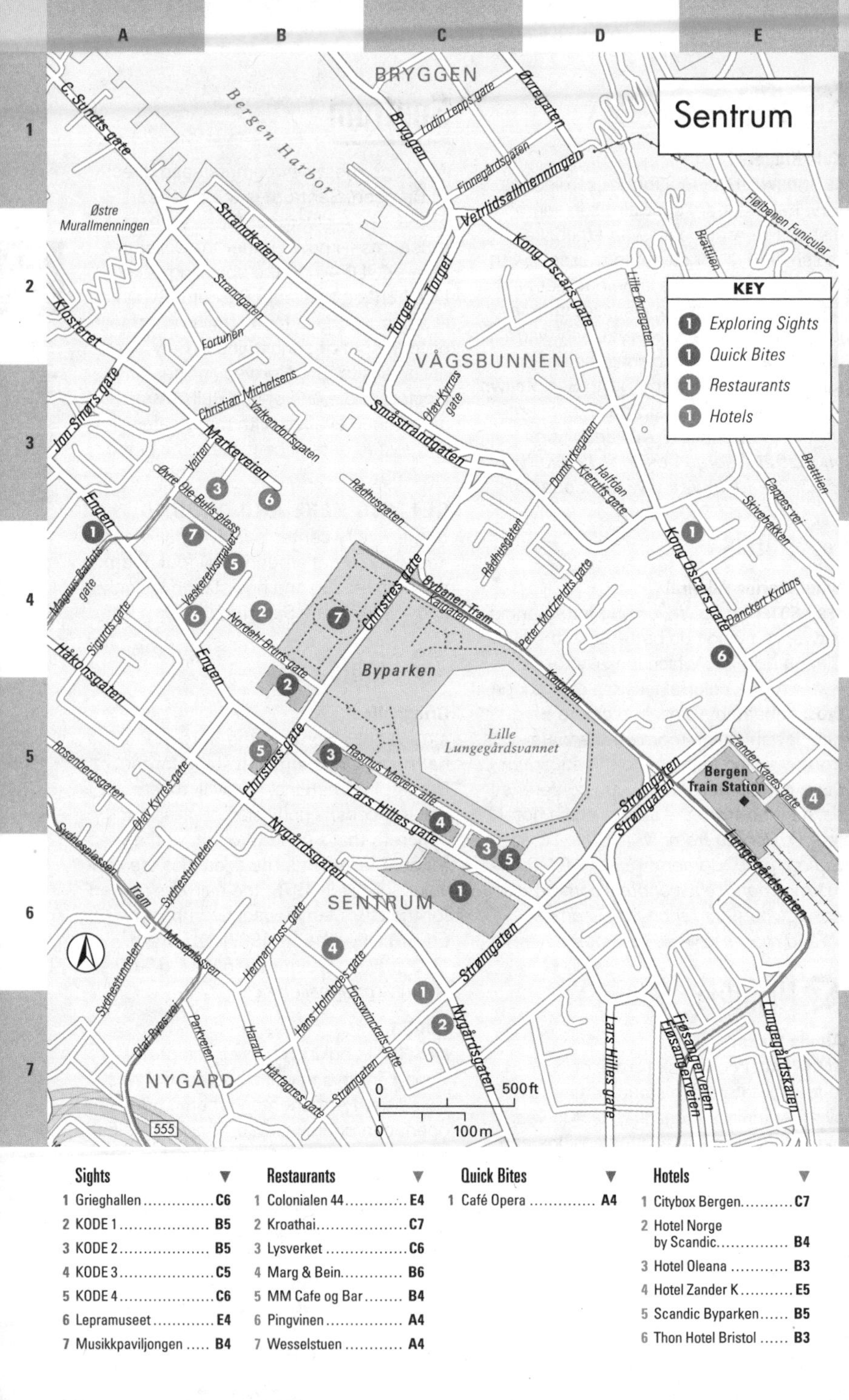

Sights

1 Grieghallen.............. C6
2 KODE 1.................. B5
3 KODE 2.................. B5
4 KODE 3.................. C5
5 KODE 4.................. C6
6 Lepramuseet............ E4
7 Musikkpaviljongen..... B4

Restaurants

1 Colonialen 44............ E4
2 Kroathai................... C7
3 Lysverket.................. C6
4 Marg & Bein.............. B6
5 MM Cafe og Bar......... B4
6 Pingvinen.................. A4
7 Wesselstuen.............. A4

Quick Bites

1 Café Opera.............. A4

Hotels

1 Citybox Bergen.......... C7
2 Hotel Norge by Scandic.............. B4
3 Hotel Oleana............ B3
4 Hotel Zander K........... E5
5 Scandic Byparken...... B5
6 Thon Hotel Bristol...... B3

on-site. ✉ *Nordahl Bruns gt. 9, Sentrum* ☎ *53–00–97–04* 🌐 *kodebergen.no/en/find-us/kode-1* 🎫 *NKr 130 (includes 2-day admission to all KODE museums)* 🕑 *Closed Mon. mid-Sept.–mid-June.*

KODE 2

MUSEUM | Opening its doors in 1978, the newest of the museums in the KODE complex hosts temporary art exhibitions. The biggest draw here is the bookstore, which has an impressive collection of volumes on art, architecture, and design. Cafe Smakverket is a casual eatery that's perfect for a lunchtime repast or coffee in the afternoon. ✉ *Rasmus Meyers allé 3, Bryggen* ☎ *53–00–97–02* 🌐 *kodebergen.no/en/find-us/kode-2* 🎫 *NKr 130 (includes 2-day admission to all KODE museums)* 🕑 *Closed Mon. mid-Sept.–mid-May.*

KODE 3

MUSEUM | If you're here to see the amazing works by Edvard Munch—the painter who gave the world *The Scream*—this is the museum for you. The museum is dedicated to Munch and other Norwegian artists like J.C. Dahl, Harriet Backer, Erik Werenskiold, and Gerhard Munthe. The building itself was designed by architect Ole Landmark in 1916 to house the huge collection amassed by businessman Rasmus Meyer. ✉ *Rasmus Meyers allé 7, Sentrum* ☎ *53–00–97–03* 🌐 *kodebergen.no/en/find-us/kode-3* 🎫 *NKr 130 (includes 2-day admission to all KODE museums)* 🕑 *Closed Mon. mid-Sept.–mid-May.*

KODE 4

MUSEUM | In a building strongly resembling a huge battery—it was originally the headquarters for an electrical power company—KODE 4 lets you travel through art history with a collection ranging from the 13th to the 20th centuries, including works by international luminaries like Pablo Picasso and Norwegian favorites like Nikolai Astrup. KunstLab, an art museum geared toward children, in on the ground floor. Foodies will find themselves drawn to Lysverket, a restaurant specializing in seafood. ✉ *Rasmus Meyers allé 9, Sentrum* ☎ *53–00–97–04* 🌐 *kodebergen.no/en/find-us/kode-4* 🎫 *NKr 130 (includes 2-day admission to all KODE museums)* 🕑 *Closed Mon. mid-Sept.–mid-May.*

Lepramuseet (*The Leprosy Museum*)

MUSEUM | St. George's Hospital tended to lepers for more than 500 years, and this unusual museum is now a memorial to the thousands who suffered from the disease as well as a testament to Norway's contribution to leprosy research. The building is surprisingly beautiful, especially the main ward with its tiny examining rooms and the hand-carved wood of the chapel. Many Norwegian doctors have been recognized for their efforts against leprosy, particularly Armauer Hansen, who discovered the leprosy bacteria, and after whom Hansen's disease is named. ✉ *Kong Oscars gt. 59, Sentrum* ☎ *55–30–80–37* 🌐 *www.bymuseet.no/en/museums/the-leprosy-museum-st-jo-ergen-hospital* 🎫 *NKr 100* 🕑 *Closed early Sept.–mid-May.*

Musikkpaviljongen

PLAZA | Erected in 1888, this cast-iron bandstand sits in the middle of a surprisingly quiet park. The bandstand itself reflects the Moorish design popular at the time. ✉ *Byparken, Olav Kyrres gt. 27, Sentrum.*

Coffee and Quick Bites

Café Opera

$$ | **NORWEGIAN** | A classic, this eatery sits in a pretty clapboard across from the National Theater. During the day it's the place to grab a bowl of fish soup for lunch or more substantial fare like panfried salmon for dinner. **Known for:** pretheater dinner or drinks; central location; draws a hip crowd. $ *Average main: NKr175* ✉ *Engen 18, Sentrum* ☎ *55–23–03–15* 🌐 *www.cafeopera.org.*

Restaurants

Colonialen 44
$$$$ | **NORWEGIAN** | If you want to sample the best local dishes, Colonialen 44 Restaurant should be on your list. The four-course tasting menu focuses on traditional Norwegian recipes paired with international cooking techniques. **Known for:** wine pairings complement your meal; bold mixing of flavors and colors; casual seating in bar area. *Average main: NKr 550* *Kong Oscars gt. 44, Sentrum* *55–90–16–00* *colonialen.no/restaurant* *Closed Sun.*

Kroathai
$$ | **THAI** | With a view of the Lille Lungegårdsvann Lake, this longtime favorite offers delicious, authentic Thai dishes—some, like chicken soup with lemongrass, that you already know, and others, like steamed mussels in a pineapple sauce, that you might be meeting for the first time. There's an unusually wide range of vegetarian dishes. **Known for:** great location in the city center; surprising selection of soups; small but cozy dining room. *Average main: NKr 175* *Nygårdsgaten 29, Sentrum* *55–32–58–50* *www.kroathai.com.*

★ **Lysverket**
$$$$ | **NORWEGIAN** | With an artful location in the KODE 4 museum and next to the Grieghallen concert hall, Lysverket offers New Nordic cuisine that makes clever use of seasonal, local ingredients in dishes like roasted redfish with grilled lettuce or king crab with nasturtium purée. The spare dining room is the best of Scandinavian design, making a meal here a pleasure for both the eyes and the mouth. **Known for:** wine pairings finish your meal in style; creative dishes using fresh ingredients; cozy and stylish interior. *Average main: NKr 369* *KODE 4, Rasmus Meyers allé 9, Sentrum* *55–60–31–00* *lysverket.no* *Closed Mon.*

Marg & Bein
$$$ | **NORWEGIAN** | The casual, uncomplicated dining room at Marg & Bein is just a taste of what you're going to experience: a meal where the dishes are simple and straightforward. The kitchen here focuses on keeping the old food traditions alive and utilizing all parts of the animal, like the cheek or the marrow. **Known for:** rustic, home-cooked meals; sunny storefront location; great wine selection. *Average main: NKr 289* *Fosswinckels gt. 18, Sentrum* *55–32–34–32* *www.marg-bein.no.*

MM Cafe og Bar
$$ | **INTERNATIONAL** | At the end of Torgalmenningen, the massive square where everyone in town seems to meet, this is the kind of place where you should ask for a table by the window or in the glassed-in terrace so you can people-watch. Using the best local ingredients, the kitchen is inspired by cuisines from around the world. **Known for:** huge and varied menu; friendly and attentive staff; look for the huge neon sign. *Average main: NKr 199* *Kong Olav Vs pl. 4, Sentrum* *468–38–034* *www.mmcafeogbar.no/bergen.*

Pingvinen
$$ | **NORWEGIAN** | Traditional Norwegian meals served in generous portions are on offer at this street-corner eatery. Grab one of the stools facing the street and enjoy a hearty meal as you watch the passing parade. **Known for:** traditional dishes; fun and funky atmosphere; student hangout. *Average main: NKr180* *Vaskerelven 14, Sentrum* *55–60–46–46* *www.pingvinen.no.*

Wesselstuen
$$ | **NORWEGIAN** | Housed in a 18th-century wine cellar, this atmospheric restaurant is known for its convivial atmosphere and unpretentious, authentic Norwegian fare. This is a good place to try reindeer steak or whale carpaccio. **Known for:** one of those longtime favorites that never seem to change; a great outdoor garden

protected from the weather; perfect spot to try traditional dishes. $ *Average main: NKr 250* ✉ *Øvre Ole Bulls pl. 6, Sentrum* ☎ *55–55–49–49* 🌐 *www.wesselstuen.no.*

Hotels

Citybox Bergen

$ | **HOTEL** | If all you need is a place to crash in at the end of the day, Citybox has streamlined rooms at hard-to-beat prices. **Pros:** smart, sophisticated design; easy self-service check-in; coin-operated laundry. **Cons:** no phones or TVs in the rooms; staff not always on the premises; you can't pay with cash after hours. $ *Rooms from: NKr 579* ✉ *Nygårdsgt. 31, Sentrum* ☎ *55–31–25–00* 🌐 *citybox.no/bergen-en* *55 rooms* *No meals.*

Hotel Norge by Scandic

$$$ | **HOTEL** | With a top-to-bottom face-lift, this Bergen classic is now one of the loveliest lodgings in town. **Pros:** ideal location in the heart of Bergen; excellent seafood restaurant on-site; ask for a room with a balcony. **Cons:** front-facing rooms can be noisy; rates on the pricey side; chain hotel feel. $ *Rooms from: NKr 1900* ✉ *Nedre Ole Bulls pl. 4, Sentrum* ☎ *55–55–40–00* 🌐 *www.scandichotels.no/hotell/norge/bergen/hotel-norge-by-scandic* *415 rooms* *Free breakfast.*

Hotel Oleana

$$$ | **HOTEL** | A stylish boutique lodging located in Bergen's theater district, Hotel Oleana's interior design is inspired by Ole Bull, one of the city's most famous composers and musicians. **Pros:** great location close to theater and nightlife; the sophisticated design catches the eye; excellent restaurant. **Cons:** some noise on the weekends; bar can get crowded at times; not much of a view. $ *Rooms from: NKr 1642* ✉ *Øvre Ole Bulls pl. 5, Sentrum* ☎ *55–21–58–70* 🌐 *www.hoteloleana.com* *97 rooms* *Free breakfast.*

Hotel Zander K

$$$ | **HOTEL** | **FAMILY** | You notice the sophisticated Scandinavian design when you enter the inviting lobby of the stylish Hotel Zander K, located just a short walk from the main train station. **Pros:** modern and practical rooms; near public transportation; inviting and vibrant lobby. **Cons:** a long walk to the city center; no closets in standard rooms; some rooms can be noisy. $ *Rooms from: NKr 1265* ✉ *Zander Kaaes gt. 8, Sentrum* ☎ *55–36–20–40* 🌐 *www.zanderk.no* *249 rooms* *Free breakfast.*

Scandic Byparken

$$ | **HOTEL** | **FAMILY** | Near the city's bustling main square of Torgalmenningen, this popular and stylish hotel is a stone's throw from the city's top-notch cultural attractions. **Pros:** kids get a welcome present when you check in; well-appointed rooms; excellent breakfast. **Cons:** some rooms are small; can be noisy in summer; dull exterior. $ *Rooms from: NKr 1100* ✉ *Christiesgt. 5–7, Sentrum* ☎ *55–36–29–00* 🌐 *www.scandichotels.com/hotels/norway/bergen/scandic-byparken* *159 rooms* *Free breakfast.*

★ Thon Hotel Bristol

$$ | **HOTEL** | Built in the 1920s, the elegant Hotel Bristol has an enviable location that puts you within walking distance of the city's main sights. **Pros:** perfect location if you like shopping or nightlife; plenty of charm and character; great on-site eatery. **Cons:** rooms overlooking the street can be noisy; no air-conditioning, so rooms can get hot in summer; some rooms are a bit small. $ *Rooms from: NKr 1250* ✉ *Torgallmenningen 11, Sentrum* ☎ *55–55–10–00* 🌐 *www.thonhotels.com/hotels/countrys/norway/bergen/thon-hotel-bristol-bergen/* *123 rooms* *Free breakfast.*

Nightlife

Fincken

CAFES—NIGHTLIFE | The only gay bar in Bergen, Fincken packs a lot into a compact space: a friendly bar on the ground level, a dance floor and performance space up the spiral staircase, and even a pleasant patio in the back. ✉ *Nygårdsgaten 2A, Sentrum* 🌐 *www.fincken.no* ⏲ *Closed Sun.-Tues.*

Jacob Aall

PIANO BARS/LOUNGES | With a clubby atmosphere, Jacob Aall lets you sink into a leather armchair and enjoy a glass of beer or wine. But the big draw is the huge rooftop terrace, open throughout the year on the top floor of a shopping center. ✉ *Xhibition Shopping Center, Småstrandgaten 3, Bergen* ☎ *55–30–71–00* 🌐 *www.jacobaall.no/bergen/kirsebaerhagen.*

Kava Roofgarden

BARS/PUBS | With two stylish bars inside and a rooftop terrace with views of the fjord, Kava attracts a young and hip crowd. The place is known for its fishbowl-sized drinks with enough straws for everyone in your group to share. ✉ *Strandgaten 15, Bergen* 🌐 *www.kava-roofgarden.no* ⏲ *Closed Sun.–Fri.*

LouLou

DANCE CLUBS | In the basement of the Hotel Norge by Scandic, this surprisingly sophisticated club is the location of hundreds of selfies every week. The cocktails are some of the most creative in town, and the dance floor is illuminated by a futuristic light show. DJs play at ear-splitting decibels, which is just right for the young crowd. ✉ *Hotel Norge by Scandic, Nedre Ole Bullsplass 4, Sentrum* ☎ *55–55–40–00* 🌐 *loulou.no* ⏲ *Closed Sun.–Thurs.*

Storm Bar

BARS/PUBS | The downstairs brasserie has plenty of aficionados, but for our money, the upstairs bar is the place to be. The heated terrace is great no matter what time of year, and the views are stellar. This is the perfect place for a drink before a show at the adjacent Ole Bull Theater. ✉ *Øvre Ole Bullsplass 3, Bergen* ☎ *55–32–11–45* 🌐 *www.olebullhuset.no/storm-bar.*

Performing Arts

★ Bergen Jazzforum

MUSIC | Bergensers love jazz. The Bergen Jazz Forum is *the* place to find it—there are concerts every Friday from September to May. Also, more than 40 concerts are offered in the 10-day international **Nattjazz** festival in late May and early June. ✉ *Sardinen, Georgernes Verft 12, Nordnes* ☎ *55–30–72–50* 🌐 *www.bergen-jazzforum.no.*

★ Den Nationale Scene (*National Theater*)

THEATER | One of the city's most majestic buildings, the Art Nouveau Den Nationale Scene first opened its doors in 1906 with a performance before the royal family. The National Theater is worth a visit just to see the opulent main theater, which hosts lavish Broadway-style productions. Smaller venues inside the august building include the 250-seat Småscenen and the 90-seat Lille Scene. ✉ *Engen 1, Sentrum* ☎ *55–54–97–00* 🌐 *dns.no/dns-in-english.*

Det Akademiske Kvarter

MUSIC | At this student-run venue in a handsome brick building, there are pop, rock, and jazz concerts most of the year. ✉ *Olav Kyrresgate 49, Bergen* ☎ *55–58–99–10* 🌐 *www.kvarteret.no.*

Hordaland Teater

THEATER | This popular concert and theater venue sits on Bergen's main drag. Edvard Grieg performed here, and so have artists from Sergei Rachmaninoff to Rickie Lee Jones. ✉ *Øvre Ole Bulls pl. 6, Sentrum* ☎ *55–23–20–15* 🌐 *hordalandteater.no.*

Hulen

MUSIC | During the academic year, college students and other music fans head

Composer Edvard Grieg entertained guests at Troldhaugen, an elegant country estate that is now a museum south of Bergen.

here for rock concerts in a rebuilt air-raid shelter. ✉ *Olaf Ryes vei 48, Møhlenpris* ☎ *55–32–31–31* 🌐 *www.hulen.no.*

Ole Bull Scene

MUSIC | On the largest theaters in Bergen, the Ole Bull Scene mounts an impressive variety of stand-up performances, rock concerts, and theatrical events. Smaller shows are presented in the Lille Ole Bull, which becomes a nightclub on weekends. ✉ *Øvre Ole Bullsplass 3, Sentrum* ☎ *55–32–11–45* 🌐 *www.olebullhuset.no.*

Shopping

Bergen Storsenter

SHOPPING CENTERS/MALLS | The largest shopping center in the city, Bergen Storsenter has the types of shops you'd expect to find along a main street, including bookstores and wineshops. It's located near the bus terminal and the train station. ✉ *Strømgt. 8, Sentrum* ☎ *55–21–24–60* 🌐 *www.bergenstorsenter.no/* 🕓 *Most shops closed Sun.*

Galleriet

SHOPPING CENTERS/MALLS | The most centrally located of the downtown shopping malls, Galleriet has more than 70 shops, including a wide range of smaller designer boutiques. ✉ *Torgallmenningen 8, Sentrum* ☎ *55–30–05–00* 🌐 *www.galleriet.com* 🕓 *Closed Sun.*

Hjertholm

CERAMICS/GLASSWARE | At this gift shop, most everything is of Scandinavian design. The pottery and glassware are of the highest quality—much of it is made by local artisans. ✉ *Galleriet, Torgallmenningen 8, Sentrum* ☎ *55–31–70–27* 🌐 *www.hjertholm.no* 🕓 *Closed Sun.*

Kløverhuset

SHOPPING CENTERS/MALLS | Dating back to 1852, Kløverhuset is the country's oldest shopping center. These days there are several dozen shops and restaurants under one roof. It's next to the fish market. ✉ *Strandgaten 13–15, Sentrum* ☎ *55–31–37–90* 🌐 *www.kløverhuset.no* 🕓 *Closed Sun.*

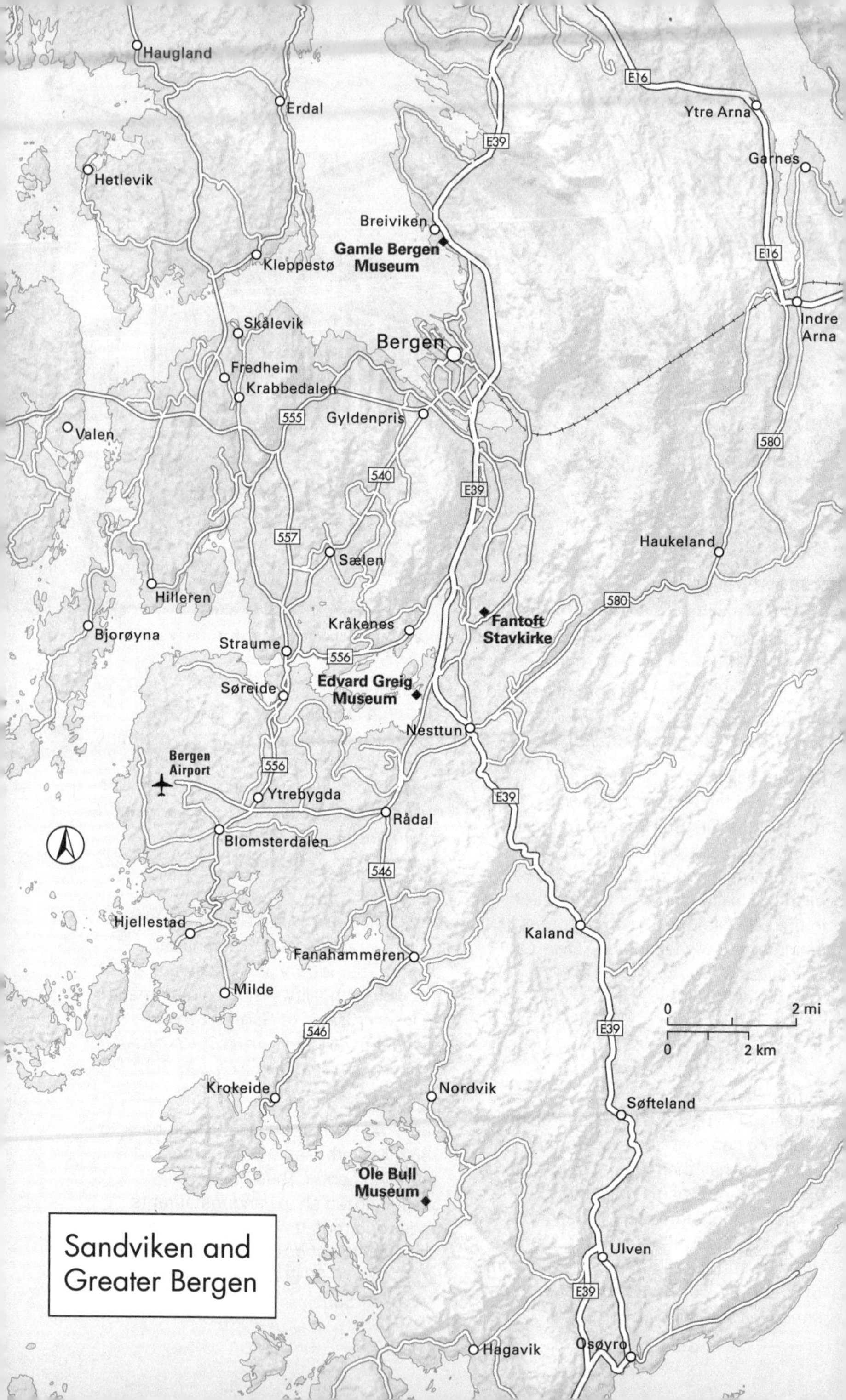

Sandviken and Greater Bergen

Norsk Flid Husfliden
CRAFTS | Established in 1895, this famous boutique sells Norwegian handicrafts, including sweaters, blankets, and leather items. You can also grab some last-minute souvenirs. ✉ *Vågsallmenningen 3, Sentrum* ☎ *55–54–47–40* 🌐 *www.norskflid.no/bergen* ⏲ *Closed Sun.*

Sundt
DEPARTMENT STORES | The closest thing Norway has to a traditional department store, Sundt focuses primarily on fashion. It's been in business since the 1880s. ✉ *Torgallmenningen 14, Sentrum* ☎ *55–32–47–24* 🌐 *sundtmotehus.no* ⏲ *Closed Sun.*

Theodor Olsens
CRAFTS | Run by the fourth generation of the same family, this venerable company sells some of the finest jewelry in the city. ✉ *Chr. Michelsensgate 2B, Sentrum* ☎ *55–55–14–80* 🌐 *www.theodor-olsen.no* ⏲ *Closed Sun.*

Sandviken

The neighborhood of Sandviken begins just past Bergenhus Festning, the huge fortress of the edge of Bryggen, and follows the coastline northward. It's a pleasant community, but most travelers head this way to see the Gamle Bergen Museum.

GETTING HERE AND AROUND

Sandviken is about 3 km (2 miles) north of Bryggen, so a taxi is the quickest way to get here. Buses also run here from Bryggen.

Sights

★ **Gamle Bergen Museum** (*Old Bergen Museum*)
MUSEUM VILLAGE | **FAMILY** | This open-air museum transports you to the 19th century, when Bergen consisted mostly of wooden houses. Streets and narrow alleys are lined with more than 50 buildings, including a baker, dentist, photographer, and jeweler. Local artists often hold exhibitions here. The grounds and park are open free of charge year-round. ✉ *Nyhavnsveien 4, Bergen* ☎ *55–30–80–30* 🌐 *www.bymuseet.no/en/museums/old-bergen-museum/* 🎫 *NKr 120* ⏲ *Closed Sept.–mid-May.*

Greater Bergen

Once you've gotten your fill of Bergen's city life, you can head out to the countryside to tour some of the area's lesser-known yet still interesting attractions. Music aficionados come from far and wide to see the homes of Edvard Grieg, Norway's foremost composer, and that of legendary violinist Ole Bull. The Fantoft Stave Church is also worth a visit if you're interested in Viking-era architecture or the Middle Ages.

GETTING HERE AND AROUND

These sights are farther from the city than they appears on a map. Join a guided tour, or splurge on a taxi.

Sights

★ **Edvard Grieg Museum**
HOUSE | Built in 1885, Troldhaugen was the home of Norway's most famous composer, Edvard Grieg. He composed many of his best-known works in a garden cottage by the lakeshore. In 1867 he married his cousin Nina, a Danish soprano. They lived in the white clapboard house with green gingerbread trim for 22 years. A salon and gathering place for many Scandinavian artists then, it now houses mementos—a piano, paintings, prints—of the composer's life. The interior has been kept as it was during Grieg's time here. Concerts are held both at Troldhaugen and at the very modern Troldsalen next door. ✉ *Troldhaugsveien 65, Paradis* ✣ *7 km (5 miles) south of Bergen* ☎ *55–92–29–92* 🌐 *griegmuseum.no/en* 🎫 *NKr 110* ⏲ *Closed mid-Dec.–mid-Jan.*

Fantoft Stavkirke (*Fantoft Stave Church*)
ARCHAEOLOGICAL SITE | During the Middle Ages, when European cathedrals were built in stone, Norway used wood to create unique stave churches. These cultural symbols stand out for their dragon heads, carved doorways, and walls of staves (vertical planks). Though as many as 750 stave churches may have once existed, only 30 remain standing. The original stave church here, built in Fortun in Sogn in 1150 and moved to Fantoft in 1883, burned down in 1992. Since then, the church has been reconstructed to resemble the original structure. Take the light rail to the town of Paradis and walk up Birkelundsbakken to the parking lot on the left hand side and follow the trail to get to the church ✉ *Fantoftvn. 38, Paradis* ☎ *55–28–07–10* 🌐 *fantoft-stavkirke.com* 🎫 *NKr 55* ⊙ *Closed mid-Sept.–mid-May.*

Ole Bull Museum (*Lysøen Island and Ole Bull's house*)
HOUSE | From 1873 onward, Lysøen ("island of light") was the home of the Norwegian violin virtuoso Ole Bull (1810–80). His over-the-top mansion has an onion dome, gingerbread gables, curved staircases, and cutwork trim, and it's surrounded by 13 km (8 miles) of pathways created by Bull; it's great for picnics, rowing, and swimming in secluded spots. During Bull's long career, he performed frequently throughout Europe and the United States, and even started a short-lived utopian colony—Oleana—in Pennsylvania. After founding the first national theater in Norway, he chose the young playwright Henrik Ibsen to write full-time for the theater, and later encouraged and promoted another neophyte—Edvard Grieg, then 15 years old. If you drive or take a bus here, the last part of the journey is on a ferry from Buena quay at Lysekloster. In the summer there are guided tours sponsored by the KODE museum in Bergen. ✉ *Museet Lysøen, Lysekloster* ✣ *25 km (13 miles) south of Bergen* ☎ *56–30–90–77* 🌐 *lysoen.no/en* 🎫 *NKr 60; ferry NKr 60 round-trip* ⊙ *Closed mid-Sept.–mid-May.*

Activities

HIKING

Mt. Ulriken
HIKING/WALKING | Mt. Ulriken is popular with walkers and hikers of all levels. The easiest way to reach the summit is via the cable car from Haukeland University Hospital. (To get there, take the double-decker bus that leaves from Torget every day between May and September.) Once you get off the cable car, you'll find trails leading across the mountain plateau, Vidden, which is above the tree line. The plateau connects the Fløyen and Ulriken mountains, and you can hike between them in four to six hours. Views from the alpine trail are spectacular. Be advised that foggy and rainy weather, even in the summer months, can make hiking here dangerous. Consult the tourist information center in Bergen for maps and general advice. ✉ *Mt. Ulriken* ☎ *53–64–36–43* 🌐 *www.ulriken643.no.*

Chapter 8

THE WESTERN FJORDS

Updated by
Lisa Stentvedt

Sights	Restaurants	Hotels	Shopping	Nightlife
★★★★★	★★★★☆	★★★★☆	★★★☆☆	★★☆☆☆

WELCOME TO THE WESTERN FJORDS

TOP REASONS TO GO

★ **Explore the Nærøyfjord:** When you visit Norway's narrowest fjord, make sure to meet the Vikings in Gudvangen.

★ **The Geirangerfjord:** The country's most popular fjord is a natural wonder that's a UNESCO World Heritage Site.

★ **Ride the Flåm Railway:** Among the most beautiful train rides in the world, it takes in magnificent mountain scenery.

★ **Hike Trolltunga:** This sliver-like rock formation jutting out over Ringedalsvatnet Lake is well worth the daylong hike.

★ **Drive the scenic routes:** These roads are known for hairpin turns, steep mountain passes, and breathtaking views.

The scenery of the western fjords is like nowhere else on Earth. From the shimmering waterways, lush green farmlands edge up the rounded mountainsides and the chiseled, cragged, steep peaks, some of Norway's tallest, seem to touch the blue skies. Most of these towns are at the water's edge.

1 **Utne.** An excellent base when exploring the Hardangerfjord.

2 **Odda.** The best gateway for Folgefonna National Park.

3 **Kinsarvik.** Easy access to some of the area's best hiking.

4 **Eidfjord.** A horse-loving village on northern Europe's deepest lake.

5 **Ulvik.** The center for the region's apple cider industry.

6 **Voss.** The region's extreme sports capital.

7 **Stalheim.** Take in the breathtaking views of the Nærøy Valley.

8 **Gudvangen.** Where the Vikings still roam free.

9 **Flåm.** Popular little village by the fjords.

10 **Myrdal.** Starting point of the Flåm Railway.

11 **Undredal.** Know for two things: goats and goat cheese.

12 **Aurland.** Home of the original penny loafer.

13 **Solvorn.** Visit its pair of lovely churches.

14 **Balestrand.** A haven for artists for more than a century.

15 **Fjærland.** Norway's destination for book lovers

16 **Vik.** Pretty churches and lovely scenery.

17 **Olden.** Close to the Briksdal Glacier.

18 **Loen.** Ride the spectacular skylift.

19 **Grodås.** Great hikes among the mountain peaks.

20 **Hellesylt.** A waterfall in the village.

21 **Åndalsnes.** Easy access to Troll Ladder.

22 **Ålesund.** On three islands between two fjords.

23 **Florø.** The area's westernmost municipality.

24 **Kristiansund.** Don't miss the opera house.

8

The Western Fjords WELCOME TO THE WESTERN FJORDS

The intricate outline of the fjords makes Norway's coastline of 21,347 km (13,264 miles) longer than the distance between the north and south poles. Majestic and magical, the fjords can take any traveler's breath away in a moment. In spectacular inlets like Nærøyfjord and the Geirangerfjord—both UNESCO World Heritage Sites—walls of water shoot up the mountainsides, jagged snowcapped peaks blot out the sky, and water tumbles down the mountains in an endless variety of colors.

The farther north you travel, the more rugged and wild the landscape. The still, peaceful Sognefjord is the longest inlet, snaking 190 km (110 miles) inland. At the top of Sogn og Fjordane county is a group of fjords referred to as Nordfjord, with the massive Jostedalsbreen, mainland Europe's largest glacier, to the south. In the county of Møre og Romsdal, you'll see mountains that would seem more natural on the moon—all gray rock—as well as cliffs hanging over the water below.

MAJOR REGIONS

Hardangerfjord Area. Trolltunga, one of the most spectacular mountains in Norway, makes this region especially popular with hikers. Outdoor enthusiasts also love Hardangervidda National Park and Folgefonna National Park. The Hardangerfjord has been popular for centuries, and one of the most famous paintings in Norway pictures a newlywed couple rowing across the fjord. The painting is from 1848, proof that this area has been popular for a long, long time.

Sognefjord Area. The continent's longest fjord stretches 200 km (124 miles) through what is perhaps Norway's most beautiful scenery. Here you'll find Jotunheimen National Park, with some of the country's highest and wildest mountains, and Jostedalsbreen Glacier National Park, home to the region's largest glacier. In summer the area draws mountain sports enthusiasts who climb, hike, and walk along the glaciers.

Nordfjord Area. In between the Sognefjord and the Geirangerfjord lies Nordfjord. Olden and Loen are considered parts of the Inner Nordfjord, and Grodås is located at the end of the picturesque Hornindalsvatnet. This is a popular destination for photographers, nature lovers, and hiking enthusiasts.

Geirangerfjord Area. On the list of UNESCO World Heritage Sites, the Geirangerfjord is Norway's most spectacular and perhaps best-known fjord. The 16-km-long (10-mile-long) waterway is known for its roaring waterfalls: the Seven Sisters, the Bridal Veil, and the Suitor. Perched on mountain ledges along the fjord, deserted farms at Skageflå and Knivsflå are being restored and maintained by local enthusiasts.

Nordvestlandet. The coastal fjord country that extends from Kristiansund to Selje is called Nordvestlandet, or "Northwest Land," by Norwegians, even though it's located toward the middle of the western coastline. Small weather-beaten islands dot the coastline, and if you follow the fjords as they wend their way inland, you quickly come to steep, jagged, beautiful mountains. This region is traditionally where some of Norway's most successful fishing companies were based—halfway between the rich waters of the north and the important commercial center of Bergen. It's also where some of Norway's most spectacular scenery is most accessible.

Planning

As the area is quite rural, with few major cities, it is necessary to plan ahead for your visit. Whether you are renting a car or using public transportation, it is important to do your research before and during your trip. This way you avoid meeting any surprise road closures or route changes and you can make the most of your time and trip to the fjords.

When to Go

The fjords are beautiful all year round, and depending on your preferences you'll find that there are reasons to visit in any season. However, high season is the summer months, from June to August, with the shoulder season (April, May, September, and October) becoming more and more popular for visitors. You'll find in the summer months that the area is very busy, with most establishments open every day.

Norway is beautiful in the winter, and winter tourism is becoming more common. But if you visit from November to March, plan ahead and prepare for less frequent departures and limited opening hours.

Getting Here and Around

Boat cruises are the classic way of exploring this region, but this only takes you to the communities along the coast. If you want to explore the countryside, a car is probably a must. It's possible to use public transportation, but it will require a lot more advance planning.

AIR TRAVEL

Air travel is not the most common way to explore in this region, although there are domestic airports in Florø, Kristiansund, Molde, and Sogndal and a small international airport at Ålesund.

BOAT TRAVEL

Boat cruises are the classic way of exploring this region. It's possible to travel all the way from Bergen to the Sognefjord by boat.

If you're driving through the fjords, you probably will encounter at least one car ferry along the way. Car ferries can't be booked in advance, and you will pay upon arrival on the dock. Express boats do not take cars. These smaller and faster boats run more frequently in high season.

BUS TRAVEL

Traveling by bus between towns is completely doable, and a preferred way to travel along the fjords. Not all towns and villages have train connections, so buses run more frequently. Tickets can be purchased both online in advance and on the bus, but it is always recommended to book online to be guaranteed a seat on your preferred bus.

There is no bus company that covers the whole region, as this chapter covers several counties. However, Tide and Vy (formerly Nettbuss) both have long-distance buses traveling across the counties.

CONTACTS Tide Buss. ☎ *55–23–87–00* 🌐 *www.tide.no.* **Vy.** ☎ *40–70–50–70* 🌐 *www.vy.no.*

CAR TRAVEL

Many of Norway's National Tourist Routes traverse this area, making driving in the western fjords a truly beautiful experience. Hardanger and Hardangervidda wind through spectacular scenery, and Aurlandsfjellet and Sognefjellet are mountain passes that have eye-popping views. Don't forget the famous Trollstigen in the Geiranger area.

That's not to say driving here is without challenges. The roads in certain places along the fjords are narrow and windy, and you likely encounter hairpin curves when crossing over mountains.

TRAIN TRAVEL

Voss can be reached by train from Oslo or Bergen via the Bergensbanen, and in summer it is possible to reach Åndalsnes via the Raumabanen. Other than that, trains don't cover much of this region, making buses a better option.

CONTACTS Vy. ☎ *61–05–19–10* 🌐 *www.vy.no.*

Restaurants

In the western fjords you are likely to encounter both traditional Norwegian restaurants and eateries that have put a modern twist on old-fashioned recipes. Meals here include a lot of seafood, often fresh from the fjord or the ocean, and potatoes are usually piled on the side.

Restaurants in the smaller villages are often open longer hours during the summer, but will have much more limited hours in winter. Most kitchens close by 9 pm, so don't plan on a late dinner.

Hotels

The more popular towns, such as Flåm, Geiranger, and Ålesund, have the widest selection of accommodations across different budgets. The smaller the village, the more likely you'll just have one or two options. Many of the hotels in the area are family run and have been for generations, so expect a warm welcome and personalized service. You'll find that the more expensive hotels are usually located in places offering unique views of the landscape, whether it's on the fjords, near the lakes, or in the mountains.

Restaurant and hotel reviews have been shortened. For full information, visit Fodors.com.

What It Costs in Norwegian Krone

	$	$$	$$$	$$$$
RESTAURANTS				
	under NKr 125	NKr 125–NKr 250	NKr 251–NKr 350	over NKr 350
HOTELS				
	under NKr 750	NKr 750–NKr 1250	NKr 1251–NKr 1900	over NKr 1900

Tours

★ FjordSafari

This tour takes you closer to nature in a RIB boat, on a guided tour of the Aurlandsfjord and Nærøyfjord. The boats have a smaller capacity than the larger tourist ferries, and it gives an intimate and rather unique experience of the fjords. The guide is also the driver of the boat, and will stop at any time if you encounter any local animals along the way. ☎ *99–09–08–60* 🌐 *www.fjordsafari.com.*

Visitor Information

CONTACTS Visit Hardangerfjord. ☎ *56–55–38–70* 🌐 *www.hardangerfjord.com.* **Visit Nordfjord.** ☎ *57–87–40–40* 🌐 *www.nordfjord.no.* **Visit Nordvest.** ☎ *70–23–88–00* 🌐 *www.visitnorthwest.no.* **Visit Sognefjord.** 🌐 *www.sognefjord.no.*

Utne

131 km (81 miles) east of Bergen.

In the heart of the Hardangerfjord area lies Utne, a tiny village that rests at the tip of the peninsula dividing the inlet of Hardangerfjord from the arm that stretches south towards Odda, the Sørfjord. It's an excellent starting point for exploring the area. Going south on both sides of the fjord, you can explore farming communities with traditions dating back centuries, or go hiking in the steep mountainsides and the plateaus or glaciers beyond. A popular destination here is the Hardanger Folkemuseum, consisting of several buildings from the Middle Ages.

GETTING HERE AND AROUND

Utne can be reached by ferry from either Kinsarvik (via Route 13) or Kvanndal (via Route 7). It's also possible to drive along the fjord from Odda.

Sights

Hardanger Folkemuseum (*Hardanger Folk Museum*)
MUSEUM | Focusing primarily on local heritage, the Hardanger Folk Museum is one of the largest and best of its kind in western Norway. Here you can walk around a cluster of old houses and get an idea of what life was like in Norway in the 1800s. Hardanger is home to many national symbols of Norway, such as the *Hardingfele* (an eight-stringed fiddle that inspired Norwegian composers like Edvard Grieg), *Hardangerbunad* (traditional dress from the region), and *Hardangersaum* (an intricate type of embroidery), and you can see examples of them here. ✉ *Museumsvegen 36, Utne* ☎ *474–79–884* 🌐 *hardangerfolkemuseum.no.*

Utne Kyrkje (*Utne Church*)
RELIGIOUS SITE | Completed in 1895, this squat parish church was designed by the well-known architect Peter Blix, who also restored two of the churches in Vik. Primarily made of wood and painted a creamy white, it seats up to 400 people. ✉ *Utne Kyrkje, Fv 550 340, Utne* 🌐 *www.ullensvang.herad.no/krk.*

Restaurants

Utne Hotel Restaurant
$$$$ | **NORWEGIAN** | At Utne Hotel, this quaint restaurant is known for its menu based on local ingredients, such as veal from Folkedal and lamb from Hardanger, and the freshest produce. Don't pass up a chance to sample the "Flavors of Hardanger," a three-course set menu focusing on traditional dishes. **Known for:** cider tastings; local produce; traditional decor. 💲 *Average main: NKr 595* ✉ *Utne Hotel, Fv 550 11, Utne* ☎ *53–66–64–00* 🌐 *utnehotel.no/restaurant-i-hardanger* 🕒 *Price is for the 3-course menu of the day.*

Hotels

★ Utne Hotel
$$$$ | **HOTEL** | One of the oldest lodgings in Norway, this graceful wooden structure with flower boxes on the windowsills and a tile roof above first opened its doors in 1722. **Pros:** serves local cider in the restaurant; modern bathrooms in

Western Fjords
Nordfjord, Geirangerfjord, and Nordvestlandet
see detail map
Alesund
see detail map
Sognefjord
see detail map
Hardangerfjord
see detail map
NORWEGIAN SEA
0
20 mi
0
20 km
Kristiansund
Knarrvik
Edoyfjord
Karvag
Bud
Gjemres
E39
Vulvik
Botnfjordsora
Koksvik
Nordvestlandet
Kleive
Tjelle
Flem
Heggdal
Rovik
Nesse
Midfjord
Hildrestrand
Vestnes
Vistdal
Fiksdal
Afarnes
Gjosund
Tennfjord
Åndalsnes
E39
Noringset
Blindheim
Tresfiord
Storfjord
Marstein
MØRE OG ROMSDAL
Vartdal
Beril
Leikanger
E39
Ervik
Linge
Gronning
Verma
Orsta
Volda
Oyo
Selje
Syvde
Dalsfjord
Geirangerfjord
E316
Bjolverud
Maurstad
Bjorkedal
Geiranger
Fid
Grodås
Lindevik
Billingen
Nordfjord
Loen
Folva
OPPLAND
Nordfjord
Hyen
E39
Olden
Skjak
Florø
Breim
Lom
Briksdalsbreen
Fordefjord
Ardal
SOGN OG FJORDANE
Forde
Bygstad
Bolstad
Jotunheimen Nasjonalpark
Vik
Fjærland
Skor
E39
Vadheim
Solvorn
Torvund
Balestrand
Ardal
Sognefjord
Ortnevik
Seim
Kvamme
E16
Nystova
Vang
E39
Undredal
Fensfjord
Gudvangen
Aurland
Stalheim
Flåm
Manger
Tuv
Myrdal
Seim
Evanger
Voss
Granvin
Ulvik
Liagarda
HORDALAND
Hol
Bergen
Eidfjord
Hardangerfjord
E39
Soere
Kinsarvik
Fusafjord
Krossfjord
BUSKERUD
Bjørnafjord
Sorfjord
Odda
Neset
Sildefjord
E39
TELEMARK

every room; authentic period decor. **Cons:** very simple furnishings in the rooms; not all rooms have a fjord view; expensive rates. *Rooms from: NKr 2580* *Utne Hotel, Fv 550 11, Utne* *53–66–64–00* *www.utnehotel.no* *17 rooms* *Free breakfast.*

Odda

43 km (27 miles) south of Utne, 135 km (84 miles) southeast of Bergen.

A beautiful town along the Hardangerfjord, Odda is where many people choose to stay as a base for visiting Folgefonna National Park and Glacier and Trolltunga. The town is larger than any of the surrounding villages, so you'll find several restaurants and cafés where you can relax after exploring the region. Beautiful waterfalls, blue glaciers, and deep green fjords are just some of the sights that await you in Odda.

GETTING HERE AND AROUND

The main road E134 passes through Odda, and meets Route 13 in the middle of the town. It is possible to reach Odda by public transportation, with the Haukeliekspressen bus traveling from Oslo to Odda several times a day, including one transfer at Seljestad. Line 930 takes you from Bergen to Odda.

Eidesnuten

TRAIL | This hike leads you to a peak nearly 3,000 feet above sea level. The hike itself is clearly marked with red Ts along the trail, and you can enjoy some spectacular views over Sandvinsvatnet and the Sørfjord. There are some steep parts, so you should be in relatively good shape for the hike, which takes around three to four hours round-trip. The address takes you to a small parking lot (near a playground), close to the start of the trail. *Eidesåsen 100, Odda* *48–07–07–77.*

★ Folgefonna National Park

NATIONAL/STATE PARK | **FAMILY** | Home to Norway's third-largest glacier, Folgefonna National Park is popular for its kayaking, hiking, and, of course, hiking on the glacier. From the top of the glacier there are beautiful valleys stretching all the way down to the fjord, and visiting Folgefonna is something you will remember. The National Park has several places of entry, with Odda and Rosendal (with the visitor center) being two popular ones, and several hikes and glacier arms you can explore, in addition to beautiful valleys with waterfalls of melting water from the glacier. *Skålafjæro 17, Rosendal* *53–48–42–80* *folgefonna.info.*

Trolltunga

MOUNTAIN—SIGHT | This rock formation about 3,600 feet above sea level is one of the most breathtaking sights in Norway. From the tip of a huge sliver of stone jutting out from the mountain you can gaze down at the valley and fjord below. The hike itself takes around 10 to 12 hours, and many people find that they underestimated the level of fitness and endurance needed to make the trip. Always check weather conditions a few days ahead of time, then again the morning of the hike. The main starting point is at P2 in Skjeggedal, but it is also possible to start from P3 Mågelitopp (saving two or three hours). From Odda there are shuttle buses to P2, and between P2 and P3 there is a smaller shuttle operating in the summer season. There is parking at both P2 and P3, the latter with more limited spaces that should be booked in advance. *Skjeggedal Carpark, Tyssedal* *www.hardangerfjord.com/odda/trolltunga.*

Glacier Restaurant

$$ | **INTERNATIONAL** | **FAMILY** | In the center of Odda, the Glacier Restaurant couldn't be more relaxed: there are picnic tables outside, a casual eatery on the main

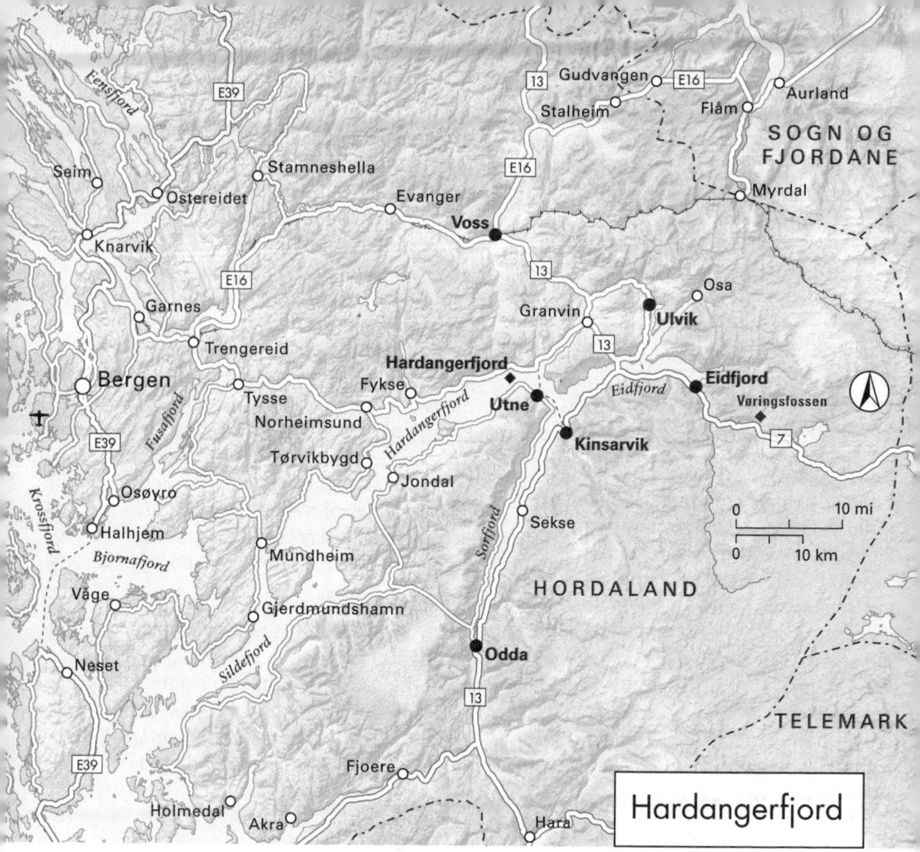

Hardangerfjord

level, and a slightly more formal dining room downstairs. With Asian, European, and even Middle Eastern dishes on the menu, everyone in the family will find something they like. **Known for:** varied menu; vegetarian options; one of the few places serving cocktails. $ *Average main: NKr 239* ✉ *Eitrheimsveien 9, Odda* ☎ *53–50–00–22* 🌐 *glacier-as.no/g/* 🕒 *No lunch Mon. or Thurs.*

Hotels

Hardanger Hotel

$$$ | **HOTEL** | **FAMILY** | In the center of Odda, this lodging has a couple of things going for it: sweeping views of the water and a location that puts you within walking distance of most attractions. **Pros:** free parking; central location; complimentary Wi-Fi. **Cons:** parking fills up in high season; rooms aren't soundproofed; no ironing facilities. $ *Rooms from: NKr 1400* ✉ *Eitrheimsveien 13, Odda* ☎ *53–64–64–64* 🌐 *www.hardangerhotel.no* *50 rooms* *Free breakfast.*

Trolltunga Hotel

$$$ | **HOTEL** | **FAMILY** | The views alone—overlooking the lake and the mountains beyond—are reason enough to chose this hotel, but it also has a relaxed atmosphere and amenities ranging from packed lunches for the trail to a gear-drying service so you don't have to pack wet clothes. **Pros:** beautiful views; renovated rooms; great breakfast. **Cons:** not all rooms offer the same view; 20-minute walk to downtown Odda; free shuttle to Trolltunga only for those hiking with a guide. $ *Rooms from: NKr 1500* ✉ *Vasstun 1, Odda* ☎ *400–04–486* 🌐 *www.trolltungahotel.no* *36 rooms, 2 dormitories* *Free breakfast.*

Kinsarvik

41 km (25 miles) north of Odda.

A small village near the Hardangerfjord, Kinsarvik has a beautiful setting on the edge of the water and easy access to some of the area's best hiking.

GETTING HERE AND AROUND

Route 13 goes straight through this village, making it an easy trip from Odda or Voss (except in summer, when the route may be clogged with traffic). The ferry from Utne sails directly to Kinsarvik.

Sights

★ Husedalen

TRAIL | One of the most beautiful hikes in Norway, Husedalen takes you past four spectacular waterfalls: Tveitafossen, Nykkjesøyfossen, Nyastølsfossen, and Søtefossen. The hike takes about five or six hours if you aim to see all of the waterfalls, but you can also opt to visit just the first one and be finished in 90 minutes. From Kinsarvik, follow the river up the valley and then follow signs marking the hike, or drive to the power station to park there. The full hike is best for those who consider themselves to be of a moderate hiking level, but the first waterfall is hikeable for most people. ✉ *Kinso Kraftverk, Kinasaevik.*

Mikkelparken

AMUSEMENT PARK/WATER PARK | **FAMILY** | Named for a friendly cartoon fox, this theme park has a very popular water park, along with ziplines, playgrounds, and plenty of other diversions for the kids. ✉ *Husevegen 6, Kinasaevik* ☎ *53–67–13–13* 🌐 *mikkelparken.no* 🎫 *NKr 339* 🕑 *Call ahead for hrs in the autumn, winter, and spring.*

Restaurants

Gloyp Spiseri

$$ | **SCANDINAVIAN** | This restaurant is bright and breezy, with huge windows letting in lots of light, but the real reason to come here is what's on your plate: beautifully prepared, locally sourced meals by Norway's originator of New Nordic cuisine. The atmosphere is relaxed and the location is right across from the water. **Known for:** great atmosphere; local ingredients; fine Nordic cuisine. $ *Average main: NKr 240* ✉ *Kinsarvikvegen 45, Kinasaevik* ☎ *92–85–50–94* 🌐 *facebook.com/gloypspiseri.*

Hotels

Kinsarvik Camping

$$ | **B&B/INN** | **FAMILY** | Welcoming guests since 1950, Kinsarvik Camping has 25 rustic cabins with varying amenities. **Pros:** camping experience without camping; can accommodate groups; walking distance to town. **Cons:** books up fast; linens not included; some cabins are very simple. $ *Rooms from: NKr 795* ✉ *Kinsarvik Camping* ☎ *53–66–32–90* 🌐 *kinsarvik-camping.no* *25 cabins* 🍽 *No meals.*

Eidfjord

31 km (19 miles) northeast of Kinsarvik.

This small agricultural community town is best known for the *fjordhest* (fjord horse), an equine symbol that you'll see everywhere, including on the official town shield. This type of horse was bred for farm work and played a big role in guiding the development of western Norway. Every spring the community hosts the Hingsteutstillinga (State Stallion Show), which attracts horse enthusiasts from around the region. With a population of about 6,000, Eidfjord is a good destination if you want to see what life is like on a farm. It sits near Hornindalsvatnet, northern Europe's deepest lake.

Eidfjord's sister village, Øvre Eidfjord, some 6 km (4 miles) southeast, is home to the Hardangervidda Natursenter.

GETTING HERE AND AROUND

On the eastern edge of the Hardangerfjord, Eidfjord is a good gateway to the Hardangervidda Plateau. To get to Eidfjord from Bergen (via Voss) takes about 2 1/2 hours, and includes crossing the impressive Hardanger Bridge. From Bergen to Voss, follow main road E16. From Voss, follow Route 13, then turn onto Route 7.

Sights

Kjeåsen Farm

FARM/RANCH | Dotted around the steep hillsides flanking the fjords are a number of small, seemingly inaccessible farms. Farmers who settled there would often use a system of ropes and pulleys to haul up supplies. One of these farms, Kjeåsen, became accessible when workers built a narrow switchback road to the top of the cliff. Because the road is a single lane, traffic goes uphill for the first 30 minutes of every hour, downhill for the last 30 minutes. A more strenuous but more rewarding way up is via the footpath the inhabitants used to take. Starting at the parking lot near the Sima power station, it's a fairly strenuous 90-minute walk each way, with ropes and ladders helping you navigate the more difficult portions. The view from atop of the cliff is your reward, but if you're lucky the proprietor will offer to give you a tour. ✉ *Off Fv 103, Eidfjord.*

Norsk Natursenter Hardanger

MUSEUM | **FAMILY** | With exhibits that will interest the whole family, this nature center is spread over three floors of a gorgeous glass-and steel building. Whether you're interested in climate, nature, or the environment, there's plenty to keep you occupied. Don't miss the bird's-eye view of Norway in Ivo Caprino's 20-minute film *Fjord Fjell Foss*, meaning *Fjord, Mountain, Waterfall.* ✉ *Sæbøtunet 11, Eidfjord* ☎ *53–67–40–00* 🌐 *norsknatursenter.no* ⏲ *Closed Nov.–Mar.*

★ Vøringsfossen

VIEWPOINT | For thousands of years, this 600-foot waterfall has cut like a knife through the Hardangervidda Plateau, every year adding another fraction of an inch to the Måbødalen Valley. There are a number of ways to take in the waterfall and the valley beneath it, the most accessible being the cliff-top lookout points along Route 7 between Eidfjord and Fossli. For a dazzling and damp view from beneath the waterfall, take a half-hour hike from the road to the bottom of the waterfall. The trail is slippery, even in dry weather, but is well worth it. The Eidfjord Tourist office can help plan your trip. ✉ *Rte. 7, 20 mins from Eidfjord, Eidfjord* ☎ *53–67–34–00.*

Restaurants

Fjell og Fjord Kafè

$ | **CAFÉ** | **FAMILY** | Centrally located in Eidfjord, this charming café with a handful of tables outside bakes some of the best pastries around—make sure to to get some cinnamon rolls to take along on your adventures. This is the perfect place for a light lunch, using the best local produce, a filling snack, or a great cup of coffee. **Known for:** delectable cinnamon rolls; edible souvenirs; friendly staff. [$] *Average main: NKr 100* ✉ *Fjell og Fjord Kafè, Eidfjordvegen 277, Eidfjord* ☎ *53–66–52–64* 🌐 *eidfjordhotel.no.*

Hotels

Eidfjord Fjell og Fjord Hotel

$$$ | **HOTEL** | **FAMILY** | The views are stunning at this small lodging—half of the rather rustic rooms gaze out over the fjord—but the cozy atmosphere, with a fireplace warming up the comfortable lobby, is another reason to make this your base in the area. **Pros:** charming atmosphere; friendly hosts; good base for exploring. **Cons:** not all rooms have fjord views; basic decor in the rooms; no bathtubs. $ *Rooms from: NKr 1850* ✉ *Lægreidsvegen 7, Eidfjord* ☎ *53–66–52–64* 🌐 *eidfjordhotel.no* 28 *rooms* 🍽 *Free breakfast.*

★ Quality Hotel Vøringfoss
$$$ | HOTEL | A stone's throw from the port, this contemporary lodging with grand gables and other architectural flourishes that call to mind the region's rich history gives you a choice between a spectacular view of the Hardangerfjord or a less-impressive one of the valley (some rooms have private balconies, which are worth requesting). **Pros:** unbeatable views; restaurant uses local ingredients; good for business travelers. **Cons:** does not accept cash payments; a bit expensive. $ *Rooms from: NKr 1845* ✉ *Ostangvegen 20, Eidfjord* ☎ *53–67–41–00* 🌐 *nordicchoicehotels.no/hotell/norge/eidfjord/quality-hotel-voringfoss* *81 rooms* 🍽 *Free breakfast.*

Ulvik

31 km (19 miles) north of Kinsarvik, 33 km (21 miles) northwest of Eidfjord.

Ulvik can be found at the end of the Hardangerfjord, amidst tall mountains and rather dramatic scenery. Ulvik is known for its production of apple cider, with three private farms producing this Hardanger based product. There are some beautiful hiking trails in the area, and Ulvik is a good place to stay as a base for your Hardanger adventures.

GETTING HERE AND AROUND

Ulvik can be reached from Voss by following Route 572, or driving on Route 13 towards the Hardanger Bridge and taking the exit towards Ulvik on Route 572 along the fjord. The latter is a very scenic drive, and takes about 45 minutes.

Sights

Hardanger Bridge
BRIDGE/TUNNEL | This spectacular suspension bridge crossing the Eidfjorden branch of the Hardangerfjord quickly became a symbol of Hardanger when it opened in 2013. It's an impressive feat of engineering, with the central span the longest of any suspension bridge in the world. Tunnels at either end ensure that your first glimpse will be unforgettable. ✉ *Rte. 13, 16 km (10 miles) south of Ulvik, Ulvik.*

Ulvik Kyrkje (*Ulvik Church*)
RELIGIOUS SITE | Dating back to 1859, this cross-shaped house of worship is worth seeing for its architect alone. It was designed by Danish-Norwegian architect Hans Ditlev Franciscus von Linstow, who is most famous for being the man behind the Norwegian Royal Palace in Oslo. ✉ *Storøyni 6, Ulvik.*

Restaurants

Den Grøne Kafe
$$ | SCANDINAVIAN | Facing the dock in Ulvik, the Green Cafe has big windows with amazing views of the fjord and the mountains beyond, but in warm weather you'll want to head outside to one of the tables just feet from the water's edge. Given the name, you won't be surprised at the number of vegetarian and vegan options, but there is also a wide range of dishes for meat-eaters, from burgers to fish-and-chips. **Known for:** varied menu; friendly staff; great views. $ *Average main: NKr 130* ✉ *Promenaden 7, Ulvik* ☎ *56–52–61–87* 🌐 *fjordkafe.no* ⏲ *Closed Mon.*

Hotels

★ Brakanes Hotel
$$$ | HOTEL | With a beautiful location along the Hardangerfjord, this modern hotel makes sure that the rooms along the waterfront have expansive windows

Did You Know?

Trolltunga, which literally mean "Troll's Tongue," juts out from a mountain hundreds of feet above Lake Ringedalsvatnet.

and balconies where you can enjoy your morning coffee or a drink after dinner; these rooms have also been nicely renovated, making them far superior to the older rooms facing the other direction. **Pros:** lovely views of the fjord; allergy-friendly rooms; friendly staff. **Cons:** half of the rooms face the parking lot; some areas need refurbishing; popular with tour groups. *Rooms from: NKr 1700* *Promenaden 3, Ulvik* *56–52–61–05* *brakanes-hotel.no* *142 rooms* *Free breakfast.*

Voss

43 km (19 miles) northwest of Ulvik, 107 km (66 miles) northeast of Bergen.

Between the Hardangerfjord and the Sognefjord, Voss is in a handy place to begin an exploration of the fjords. Once considered just a stopover, it now has a wide range of activities that invite people to linger. Its reputation is burnished by Vossajazz, an annual jazz festival, and the Sheep's Head Festival, a celebration of the region's culinary delicacies. Voss is known as the extreme sports capital of Norway. Ekstremsportveko, taking place every June, draws adrenaline enthusiasts from all over the world for paragliding, kitesurfing, base jumping, and other activities. The famous "Horgi Ned" competition includes three sports: skiing, biking, and kayaking

GETTING HERE AND AROUND

From Bergen, Voss is a 1 1/2- to 2-hour drive along the E16. It's located on the Oslo-Bergen line, and trains are about 1 1/2 hours from Bergen, 5 1/2 hours from Oslo. Express trains run several times daily.

Sights

Voss Gondol

VIEWPOINT | This gondola is an exciting way to see Voss and the surrounding region. At the top is Hangurstoppen, which sits at 820 meters (2,690 feet) above sea level. Here you can enjoy a panoramic view from the restaurant or set off on hikes of different skill levels. *Evangervegen 5, Voss* *47–00–47–00* *vossgondol.no* *Nkr 750.*

Restaurants

Elvatun Restaurant

$$$ | **NORWEGIAN** | If you're looking to eat like a Viking, this long dining hall with soaring wood beams and a central fireplace should be on your list. The atmosphere is extremely cozy, especially when it's cold outside and you want to warm up by the open fire; at other times of the year, the tables out on the deck facing the lake are the most desirable (especially if you take advantage of the three outdoor hot tubs). **Known for:** an old-school vibe; plenty of local dishes; lovely location. *Average main: NKr 300* *Nedkvitnesvegen 25, Voss* *56–51–05–25* *vossactive.no.*

Hotels

★ Fleischer's Hotel

$$$$ | **HOTEL** | By the train station in the center of the city, this hotel dating from 1864 has plenty of details that call to mind a bygone era—bay windows, wooden balconies, and steeply pitched mansard roofs; even the newer wings have a pleasingly traditional look. **Pros:** indoor pool and sauna; central location; period charm. **Cons:** some noise from the train station; expensive rates; some amenities only open in summer. *Rooms from: NKr 2100* *Evangerveien 13, Voss* *56–52–05–00* *fleischers.no* *110 rooms* *Free breakfast.*

Myrkdalen Hotel

$$$$ | **HOTEL** | **FAMILY** | In the Myrkdalen Valley about a half-hour drive from the center of Voss, this year-round destination is particularly popular in winter thanks to the popular cross-country and downhill

skiing facilities. **Pros:** superb location for ski enthusiasts; family activities throughout the year; great winter destination. **Cons:** not very close to Voss; not ideal for non-skiers; expensive rates. *Rooms from: NKr 2200* *Klypeteigane, Vossestrand, Voss* *47–47–16–00* *myrkdalen.no* *112 rooms* *Free breakfast.*

Activities

★ Voss Active

WHITE-WATER RAFTING | White-water rafting is just one of the activities at Voss Active, where the guides are enthusiastic about showing off what the area has to offer. They are knowledgeable about these sports and will make you feel comfortable and well taken care of, regardless of which adventure you pick. Fishing expeditions and ropes courses are among the favorite outings. *Nedkvitnesvegen 25, Skulestadmo, Voss* *56–51–05–25* *vossactive.no.*

Stalheim

37 km (23 miles) northeast of Voss.

The best reason to visit Stalheim is to take in the breathtaking views of the Nærøy Valley and drive along the eye-popping Stalheimskleiva. Before the highway was built, this farming community was a natural resting place for anyone traveling to the fjords. The mail route between Oslo and Bergen opened in 1647, and since then Stalheim became one of several "mailing farms" along the route.

GETTING HERE AND AROUND

Stalheim is easily accessible by car. Be aware that Stalheimskleiva, a series of 13 hairpin turns, is a one-way road, so plan your journey carefully.

Sights

Stalheimskleiva

SCENIC DRIVE | A pair of majestic waterfalls are among the thrilling sights along this mountain road, built in the first half of the 19th century. With a nerve-jangling series of 13 hairpin curves, it is said to be one of the steepest roads in northern Europe. Today the road is one-way only, so plan to drive down them from Stalheim. *Stalheim.*

Hotels

Stalheim Hotel

$$$$ | **HOTEL** | Originally a coach station on the old postal route from Oslo to Bergen, this hotel is perched high over the 13 hairpin turns of the dramatic Stalheimskleiva road, halfway between Voss and Flåm. **Pros:** breathtaking views; charming atmosphere; good location for travelers. **Cons:** the drive is difficult; furnishings are very simple; expensive rates. *Rooms from: NKr 2000* *Stalheim Hotel, Stalheimsvegen 131, Stalheim* *56–52–01–22* *stalheim.com* *124 rooms* *Free breakfast.*

Gudvangen

8 km (5 miles) northeast of Stalheim.

This small village at the end of the Nærøyfjord is the final stop for cruises from both Flåm and Kaupanger. The village is a very popular destination because of the lovely views and the viking heritage.

GETTING HERE AND AROUND

Gudvangen is located along E16, the main road from Bergen and Voss. From Bergen, it takes about 2 1/2 hours by car or bus. From Flåm and Kaupanger, the most relaxing way to get here by boat.

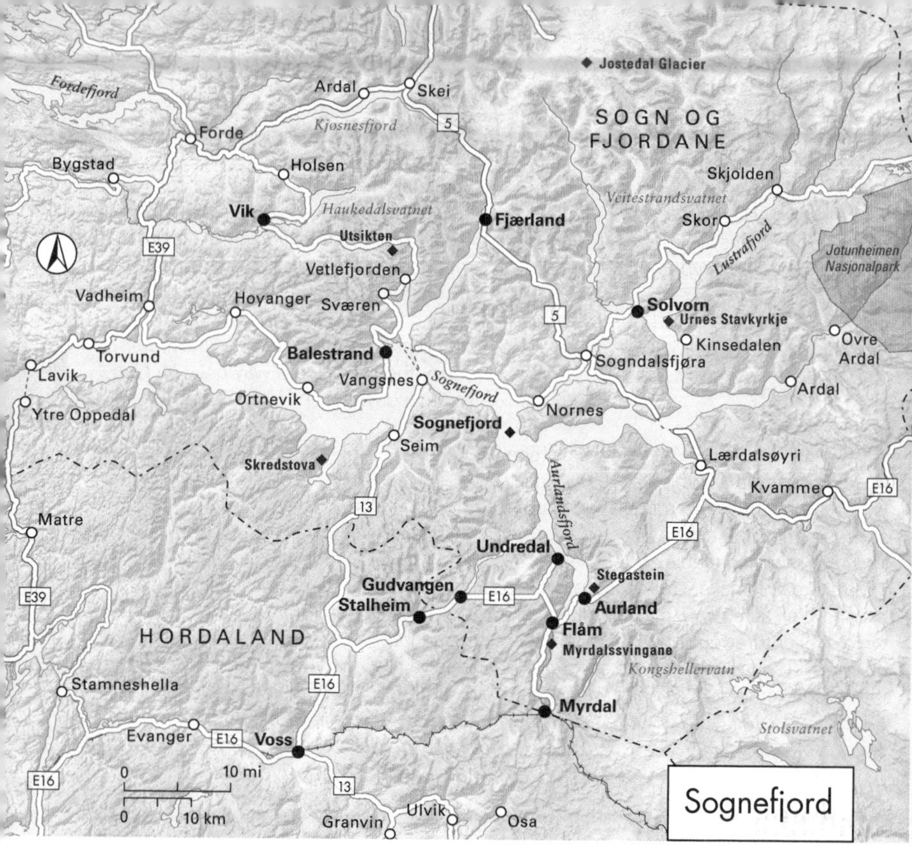

Sognefjord

Sights

★ Njardarheimr Viking Village

MUSEUM VILLAGE | You can completely immerse yourself in Viking culture at this village named for the northern god Njord. You won't be speaking with costumed performers here—the international community here is living as the Vikings did 1,000 years ago. Try your hand at axe throwing or archery, then chow down on authentic Viking grub. ✉ *Gudvangen* ☎ *46–24–54–62* 🌐 *vikingvalley.no* 🎫 *NKr 200.*

Hotels

Gudvangen Fjordtell

$$$$ | **HOTEL** | **FAMILY** | How about staying in a Viking-themed room, just a stone's throw from Norway's own Viking village of Njardarheimr? That's one of the joys of Gudvangen Fjordtell, in addition to the great location in the center of Gudvangen. **Pros:** great way to explore Viking history; lovely outdoor terrace; close to cruise ship dock. **Cons:** some rooms are drab; very remote location; restaurant has limited hours. $ *Rooms from: NKr 1990* ✉ *Gudvangen Fjortdell, Fv 241, Gudvangen* ☎ *48–07–55–55* 🌐 *gudvangen.com* 🛏 *30 rooms* 🍽 *Free breakfast.*

Flåm

20 km (12 miles) east of Gundvagen, 64 km (40 miles) northeast of Voss.

One of the most scenic train routes in Europe zooms high into the mountains between the towns of Myrdal and Flåm. After the day-trippers have departed, it's a wonderful place to extend your tour and spend the night. Located at the end of the Sognefjord, Norway's longest fjord, this beautiful village is an ideal base for exploring the area.

GETTING HERE AND AROUND

From Voss take the E16 heading northeast—it takes about an hour to get to Flåm. The road passes the Nærøyfjord, Norway's narrowest fjord, and one of the most spectacular. Buses also link Flåm with Voss (1 hour 15 minutes) and Bergen (3 hours).

Flåm railway station is the starting point (or terminus) of the famous Flåmsbana. Trains go to Myrdal, with connections to Voss, Geilo, Oslo, and Bergen, but you take this train for the views rather than merely for transportation.

BUS CONTACTS NOR-WAY Bussekspress. ☎ *22–31–31–50* 🌐 *www.nor-way.no.*

CRUISE SHIP TRAVEL

Ships dock directly in the harbor of Flåm, within walking distance of all the sights. The train station is a five-minute walk from the pier.

VISITOR INFORMATION

CONTACTS Visit Flåm. ✉ *A-Feltvegen 11, Flåm* ☎ *57–63–14–00* 🌐 *visitflam.com.*

Sights

★ **Flåmsbana** (*Flåm Railway*)
SCENIC DRIVE | Although this trip covers only 20 km (12 miles), the one-way journey takes nearly an hour to travel through 20 tunnels and up the 2,850 feet up the steep mountain gorge. The masterpiece of Norwegian engineering took 20 years to complete, and today it's one of Norway's prime tourist attractions, drawing more than 1 million travelers each year. The train runs year-round, with 8 to 10 round-trips from mid-April through mid-October and 4 round-trips the rest of the year. Most tourists take the train round-trip, returning on the same train a few minutes after arriving in Myrdal. ✉ *Flåm Train Station, A-Feltvegen, Flåm* ☎ *57–63–14–00* 🌐 *www.visitflam.no/flamsbana* 🎟 *NKr 590.*

Flåmsbana Museet
MUSEUM | If you have a little extra time in Flåm, make sure you visit the Flåm Railway Museum. Building the railway was a remarkable feat of engineering, and this museum details the challenges the builders faced. You'll find it in the old station building, 300 feet from the one now in use. ✉ *Stasjonsvegen 8, Flåm* ☎ *57–63–14–00* 🌐 *visitflam.com/flamsbana/flamsbana-museet* 🎟 *Free.*

Coffee and Quick Bites

Flåm Bakeri
$ | CAFÉ | FAMILY | This bakery serves up some of the best cinnamon rolls you have ever tasted, and of course the famous Norwegian *skolebolle* (buns with custard and coconut). In the summer, they move the chairs and tables outside so you can enjoy the sunshine. **Known for:** baked goods daily; unbelievable cinnamon rolls; great place for a quick bite. Ⓢ *Average main: NKr 60* ✉ *Flåm* ☎ *992–02–604* 🌐 *visitflam.com/no/restaurants/flam-bakery/.*

Restaurants

★ **Ægir Bryggeri og Pub**
$$$$ | NORWEGIAN | It started out as a straightforward microbrewery, but Ægir has been transformed into a complete culinary experience. Conveniently located near the cruise port in Flåm, its local dishes pair beautifully with the award-winning beer. **Known for:** interesting architecture; some of the region's best beer; local meats. Ⓢ *Average main: NKr 400* ✉ *A-feltvegen 23, Flåm* ☎ *57–63–20–50* 🌐 *flamsbrygga.no/aegir-bryggeripub.*

Arven
$$$ | SCANDINAVIAN | At the Fretheim Hotel, the Arven offeres dishes based on local ingredients—think mussels steamed in cider and herbs or monkfish

with seaweed—in a sophisticated and cozy atmosphere. From the second-floor windows you can enjoy beautiful views of the Aurlandsfjord and the mountains beyond. **Known for:** views of the village; locally sourced products; top-notch service. *Average main: NKr 330 ✉ Fretheim Hotel, Vikjavegen, Flåm ☎ 57–63–63–00 🌐 fretheimhotel.no/nb/mat/restaurant-arven.*

★ Flåm Marina Restaurant

$$ | INTERNATIONAL | With relaxing views of the fjord, this popular eatery serving well-prepared local fare can be found a short walk from the train station. The terrace is the perfect place in warmer weather, and locals and travelers alike find their way to the glassed-in pavilion all year. **Known for:** great views; cozy terrace; "milk shakes" for grown-ups. *Average main: NKr 250 ✉ Vikjavegen 4, Flåm ☎ 57–63–35–55 🌐 flammarina.no.*

★ Flåmstova

$$$ | NORWEGIAN | Looking for all the world like a traditional chalet, thanks to the massive beams and honey-colored wood floors, you'll feel the Scandinavian *hygge* (coziness) as soon as you walk inside. The restaurant focuses on fresh local ingredients while encouraging creativity among its chefs. **Known for:** cooks with local beer; new takes on traditional dishes; locally sourced ingredients. *Average main: NKr 285 ✉ Flåmsbrygga Hotell, A-Feltvegen 25, Flåm ☎ 57–63–20–50 🌐 flamsbrygga.no.*

Furukroa Restaurant

$$ | INTERNATIONAL | FAMILY | Occupying a traditional Nordic structure, this casual eatery is the kind of place where families head to the picnic tables on the terrace in warmer months and booths in the homey interior when it's cooler. It serve a variety of dishes, most of which are pictured on the wall. **Known for:** speedy service; wide variety of dishes; tasty soups. *Average main: NKr 150 ✉ A-Feltvegen 24 ☎ 57–63–20–50 🌐 flamsbrygga.no.*

★ Toget Cafe

$$ | INTERNATIONAL | With a name that means "The Train," this unique café lets you choose between tables in two converted train carriages or outside on the platform. For several summers in a row this casual eatery has served some of the best pizzas in the area. **Known for:** great pizza; unusual location; quick and efficient service. *Average main: NKr 180 ✉ A-Feltvegen, Flåm ☎ 57–63–14–00 🌐 visitflam.com/no/restaurants/toget-cafe ⏲ Closed Nov.–Mar.*

Hotels

Flåm Marina and Apartments

$$$ | HOTEL | On the edge of the water, these self-serviced apartments have breathtaking views of the fjord. **Pros:** great fjord views; tasty on-site restaurant. **Cons:** breakfast not included; bunk beds in the apartment; decor is a bit plain. *Rooms from: NKr 1850 ✉ Vikjavegen 4, Flåm ☎ 57–63–35–55 🌐 flammarina.no 8 apartments, 2 rooms No meals.*

Flåmsbrygga Hotel

$$$$ | HOTEL | With a wooden exterior and peaked roof that makes it look like a chalet—an extremely large chalet—this handsome lodging makes you feel right at home in no time. **Pros:** All rooms have views; delicious breakfast; central location. **Cons:** not all views are the same; very expensive rates; books up fast. *Rooms from: NKr 2600 ✉ A-Feltvegen 25, Flåm ☎ 57–63–20–50 🌐 flamsbrygga.no 41 rooms No meals.*

Fretheim Hotel

$$$$ | HOTEL | One of western Norway's most beautiful hotels, the Fretheim has a classic, timeless look thanks to its whitewashed facade topped with a tower. **Pros:** superb location; excellent food; long history. **Cons:** not all the rooms have fjord views; expensive rates; simple decor in some rooms. *Rooms from: NKr 2000 ✉ Nedre Fretheimsvegen, Flåm*

☎ 57–63–63–00 🌐 *fretheimhotel.no/en* 🛏 *122 rooms* 🍽 *Free breakfast.*

Heimly Pensjonat
$$ | **B&B/INN** | Located a little outside the center of town, this local lodging has a quiet vibe. **Pros:** affordable rates; plenty of peace and quiet; looks spiffy after a recent renovation. **Cons:** basic furnishings; not all rooms have views; not as close to the sights. 💲 *Rooms from: NKr 1000* ✉ *Vikjavegen 15, Flåm* ☎ *57–63–23–00* 🌐 *heimly.no* ⏲ *Closed Oct.–Apr.* 🛏 *22 rooms* 🍽 *Free breakfast.*

Shopping

★ Flåm Store Exclusive
GIFTS/SOUVENIRS | In Flåm Station, this souvenir store stocks one-of-a-kind gifts from around the region. It's a good place to try on the locally made Aurland shoes, called the "original penny loafer." ✉ *A-Feltvegen 11, Flåm* ☎ *57–63–14–00.*

Activities

BOATING

Fjord Cruise Nærøyfjord
BOATING | These ships have plenty of glass, ensuring that no matter the temperature you get great views of the water and the mountains on either side. Taking between 1 1/2 to 2 1/2 hours, depending on which vessel you choose, the journey takes you through the Nærøfjord, designated a UNESCO World Heritage Site. ✉ *Fjord Cruise Nærøyfjord, Flåm Pier, Flåm* ☎ *57–63–14–00* 🌐 *visitflam.com.*

FjordSafari
BOATING | **FAMILY** | Zoom past the slower fjord cruises on a 12-person boat, with the pilot also serving as your personal guide. This is a great way to get closer to nature, and is a truly unique experience. ✉ *Inner Harbour Flåm Center, Flåm* ✥ *next to Pier 1* ☎ *57–63–33–23* 🌐 *fjordsafari.com.*

DRIVING

eMobility Flåm
TOUR—SPORTS | These speedy little electric cars, with just enough room for two people, are a fun way to explore the area. Routes are already in the GPS, so there's no chance of getting lost. ✉ *Nedre Fretheim 15, Flåm* ☎ 🌐 *emobflam.no.*

KAYAKING

Njord
KAYAKING | Based on the beach in Flåm, this local company offers guided kayak tours ranging from several hours to several days. If you need to learn the ropes, they offer courses as well. ✉ *Flåm Beach, Flåm* ☎ *91–32–66–28* 🌐 *seakayaknorway.com.*

Myrdal

47 minutes from Flåm via the Flåm Railway, 47 minutes from Voss by train.

While there used to be a small mountain village here, few people actually lives in Myrdal today. This train station along the Oslo-Bergen Railway is where you connect to the Flåm Railway. It's also starting point for anyone wanting to hike the Flåm Valley.

GETTING HERE AND AROUND

Express trains between Oslo and Bergen stop in Myrdal several times a day, connecting to the Flåm Railway. By foot, Myrdal is accessible from Flåm via the Myrdalssvingane, a series of hairpin turns down the mountainside.

Sights

Myrdalssvingane
TRAIL | This impressive series of 21 hairpin turns takes you from Myrdal to Flåm. It's popular among hikers and cyclists, who are rewarded with spectacular views of the Kjosfossen Waterfall. Most of the trail is made up of gravel and rocks. To get to the trailhead, follow the train tracks out of Myrdal.

Restaurants

Cafe Rallaren
$ | **NORWEGIAN** | In Myrdal Station, Cafe Rallaren caters to travelers during the busy summer season. It serves local dishes in a diner-style atmosphere, and also offers bicycle rentals and luggage storage. **Known for:** great waffles; friendly staff; quick service. *Average main: NKr 90* *Myrdal Station* *57–63–37–56* *caferallaren.no* *Closed in the winter season.*

Rallarrosa Mountain Cheeses
$$ | **CAFÉ** | Rallarrosa is located at the end of the Flåm zipline, and is a great place for a bite after your adrenaline-infused trip. Those hiking or cycling the Flåm Valley will also pass Rallarrosa during their journey. **Known for:** goats roaming freely outside the fence; waffles with homemade goat cheese; traditional cheese from unpasteurized goat milk. *Average main: NKr 150* *Rallarrosa Stølsysteri* *Located a 2-km (1-mile) walk from Myrdal* *48–20–95–20* *rallarrosa.no* *Closed in the low season.*

Hotels

Vatnahalsen Hotel
$$$ | **HOTEL** | Along the Flåm Railway, this lodging feels like a proper alpine resort (think antlers on the wall, wooden benches for seating, and lots of colorful blankets). **Pros:** mountain views; cozy and warm atmosphere; beautiful fireplaces. **Cons:** very simple furnishings; cold rooms in the winter; needs some refurbishing. *Rooms from: NKr 1900* *Vatnahalsen Hotel, Aurland* *57–63–75–10* *vatnahalsen.no* *40 rooms* *No meals.*

Activities

ZIPLINE

★ Flåm Zipline
ZIP LINING | Scandinavia's longest zipline—nearly a mile long— takes you from the top of the Myrdalssvingane all the way down to Kårdal and Rallarrosa. It's a thrilling ride, with speeds reaching 60 miles per hour. Take the Flåm Railway to Vatnahalsen for the start of the zipline. The starting point is a two-minute walk from the end of the train platform. *Vatnahalsen Train Station, Aurland* *at the end of the trail platform* *48–20–95–20* *flaamzipline.no.*

Undredal

63 km (39 miles) northeast of Voss, 19 km (12 miles) northeast of Gundvagen.

This small village is known for two things around Norway; goats and goat cheese. The village has only around 80 inhabitants, but more than 400 goats. In the summer, many of the goats herd at Langhuso, an area you will drive through on your way to Undredal. (There are no fences, so drive slowly.) Undredal is absolutely beautiful, nestled below steep mountains along the fjord. It's a photographer's dream, and perfect if you want to unwind.

GETTING HERE AND AROUND

In the summer, boats are the only public transportation to Undredal. The fjord cruise between Flåm and Gudvangen stops in Undredal, as does the express boat from Bergen. By car, follow E16 from Bergen and Voss past Gudvangen, drive through the 11-km (7-mile) Gudvangen tunnel to Langhuso, and turn onto the E16. When driving from Oslo, Gol, and Aurland, turn right off E16 after Flåm and Flenjatunnelen.

Sights

Undredal Stavkyrkje (*Undredal Stave Church*)
RELIGIOUS SITE | This is the smallest stave church in Scandinavia, and most likely the smallest in northern Europe. (It's hard to spot from the fjord because of its size.) It dates back to the 1100s and seats barely

40 people. The church is painted white, unlike most stave churches that retain their original dark brown color. ✉ *Hjødna 14, Undredal* 🌐 *undredal-stavkyrkje.com.*

Restaurants

Osteklokke Kafe

$ | **CAFÉ** | Brown goat cheese is a Norwegian delicacy, and there is no better place to try it than at Osteklokka, whose name translates as the "cheese bell jar." On the docks in Undredal, this small café serves local dishes and cheese with stunning surroundings. **Known for:** place to sample local delicacies; stunning location by the fjord; right on the water. 💲 *Average main: NKr 100* ✉ *Undredalvegen, Undredal.*

Hotels

Undredal Gjestehus

$$$ | **RENTAL** | **FAMILY** | Run by the villagers, this small guesthouse consists of several simply furnished apartments with their own small kitchenettes. **Pros:** beautiful surroundings; close to the sights; friendly check-in. **Cons:** simple furnishings; no breakfast; not all apartments have views. 💲 *Rooms from: NKr 1800* ✉ *Undredalsvegen, Aurland* ✣ *in the center of Undredal* 🛏 *4 apartments* 🍽 *No meals.*

Aurland

12 km (7 miles) northeast of Flåm.

This village is perfectly situated along the Aurlandsfjord, just a 10-minute drive from busy Flåm. People visit for the serenity of life by the fjords, to use it as a starting point for the Aurlandsfjellet National Tourist Route, and to visit the Stegastein Viewpoint. The latter has one of the most spectacular views in Norway, allowing you to truly take in the beauty of the fjords.

GETTING HERE AND AROUND

Aurland is located just off the E16 main road, about a three-hour drive from Bergen. Aurland is also reachable by boat, and both the express boat from Bergen and the fjord cruise between Flåm and Gudvangen stop in Aurland.

Sights

Aurland Shoe Factory

STORE/MALL | The only shoe factory left in Norway, this is said to be where the first penny loafers were made. (The term "Weejuns," often used to describe this type of shoe, comes from the word Norwegians.) If you want to learn more about the history of this popular shoe, the working factory has a small museum. ✉ *Odden 13* ☎ *57–63–32–12* 🌐 *aurlands.no.*

Snow Road

SCENIC DRIVE | Route 243 from Aurland to Lærdal is nicknamed the Snow Road, as this mountain pass is closed for much of the year due to massive amounts of snow. It is one of Norway's most scenic drives in the summer. ✉ *Rte. 243* 🌐 *nasjonaleturistveger.no.*

Stegastein

VIEWPOINT | A 20-minute drive from Aurland, this scenic overlook has panoramic views of the Aurlandsfjord and all the way to Flåm. It's a rather challenging drive along a winding road, but there are also buses running here. ✉ *Bjørgavegen 83.*

Vangen Kyrkje

RELIGIOUS SITE | This beautiful stone church was built in 1202, and has since been nicknamed Sognedomen, meaning the "Sogn Cathedral." This is the largest stone church in the area, and well worth a visit. ✉ *Vangen 9.*

Restaurants

Marianne Bakeri og Kafe

$ | CAFÉ | The local bakery, named for its owner, is located beside the river in Aurland, with an outdoor seating area that is perfect on warm days. Enjoy the homemade bread and a bowl of soup here, or take an armload of pastries to go. **Known for:** delicious stuffed focaccia; cozy atmosphere; perfect meeting spot. *Average main: NKr 50 ✉ Ohnstadvegen 2A ☎ 90–51–29–78.*

★ **Vangsgaarden Gastropub**

$$ | INTERNATIONAL | The outdoor seating area boasts spectacular views of the fjord, making this eatery in the village's former bakery well worth a visit. The menu includes pub classics as well as local dishes, so you are bound to find something for the whole family. **Known for:** fish from the nearby mountain lakes; historic building; local cuisine. *Average main: NKr 250 ✉ Vangsgaarden Gjestgiveri, Nedstagata 1 ☎ 57–63–35–80 🌐 vangsgaarden.com/mat-og-drikke.*

Hotels

Vangsgaarden Hotel

$$$ | HOTEL | Staying here is like being transported back in time, as the owners have done their utmost to preserve the charm on this building dating back to the 1700s. **Pros:** beautiful gardens; well-regarded restaurant; nicely designed rooms. **Cons:** you're not guaranteed a fjord view; all rooms have twin beds; some rooms are a little far from the reception. *Rooms from: NKr 1800 ✉ Nedstagata 1 ☎ 57–63–35–80 🌐 vangsgaarden.no 18 rooms, 6 cabins Free breakfast.*

Shopping

★ **Merete Rein Glassblåsing**

CERAMICS/GLASSWARE | You can often watch local glassblower Merete Rein hard at work in her shop. She sells some unique souvenirs, all made on the premises. *✉ Aurlandsvangen 12 ☎ 47–24–62–40 🌐 reinglass.no Closed Sun.; by appointment only Jan. and Feb.*

Solvorn

78 km (48 miles) northeast of Aurland.

This picturesque village puts you close to two lovely churches, Solvorn Church and Urnes Stave Church. The latter is located just across the fjord and can be reached by ferry.

GETTING HERE AND AROUND

No matter what direction you're coming from, you're like to require a ferry to reach Solvorn. Driving from the east, take the ferry from Ornes directly to Solvorn. From the south, take the Fodnes-Mannheller ferry, then follow Route 5 to Sogndal and Route 55 and Route 338 towards Solvorn.

Sights

Solvorn Kyrkje (*Solvorn Church*)

RELIGIOUS SITE | Built in 1883, this beautiful white wooden church has an impressive spire. It's the first thing you see when approaching Solvorn. *✉ Løteigane 8, Solvorn.*

Urnes Stavkyrkje (*Urnes Stave Church*)

RELIGIOUS SITE | In the village of Ornes, this beautiful stave church is one of the oldest in the area. It's believed to have been completed in 1132 (although some say 1140). Take the ferry to get here. *✉ Fv 331, Solvorn 🌐 www.stavechurch.com/urnes-stave-church.*

Restaurants

Bryggehuset Solvorn

$$ | CAFÉ | FAMILY | This friendly gathering spot in the corner of a wooden building has a scattering of tables on the terrace for when the sun is shining. It serve lighter fare for lunch, and adds some

heartier dishes to the menu later in the afternoon. **Known for:** lively atmosphere; affordable dishes; great burgers. *$ Average main: NKr 129 ✉ Solvornvegen 314, Solvorn ☎ 91–72–17–19 🌐 bryggehuset.no ⏲ Closed Mon. and Tues.*

Hotels

Villa Solvorn

$$$ | B&B/INN | FAMILY | Despite being in the middle of Solvorn, this family-run guesthouse feels like it's somewhere in the countryside. **Pros:** picturesque building; friendly owners; beautifully decorated. **Cons:** shared bathrooms; some rooms are very small; family's cat isn't great for allergy sufferers. *$ Rooms from: NKr 1500 ✉ Solvornvegen 310, Solvorn ☎ 99–29–66–72 🌐 villasolvorn.com 6 rooms Free breakfast.*

★ Walaker Hotel

$$$$ | HOTEL | Norway's oldest hotel dating back to 1690, this longtime favorite has been run by the Walaker family for nine generations. **Pros:** proud of its history; garden is beautiful in summer; wonderful restaurant. **Cons:** modern rooms not as nice; not all rooms have bathtubs; annex not as charming. *$ Rooms from: NKr 3200 ✉ Fv 338, Solvorn ☎ 57–68–20–80 🌐 walaker.com 25 rooms Free breakfast.*

Balestrand

78 km (48 miles) west of Solvorn.

One of the most picturesque villages along the Sognefjord, Balestrand has been a haven for painters and artists for more than a century because of its old wooden houses. Beside the larger fjord, three smaller arms stretch farther inland, making this a destination for all types of outdoors enthusiasts.

GETTING HERE AND AROUND

Balestrand is easily reachable by boat or car. When driving from Bergen, Voss, or Vik, take the car ferry from Vangsnes to Dragsvik and then follow Route 55 to Balestrand. From Oslo and Sogndal, take the car ferry from Hella to Dragsvik before continuing on Route 55. The express boat from Bergen stops in Balestrand.

Sights

Nature Trail Kreklingen

TRAIL | FAMILY | Suitable for families and experienced hikers alike, this trail takes between two and four hours, depending on which particular trail you choose. Along the way there is information about the local flora and fauna, and from the highest point you get a nice view of the village. *✉ Kreklingevegen 3-5, Balestrand.*

St. Olaf's Church

RELIGIOUS SITE | Also called the English Church, this Anglican house of worship was the dream of Margaret Sophia Green. The daughter of an English minister who married a local man, she spoke on her death bed about her vision of an English church in the village. Built in a stave church style, it was completed in 1897. *✉ Kong Beles Veg 35, Balestrand.*

Utsikten

VIEWPOINT | This famous viewpoint is a 40-minute drive from Balestrand, on Gaularfjellet. The viewing platform offers spectacular views of the valley and mountains surrounding it, in addition to the impressive hairpin turns below. *✉ Rv 13, Balestrand ✣ follow signs for Gaularfjellet Tourist Rte. 🌐 www.nasjonaleturistveger.no/en/routes/gaularfjellet?attraction=utsikten.*

Restaurants

Ciderhuset

$$ | MEDITERRANEAN | This place makes its own cider and expertly pairs it with creative Norwegian and Mediterranean dishes. Dry cider and herbs from the garden fill the soups, while fruit from the garden finds its way into the desserts. Join a cider tasting and learn how they make sparkling cider using traditional methods. **Known for:** region's best cider; uses local ingredients; creative cooking. *$ Average main: NKr 170 ✉ Sjøtunsvegen 32, Balestrand ☎ 90–83–56–73 ⊕ ciderhuset.no ⏲ Closed weekdays and Sun. and Sept.–May.*

Hotels

★ Kviknes Hotel

$$$ | **HOTEL** | Kings, presidents, and movie stars have stayed at this historic hotel known for its unforgettable views of the Sognefjord. **Pros:** stunning historic hotel; breathtaking scenery; beautiful decor. **Cons:** not all rooms have fjord views; can be expensive; books up early. *$ Rooms from: NKr 1600 ✉ Kviknevegen 8, Balestrand ☎ 57–69–42–00 ⊕ kviknes.no 190 rooms Free breakfast.*

Fjærland

54 km (34 miles) northwest of Solvorn.

Fjærland is known for its proximity to the Jostedal Glacier, as well as its beautiful green fjord. The color is due to the melting glaciers nearby, and it gives the water a serene look you won't find anywhere else.

GETTING HERE AND AROUND

From Olden it's 62 km (37 miles) south to Skei, at the base of Lake Jølster, where Route 5 goes under the glacier for more than 6 km (4 miles) of the journey to Fjærland. In the summer months there are express boats running from Flåm and Balestrand to Fjærland, in addition to a "glacier bus" traveling from Fjærland to the Jostedal Glacier.

Sights

Fjærland Kyrkje (*Fjærland Church*)

RELIGIOUS SITE | This beautiful wooden church, painted a deep shade of red, dates back to 1861. It's a popular photo stop because of the snow-covered mountain peaks in the background. *✉ Mundalsvegen 6, Mundal.*

Jostedal Glacier

SCENIC DRIVE | Covering the mountains between the Sognefjord and Nordfjord, Jostedal Glacier is the largest in Europe. Unlike many around the world, it has actually grown in recent years due to increased snowfall. There are about 100 known routes for crossing Jostedal Glacier: if you want to hike it, you must have a qualified guide. Contact the Jostedalsbreen Glacier National Park Center. Getting to Jostedalsbreen Glacier is easiest by car: from Solvorn, head north on Route 55 to Route 604. Glacier Express buses run in the summer months. *✉ Breheimssenteret ☎ 57–68–32–50 ⊕ jostedal.com ⏲ Glacier Centre closed Oct.–Apr.*

★ Norsk Bremuseum (*Norwegian Glacier Museum*)

MUSEUM | One of Norway's most innovative museums, the Norsk Bremuseum lets you study glaciers up close by conducting experiments with thousand-year-old glacial ice. Take the time to watch Ivo Caprino's unforgettable film of the Jostedal Glacier. *✉ Fjærlandsfjorden 13, Mundal ☎ 57–63–32–88 ⊕ bre.museum.no NKr 130 ⏲ Closed Nov.–Mar.*

Restaurants

Kaffistova

$ | **NORWEGIAN** | **FAMILY** | Part of the Norwegian Book Town, Kaffistova draws travelers from all over the world who want to grab a coffee and a light bite while having a read. **Known for:** a favorite of book lovers; rustic charm; great coffee. *$ Average main: NKr 60 ✉ Den norske*

A river running through the Jostedal Glacier, the centerpiece of sprawling Jostedalsbreen Glacier National Park

bokbyen, Fv 152 Across the street from the tourist information 57–69–22–10 bokbyen.no Closed Oct.–May.

Mikkel

$ | CAFÉ | FAMILY | In the same building as Hotel Mundal, this café serves light snacks throughout the day. It has a charming interior, including an interesting map of routes through the area. **Known for:** homemade soups; great place to stock up on snacks; simple yet charming decor. *Average main: NKr 90 Hotel Mundal, Fv 152, Mundal 91–90–99–90 hotelmundal.no/no/mat.*

Hotels

Fjærland Fjordstove

$$$ | HOTEL | Sitting beside the fjord, this charming boutique hotel is a little like stepping back in time. **Pros:** historic building; the best service; unique rooms. **Cons:** no elevator; very narrow stairs; simple furnishings. *Rooms from: NKr 1800 Fjærland Fjordstove, Fv152, Mundal 41–00–02–00 fjaerlandhotel.com Closed Oct.–Mar. 14 rooms Free breakfast.*

Mundal Hotel

$$$ | HOTEL | Artists, mountaineers, and travelers first began coming to this region in the late 1800s, many of them destined for this majestic yellow-and-white hotel. **Pros:** beautiful historic building; lovingly restored; great location on the fjord. **Cons:** some bathrooms are dated; restaurant fills up with large groups; books up fast. *Rooms from: NKr 1900 Hotel Mundal, Fv 152, Mundal 91–90–99–90 hotelmundal.no 35 rooms No meals.*

Shopping

★ Den Norske Bokbyen

ANTIQUES/COLLECTIBLES | Even if you can't read Norwegian, you may still be fascinated by Den Norske Bokbyen. If you look around, you may find some titles in English. In the warmer months, Norwegian Book Town has 150,000 used books, magazines, and records for sale in buildings around town, and even in little huts along the fjord. ✉ *Den Norske Bokbyen, Fv 152* ☎ *57–69–22–10* 🌐 *bokbyen.no.*

Vik

26 km (16 miles) south of Balestrand, 58 km (42 miles) north of Voss, 170 km (105 miles northeast) northeast of Bergen.

This municipality along the Sognefjord is known for its three beautiful churches. The nearby river is a popular destination for anyone hoping to hook a salmon, and there are several great hikes in the area. Most of all, travelers add Vik to their itineraries for the breathtaking scenery.

GETTING HERE AND AROUND

It takes a little over an hour to drive from Toss to Vik along Route 13, although in winter you should check for road closures. From Sogndal and Balestrand, the most direct route includes a ferry ride across the fjord. From Bergen, an express boat operates in the summer months.

Sights

Hopperstad Stavkyrkje (*Hopperstad Stave Church*)
RELIGIOUS SITE | This beautiful house of worship stands on its original foundation from around 1130. Visitors in the summer months can join a guided tour around the interior and learn about how it has changed throughout the centuries. ✉ *Hopperstadvegen 61, Vik* ☎ *57–69–52–70* 🌐 *stavechurch.com/hopperstad-stavkirke* 🎫 *NKr 70* ⏲ *Closed Oct.–May.*

Hove Steinkyrkje (*Hove Stone Church*)
RELIGIOUS SITE | Dating back to the Middle Ages, this parish church is a prime example of Roman architecture. It was built in 1170, and Peter Andreas Blix, who restored it in the late 1800s, is buried below the nave. The church has a capacity of only 35 people. ✉ *Hovevegen, Vik* ☎ *57–67–88–40* 🎫 *NKr 50* ⏲ *Closed mid-Aug.–late June.*

Skredstova (*Avalanche House*)
MUSEUM | This miniature museum is dedicated to the landslide (or skred) that devastated Vik in 1811. It killed 45 people, a large percentage of the population at the time. Although it's tiny, the museum in a one-room log cabin is surprisingly informative. ✉ *Rte. 92* ✥ *between Vik and Arnafjord* 🌐 *www.visitnorway.com/listings/skredstova-the-avalanche-house/12246/* 🎫 *Free.*

Hotels

Blix Hotel
$$ | **HOTEL** | In the center of the city, this mid-century-modern hotel is named after engineer and architect Peter Andreas Blix, who used his own money and resources to restore two local gems: Hove Stone Church and Hopperstad Stave Church. **Pros:** centrally located; good restaurant; serves a great breakfast. **Cons:** old-fashioned decor; expensive rates; some small bathrooms. $ *Rooms from: NKr 1250* ✉ *Vikøyri, Vik* ☎ *57–69–65–50* 🌐 *blizhotell.no* *27 rooms* 🍽 *Free breakfast.*

Olden

91 km (57 miles) northwest of Fjærland.

At the eastern end of Nordfjord, Olden was among the first travel destinations in the region. The first were English fishermen who came in search of salmon in the 1860s. By the end of the 19th century, more and more hotels were springing up in the region.

The most famous attraction in the area is the Briksdal Glacier, an arm of the Jostedal Glacier. It's about 20 km (12 miles) south of Olden, and can be visited by car, by bicycle, or on foot from April to October.

GETTING HERE AND AROUND

If you're driving, Olden is accessible by following Route 60 from Stryn and Loen.

TOURS

Troll Shuttle

A popular (and fun) way to explore the glacier is hopping aboard these open-air cars that take you there and back in 90 minutes. Dress warmly, as it can get cold during the drive. This trips run from May to October, and advance reservations are recommended. ✉ *Briksdalbre, Briksdalsbreen* ✣ *tours depart from the souvenir shop parking lot* ☎ *57–87–68–05* 🌐 *oldedalenskysslag.com.*

Briksdal Glacier

NATIONAL/STATE PARK | Many of the Jostedal Glacier's smaller arms are tourist attractions in their own right. The best known of them, Briksdal Glacier, lies at the end of Oldedal Valley, about 20 km (12 miles) south of Olden. It can be visited by bicycle, by car, or on foot from April to October. From Olden, the Brebussen takes you to the glacier. ✉ *Briksdalsbre Fjellstove, Briksdalsbreen* ☎ *57–87–68–00* 🌐 *briksdalsbre.no.*

Olden Gamle Kyrkje (*Olden Old Church*)

RELIGIOUS SITE | Olden Old Church dates back to the 1700s, where a stave church once sat on the same spot. The pretty white structure was originally owned by a merchant, and the village didn't buy it until the late 1800s. ✉ *Fv 724 169, Olden.*

Mølla Gjestehus

$$ | **NORWEGIAN** | **FAMILY** | If you want a friendly atmosphere and superb local dishes, this is a great choice. Mølla is located in a handsome building on the dock in Olden, and you can't miss the tall red letters spelling out the name. **Known for:** fresh fish from the area; waterfront location; lively staff. [$] *Average main: NKr 200* ✉ *Rv60 19, Olden* ☎ *90–13–83–08* 🌐 *briksdaladventure.com* ⏲ *Closed Sun.–Thurs.*

Olden Fjordhotel

$$$ | **HOTEL** | **FAMILY** | Close to the cruise ship terminal, this modern hotel has simple, comfortable rooms with balconies overlooking the fjord. **Pros:** larger family rooms; very friendly staff; good restaurant. **Cons:** not all rooms have balconies; not much in the way of decor; plain rooms. [$] *Rooms from: NKr 1450* ✉ *Solstrandvegen 1, Olden* ☎ *57–87–04–00* 🌐 *olden-hotel.no* *60 rooms* *Free breakfast.*

Briksdalsbre Mountain Lodge

HIKING/WALKING | Hiking to the glacier is one of the best ways to experience it. The hike starts at Briksdalsbre Mountain Lodge and is about 3 km (2 miles) in total. The hike takes around one hour each way. ✉ *Briksdalsbre Fjellstove AS, 6792 Briksdalsbre* ☎ *57–87–68–00* 🌐 *briksdalsbre.no.*

Loen

6 km (4 miles) north of Olden.

Thanks to its location near the Briksdal Glacier, Loen is a short drive from some of Norway's most spectacular hikes. It also has an unbeatable location on the eastern edge of the fjord.

GETTING HERE AND AROUND

Loen is less than a 10-minute drive from Olden along Route 60.

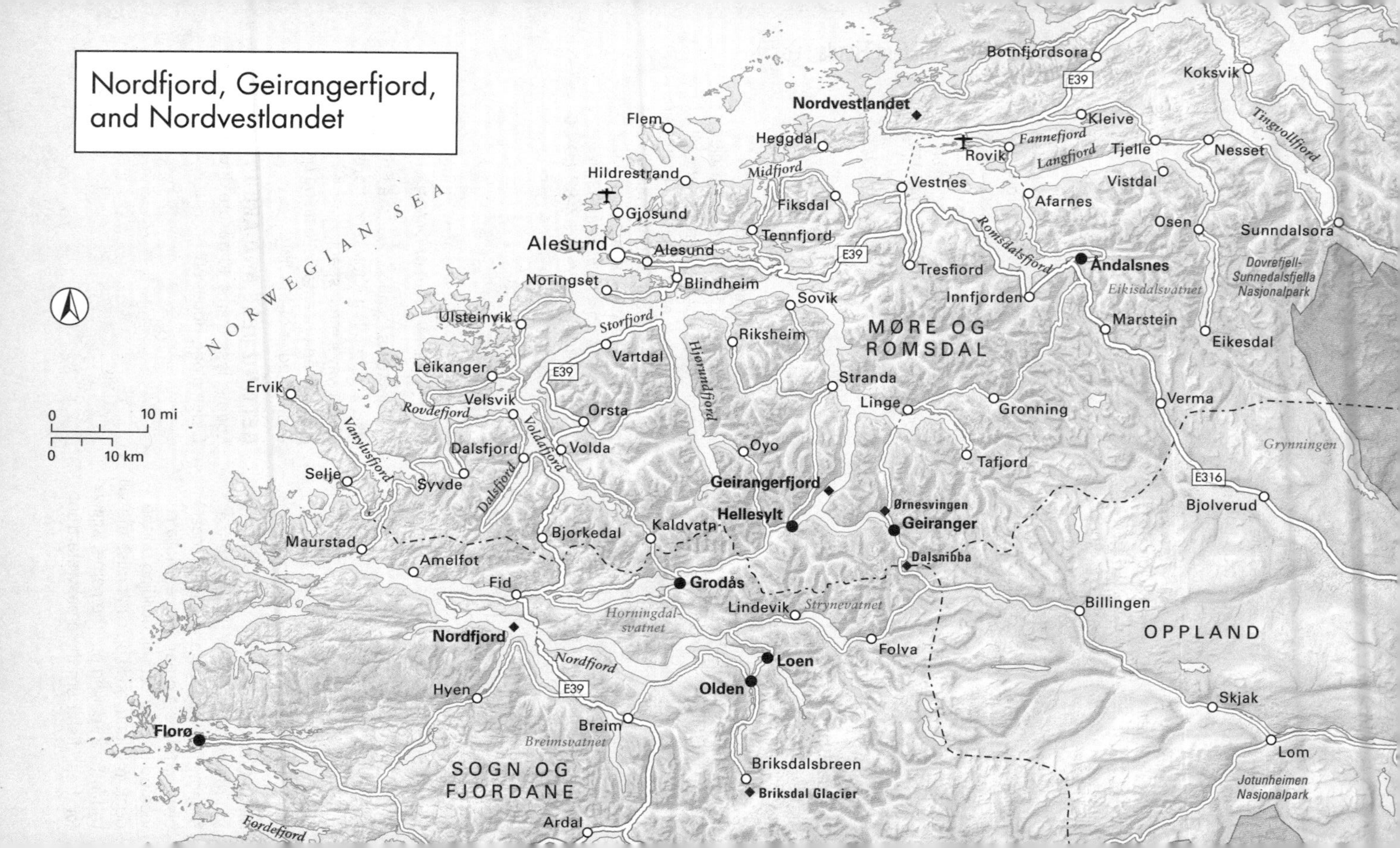

Nordfjord, Geirangerfjord, and Nordvestlandet
NORWEGIAN SEA
0
10 mi
0
10 km
Botnfjordsora
Koksvik
E39
Nordvestlandet
Kleive
Tingvollfjord
Flem
Heggdal
Rovik
Fannefjord
Langfjord
Tjelle
Nesset
Hildrestrand
Midfjord
Vestnes
Vistdal
Fiksdal
Afarnes
Gjosund
Osen
Sunndalsora
Tennfjord
Romsdalsfjord
Alesund
Alesund
E39
Tresfiord
Åndalsnes
Noringset
Blindheim
Dovrefjell-Sunnedalsfjella Nasjonalpark
Eikisdalsvatnet
Sovik
Innfjorden
Ulsteinvik
Storfjord
MØRE OG ROMSDAL
Marstein
Riksheim
Eikesdal
Vartdal
Hjørundfjord
Leikanger
E39
Stranda
Ervik
Linge
Gronning
Verma
Velsvik
Rovdefjord
Orsta
Voldafjord
Dalsfjord
Volda
Oyo
Tafjord
Grynningen
Selje
Vanylvsfjord
Syvde
Geirangerfjord
E316
Dalsfjord
Ørnesvingen
Bjolverud
Hellesylt
Geiranger
Kaldvatn
Maurstad
Bjorkedal
Dalsnibba
Amelfot
Fid
Grodås
Billingen
Lindevik
Strynevatnet
Horningdalsvatnet
OPPLAND
Nordfjord
Folva
Nordfjord
Loen
Hyen
E39
Olden
Skjak
Breim
Florø
Breimsvatnet
Lom
Briksdalsbreen
SOGN OG FJORDANE
Briksdal Glacier
Jotunheimen Nasjonalpark
Ardal
Fordefjord

Sights

★ Loen Skylift

VIEWPOINT | This cable car whisks you to the top of Hoven Mountain, offering spectacular views of the fjord. Some people prefer to take the cable car up and walk back down the mountain. At the top there is a viewpoint and a restaurant. ✉ *Loen Skylift, Fv 60, Loen* ☎ *57–87–59–00* 🌐 *loenskylift.com* 🎫 *NKr 520* ⏲ *Closed Mon.–Thurs. Nov. and Jan.*

Lovatnet

BODY OF WATER | This beautiful lake is worth a visit for the photo ops alone. Some say it's the most beautiful lake in Norway, with its brilliant green color coming from the melting glacier water. ✉ *Lovatnet, Fv 723.*

Restaurants

★ Hoven Restaurant

$$$ | SCANDINAVIAN | At the top of Loen Skylift, this strikingly modern restaurant is perched off the edge of a cliff. One one side of the dining room is an entire wall of glass, so every table has a spectacular view. **Known for:** delicious traditional foods; a grill is open for summer lunches; rooftop café serves light fare. 💲 *Average main: NKr 255* ✉ *Hoven Restaurant* ☎ *57–87–59–00* 🌐 *loenskylift.com* ⏲ *Closed Mon.–Thurs. Nov. and Jan.*

Kjenndalstova

$$ | NORWEGIAN | This region's best-kept secret, this little red house perched at the water's edge serves up delicious traditional dishes. Close to a pristine glacier, towering mountains, cascading waterfalls, and a shimmering lake, the scenery makes a visit to this laid-back eatery well worthwhile. **Known for:** fresh trout; homemade dishes; lovely views. 💲 *Average main: NKr 220* ✉ *Kjenndalstova, Hogrenning, Loen* ☎ *91–84–87–67* 🌐 *kjenndalstova.no* ⏲ *Closed Sept.–Apr.*

Hotels

Hotel Alexandra

$$$$ | HOTEL | Originally built in 1884, this longtime favorite has been transformed into a modern luxury hotel made of stone and oak. **Pros:** relaxing spa area; beautiful grounds; views are astounding. **Cons:** very expensive rates; pool can get crowded; affordable rooms book up early. 💲 *Rooms from: NKr 3500* ✉ *Loen* ☎ *57–87–50–00* 🌐 *alexandra.no* 🛏 *343 rooms* 🍽 *No meals.*

Grodås

33 km (21 miles) west of Loen.

A tiny village at the water's edge, Grodås sits on the deepest lake in northern Europe. It's known for its stunning views and great hikes among the mountain peaks. This is home of the Hornindal Rundt, the country's toughest mountain race.

GETTING HERE AND AROUND

The E39 goes straight through Grodås and Hornindal.

Restaurants

Dølen Eteri

$$ | INTERNATIONAL | This restaurant's unusual name comes from the steamship *Dølen*, which used to chug along the Hornindalsvatnet between 1880 and 1950. With a rustic feel, it serves dishes made with local produce. **Known for:** delicious chocolate; top-quality ingredients; homemade pastries. 💲 *Average main: NKr 250* ✉ *Havila Hotel Raftevold, Sanden 27, Grodås* ☎ *57–87–99–99* 🌐 *havilahotelraftevold.no/mat-og-drikke.*

Hotels

Havila Hotel Raftevold

$$ | HOTEL | FAMILY | The Havila Hotel Raftevold has been welcoming guests since 1867, which is evident from the warm welcome you get from the minute you walk in the door. **Pros:** great service; private balconies; waterfront location. **Cons:** small sink in bathrooms; some rooms are noisy; not much variety in the breakfast. *Rooms from: NKr 1200 ✉ Sanden 27, Grodås ☎ 57–87–99–99 🌐 havilahotelraftevold.no 44 rooms Free breakfast.*

Hellesylt

28 km (17 miles) northeast of Grodås, 75 minutes by ferry west of Geiranger.

People have been trekking through Hellesylt since the end of the last ice age, but tourists began staying overnight only in 1875, when the village's first hotel was built. There's not that much to do in the village itself besides look at the waterfall, oddly wedged between two bridges.

GETTING HERE AND AROUND

Most travelers visit Hellesylt because this is where the fjord cruises end. If you're traveling by car, Hellesylt is reached via Route 60.

Sights

Hellesyltfossen

BODY OF WATER | In the center of Hellesylt, this waterfall is the main sight in the village. It is wedged between two bridges: Høge Bro and Hellesylt Bro, both from the early 1900s. *✉ Fv 60, Hellesylt.*

Peer Gynt Galleriet (*Peer Gynt Gallery*)

MUSEUM | FAMILY | Playwright Henrik Ibsen is said to have been inspired by the natural beauty around Hellesylt, and the main exhibit in this gallery contains wooden carvings inspired by his play *Peer Gynt. ✉ Peer Gynt Galleriet, Hellesylt ☎ 95–01–31–70 🌐 peergyntgalleriet.no.*

Sunnylven Kirke

RELIGIOUS SITE | Near the Hellesyltfossen, this church is said to have been visited by Henrik Ibsen during his trip to Hellesylt in 1862. The white wooden structure was completed in 1859. *✉ Hellesylt ⏲ Closed Sept.–June.*

Restaurants

Hellesylt Boutique and Bar

$ | CAFÉ | This cozy bookshop and café serves homemade baked goods, great coffee, and local beer. You'll find yourself surrounded by interesting books and some lovely antiques, much of it for sale. **Known for:** coffee and tea for take-out; local ice cream; charming atmosphere. *Average main: NKr 40 ✉ Gatå 29, Hellesylt ☎ 40–51–65–35.*

Øcal Restaurant

$$ | INTERNATIONAL | Looking spiffy after a renovation, this eatery offers a variety of local and international fare. They've been making the best pizza in town for decades. **Known for:** vintage photos of the region; central location; family fare. *Average main: NKr 180 ✉ Øcal Restaurant, Fv 60, Hellesylt.*

Geiranger

85 km (52½ miles) southwest of Åndalsnes, 86 km (53 miles) northeast of Loen, 75 minutes by ferry east of Hellesylt.

The village of Geiranger, at the end of the fjord, is home to fewer than 300 year-round residents, but in spring and summer its population swells to 5,000 due to visitors traveling here to see the famous Geirangerfjord. In winter, snow on the mountain roads makes the village isolated.

GETTING HERE AND AROUND

The best way to take in the area's spectacular scenery is to travel by boat or ferry. The ferry between Geiranger and Hellesylt runs frequently in summer and offers stupendous views of Geirangerfjord's mighty waterfalls.

By car, the most scenic route to Geiranger from Åndalsnes is the two-hour drive along Route 63 over Trollstigen (Troll's Ladder). After that, the Ørneveien (Eagles' Road) to Geiranger, which has 11 hairpin turns, leads to the fjord.

TOURS

★ eMobility

TOUR—SIGHT | A fun way of exploring the area, eMobility lets you take small electric vehicles around preset routes with GPS to guide you. Each car has (just enough) space for two people. ✉ *Geirangervegen 2, Geirangerfjord* ☎ *45–50–02–22* 🌐 *emobgeiranger.no.*

Sights

Dalsnibba

VIEWPOINT | Europe's highest roadside viewpoint, Dalsnibba lets you look straight down at the village of Geiranger, as well as the famous Geirangerfjord. ✉ *Dalsnibba Utsiktspunkt, Nibbevegen* ✣ *Follow Nibbevegen from Geiranger for about 30 mins* ☎ *45–48–13–01* 🌐 *dalsnibba.no.*

Flydalsjuvet

VIEWPOINT | One of the best-known photo ops in Norway, this dramatic mountain plateau has two viewing platforms that put you high above Geiranger. The breathtaking views from Flydalsjuvet are well worth the trip. ✉ *Flydalsjuvet, Geirangerfjord* ✣ *Drive approximately 4 km (2 1/2 miles) from the center of Geiranger, towards Grotli* ☎ *70–26–30–09* 🌐 *www.visitnorway.com/listings/flydalsjuvet/5904.*

Geiranger Kyrkje (*Geiranger Church*)

RELIGIOUS SITE | This church is interesting (and quite peculiar) because of its octagonal shape. Designed by architect Hans Klipe, the wooden church dating from 1842 is the third to have stood on this spot. It's especially beautiful because of the backdrop of the fjords. ✉ *Geiranger Kirke, Geirangerfjord.*

★ Norsk Fjordsenter (*Norwegian Fjord Centre*)

COLLEGE | An invaluable introduction to the Geirangerfjord UNESCO World Heritage Site, this excellent contemporary museum expounds on the area's natural and cultural history, its flora and fauna, and latest technologies effecting the environment, from hydroelectric power to landslide control. Walk through the old farm buildings and learn about the old villages of the Geiranger region. Multimedia exhibits, a café, and bookshop make this a fun and interesting hour for the whole family. ✉ *Gjørvahaugen 35, Geiranger* ☎ *70–26–38–10* 🌐 *fjordsenter.com* 🎟 *NKr 130.*

Ørnesvingen

VIEWPOINT | At the end of a dramatic route with 11 hairpin turns called the Ørnevegen, or Eagle Road, Ørnesvingen gives you breathtaking views of Geiranger. One of the first viewpoints in the area, it's still one of the most impressive. ✉ *Fv 63 27, Geirangerfjord* ☎ *70–26–30–99.*

Westerås Gard (*Westerås Farm*)

FARM/RANCH | One of three working farms left in Geiranger, Westerås Farm is located just a few miles from the village. The farm itself is beautifully situated along the hillside above the fjord and offers stunning views. There is a simple restaurant in the barn where you can have a bite during your visit, and you can also pick up some local produce. ✉ *Geirangervegen 320, Geirangerfjord* ☎ *92–64–95–37* 🌐 *hanen.no/bedrift/625* ⏲ *Closed Oct.–Apr.*

Restaurants

★ Brasserie Posten

$$$ | **MODERN EUROPEAN** | Being one of the best restaurants in Geiranger may not seem such a feat (there's only a handful), but this place distinguishes itself with a stunning fjordside setting and excellent, no-nonsense cuisine that capitalizes on the area's abundant fresh, local seafood, artisanal cheeses, wild game, and produce, not to mention a huge selection of local beers. **Known for:** lovely terrace for summertime dining; great view of the fjord; central location. *Average main: NKr 300* ✉ *Geirangervegen 4, Geiranger* ☎ *70–26–13–06* 🌐 *brasserieposten.no* *Closed Nov.–Mar.*

★ Olebuda and Cafe Ole

$$$ | **MODERN EUROPEAN** | In a picturesque white clapboard house that was Geiranger's first grocery store, this restaurant is a popular choice for sophisticated, modern fare. A bright, cozy dining room on the second floor focuses on small plates with an emphasis on local veggies, seafood, and meats: wild poached salmon with parsley butter, scallops, and cauliflower purée; venison medallions with bacon and buttered beets. **Known for:** downstairs café is popular with families; homemade desserts; good coffee and pastries. *Average main: NKr 325* ✉ *Gjørvahaugen, Geiranger* ☎ *70–26–32–30* 🌐 *olebuda.no* *Restaurant closed Sept.–May. Café closed Oct.–Apr.*

Restaurant Julie

$$ | **NORWEGIAN** | If you are looking for a friendly atmosphere and a menu based on regional favorites, this is the restaurant for you. Expect original dishes with a traditional touch and great views of the Geirangerfjord. **Known for:** excellent brasserie menu; waterfront views; laid-back atmosphere. *Average main: NKr 230* ✉ *Hotel Union, Geirangervegen 101, Geiranger* ☎ *70–26–83–00* 🌐 *hotelunion.no.*

Hotels

Grande Fjord Hotel

$$$$ | **HOTEL** | **FAMILY** | The hotel's majestic setting on the cliffs overlooking the Geiranger fjord assures stunning views from almost every room. **Pros:** good hiking on the grounds; free coffee, tea, and hot chocolate; free parking. **Cons:** sporadic Wi-Fi; it's a trek up to the hotel; not all rooms face the fjord. *Rooms from: NKr 2200* ✉ *Ørnevegen 200, Geiranger* ☎ *70–26–94–90* 🌐 *grandefjordhotel.com* *48 rooms* *Free breakfast.*

Hotel Union Geiranger

$$$$ | **HOTEL** | **FAMILY** | The largest hotel in the area, Hotel Union is Geiranger's closest thing to a luxury hotel. **Pros:** excellent buffet breakfast; fun classic car museum; free parking. **Cons:** pool can get crowded in summer; dining room can get uncomfortably packed; some rooms are a bit dated. *Rooms from: NKr 1980* ✉ *Geirangervegen 101, Geiranger* ☎ *70–26–83–00* 🌐 *hotelunion.no* *197 rooms* *Free breakfast.*

Nightlife

The Lobby Bar

BARS/PUBS | Hotel Union's huge lobby bar is a comfortable place to start your evening in an overstuffed sofa or at the bar admiring panoramic views of the fjord. Downstairs, the Vognfabrikken Bar, set among the hotel's collection of vintage cars, has an atmosphere all its own. ✉ *Hotel Union Geiranger, Geirangervegen 101, Geiranger* ☎ *70–26–83–00* 🌐 *hotelunion.no/fasilitetar.*

Shopping

Geiranger Gallery

ART GALLERIES | Located in a historic school at the heart of Geiranger, the gallery features three floors hung floor-to-ceiling with the work of local artists, artisans, and craftspeople. There's everything from ceramics and glass to paintings and tapestries. ✉ *Maråkvegen 24, Geiranger* ⏲ *Closed Oct.–Apr.*

Activities

BOATING

Fjord Cruise Geiranger

BOATING | This classic car ferry takes you on a one-hour fjord cruise through the Geirangerfjord. Car spaces are limited, especially in the high season, so book in advance. ✉ *Geiranger ferjekai, Geiranger* ✥ *The cruise leaves from the pier in Geiranger* ☎ *57–63–14–00* 🌐 *visitflam.com/no/activities/fjord-cruise-geirangerfjord.*

★ Geirangerfjord Safari

BOATING | This fast-paced boat tour allows you to get closer to the famous waterfalls of the Geirangerfjord than with any other tour. The pilot is also your guide on this adventure, and it is fun and thrilling to speed along the fjord. ✉ *Geiranger Fjordservice, Fv 63, Geiranger* ✥ *tours meet at tourist information office in Geiranger* ☎ *70–26–30–07* 🌐 *geirangerfjord.no.*

Åndalsnes

105 km (53 miles) northwest of Dombås.

Novelist Jo Nesbø's book *The Bat* says that when God created the world, he started with Åndalsnes. He spent so long crafting the scenery that he had to rush everything else in order to finish by Sunday. Åndalsnes truly is a beautiful area, nicknamed "the Mountain Peak Capital" by Norwegians. Here you'll find dramatic, snow-covered behemoths that will take your breath away.

Åndalsnes is the last stop on the railway, making it a great gateway to fjord country. Here you'll also find the Trollstigen (Troll Ladder), a serpentine roadway through the mountains, and the Trollveggen (Troll Wall), Europe's highest vertical rock face and the birthplace of rock climbing in Scandinavia.

GETTING HERE AND AROUND

Molde Airport is a 90-minute drive from Åndalsnes and has daily flights from Oslo, Bergen, and Trondheim. There are also buses running daily from Bergen and Trondheim to Åndalsnes. The Raumabanen train gets you from Oslo to Åndalsnes in approximately 5 1/2 hours.

If you're driving to Åndalsnes, follow E136 through Romsdalen Valley.

Sights

★ Norsk Tindemuseum (*The Norwegian Mountaineering Museum*)

MUSEUM | One of Norway's most famous mountaineers, Arne Randers Heen (1905–91), and his wife, Bodil Roland, founded this fascinating museum dedicated to mountain climbing. Displays of Heen's equipment and descriptions of his many triumphs are among the highlights here. The mountain nearest to his heart was Romsdalshorn, rising 5,101 feet into the air. He climbed that mountain 233 times, the last time when he was 85. He was the first to reach the top of several other mountains in northern Norway. ✉ *Norsk Tindemuseum, Havnegata 2, Åndalsnes* ☎ *73–60–45–57* 🌐 *tindemuseet.no* 🎫 *NKr 160.*

Trollstigen

SCENIC DRIVE | Norway's most popular scenic drive is in Åndalsnes. Starting in 1916, Trollstigen took 100 men 20 summers to build, and they constantly struggled against the forces of rock and water. Often described as a masterpiece of construction, the road snakes its way through 11 hairpin curves up the mountain to the peaks named Bispen (the Bishop), Kongen (the King), and Dronningen (the Queen). The road is only open in summer. ✉ *Trollstigen, Åndalsnes.*

Restaurants

Trollstigen Kafe

$ | **CAFÉ** | After navigating the hairpin turns of the Trollstigen, reward yourself with a stop at this café. Here you can expect an exciting menu of local dishes and spectacular views of road you just conquered. **Known for:** wide-open views; a variety of quick bites; next to a shop where you can stock up on supplies. *Average main: NKr 120* *Trollstigen, Åndalsnes* *trollstigen.no.*

Hotels

Grand Hotel Bellevue

$$$ | **HOTEL** | Travelers often begin their exploration of the region by basing themselves at this handsome hotel in the center of Åndalsnes. **Pros:** bright and beautiful rooms; close location to Trollstigen; great on-site restaurant. **Cons:** expensive rates; small lobby; so-so breakfast. *Rooms from: NKr 1695* *Åndalgata 5, Åndalsnes* *71–22–75–00* *grandhotel.no* *86 rooms* *Free breakfast.*

Ålesund

116 km (72 miles) west of Åndalsnes.

On three islands and between two brilliant blue fjords lies Ålesund, one of Norway's largest harbors for exporting dried and fresh fish. About two-thirds of its 1,040 wooden houses were destroyed by a fire in 1904. In the rush to shelter 10,000 people, Germany's Kaiser Wilhelm II, who often vacationed here, led a swift rebuilding that married Art Nouveau design with Viking flourishes. Winding streets are crammed with buildings topped with turrets, spires, gables, dragon heads, and curlicues. Today it's considered one of the few Art Nouveau cities in the world. Inquire at the tourism office for one of the insightful walking tours.

GETTING HERE AND AROUND

Vigra Airport is 15 km (9 miles) from the center of town. An airport bus drops you in town in 25 minutes. Buses are scheduled according to flights, leaving the airport about 10 minutes after all arrivals. SAS has nonstop flights to Ålesund from Oslo, Bergen, Trondheim, Stavanger, and several cities in Europe. Low-cost airlines Norwegian and WizzAir fly to Ålesund from Oslo, Bergen, Trondheim, London, and other European cities. KLM flies from Amsterdam.

In addition to regular ferries to nearby islands, the Hurtigruten and other boats connect Ålesund with other points along the coast. Excursions by boat can be booked through the tourist office.

From Oslo to Ålesund it's 550 km (342 miles) on E6 to Dombås and then E136 through Åndalsnes to Ålesund. From Bergen via the E39 it's a 390-km (242-mile) drive. It's open most of the year, and involves two ferry crossings and a few toll roads.

VISITOR INFORMATION

CONTACTS Ålesund Taxi. *70–10–30–00* *alesund-taxi.no.* **Destinasjon Ålesund og Sunnmøre.** (*Destination Ålesund and Sunnmøre*) *Skateflukaia, Ålesund* *70–16–34–30* *visitalesund.com.*

Sights

Ålesunds Museum

MUSEUM | This gem of a museum highlights the city's past, including the great fire of 1904 and the dangerous escape route that the Norwegian Resistance established in World War II. Handicrafts on display are done in the folk-art style of the area. You can also visit the Art Nouveau room and learn more about the town's unique architecture. *Rasmus Rønnebergs gt. 16, Ålesund* *70–16–48–42* *aalesunds.museum.no* *NKr 60.*

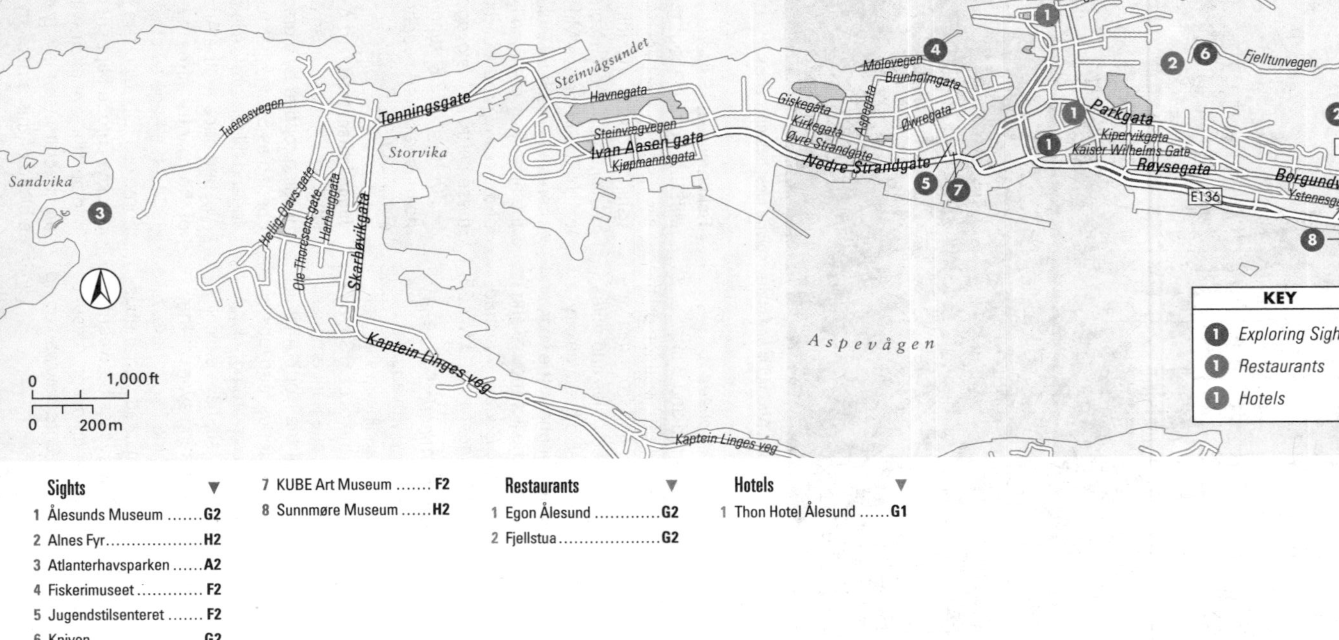

Sights

1 Ålesunds Museum G2
2 Alnes Fyr H2
3 Atlanterhavsparken A2
4 Fiskerimuseet F2
5 Jugendstilsenteret F2
6 Kniven G2
7 KUBE Art Museum F2
8 Sunnmøre Museum H2

Restaurants

1 Egon Ålesund G2
2 Fjellstua G2

Hotels

1 Thon Hotel Ålesund G1

Spread across three islands, Ålesund is one of the region's most beautiful cities.

Alnes Fyr (*Alnes Lighthouse*)
LOCAL INTEREST | This red-and-white lighthouse has a beautiful location on the Norwegian coastline, and from this vantage point you can see miles and miles of ocean. Alnes Fyr also has a gallery, a café that's open throughout the year, and an exhibition about the lighthouse and its history. ✉ *Alnesgard, Godøya, Ålesund* ☎ *70–18–50–90* 🌐 *alnesfyr.no* 🎟 *Nkr 25.*

Atlanterhavsparken (*Atlantic Sea Park*)
ZOO | **FAMILY** | Teeming with aquatic life, this is one of Scandinavia's largest aquariums. Right on the ocean, 3 km (2 miles) west of town, the park emphasizes aquatic animals of the North Atlantic, including anglers, octopus, and lobster. The Humboldt penguins are popular with children. After your visit, have a picnic, hike, or take a refreshing swim at the adjoining Tueneset Park. To get here, take the Aquarium Bus (marked "Akvariebussen") from St. Olav's Plass between April and October. ✉ *Tueneset, Ålesund* ☎ *70–10–70–60* 🌐 *atlanterhavsparken.no* 🎟 *NKr 195.*

Fiskerimuseet (*Fisheries Museum*)
MUSEUM | Learn about the people who've always been the backbone of Ålesund's fishing industry, including those who remained on shore to process the daily catch. The Fisheries Museum has several interesting exhibits, including one tracing the history of *tran* (cod liver oil), one of the many products that came from these parts. ✉ *Molovegen 10, Ålesund* ☎ *70–16–48–42* 🌐 *sunnmore.museum.no/musea/fiskerimuseet* 🎟 *NKr 60* 🕓 *Closed Sept.–Apr.*

Jugendstilsenteret (*Art Nouveau Center*)
MUSEUM | Housed in an eye-catching building topped by a graceful turret—it opened as Swan Pharmacy in 1907—the Jugendstilsenteret tells the story of how Ålesund became the Art Nouveau capital of the country. After the great fire of 1904 left a huge swath of the population homeless, city planners had to rebuild quickly. Europe happened to be in the middle of a love affair with Art Nouveau architecture, so the city ended up with a blend of this ornate style with the

occasional Viking flourish. The KUBE Art Museum is part of the same complex. ✉ *Apotekergata 16, Ålesund* ☎ *70–10–49–70* 🌐 *jugendstilsenteret.no* 🎫 *NKr 70, includes Kube Art Museum.*

★ Kniven

VIEWPOINT | For a splendid view of the city, one that absolutely glitters at night, take this scenic drive up the city's mountain. Most photos you've seen of Ålesund have been taken from this vantage point. ✉ *Fjellstua Aksla, Ålesund.*

KUBE Art Museum

MUSEUM | **FAMILY** | In a branch of Norges Bank dating from 1906, this museum aims to promote the work of contemporary Norwegian artists. It is part of the complex that holds the Jugendstilsenteret. ✉ *Apotekergata 16, Ålesund* ☎ *70–10–49–70* 🌐 *jugendstilsenteret.no* 🎫 *NKr 70, includes the Jugendstilsenteret.*

Sunnmøre Museum

MUSEUM VILLAGE | **FAMILY** | This open-air museum focuses on the traditions and history of the people who make their home on the Norwegian coast. A five-minute drive from Ålesund, it's spread over 50 acres and consists of 55 well-kept buildings ranging from cow sheds to schoolhouses, giving insight into people's lives in this region. ✉ *Museumsvegen 1, Ålesund* ☎ *70–16–48–70* 🌐 *sunnmore.museum.no/musea/sunnmoere-museum* 🎫 *NKr 80* ⏲ *Closed Sat. Oct.–Apr.*

Restaurants

Egon Ålesund

$$ | **INTERNATIONAL** | **FAMILY** | The atmosphere is casual and relaxed, and perhaps a little loud at peak hours, but you won't find a better spot for a quick meal. There are wood beams, exposed brick walls, and cozy booths with rough-hewn furnishings. **Known for:** you order at the bar; great selection of starters; several vegetarian options. 💲 *Average main: NKr 210* ✉ *Løvenvoldgt. 8, Ålesund* ☎ *70–15–78–15* 🌐 *egon.no.*

Off the Beaten Path

Runde. Perhaps Norway's most famous "bird rock"—it also happens to be one of the largest in Europe—Runde is the breeding ground for some 200 species, including puffins, gannets, and cormorants. The region's wildlife managers maintain many observation posts here. It can get quite windy during a hike, so dress accordingly. ✉ *Ålesund* ☎ *70–16–34–30* 🌐 *www.visitalesund-geiranger.com/en/The-bird-island-Runde.*

Fjellstua

$$$ | **NORWEGIAN** | **FAMILY** | This mountaintop restaurant covered with a dramatic glass canopy has tremendous views over the surrounding peaks, islands, and fjords. It serves a mix of national and international dishes, and on the menu might be Norwegian salt cod or baked salmon. **Known for:** spectacular city views; wide variety of options; great service. 💲 *Average main: NKr 300* ✉ *Fjellstua Aksla, Ålesund* ☎ *70–10–74–00* 🌐 *fjellstua.no.*

Hotels

Thon Hotel Ålesund

$$ | **HOTEL** | **FAMILY** | This gleaming white hotel is known for its homey and casual atmosphere, with rooms that feel much more cozy than your usual chain offerings. **Pros:** lovely indoor pool; great breakfast; smart bathrooms. **Cons:** evening buffet not always available in low season; welcomes pets, so it's not for allergy sufferers; a business hotel feel. 💲 *Rooms from: NKr 900* ✉ *Kongensgate 27, Ålesund* ☎ *70–15–77–00*

⊕ *thonhotels.no/hoteller/norge/alesund/thon-hotel-alesund* ⮒ *106 rooms* 🍽 *Free breakfast.*

Shopping

Moloveien

SHOPPING NEIGHBORHOODS | This is one of the oldest streets in Ålesund, and in these old wooden buildings you'll find antiques shops and a glass art gallery. ✉ *Moloveien, Ålesund.*

Florø

216 km (134 miles) south of Ålesund, 230 km (142 miles) north of Bergen.

Norway's westernmost city, the seaside community of Florø is the place to enjoy fresh seafood, stroll along the docks, and stare out towards the horizon,

GETTING HERE AND AROUND

Getting to Florø is not a huge challenge, and there are daily departures from Bergen by express boat. This is also one of the stops for the Hurtigruten. Daily flights from both Oslo and Bergen arrive at the airport located just minutes from the center of town. There's bus service from Trondheim, Ålesund, Bergen, and Oslo.

Sights

Brandsøyåsen

VIEWPOINT | This scenic overlook in the center of Florø is best reached by foot or bicycle. From the top you'll have great views of the city and of the ocean beyond. There are several hiking trails at the top, most of them well marked. The hike to the top takes about 45 minutes, depending on which trail you take. ✉ *Krokavegen 41, Florø.*

Kystmuseet i Sogn og Fjordane (*Coastal Museum*)

MUSEUM | You really get a sense of what life must have been like over the years for Norway's coastal dwellers at this seaside museum. It's a mix of indoor exhibits and open-air strolls to buildings like the *bataldebua*, a 17th-century structure used for curing herring. You can walk to the museum in 20 minutes from the center of Florø. ✉ *Brendøyvegen, Florø* ☎ *98–26–98–54* ⊕ *web.kyst.museum.no.*

Restaurants

Bryggekanten Restaurant

$$$ | **NORWEGIAN** | Decorated in a maritime style, it's no surprise that Bryggekanten has such close proximity to the ocean. Naturally it has lovely views from the dozens of windows. **Known for:** tasty fish soup; friendly staff; a buffet for hearty eaters. [$] *Average main: NKr 300* ✉ *Quality Hotel Florø, Hamnegata 7, Florø* ☎ *57–75–75–75* ⊕ *bkfloro.no.*

Vesle Kinn

$ | **SPANISH** | This casual eatery has one thing on its mind: beer. It was opened by the Kinn Bryggeri as a way to showcase its wide range of beers and the foods that pair so naturally with them, and you can expect an impressive array of small dishes that are the perfect size to share. **Known for:** friendly atmosphere; locally brewed beer; light snacks. [$] *Average main: NKr 110* ✉ *Strandgata 28, Florø* ☎ *900–90–465* ⊕ *kinn.no.*

Hotels

Quality Hotel Florø

$$$ | **HOTEL** | **FAMILY** | With a perfect location right on the docks of Florø, this hotel's interior design and laid-back atmosphere are inspired by its maritime origins. **Pros:** very central location; breakfast included; delightful restaurant. **Cons:** service gets mixed reviews; some rooms are quite small; a bit expensive. [$] *Rooms from: NKr 1400* ✉ *Hamnegata 11, Florø* ☎ *57–75–75–75* ⊕ *nordicchoicehotels.no/hotell/norge/floro/quality-hotel-floro* ⮒ *79 rooms* 🍽 *Free breakfast.*

Kristiansund

151 km (94 miles) northeast of Ålesund, 198 km (123 miles) southwest of Tondheim.

By the 19th century, timber and *klippfisk* (fish salted and dried in the sun on slabs of rock) had made Kristiansund one of Norway's biggest ports. Today Kristiansund's lively harbor, Vågen, has a wonderful collection of historic boats. During World War II almost everything in town was destroyed except for Vågen, where some well-preserved buildings remain.

GETTING HERE AND AROUND

Kristiansund is one of the ports of call for the Hurtigruten, making this a perfect place to arrive by boat. The city's domestic airport has several daily flights from Oslo and Bergen.

This is a long drive from the country's larger cities: 8 hours from Oslo, 10 from Bergen. There are buses from most places around the country (though not very frequently).

Sights

★ **Grip Stavkyrkje** (*Grip Stave Church*)
RELIGIOUS SITE | The island of Grip is a delight, especially the little red stave church that stands at the island's highest point and dates to 1470. The fishing community itself was mostly abandoned after World War II, but locals return in summer, along with many tourists. Ferries run from Kristiansund at least once a day between June and August. If the church is closed, locals can get the key. ✉ *Grip* ☎ *70–23–88–00.*

Kvalvik Fort
MILITARY SITE | One of Kristiansund's most beaten hiking paths is to this well-preserved World War II submarine base and fortress built by German forces. At its height, it housed 5,000 soldiers, who left several bunkers, a battery of artillery guns, and a submarine, all of which are visitable today. Tours and exhibits tell the fort's story. The pristine setting among wooded seaside hills is the second highlight and attracts many locals for fishing and barbecues. ✉ *Kristiansund* ✣ *13 km (8 miles) east of Kristiansund.*

★ **Sundbåten**
TRANSPORTATION SITE (AIRPORT/BUS/FERRY/TRAIN) | The ferry service to connect Kristiansund's four main islands was established in 1876 and has not stopped since, making it the world's oldest public transportation in continuous use. Ferries depart two or three times per hour and provide visitors with a nice overview of the city's layout as well as views of the region's distinctive architecture, whose bright colors reflect charmingly in the water. A round-trip takes 17 minutes. ✉ *Kirkelandet Sundbåtkai, Kristiansund* ☎ *92–85–17–44* 🌐 *sundbaten.no* 🎟 *NKr 40.*

Restaurants

Bryggekanten Restaurant/Brasserie og Bache Bar
$$$ | **NORWEGIAN** | Today's catch is all over the menu—crayfish, klippfisk, and grilled monkfish, to name a few—at this casual eatery. The seemingly mismatched, umbrella-shaped roof atop this rectangular blue waterfront restaurant offers a lesson in Norwegian history, culture, and cuisine: it's where locals of yesteryear dried fish by night. **Known for:** waterside patio; freshest fish available; great views of the harbor. 💲 *Average main: NKr 345* ✉ *Storkaia 1, Kristiansund* ☎ *71–67–61–60* 🌐 *fireb.no* 🕒 *Closed Sun. and Mon.*

Sjøstjerna
$$$ | **NORWEGIAN** | Another contender for the best fish restaurant crown in Kristiansund, Sjøstjerna matches its zeal for klippfisk with major skills in hospitality to create an exceedingly warm and convivial environment. In addition to intimacy of the relatively small space, the vast assortment of Norwegian folk

art and fishing-related artifacts hanging from the walls adds a refreshing and well-designed layer of intrigue on an otherwise typical menu of bacalao, *blandaball* dumplings, and klippfisk. **Known for:** best bacalao in the area; live piano music in the bar; Norwegian dishes with international flair. *Average main: NKr 300 Skolegata 8, Kristiansund 71–67–87–78 sjostjerna.no Closed Sun. No lunch.*

Hotels

Quality Hotel Grand Kristiansund

$$$ | **HOTEL** | This downtown hotel has modern, unfussy rooms and is well placed for local attractions, shopping, and the Caroline Cinema and Conference Center, just around the corner. **Pros:** good location; decent breakfast choices; free Wi-Fi. **Cons:** public areas full of convention attendees; cash not accepted; no in-room safes. *Rooms from: NKr 1700 Bernstorffstredet 1, Kristiansund 71–57–13–00 nordicchoicehotels.no/hotell/norge/kristiansund/quality-hotel-grand-kristiansund 158 rooms Free breakfast.*

Scandic Hotel Kristiansund

$$$ | **HOTEL** | It's difficult to sleep in late at this downtown hotel—the spread of one of Norway's best breakfast buffets makes a hungry stomach stand at attention. **Pros:** excellent breakfast; river views; free Wi-Fi. **Cons:** rooms under the bar suffer noise bleed; service gets mixed reviews; quite expensive. *Rooms from: NKr 1800 Storgata 41, Kristiansund 71–57–12–00 scandichotels.no/hotell/norge/kristiansund/scandic-kristiansund 102 rooms Free breakfast.*

Thon Hotel Kristiansund

$$$ | **HOTEL** | On the north edge of Innlandet Island, this hotel is one of the region's best, with views of the harbor that receive so much praise for its natural beauty that it keeps people awake at night. **Pros:** amazing views from most rooms; popular restaurant; private beach. **Cons:** small rooms; outside city center; no gym. *Rooms from: NKr 1300 Fiskergata 12, Kristiansund 71–57–30–00 thonhotels.no/hoteller/norge/kristiansund/thon-hotel-kristiansund 98 rooms Free breakfast.*

Performing Arts

Kristiansund Opera

OPERA | Kristiansund is home to Norway's oldest opera house. There are performances throughout the year, both by local troupes and visiting entertainers. *Kong Olav V's gt. 1, Kristiansund 71–58–99–60 oik.no.*

Shopping

Klippfiskbutikken

FOOD/CANDY | Pay tribute to and stock up on the mighty klippfisk at this shop, where proprietor Knut Garshol carries on the family business begun by his grandfather. A visit is also an education in the types of cod used and methods of preparation. *Kaibakken 2, Kristiansund 71–67–12–64 klippfiskbutikken.no.*

Norsk Flid Husfliden Kristiansund

CLOTHING | Go native at this Norwegian arts-and-crafts store, which specializes in national costumes in nearly 150 varieties, all made with top-quality fabrics and intended to last for generations. Sewing and knitting supplies are also available, as are sweaters, jackets, carpets, and other textiles. *Hauggata 15, Kristiansund 71–67–17–70 norskflid.no/kristiansund/ Closed Sun.*

Chapter 9

TRONDHEIM TO THE LOFOTEN ISLANDS

Updated by
Megan Starr and
Aram Vardanyan

Sights ★★★★★ | Restaurants ★★★★☆ | Hotels ★★★★☆ | Shopping ★★★☆☆ | Nightlife ★★☆☆☆

WELCOME TO TRONDHEIM TO THE LOFOTEN ISLANDS

TOP REASONS TO GO

★ **Sleep near the fishes.** On the Lofoten Islands, which have a long and proud maritime history, spend the night in one of the traditional *rorbuer* (fishermen's cabins) on the waterfront.

★ **Have a whale of a time.** Feast your eyes on one (or hopefully many) of the majestic sperm whales in their favorite feeding grounds off the coast of the remote Vesterålen Islands.

★ **Explore the northern landscape.** A gem on the Nordland coast, the former trading post of Kjerringøy is famous for its pristine fjord landscape and outdoor activities.

★ **Get lost in a whirlpool.** Saltstraumen is one of Norway's legendary maelstroms, and there's no better place to witness the awesome power of the normally placid fjords.

★ **Head back to the Middle Ages.** Located in Trondheim, Nidaros Cathedral boasts the title of the northernmost medieval cathedral in the world.

At the forefront of Norway's fishing industry, the Lofoten Islands have a full, rich history. It has a culture all its own and is consistently rated one of the most beautiful places in the world. The nearby Vesterålen Islands offer a quieter, more relaxing experience than in the Lofoten Islands.

1 **Trondheim.** Norway's third-largest city is a center for maritime research, and the wide streets of the historic city center are still lined with brightly painted wood houses and striking warehouses.

2 **Bodø.** The strikingly modern city of Bodø sits just above the Arctic Circle and is the gateway to the Lofoten Islands, the Vesterålen Islands, and all points north.

3 **Harstad.** On one of Norway's largest islands, Harstad is the gateway to the remote Vesterålen Islands.

4 **Sortland.** A city painted vivid shades of blue, Sortland is known for its musical traditions and cultural institutions.

5 **Stokmarknes.** If you're interested in this region's maritime history, Stokmarknes is a must-see destination.

6 **Henningsvær.** A charming coastal town, Henningsvær is likely to be your first stop in the Lofoten Islands.

7 **Svolvær.** An important hub of the fishing industry, Svolvær sits near Norway's oldest settlement.

8 **Stamsund.** This colorful community is where you can spend the night in a fisherman's cabin.

9 **Leknes.** The dramatic landscape around Leknes draws travelers from around the world.

10 **Nusfjord.** One of the most remote villages in the islands, this is the place to find serenity.

11 **Reine.** If you love outdoor activities, Reine is the right destination summer or winter.

12 **Å.** The end of the road, photogenic Å has some of the best views in Norway.

VESTERÅLEN ISLANDS
LOFOTEN ISLANDS
Finnsnes
TRØMS
3 Harstad
4 Sortland
Gausvik
E6
Stokmarknes
5
Herjangen
7
6
8
Narvik
9
Svolvær
Korsnes
Leknes
Henningsvær
10
Stamsund
Nusfjord
Skutvik
Reine
11
Å
Vestfjord
12
Kjerringøy
2
NORWEGIAN SEA
Bodø
Saltstraumen
Setsa
Rognan
E6
NORDLAND
Mo i Rana
E12
Mosjoen
E6
E45
E12
0
50 mi
0
50 km
SWEDEN
Rørvik
E45
Namsos
NORD-TRØNDELAG
Steinkjer
E6
1
Trondheim
E45
E14
E39

The mind-blowing scenery and the feeling that you're discovering something for the first time makes the area of Norway directly above and below the Arctic Circle the perfect gateway to the magical north. From the vibrance of Trondheim to the dramatic landscapes of the Lofoten Islands, the popularity of this Norwegian region is beginning to skyrocket, and it's not difficult to see why. Often overlooked by travelers, it's your best bet for world-class dining, undiscovered beaches, unparallelled views, and villages that echo the old ways of life.

A narrow but immensely long strip of land stretches between Trondheim and Kirkenes in northern Norway. In this vast territory you'll encounter the sawtooth, glacier-carved peaks of the Lofoten Islands and the world's strongest tidal current, in Bodø. Thousands of islands and skerries hug the coast of northern Norway, and the provinces of Nordland, Troms, and Finnmark, up to the North Cape. Along this wild, unpredictable coast, the weather is as dramatic as the scenery: in summer you can see the midnight sun, and in winter experience aurora borealis, the northern lights.

Northern Norwegians still make their living in the fishing villages of the Lofoten Islands, in small, provincial towns, and in modern cities like Tromsø. Tourism plays an important role in the region, especially with those seeking wild landscapes, outdoor activities, and adventure, whether it's mountaineering, dogsledding, skiing, caving, or wreck-diving. Basking in the midnight sun is one of Norway's most popular attractions; every year, thousands of people flock to Nordkapp (the North Cape) for it. To cater to the large number of visitors, northern Norway has well-run tourist offices which stock excellent maps and travel literature on the area.

Planning

When to Go

For hiking enthusiasts and those looking to partake in an epic road trip, the mild summer months make this part of Norway special because the midnight sun allows for endless days of exploring. If you're more interested in winter sports and seeing the northern lights, winter is undoubtedly the best season to visit. From snowshoeing to cross-country skiing, this region doesn't slow down once temperatures dip below freezing.

If you want a little bit of everything, shoulder season may be the right time of year for you. The weather in autumn and spring can be slightly unpredictable, but the scenery is in transition and you have a chance to both hike and see the northern lights.

Getting Here and Around

When you looks at a map of Norway, everything looks pretty close together. It's actually quite the opposite: From Trondheim to Bodø, the drive is nearly 13 hours. Norway has deeply cut fjords, wide mountain passes, and a jagged coastline that make the country especially difficult to navigate.

AIR TRAVEL

The distances between these destinations can be daunting, so the best way to get around this part of Norway is often by plane. Remember that the airports in the Vesterålen and Lofoten islands are extremely small and have few flights in or out.

CONTACTS Norwegian. ☎ *815–21–815* 🌐 *www.norwegian.no.* **SAS.** ☎ *05400* 🌐 *www.flysas.com.* **Widerøe.** ☎ *810–01–200* 🌐 *www.wideroe.no.*

BOAT TRAVEL

The Hurtigruten is a cruise ship that navigates the coast of Norway. While many passengers use it to travel long distances, you can also book passage from port to port.

CONTACTS Hurtigruten. ☎ *810–30–000* 🌐 *www.hurtigruten.com.*

BUS TRAVEL

In northern Norway, buses are not usually the best way to travel. The distances are long, and the departures are few. Most bus companies run local routes.

CONTACTS NOR-WAY Bussekspress. ☎ *815–44–444* 🌐 *www.nor-way.no.*

CAR TRAVEL

Renting a car is an appealing option in this part of Norway, but do your homework before you sign on the dotted line. Distances are not what they seem on a map, and it can take an entire day to reach certain destinations. Fuel isn't cheap, and rentals are much more expensive than they probably are back home.

Most roads in northern Norway are quite good, although there are always narrow and winding stretches, especially along fjords. Distances are formidable. Route 17—the Kystriksveien (Coastal Highway) which goes from Namsos to Bodø—is an excellent alternative to the E6. Getting to Tromsø and the North Cape involves additional driving on narrower roads off E6. In winter, near-blizzard conditions and icy roads sometimes make it necessary to drive in a convoy. You must also drive with special studded winter tires.

TRAIN TRAVEL

One viable option, particularly in Tromsø and Bodø, is taking a train. The northernmost station is Bodø, so you'll have to make other plans if your journey takes you farther north.

CONTACTS VY. *(Norwegian state railways)* ☎ *815–00–888* 🌐 *www.vy.no/en.*

Restaurants

It's no surprise that menus in this part of the country incorporate a lot of fresh seafood. You will find a lot of Arctic char, king crab, salmon, whale, and other seafood, usually topped with a buttery or creamy sauce and served with a side of potatoes. Many areas, especially around the Lofoten Islands, have a tradition of dried or salted fish. One example is stockfish, often referred to as *klippfisk*. In past years this type of dried cod was hung out to dry to make sure there was always food when the weather was uncooperative or catch was poor. Today even the most modern chefs include it in their repertoires, often with a European or Asian twist. The regional specialty *lutefisk* (a gelatin-like fermented fish) is also popular. Other delicious items you might not recognize are *multe* (cloudberries) and *skogsbær* (forest berries).

Restaurant and hotel reviews have been shortened. For full information, visit Fodors.com.

What It Costs in Norwegian Krone

$	$$	$$$	$$$$
RESTAURANTS			
under NKr 125	NKr 125–NKr 250	NKr 251–NKr350	over NKr 350
HOTELS			
under NKr 750	NKr 750–NKr 1250	NKr 1251–NKr 1900	over NKr 1900

Hotels

Outside of the major cities, hotels in this part of Norway tend to offer few frills and only the most basic amenities. Breakfast is usually the standard Norwegian fare (bread with various toppings), but may also have some of the items that would be on a full English breakfast.

Visitor Information

CONTACTS Nord-Norge. ☎ *90–17–75–00* 🌐 *www.nordnorge.com.*

Trondheim

494 km (307 miles) north of Oslo, 657 km (408 miles) northeast of Bergen.

One of Scandinavia's oldest cities, Trondheim was the first capital of Norway, from 997 to 1380. Founded in 997 by Viking king Olav Tryggvason, it was first named Nidaros (still the name of the cathedral), a composite word referring to the city's location at the mouth of the Nidelva River. Today, it's central Norway's largest (and Norway's third-largest) city. The wide streets of the historic city center remain lined with brightly painted wood houses and striking warehouses. But it's no historic relic: it's also the home to NTNU (Norwegian University of Science and Technology) and is Norway's technological capital.

AIR TRAVEL

There are daily flights from Trondheim to several European cities and numerous flights to other cities in Norway. Trondheim's Værnes Airport is 32 km (21 miles) northeast of the city. SAS, Norwegian, and Widerøe offer connections throughout northern Norway. Widerøe flies to 27 destinations in the region, including Honningsvåg, the country's northernmost airport and the one closest to North Cape.

BOAT AND FERRY TRAVEL

The Hurtigruten (the coastal express boat, which goes to 35 ports from Bergen to Kirkenes) stops at Trondheim. Stops between Trondheim and North Cape include Bodø, Stamsund, and Svolvær (Lofoten Islands), Sortland (Vesterålen Islands), Harstad, Tromsø, Hammerfest, and Honningsvåg.

BUS TRAVEL

The Østerdalsekspressen and Lavprisekspressen buses run from Oslo to Trondheim. Buses also connect Bergen and Ålesund with Trondheim. All local Trondheim buses stop at the Munkegata–Dronningens Gate intersection. Some routes end at the bus terminal at Trondheim Sentralstasjon.

CAR TRAVEL

Trondheim is about 494 km (308 miles) from Oslo: a seven- to eight-hour drive. The two alternatives are the E6 through Gudbrandsdalen Valley or Route 3 through Østerdalen Valley. It's 723 km (448 miles) from Trondheim to Bodø on E6, which goes all the way to Kirkenes. There are several toll roads in and around Trondheim. As is usual in Norway, you drive through the toll areas. If you're in a rental car, the toll will be charged directly to your credit card.

CRUISE-SHIP TRAVEL

Cruise ships dock at one of two piers, both within easy walking distance of the city center. There are no facilities at the piers, but you'll find everything you need in the city.

TAXI TRAVEL

CONTACTS Trøndertaxi. *07373 in Norway* *www.07373.no.*

TRAIN TRAVEL

Dovrebanen has frequent departures daily on the Oslo–Trondheim route. Trains leave from Oslo Central Station (Oslo S) for the seven- to eight-hour journey. Two trains run daily in each direction on the 11-hour route between Trondheim and Bodø, to the north. The Ofotbanen has two departures daily in each direction on the Stockholm–Narvik route, a 21-hour journey.

VISITOR INFORMATION

CONTACTS Visit Trondheim. *Nordre gt. 11, Trondheim* *73–80–76–60* *visittrondheim.no/en.*

Sights

Erkebispegården (*Archbishop's Palace*)
CASTLE/PALACE | The oldest secular building in Scandinavia, Erkebispegården dates from around 1160. It was the residence of the archbishop until the Reformation in 1537. The Archbishop's Palace Museum has original sculptures from Nidaros Cathedral and archaeological pieces from throughout its history. Within Erkebispegården's inner palace is the Rustkammeret/Resistance Museum, which traces military development from Viking times to the present through displays of uniforms, swords, and daggers. The dramatic events of World War II get a special emphasis. ■ **TIP→ Opening times for the various museums and wings in the Erkebispegården and for the cathedral vary greatly by season.** *Kongsgårdsgt. 1, Trondheim* *73–89–08–00* *www.nidarosdomen.no* *NKr 200, includes entry to Nidaros Cathedral* *Closed Mon. Sept.–Apr.*

Korsvika
BEACH—SIGHT | This little beach is the perfect place to take in the views of the fjord after conquering one of the many hiking trails in the area. Swimming is possible during the summer months, although the water is still pretty cold. The beach is a popular place among locals, especially around sunset. *Ladestien, Trondheim.*

Kristiansten Festning (*Kristiansten Fort*)
MILITARY SITE | Built by J. C. Cicignon after the great fire of 1681, the Kristiansten Fort saved the city from conquest by Sweden in 1718. During World War II, the German occupying forces executed members of the Norwegian Resistance here; there's a plaque in their honor. The fort has spectacular views of the city, the fjord, and the mountains. Some walls are unsecured, so take care when walking, and mind your children. *Trondheim* *815–70–400* *www.forsvarsbygg.no/no/festningene/finn-din-festning/kristiansten-festning* *Free.*

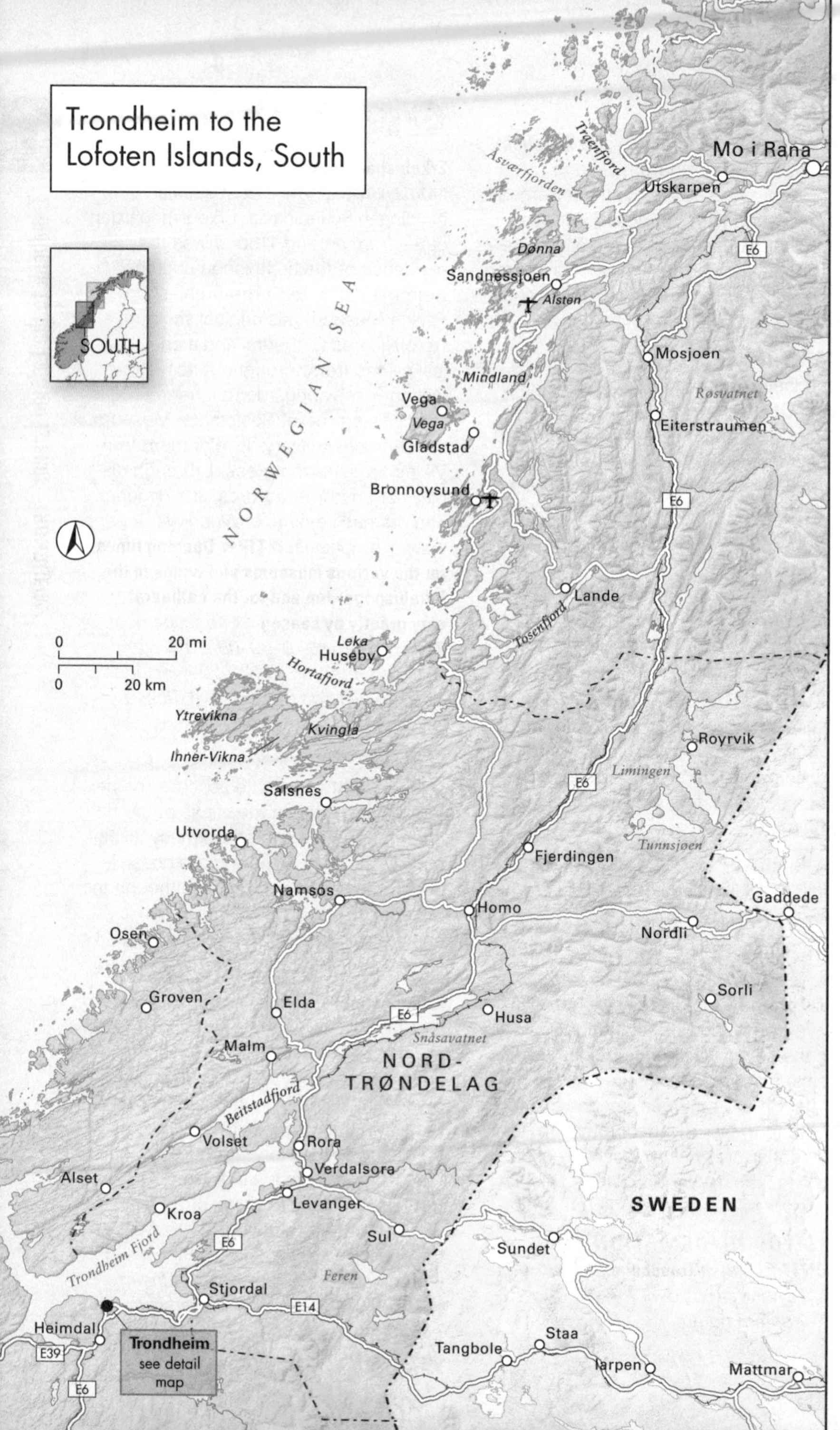

Trondheim to the Lofoten Islands, South
SOUTH
0
20 mi
0
20 km
NORWEGIAN SEA
Træenfjord
Åsværfjorden
Mo i Rana
Utskarpen
E6
Dønna
Sandnessjoen
Alsten
Mosjoen
Røsvatnet
Mindland
Vega
Vega
Gladstad
Eiterstraumen
Bronnoysund
E6
Lande
Tosenfjord
Leka
Huseby
Hortafjord
Ytrevikna
Kvingla
Ihner-Vikna
Royrvik
Limingen
E6
Salsnes
Utvorda
Fjerdingen
Tunnsjøen
Namsos
Homo
Gaddede
Osen
Nordli
Sorli
Groven
Elda
E6
Husa
Snåsavatnet
Malm
NORD-
TRØNDELAG
Beitstadfjord
Volset
Rora
Verdalsora
Alset
Levanger
SWEDEN
Kroa
Sul
Sundet
E6
Trondheim Fjord
Feren
Stjordal
E14
Heimdal
E39
E6
Trondheim
see detail
map
Staa
Tangbole
Iarpen
Mattmar

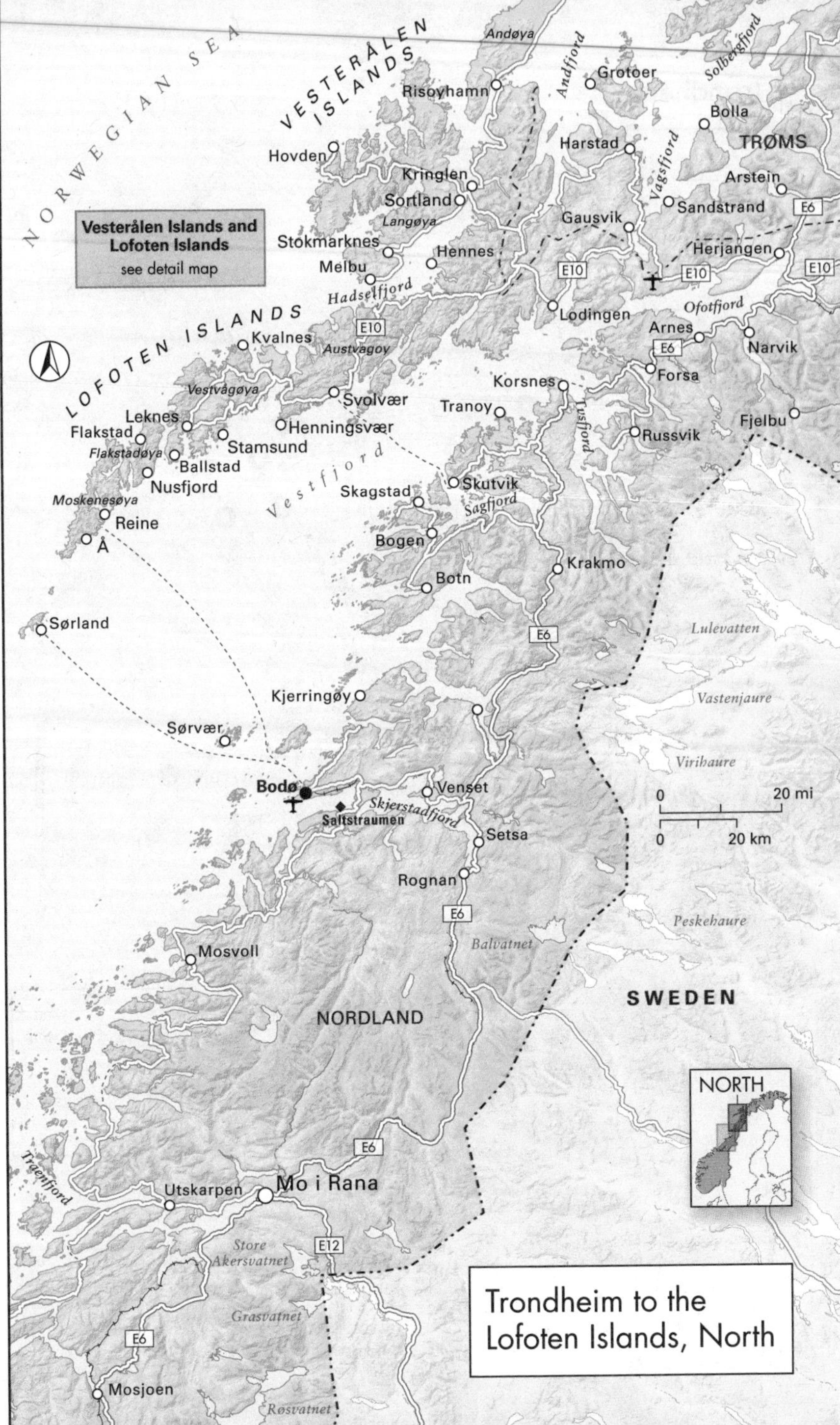

Trondheim to the Lofoten Islands, North

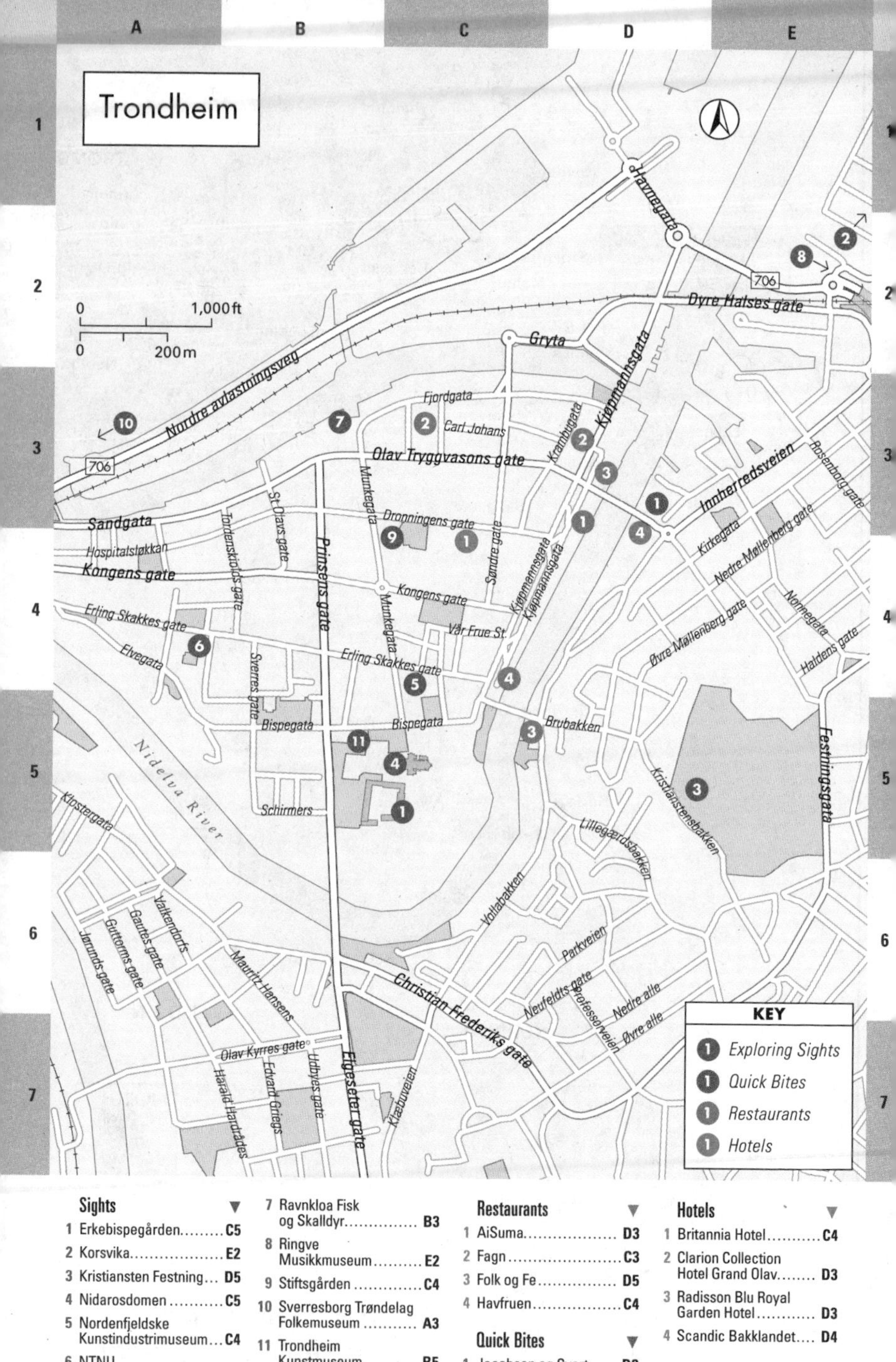

Sights

1 Erkebispegården......... C5
2 Korsvika.................... E2
3 Kristiansten Festning... D5
4 Nidarosdomen........... C5
5 Nordenfjeldske Kunstindustrimuseum... C4
6 NTNU Vitenskapsmuseet...... A4
7 Ravnkloa Fisk og Skalldyr.............. B3
8 Ringve Musikkmuseum.......... E2
9 Stiftsgården.............. C4
10 Sverresborg Trøndelag Folkemuseum........... A3
11 Trondheim Kunstmuseum........... B5

Restaurants

1 AiSuma.................... D3
2 Fagn........................ C3
3 Folk og Fe................ D5
4 Havfruen.................. C4

Quick Bites

1 Jacobsen og Svart..... D3

Hotels

1 Britannia Hotel........... C4
2 Clarion Collection Hotel Grand Olav........ D3
3 Radisson Blu Royal Garden Hotel............ D3
4 Scandic Bakklandet.... D4

★ **Nidarosdomen** (*Nidaros Cathedral*)
RELIGIOUS SITE | Trondheim's cathedral was built on the grave of King Olav, who formulated a Christian religious code for Norway in 1024. The town quickly became a pilgrimage site for Christians from all over northern Europe, and Olav was canonized in 1164. Construction of Nidarosdomen began in 1070, but the oldest existing parts of the cathedral date from around 1150. It has been ravaged on several occasions by fire and rebuilt each time, generally in a Gothic style. Since the Middle Ages, Norway's kings have been crowned and blessed in the cathedral, and the crown jewels are on display here. Guided tours lasting 45 minutes are offered in English from mid-June to mid-August. ✉ *Kongsgårdsgt. 2, Trondheim* ☎ *73–89–08–00* 🌐 *www.nidarosdomen.no* 🎫 *NKr 80.*

Nordenfjeldske Kunstindustrimuseum
MUSEUM | The Tiffany windows are magnificent at this museum of decorative arts, which houses an impressive collection of furniture, silver, and textiles. The permanent collection includes exhibitions on the history of crafts and industrial design, Henry van de Velde interiors, contemporary Norwegian fashion, Japanese miniatures and samurai armor, and works by textile artist Hannah Ryggen. ✉ *Munkegt. 5, Trondheim* ☎ *73–80–89–50* 🌐 *www.nkim.no* 🎫 *NKr 110* ⏲ *Closed Mon.*

NTNU Vitenskapsmuseet (*NTNU Museum of Natural History and Archaeology*)
MUSEUM | This highly regarded university museum covers flora and fauna, minerals and rocks, archaeological and cultural discoveries—even church history. The eclectic exhibits include relics from the Stone Age as well as Viking artifacts and ecclesiastical articles from the 13th to 18th century. There's also a permanent exhibit showing daily life in medieval Trondheim. ✉ *Norwegian University of Science and Technology, Erling Skakkes gt. 47A, Trondheim* ☎ *73–59–21–45* 🌐 *www.ntnu.edu/museum* 🎫 *NKr 80* ⏲ *Closed Mon.*

Ravnkloa Fisk og Skalldyr (*Fish Market*)
MARKET | An immense variety of seafood is sold at Trondheim's fish and seafood market. It's also a great place to stop for a bite. ✉ *Munkegt. 70, Trondheim* ☎ *73–52–55–21* 🌐 *www.ravnkloa.no.*

Ringve Musikkmuseum (*Ringve Music Museum*)
MUSEUM | FAMILY | Taking you through the history of musical instruments in Norway and the rest of the world, the brilliant Ringve Music Museum covers just about every type of music you can imagine. Interactive displays allow you to "play" some of the most famous instruments. After exploring the museum, take the time to explore the beautiful botanical gardens surrounding the museum. The building is over 400 years old. ✉ *Lade alle 60, Trondheim* ☎ *73–87–02–80* 🌐 *www.ringve.no* 🎫 *NKr 130* ⏲ *Closed on Mon. Sept.–May.*

★ **Stiftsgården**
BUILDING | Built in the 1770s, Stiftsgården is now the official royal residence in Trondheim. The architecture and interior are late baroque and highly representative of 18th-century high society's taste. Guided tours—the only way to see the interior— offer insight into the festivities marking the coronations and blessings of the kings in the cathedral. ✉ *Munkegt. 23, Trondheim* ☎ *73–84–28–80 guided tour information* 🌐 *www.nkim.no/stiftsgarden* 🎫 *NKr 110* ⏲ *Closed mid-Aug.–May.*

★ **Sverresborg Trøndelag Folkemuseum** (*Sverresborg Trondelag Folk Museum*)
HISTORIC SITE | FAMILY | Near the ruins of King Sverre's medieval castle is this open-air historical museum that depicts everyday life in Trøndelag during the 18th and 19th centuries. The stave church here, built in the 1170s, is the northernmost preserved church of its type in Norway. In the Old Town you can visit a 1900s dentist's office and an old-fashioned grocery store that sells sweets. In the summer there are farm

Perched on stilts, Trondheim's colorful waterfront warehouses make this one of Norway's most distinctive cities.

animals on-site, and a range of activities for children. There's a copy of the main house at Walt Disney World's Epcot in the Norway pavilion. ✉ *Sverresborg allé 13, Trondheim* ☎ *73–89–01–00* 🌐 *www.sverresborg.no* 🎫 *NKr 115* ⏲ *Closed Mon. Sept.–May.*

Trondheim Kunstmuseum (*Trondheim Art Museum*)
MUSEUM | The town's art museum houses some 4,000 works of art, including many by regional artists. It's one of the country's largest public art collections and focuses on the 19th and 20th centuries. The main building is downtown in the shadow of the city's cathedral. ✉ *Bispegt. 7B, Trondheim* ☎ *73–53–81–80* 🌐 *trondheimkunstmuseum.no/en* 🎫 *NKr 120* ⏲ *Closed Mon. and Tues. Sept.–May.*

Coffee and Quick Bites

Jacobsen og Svart
$ | **CAFÉ** | This café has taken Trondheim by storm, and most locals agree it serves the best coffee in the city. The minimalistic interior is not only inviting, but also cozy enough to make you want to linger on a cold winter's day. **Known for:** they roast their own beans; well-trained baristas; coffee-making equipment you might not find at home. 💲 *Average main: NKr 50* ✉ *Ferjemannsveien 8, Trondheim* ☎ *902–44–226* 🌐 *www.jacobsensvart.no.*

Restaurants

AiSuma
$$$$ | **STEAKHOUSE** | If you're a meat lover, there's no place better to sample a perfectly grilled steak in Trondheim. The three-course tasting menus let you start with inventive seafood dishes (smoked halibut tartar, perhaps, or black pepper crab) before moving onto the main event. **Known for:** lots of local seafood; great work at the grill; handsome dining room. 💲 *Average main: NKr 400* ✉ *Kjøpmannsgata 57, Trondheim* ☎ *73–54–92–71* 🌐 *www.aisuma.no* ⏲ *Closed Sun.*

Fagn

$$$$ | **NORWEGIAN** | One of the most famous restaurants in Trondheim, Fagn has won international awards for its inventive cuisine that harkens back to the dishes that many Norwegians ate during their childhoods, then takes them in new and unexpected directions. No need to decide among the many interesting flavor combinations: you'll have a front-row seat as the chefs in the open kitchen prepare 10- or 20-course tasting menus. **Known for:** international recognition; Trøndelag's regional cuisine; relaxed atmosphere. *Average main: NKr 1100 Ørjaveita 4, Trondheim 458–44–996 www.fagn.no/restaurant Closed Sun. and Mon.*

Folk og Fe

$$$ | **NORWEGIAN** | Many restaurants strive to use local ingredients, and Folk og Fe is no exception: everything on the inventive menu is sourced with pride from central Norway. But the chefs here take it a step further, using the entire animal in their simple yet flavorful traditional cuisine. **Known for:** modern take on traditional cuisine; beautiful setting in Bakklandet; lovely dining room. *Average main: NKr 300 Øvre Bakklandet 66, Trondheim 975–18–180 www.folkogfe-bistro.no/english.html Closed Mon. No dinner Sun.*

Havfruen

$$$ | **SEAFOOD** | The long-running Mermaid is Trondheim's best known and most stylish fish restaurant, located in one of the colorful historic buildings along the Nidelva River. The interior is surprisingly modern, reminiscent of the New Nordic design you will see across parts of Scandinavia. **Known for:** oysters come highly recommended; knowledgeable food and wine pairings; great views over the harbor. *Average main: NKr 285 Kjøpmannsgt. 7, Trondheim 73–87–40–70 www.havfruen.no Closed Sun and Mon. No lunch.*

Hotels

★ Britannia Hotel

$$$$ | **HOTEL** | This was Trondheim's first grand hotel when it opened in 1897, and more than a century later the Britannia remains one of the most luxurious places to stay. **Pros:** endless amenities; fine-dining restaurants; extensive fitness and spa area. **Cons:** free Wi-Fi only in common areas; decor is a little fussy for some; expensive rates. *Rooms from: NKr 2300 Dronningensgt. 5, Trondheim 73–80–08–00 www.britannia.no 257 rooms Free breakfast.*

Clarion Collection Hotel Grand Olav

$$$ | **HOTEL** | This reasonably priced hotel, in the same building as Trondheim's large concert hall, is nicknamed "backstage" by locals. **Pros:** central location; spacious rooms; complimentary meals. **Cons:** some rooms a bit dated; small breakfast area; parking can be difficult. *Rooms from: NKr 1800 Kjøpmannsgt. 48, Trondheim 73–80–80–80 www.nordicchoicehotels.no 106 rooms Free breakfast.*

Radisson Blu Royal Garden Hotel

$$ | **HOTEL** | This extravaganza of glass on the Nidelva River is one of Trondheim's largest hotels. **Pros:** stunning architecture; top-notch service; huge buffet breakfast. **Cons:** not for those who want something quaint; parking is extra; air-conditioning sometimes hard to operate. *Rooms from: NKr 1050 Kjøpmannsgt. 73, Trondheim 73–80–30–00 www.radissonblu.com/en/hotel-trondheim 298 rooms No meals.*

Scandic Bakklandet

$$ | **HOTEL** | **FAMILY** | Located in the heart of Trondheim, the modern Scandic Bakklandet makes the most of its waterfront location with some expansive views. **Pros:** free breakfast; parking for guests; great harbor and sea views. **Cons:** not enough outlets in some rooms; restaurant is rather small; some rooms don't have great views. *Rooms from: NKr*

1000 ✉ *Nedre Bakklandet 60, Trondheim* ☎ *729–020–00* 🌐 *www.scandichotels.com/hotels/norway/trondheim/* *169 rooms* *Free breakfast.*

Samfundet
BARS/PUBS | Young people in search of cheap drinks, live music, and dancing gravitate toward the characteristic red, round building that houses Samfundet, Trondheim's student society. ✉ *Elgesetergt. 1, Trondheim* ☎ *99–21–59–10* 🌐 *www.samfundet.no/en.*

Trondhjem Mikrobryggeri
BREWPUBS/BEER GARDENS | Trondhjem Mikrobryggeri is a spacious brewery pub where you can try a fantastic range of beers that have been brewed in-house. The ever-changing menu keeps the selection fresh and interesting for a range of preferences, from bitter to fruity and everything in between, and it is recommended to purchase a flight to sample different beers. There is also a good choice of other alcoholic and non-alcoholic drinks if you are not a beer drinker. ✉ *Prinsens gt. 39, Trondheim* ☎ *92–48–22–00* 🌐 *www.tmb.no/* *Closed Sun.*

Gullsmed Møller
JEWELRY/ACCESSORIES | Founded in 1770, this is northern Europe's oldest goldsmith. It sells versions of the Trondheim Rose, the city symbol since the 1700s. ✉ *Munkegt. 3, Trondheim* ☎ *73–52–04–39* 🌐 *www.gullsmedmoller.no* *Closed Sun.*

Jens Hoff Garn & Ide
CLOTHING | For knitted clothes and blankets, this is one of the best places in town. They sell some of the softest yarn you've ever felt. ✉ *Sirkus Shopping, Falkenborgveien 1, Trondheim* ☎ *90–26–31–40* 🌐 *www.garnkos.no* *Closed Sun.*

BIKING

Trondheim Bysykkel (*City Bikes*)
BICYCLING | Parked in more than 53 locations throughout the city, these distinctive red-and-white bikes come with shopping baskets. Sign up through the app. ✉ *Trondheim* 🌐 *trondheimbysykkel.no/en* *NKr 49 per day.*

HIKING

Bymarka (*Bymarka Forest*)
HIKING/WALKING | This wooded area on the outskirts of Trondheim has a well-developed network of more than 200 km (125 miles) of walking and skiing tracks. ✉ *Trondheim.*

Ladestien (*Lade Trail*)
HIKING/WALKING | This 14-km (9-mile) trail along the edge of Lade Peninsula has great views of Trondheimsfjord. It's a doable hike whatever your fitness level. ✉ *Trondheim.*

Nidelvstien (*Nidelvstien Trail*)
HIKING/WALKING | This trail runs along the river from Tempe to the Leirfossene waterfalls. ✉ *Trondheim.*

SKIING

Bymarka and Estenstadmarka, wooded areas on the periphery of Trondheim, are popular with cross-country skiers. The Skistua ski lodge in Bymarka also has downhill runs.

Vassfjellet Skisenter
SKIING/SNOWBOARDING | This ski center 8 km (5 miles) south of Trondheim has 6 lifts and 10 runs. There are facilities for downhill and telemark skiing as well as snowboarding and tobogganing. Cross-country trails are also nearby. In season (roughly mid-October through Easter), Vassfjellet is open daily, and buses run here every evening and weekend. Ski and snowboard rentals and lessons available, and there's a cafeteria on-site. ✉ *Trondheim* ☎ *72–83–02–00* 🌐 *www.vassfjelletvinterpark.no.*

Bodø

705 km (438 miles) north of Trondheim.

The modern city of Bodø, once an important fishing village, is situated just above the Arctic Circle at the tip of a stunning coastal route where sea eagles soar and the northern lights shimmer in full splendor. In summer, the midnight sun is visible in June and early July and the polar night descends for the last two weeks of December. As the terminus of the Nordlandsbanen railroad and the Hurtigruten coastal ferry, Bodø serves as the gateway to the beautiful Lofoten Islands and the northernmost regions of Norway. The town's position on the sea makes this city the best starting point for nature walks and boat excursions to the coastal bird colonies on the Værøy Islands.

GETTING HERE AND AROUND

Scenic routes to Bodø include the Nordlandsbanen train from Trondheim and the Hurtingruten coastal ferry: both are easy and comfortable ways to traverse some of Norway's most staggeringly beautiful coastline. By car, the Rv 80 links Bodø to the E6, the main road through Norway. You can also take the Rv 17 coastal route. SAS offers several daily flights from Oslo to Bodø (80 minutes) to the Widerøe STOL airport.

Bodø's tourist office and your hotel are the best resources for information on getting around by bus or rental bicycle. The harbor area is best explored on foot.

HEALTH AND SAFETY

Bodø's extreme northerly position means colder weather in all seasons. Be sure to check the weather and pack accordingly.

Precautions should be taken when exploring the region's many outdoor attractions. First and foremost, check the weather forecast for the entire time you plan to be outdoors before setting out. Bad weather can arrive quickly and be extreme. Always leave behind a detailed plan of your trip with a reliable party, including the precise times you plan to be away.

VISITOR INFORMATION

CONTACTS Bodø turistinformasjon. (*Visit Bodø*) ✉ *Tollbugt. 13, Bodø* ☎ *75–54–50–80* 🌐 *www.visitbodo.com/en.*

Sights

★ Kjerringøy
TOWN | Kjerringøy, located 40 km (25 miles) north of Bodø, is well worth visiting. This gem on the Nordland coast is famous for its pristine fjord landscape used as the location for several feature films. Check out the Knut Hamsun Gallery, dedicated to the Nobel Prize–winning author. Kjerringøy is great for hiking, cycling, boating, fishing, and much more. To get here, take the 10-minute ferry across a fjord at Festvåg. ✉ *RV 834, Kjerringøy* ✥ *40 km (25 miles) north of Bodø* 🌐 *www.kjerringoy.info.*

★ Kjerringøy Handelssted (*Old Kjerringøy Trading Post*)
MUSEUM VILLAGE | Amid narrow fjords edging the peninsula, the Old Kjerringøy Trading Post has 15 well-preserved 19th-century buildings where Erasmus Zahl once made handsome profits buying and selling fish. Take a guided tour of the manor—many of its original furnishings are intact. There is an on-site café where you can enjoy fresh coffee and baked goods. ✉ *RV 834, Kjerringøy* ✥ *40 km (25 miles) north of Bodø* ☎ *75–50–35–05* 🌐 *nordlandsmuseet.no/en/kjerringoy-handelssted* 🎟 *NKr 100* ⏱ *Closed Sun.–Fri. mid-Aug.–late May.*

Nordlandsmuseet (*Nordland Museum*)
MUSEUM | Housed in one of the city's oldest buildings, the Nordland Museum includes a fascinating exhibit on Sámi culture that features a 350-year-old wooden box inscribed with mysterious runes. There's also silver that dates back 1,000 years to the Rønvik era: these English and Arabic coins and jewelry

were discovered in 1919. The "Byen vårres" ("Our City") exhibition reveals the history of Bodø. An open-air section has 14 historic buildings and a collection of boats, including the *Anna Karoline af Hopen*, the sole surviving Nordland cargo vessel, or *jekt*. ✉ *Prinsens gt. 116, Bodø* ☎ *75–50–35–00* 🌐 *nordlandsmuseet.no/en/nordlandsmuseet* 🎫 *NKr 70* ⏲ *Closed weekends Sept.–May.*

★ **Norsk Luftfartsmuseum** (*Norwegian Aviation Museum*)
MUSEUM | **FAMILY** | About 15 minutes from the town's center, the massive Norwegian Aviation Museum is housed in a building shaped like a propeller. The high-ceilinged rotunda illustrates "Man's Primeval Dream of Flight." On either side are smaller exhibition halls, one for civilian aviation and the other for military aviation. Here you'll find a Spitfire, a CF-104 Starfighter, a Junkers Ju 88, a U-2 spy plane, and much more. Take a turn on the flight simulators for a glimpse of the controls of an F-16. Climb the control tower for an unforgettable view of the wild landscape. ✉ *Olav V gt., Bodø* ☎ *75–50–78–50* 🌐 *luftfartsmuseum.no/en* 🎫 *NKr 175.*

★ **Saltstraumen**
VIEWPOINT | Truly magnificent, this 3-km-long (2-mile-long) and 500-foot-wide strait joins the inner fjord basin with the sea. During high tide the volume of water rushing through the narrow sound is so great that powerful whirlpools form. This is one of Norway's legendary maelstroms, and here you can see the strongest one in the world. The rush of water brings an abundance of fish, including cod, saithe, wolffish, and halibut, making this a popular fishing spot. ✉ *Rte. 80–17, Bodø* ✣ *33 km (20 miles) southeast of Bodø.*

Skulpturlandskap Nordland (*Artscape Nordland*)
PUBLIC ART | If you're an art lover, you can plan encounters with Artscape Nordland, an art project involving artists from 18 countries. The idea behind the project was to collect modern art and place one sculpture in every municipality in Nordland, with the landscape as the backdrop to the art. Sculptures—including *Uten Tittel* by British artist Tony Cragg, which is on the breakwater in Bodø—are in beautiful locations along the coast in 33 Nordland municipalities. ✉ *Bodø marina, Bodø* 🌐 *www.skulpturlandskap.no/?sprak=3.*

Zahlfjøsen (*Zahl's Farm*)
MUSEUM | Author Knut Hamsun visited Kjerringøy in 1879 and found plenty of inspiration. Several movies based on his novels were filmed here, including *Benoni & Rosa, The Telegraphist*, and *Pan*. An exhibition here includes clips from more than 20 films made since 1921. There is also locally produced art for sale, as well as a boatbuilder's workshop. ✉ *RV 834, Kjerringøy* ✣ *40 km (25 miles) north of Bodø* 🌐 *www.zahlfjosen.no* 🎫 *NKr 30* ⏲ *Closed Wed.–Sun. in winter.*

Beaches

Mjelle Beach
BEACH—SIGHT | **FAMILY** | About 30 minutes north of the city, this beautiful beach is reached via a short hike once you reach the parking lot. It's popular during the summer months with nature enthusiasts. Mjelle Beach can be found on the way north to Festvåg. **Amenities:** parking, toilet. **Best for:** solitude, sunset, walking ✉ *Bodø.*

Quick Bites

Melkebaren
$ | **CAFÉ** | Many locals will direct you to Melkebaren to sample the *møsbrømslefse*, a local specialty of cheese melted on flatbread. The extremely popular café has an outdoor terrace and baristas adept at making various types of coffee, including the cortados and lattes you know from back home. **Known for:** regional specialties; spacious outdoor terrace; friendly

staff. $ *Average main: NKr 100 ✉ Storgata 16, Bodø ☎ 997–59–294.*

Restaurants

★ Bjørk

$$$ | ITALIAN | FAMILY | This chic, modern café-restaurant is popular for its sunny terrace and straightforward food that always hits the mark—think juicy marinated jumbo shrimp, lobster soup, and a large selection of pizzas served hot from a wood-fired oven. It's an equally good stop for lunch, dinner, or an afternoon coffee with a delicious dessert. **Known for:** satisfying burgers; homemade pasta; popular with locals. $ *Average main: NKr 300 ✉ Storgt. 8, Bodø ☎ 75–52–40–40 🌐 www.restaurantbjork.no ⏲ No lunch Sun.*

Bryggerikaia

$$$ | NORWEGIAN | FAMILY | A spacious outdoor terrace and seafront location with unparalleled views over the harbor and distant mountains assure Bryggerikaia a steady clientele. But it's the menu of fresh seafood—local mussels, shrimp, and salmon, for starters—and market-fresh produce, as well as hearty meat dishes, that keep diners coming back. **Known for:** cozy and rustic atmosphere; views of the harbor; freshly brewed coffee. $ *Average main: NKr 285 ✉ Sjøgt. 1, Bodø ☎ 75–52–28–08 🌐 www.bryggerikaia.no/meny/english/english.*

Løvolds Kafeteria

$$ | NORWEGIAN | FAMILY | If you want to eat like a local, this bustling cafeteria is the place to be. Having had plenty of time to perfect its craft, Løvolds has been serving generous helpings of homemade Norwegian food for more than 75 years. **Known for:** affordable prices; tasty desserts; ever-changing daily specials. $ *Average main: NKr 175 ✉ Tollbugt. 9, Bodø ☎ 75–52–02–61 🌐 lovoldskafeteria.no ⏲ Closed Sun.*

LystPå

$$$$ | INTERNATIONAL | An award-winning eatery in the heart of Bodø, LystPå that takes pride in presenting beautifully prepared dishes in an atmosphere that feels anything but pretentious. The signature dish is stockfish, but the wide-ranging menu features everything from scallops to monkfish. **Known for:** 150 wines in the cellar; friendly and relaxed atmosphere; well-prepared seafood. $ *Average main: NKr 500 ✉ Torghallen Postboks 417, Trondheim ☎ 75–52–70–70 🌐 lystpa.no ⏲ Closed Sun.*

Hotels

★ Clarion Collection Hotel Grand

$$ | HOTEL | FAMILY | Overlooking the harbor, this centrally located hotel is looking spiffy after a complete renovation. **Pros:** fitness room, sauna, and steam bath; pet-friendly rooms; meals and snacks are included. **Cons:** some rooms can be noisy; some bathrooms are very small; does not accept cash. $ *Rooms from: NKr 980 ✉ Storgt. 3, Bodø ☎ 75–54–61–00 🌐 www.nordicchoicehotels.no 🛏 100 rooms 🍴 Some meals.*

Scandic Havet

$$ | HOTEL | Along the waterfront, this gleaming hotel has great views of the harbor and the mountains beyond from many of its modern rooms. **Pros:** free bike rentals; extensive breakfast; handy fitness room. **Cons:** parking on the street; no swimming pool; extra charge for some business amenities. $ *Rooms from: NKr 1200 ✉ Tollbugata 5, Bodø ☎ 75–50–38–00 🌐 www.scandichotels.com/hotels/norway/bodo 🛏 234 rooms 🍴 Free breakfast.*

Skagen Hotel

$$ | HOTEL | First-class service is the hallmark of this hotel, located in downtown Bodø. **Pros:** located in the center of the city; breakfast and dinner included; dependable Wi-Fi access. **Cons:** some areas need redecorating; no dedicated parking; small showers. *$ Rooms from: NKr 945 ✉ Nyholmsgt. 11, Bodø ☎ 75–51–91–00 🌐 www.skagen-hotel.no/en ⇨ 72 rooms 🍽 Some meals.*

★ Thon Hotel Nordlys

$$ | HOTEL | Smack dab in the city center with glorious views of the sunlight reflected on the harbor, this popular Scandinavian chain hotel is a bright, modern lodging with clean, spacious rooms. **Pros:** nice outdoor terrace; friendly staff; free buffet breakfast. **Cons:** parking costs extra; some rooms are cramped; charge for some business amenities. *$ Rooms from: NKr 900 ✉ Moloveien 14, Bodø ☎ 75–53–19–00 🌐 www.thonhotels.com/our-hotels/norway/bodo ⇨ 147 rooms 🍽 Free breakfast.*

Nightlife

★ Dama Di AS

BARS/PUBS | This sassy establishment is known for its artistic decor and terrace featuring some of the city's most renowned street art. Dama Di has a cult following in Bodø, and many travelers find that they fit right in at this eclectic establishment. *✉ Sjøgata 18, Bodø ☎ 957–77–775 🌐 dama-di.no.*

★ Hundholmen Brygghus

BREWPUBS/BEER GARDENS | Spanning two floors, this spacious establishment has a nook or cranny that will appeal to every type of customer. You can watch beer being brewed on the second floor, and even sample its four favorites. The bar also serves the most kinds of grappa in Norway—there are 250 currently available. There are sea views from the upper floor, making this the perfect place to watch the northern lights or the midnight sun. *✉ Tollbugata 13, Bodø ☎ 485–02–727 🌐 hundholmenbrygghus.no ⏲ Closed Sun.*

Top 13 Sky Bar

BARS/PUBS | If you're after a panoramic view of Bodø and the surrounding islands, head to Top 13, located on the top floor of the Radisson Blu Hotel. With the mountains visible in the distance, Top 13 is a great place to relax and enjoy one of the many specialty cocktails. *✉ Radisson Blu Hotel, Storgt. 2, Bodø 🌐 www.radissonblu.com/en/hotel-bodo/bars ⏲ Closed Sun.*

Performing Arts

Nordland musikkfestuke (*Nordland Festival of Music*)

FESTIVALS | This festival, taking place the second week of August, focuses on classical musical but also hosts jazz, contemporary, folk music, and pop/rock performances. *✉ Bodø ☎ 75–54–90–40 🌐 musikkfestuka.no/en.*

★ Stormen Culture Center

ARTS CENTERS | Located right on the harbor, this cultural hub is home to theatrical performances, jazz concerts, stand-up comedy, and much more. It's not unusual to see locals hanging around the harbor enjoying ice cream and sea views on a summer's day. *✉ Storgata 1B, Bodø ☎ 75–54–90–00 🌐 stormen.no/konserthuset.*

Shopping

Norsk Flid Husfliden Bodø

CRAFTS | You'll find traditional Norwegian garb here for men, women, and kids. There's also jewelry, handsome woolen blankets, tableware, and other quality crafts made in Scandinavia. *✉ Storgt. 23, Bodø ☎ 75–54–43–00 🌐 husflidenbodo.no ⏲ Closed Sun.*

Activities

BOATING

★ Explore Salten

BOATING | This tour company that takes you on boat trips to destinations like Saltstraumen, the world's largest maelstrom. The whirlpool is at its strongest every six hours, and tours are planned accordingly. Besides safety equipment, cold-weather gear is provided if you are visiting in winter. ✉ *Dronningens gt. 18, Bodø* ☎ *941–77–962* 🌐 *exploresalten.no/Home.*

BIKING

Bike Rental Bodø

BICYCLING | Bodø Tourist Information rents bicycles starting at NKr 25 per day. Pick one up at the tourist office or at the airport. ✉ *Tollbugt. 13, Bodø* ☎ *75–54–80–00* 🌐 *booking.kystriksveien.no/en/to-do/1732757/bike-hire-bodø.*

HIKING

Bodø og Omegn Turistforening (*Bodø Trekking Association*)

HIKING/WALKING | Bodø og Omegn Turistforening—better known as BOT—owns and operates cabins at 14 sites. It also services the 600-km (373-mile) stretch from the Saltenfjord in the north to the Arctic Circle in the south. The association has youth, senior, and family groups and offers a variety of excursions, including glacier, cave-exploring, and rock-climbing. ✉ *Sandgt. 3, Bodø* ☎ *75–52–14–13* 🌐 *www.bot.no.*

The Vesterålen Islands

An often-overlooked archipelago just north of the Lofoten Islands, the Vesterålen Islands are known for their abundant wildlife and mind-blowing greenery. The region has gained a reputation as a whale-watching destination, and you can feast your eyes on the majestic sperm whale in its feeding grounds surrounding the islands. With a long maritime history and an affinity for nature, the people of the Vesterålen Islands enjoy their time at Bleikstranda, Norway's longest beach, or on the many hikes crisscrossing the islands. The larger communities here include Andenes, Sortland, Harstad, and Stokmarknes.

GETTING HERE AND AROUND

There's daily services to Harstad/Narvik Airport from Oslo, Bodø, Tromsø, Trondheim, and Andenes. Less-frequent flights touch down at two regional airports at Stokmarknes and Andenes.

The Hurtigruten ferry has three ports in the islands: Sortland, Stokmarknes, and Risøyhamn. The Hurtigruten is an easy way to get to the islands or travel from one destination to the next.

If you are keen to drive through the islands, they are connected by an easy series of roads, bridges, and ferries. You can follow the 820 or the Fv 82 through the islands to see many of the grand views or the charming towns that dot the landscape.

Harstad

Located on Norway's largest island, Hinnøya, Harstad is the gateway to the Vesterålen Islands. It has a memorable harbor, charming streets, and a laid-back atmosphere. You can easily reach Harstad by the airport the city shares with Narvik called Evenes (EVE) where there are daily connections with some of the larger cities in Norway.

GETTING HERE AND AROUND

The easiest way to get to Harstad is to fly into Harstad/Narvik Airport, about 40 minutes from the city. There are regular express buses from the airport into Harstad. You can also arrive via the Hurtigruten ferry, which docks every morning to pick up new passengers headed north toward Kirkenes or south toward Bergen. Arriving overland is also an option, as Harstad is connected by highway with other parts of Norway.

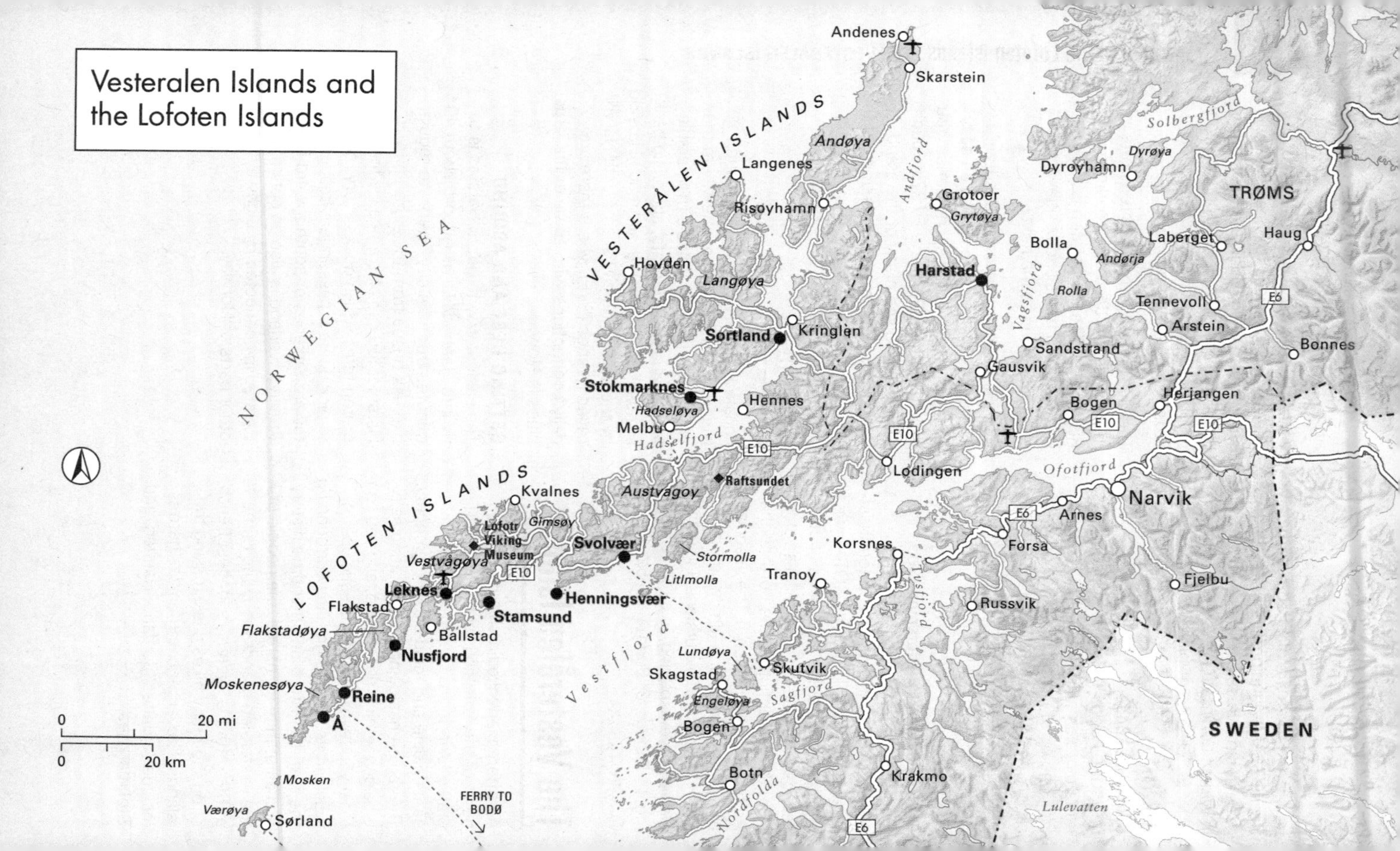
Vesteralen Islands and the Lofoten Islands
NORWEGIAN SEA
VESTERÅLEN ISLANDS
LOFOTEN ISLANDS
Andenes
Skarstein
Andøya
Langenes
Risoyhamn
Andfjord
Grotoer
Grytøya
Dyroyhamn
Dyrøya
Solbergfjord
TRØMS
Haug
Laberget
Bolla
Andørja
Rolla
Harstad
Vagsfjord
Tennevoll
Arstein
Bønnes
E6
Hovden
Langøya
Sortland
Kringlen
Sandstrand
Gausvik
Stokmarknes
Hadseløya
Melbu
Hennes
Hadselfjord
Bogen
Herjangen
E10
Lodingen
Ofotfjord
Narvik
Raftsundet
Austvagoy
Kvalnes
Gimsøy
Lofotr Viking Museum
Vestvågøya
Svolvær
Stormolla
Litlmolla
Arnes
Forsa
Korsnes
Tranoy
Tusfjord
Fjelbu
Russvik
Leknes
Flakstad
Stamsund
Henningsvær
Flakstadøya
Ballstad
Nusfjord
Vestfjord
Lundøya
Skutvik
Skagstad
Engeløya
Sagfjord
Moskenesøya
Reine
Å
Bogen
SWEDEN
0
20 mi
0
20 km
Botn
Krakmo
Nordfolda
Mosken
FERRY TO BODØ
Værøya
Sørland
Lulevatten

Sights

Adolfkanonen

MUSEUM | Part of Nazi Germany's coastal defense system, this massive naval gun was originally built to be used on a ship during World War II. The "Adolph Cannon" is now part of an interactive museum where you can explore its inner workings and see examples of the different types of missiles it could have fired. The gun is the last of its type left in the world, and is a reminder of the country's tragic history. ✉ *Harstad* ☎ *77–01–89–89* 🌐 *adolfkanonen.com/?lang=en.*

★ Trondenes Historical Center

MUSEUM | **FAMILY** | This museum covers the history of the region from the early Viking rulers to the German occupation during World War II. Although the museum's collection spans more than 2,000 years, its main focus is on the earliest eras of Scandinavian history. Using interactive displays and immersive multimedia presentations, the center really brings history to life. The grounds include many historical buildings and remnants of a long-ago way of life. ✉ *Trondenesveien 122, Harstad* ☎ *77–01–83–80* 🌐 *www.stmu.no/* *NKr 90* *Closed Sat.*

Restaurants

Big Horn Steakhouse

$$$$ | **STEAKHOUSE** | **FAMILY** | If you're feeling competitive, this American-style steak house hosts a steak-eating contest featuring a 45-ounce cut. It specializes in beef but has an extensive menu with something to appeal to everyone, even vegetarians. **Known for:** an alternative to the region's focus on fish; great selection of cocktails at the bar; mushrooms are recommended by locals. *$ Average main: NKr 500* ✉ *Strandgata 30, Harstad* ☎ *905–58–077* 🌐 *bighorn.no.*

Umami Harstad

$$$$ | **NORWEGIAN** | The decor of this extremely popular restaurant is minimalist, allowing the impressive dishes to take center stage. To add to the drama of the restaurant, the chef cooks and plates the food in full view of patrons, making for an interesting dining experience. **Known for:** delicious desserts made on-site; rotating menu of great wines; stunning presentation. *$ Average main: NKr 850* ✉ *Hans Egedes gt. 12, Harstad* ☎ *950–90–911* 🌐 *umamiharstad.no* *Closed Sun. and Mon.*

Hotels

Brygga Gjestehus

$$ | **HOTEL** | This guesthouse has a sleek, modern design that starts in the communal areas and continues into the comfortable, if a bit spartan, guest rooms. **Pros:** all the amenities you need (and none you don't); handy fitness room and sauna; breakfast and dinner included in rates. **Cons:** looks and feels like a hostel; charge for parking; not on the water. *$ Rooms from: NKr 1200* ✉ *Havnegata 3, Harstad* ☎ *77–06–50–00* 🌐 *www.brga.no* *14 rooms* *Free breakfast.*

Thon Hotel Harstad

$$$$ | **HOTEL** | This centrally located hotel overlooks the harbor, with some of the rooms having spectacular views of the shimmering water. **Pros:** sunny terrace; nice fitness center; eco-friendly vibe. **Cons:** many amenities cost extra; not all rooms have views; part of a chain. *$ Rooms from: NKr 2000* ✉ *Sjøgata 11, Harstad* ☎ *77–00–08–00* 🌐 *www.thonhotels.com* *141 rooms* *Free breakfast.*

Sortland

Located in the Vesterålen Islands, Sortland became known as the Blue City after local artists painted many of its buildings in shades ranging from azure to indigo. The dynamic city of about 10,000 people has a rich cultural history and an affinity for its musical traditions, which are celebrated in its many festivals.

Sortland also has amazing hiking trails that take you out into the surrounding countryside.

Sortland Museum

MUSEUM | **FAMILY** | This interesting museum celebrates the history and culture of Sortland and the surrounding area. Inside the city's modern Kulturfabrikken, its frequently changing exhibits range from photos of nearby communities to explorations of the local flora and fauna. A small shop stocks books and other items. ✉ *Kulturfabrikken, Strandgata 1, Sortland* ☎ *76–15–40–00* 🌐 *www.museumnord.no/en/sortland-museum* 🎫 *NKr 50* ⏲ *Closed Sun. and Mon.*

★ **Sortland Mat and Vinhus**

$$$$ | **NORWEGIAN** | Ask for a window seat at this centrally located eatery—you'll marvel at the fantastic views over the harbor and the mountains beyond. The restaurant's Scandinavian design is worked into both the decor and the aesthetically pleasing way each dish is presented. **Known for:** wine selections complement the food; extensive lunch buffet; Norwegian-style tapas. $ *Average main: NKr 400* ✉ *Torggata 27, Sortland* ☎ *76–20–12–10* 🌐 *matogvinhus.no/en/home* ⏲ *Closed Sun.*

★ **Sortland Hotell**

$$$ | **HOTEL** | This hotel has a literary pedigree: Pulitzer Prize–winning author Knut Hamsun wrote his book *Den Siste Glaede* while staying here, and there's an impressive library dedicated to writer Lars Saabye Christensen, whose works are available to read in several languages. **Pros:** allergen-free rooms; interesting history; free parking. **Cons:** not all rooms have views; extra charge for cribs; can be a bit noisy. $ *Rooms from: NKr 1700* ✉ *Vesterålsgata 59, Sortland* ☎ *76–10–84–00* 🌐 *www.sortlandhotell.no* *66 rooms* 🍽 *Free breakfast.*

★ **Hvalsafari** (*Whale Safari*)

WHALE-WATCHING | Besides seeing sperm whales in their natural environment, this outfitter lets you enjoy the rugged scenery and views with the beautiful islands of Andøya, Senja, and Bleiksøya in the background. The island of Bleiksøya is a bird sanctuary with a large puffin colony, and you'll also see fulmars, shags, and different types of gulls. Tour departs from the nearby community of Andenes. Around since 1989, the outfitter is renowned for its excellent tours. ✉ *Hamnegata, Andenes, Sortland* ☎ *761–15–600* 🌐 *www.whalesafari.no.*

Stokmarknes

The administrative center in Hadsel, Stokmarknes has a long maritime history that's well documented in the local boat museum. The hardworking town of more than 3,000 people swells when seasonal workers come to work in the fishing industry. On the way to the Vesterålen Islands, it's a great base for exploring the region.

GETTING HERE AND AROUND

Buses to and from Stokmarknes are few and far between, so getting here requires some advance planning. Stokmarknes Airport is a six-minute bus ride from the main bus terminal.

Within Stokmarknes, the best way to get around is by foot.

Days and Nights Sculpture

BUILDING | Clearly visible from the town and from passing ships, this sculpture sits on a raised platform and consists of two granite structures shaped like classic Norwegian cabins. The seemingly random holes in the cabins represent the constellations in the night sky. The walk here from town is pleasant, taking you over a bridge with jaw-dropping views of the area. ✉ *Søndregate, Stokmarknes* ☎ *75–65–00–00* 🌐 *www.skulpturlandskap.no/kunstverkene/dager-og-netter.*

★ **Norwegian Coastal Express Museum**
MUSEUM | FAMILY | At this museum of the region's maritime history, you can go aboard the MS *Finnmarken*, a ship dating from 1956 that used to make the journey along the country's rugged coast. It was among the many ships that sailed the Hurtigruten, or "Express Route." It takes you through the history of long-distance ferries and details how shipping routes came into existence. It doesn't overlook the human element; including the lives lost opening up the region to travel and commerce. ✉ *Nordnesveien 536, Stokmarknes* ☎ *76–11–81–90* 🌐 *www.museumnord.no/hurtigrutemuseet* 🎫 *NKr 100.*

Restaurants

Restaurant Isqueen
$$$$ | NORWEGIAN | A nautical theme runs through Restaurant Isqueen—not a surprise, since it's inside a handsome ship that is dry-docked near the harbor in Stokmarknes. Beamed ceilings and wide-plank floors call to mind the region's seafaring past. **Known for:** extensive wine selection; one-of-a-kind location; tasty seafood. $ *Average main: NKr 500* ✉ *Børøya, Stokmarknes* ☎ *76–15–29–99* 🌐 *isqueen.no* 🕒 *Closed Sun.–Thurs.*

Rødbrygga
BARS/PUBS | Inside a wooden cabin, this charming pub exudes plenty of coziness, or as the Norwegians like to say, *hyggelig*. Choose a local brew from the sizable beer selection, select several dishes from the extensive menu, or enjoy musicians playing songs from the region. ✉ *Markedsgata 6, Stokmarknes* ☎ *76–15–26–66* 🌐 *rødbrygga.no.*

The Lofoten Islands

Extending out into the ocean north of Bodø are the Lofoten Islands, a 190-km (118-mile) chain of jagged peaks. In summer the farms, fjords, and fishing villages draw caravans of visitors, whereas in winter the coast facing the Arctic Ocean is one of Europe's stormiest. The beaches here are remarkably clear, and travelers may think they have landed in the Caribbean instead of northern Norway. This is an adventurer's paradise with an abundance of hiking trails, boat trips, and much more. From bustling Henningsvær all the way to the photogenic village of Å, the Lofoten Islands are one of the top destinations in all of Norway.

GETTING HERE AND AROUND

Getting to the Lofoten Islands is simpler than it looks. You can take a ferry from Bodø, fly in from various other parts of Norway, or simply drive. The Islands are served by three airports: Harstad/Narvik, Leknes, and Svolvær. Once you're here, you'll want to rent a car to explore the islands at your leisure.

Henningsvær

One of the most prominent fishing villages in the Lofoten Islands, Henningsvær has a history dating back to 1556. Besides its fame as a charming fishing village, Henningsvær also offers several cafés, restaurants, workshops, and boutiques that will delight tourists. People go to Henningsvær for its quaint charm and cafés, shops, and more.

GETTING HERE AND AROUND

The nearest airport is Svolvær Helle Airport, reachable by bus or taxi. If you're driving, the E10 takes you most of the way from Svolvær to Henningsvær.

Sights

★ Galleri Lofotens Hus

MUSEUM | One of the best-known museums in the Lofoten Islands, the family-run Galleri Lofotens Hus is home to the largest collection of northern Norwegian artwork from the last century, including renowned painters like Otto Sinding, Gunnar Berg, Even Ulving, Adelsteen Normann, Einar Berger, Ole Juul, and Thorolf Holmboe. Take a load off at the on-site café. ✉ *Misværveien 18, Henningsvær* ☎ *915–95–083* 🌐 *www.galleri-lofoten.no/nb* 🎫 *NKr 60.*

KaviarFactory

MUSEUM | Run by the husband-and-wife team of Venke and Rolf Hoff, the KaviarFactory is located inside an old caviar factory. This contemporary art museum holds works from notable Norwegian artists as well as some top international talent. ✉ *Henningsværveien 13, Henningsvær* ☎ *907–34–743* 🌐 *www.kaviarfactory.com* 🎫 *NKr 100.*

Heimgårdsbrygga

MUSEUM | Henningsvær is quite possibly the most famous fishing village in the Lofoten Islands, and there's no better place to get a feel for its history than the harbor of Heimgårdsbrygga. It's also one of the most photogenic backdrops in the region, with many of its history structures still intact. ✉ *Dreyers gt. 71, Henningsvær* ☎ *76–07–11–15* 🌐 *heimgards-brygga.no/index.html.*

Restaurants

Fiskekrogen Henningsvær

$$$ | **NORWEGIAN** | You can't miss this restaurant with a huge blue fish swimming by on the whitewashed facade. It has great views over the harbor, including a glimpse of the imposing mountains in the background. **Known for:** cocktails at the bar; Lofoten lamb expertly prepared; the fish soup is spectacular. $ *Average main: NKr 300* ✉ *Dreyersgt. 29, Henningsvær* ☎ *76–07–46–52* 🌐 *www.fiskekrogen.no/home.html* 🕒 *Closed Mon.*

★ Henningsvær Lysstøperi and Cafe

$ | **CAFÉ** | In the heart of Henningsvær, this charming and delightful café is a favorite destination for both locals and visitors in search of a warming cup of coffee or hot chocolate. The café doubles as an arts-and-crafts store, with a range of lovely items available for sale. **Known for:** freshly baked cinnamon buns; candles and other gifts; cozy atmosphere. $ *Average main: NKr 100* ✉ *Gammelveien 2, Henningsvær* ☎ *76–07–70–40.*

Hotels

Henningsvær Bryggehotell

$$$ | **HOTEL** | **FAMILY** | Renowned for its impeccable customer service, the Henningsvær Bryggehotell has an unbeatable location on the docks over the harbor and is a short walk from all of the main sights in town. **Pros:** free breakfast; luggage storage; daily housekeeping service. **Cons:** older building a bit stuffy; no elevator; limited parking. $ *Rooms from: NKr 1800* ✉ *Misværveien 18, Henningsvær* ☎ *76–07–47–50* 🌐 *www.classicnorway.com/hotels/henningsvar-bryggehotell* *30 rooms* *Free breakfast.*

Lofoten Arctic Hotel Knusarn

$$$ | **HOTEL** | On a corner of Henningsvær's town square, this wooden building dating back to 1892 has been lovingly restored as a snug little inn with just eight rooms. **Pros:** luggage storage; free Wi-Fi; complimentary breakfast. **Cons:** thin walls; "cozy" means "small"; no big-hotel amenities. $ *Rooms from: NKr 1700* ✉ *Dreyers gt. 8, Henningsvær* ☎ *76–07–07–77* 🌐 *www.lofotenarctichotel.no/en* *8 rooms* *Free breakfast.*

Svolvær

An important fishing village in northern Norway, Svolvær became a destination for travelers after 19th-century painter Gunnar Berg portrayed the lives of local fishermen. A couple of miles west is the village of Vågar, known for being northern Norway's oldest settlement.

GETTING HERE AND AROUND

Svolvær Helle Airport has flights from Bodø and Oslo. Svolvær sits directly on the E10, the main highway running through the Lofoten Islands.

Sights

Kjeøya Kystbatteri

LOCAL INTEREST | History enthusiasts love this World War II bunker, although it has been swallowed up by nature and is pretty rusty. It still tells a powerful story. ✉ *Gunnar Bergs vei, Svolvær.*

Lofoten Krigsminnemuseum

MUSEUM | The Lofoten War Memorial Museum commemorates the struggles of World War II with displays of uniforms, weaponry, and other objects. ✉ *Fiskergata 3, Svolvær* ☎ *91–73–03–28* 🌐 *www.lofotenkrigmus.no* 🎫 *NKr 100.*

★ **Lofotpils**

WINERY/DISTILLERY | A labor of love, this brewery has been supplying the Lofoten Islands with refreshing craft beer since 2014. You can take a tour of the brewery and learn about the fermentation and brewing process. ✉ *Fiskergata 36, Svolvær* ☎ *906–37–383* 🌐 *lofotpils.no.*

Restaurants

Børsen Spiseri

$$$ | NORWEGIAN | Located on Svinøya, this restaurant serves traditional fare in a rustic setting with rough-hewn beams and wide-plank floors. Wildly popular among both locals and travelers, Børsen Spiseri serves dishes ranging from stockfish to *pinnekjøtt* (cured lamb and sheep ribs associated with the winter holidays). **Known for:** traditional stockfish dishes; locals head here for holidays; cozy atmosphere. $ *Average main: NKr 325* ✉ *Gunnar Bergs vei 2, Svolvær* ☎ *76–06–99–30* 🌐 *www.svinoya.no/en/restaurant.*

Paleo Arctic

$$$$ | NORWEGIAN | Exploring the culinary past of the Lofoten Islands, the kitchen here has gained credibility by using as many local ingredients as possible and employing modern cooking techniques to create spectacular dishes. The menu regularly changes based on what is available that season. **Known for:** great tasting menu; good selection of wines; tasty seasonal vegetables. $ *Average main: NKr 525* ✉ *Thon Hotel Lofoten, Torget, Svolvær* ☎ *94–86–75–67* 🌐 *paleoarctic.no* ⏲ *Closed Sun.*

Hotels

Svinøya Rorbuer

$$$$ | HOTEL | In the oldest and most atmospheric part of Svolvær Island, this cluster of *rorbuer* (fishermen's cabins) is close to the cod drying on racks and the screaming seagulls. **Pros:** cabins have a secluded feel; airport shuttle available; Wi-Fi and other amenities. **Cons:** breakfast is an extra charge; not all cabin views are the same; roads can get icy in winter. $ *Rooms from: NKr 2000* ✉ *Gunnar Bergs vei 2, Svolvær* ☎ *76–06–99–30* 🌐 *www.svinoya.no/en* *38 cabins* *No meals.*

Nightlife

Magic Ice Lofoten

BARS/PUBS | You can enjoy winter all year at this bar where you dress in an oversized parka and enter an icy world. Even the glasses your drinks are served in will be made from ice. ✉ *Fiskergata 36, Svolvær* ☎ *76–07–40–11* 🌐 *www.magicice.no.*

Did You Know?

The Lofoten Islands attract intrepid travelers who stay in the rustic waterfront cabins that once belonged to fishermen.

Shopping

Galleri Stig Tobiassen

ART GALLERIES | This gallery focuses on the works of artist Stig Tobiassen, and at any given time it has hundreds of his oil paintings of the Lofoten Islands on display. All are for sale. ✉ *Kirkegata 9, Svolvær* ☎ *476–02–722* 🌐 *www.stig-tobiassen.com* ⏲ *Closed Sun.*

Activities

BOATING

★ Lofoten Explorer

BOATING | **FAMILY** | One of the most popular tours in the Lofoten Islands is the sea eagle safari offered by Lofoten Explorer. Small boats take you to the narrow and mystical Trollfjorden to see the sea eagles in their native habitat. The company provides proper winter clothing to keep you warm in sub-freezing temperatures. ✉ *Johan E Paulsens gt. 12 N, Svolvær* ☎ *971–52–248* 🌐 *www.lofoten-explorer.no/en.*

HORSEBACK RIDING

Hov Gård

HORSEBACK RIDING | **FAMILY** | While visiting the Lofoten Islands you'll want to try Icelandic horseback riding with Hov Gård on Gimsøy Island. The company has been around for many years and takes exceptionally good care of each and every horse. Tours can be customized for the skill levels of all riders. A cozy café and restaurant here serves Norwegian specialties. ✉ *Tore Hjortsvei 471, Gimsøysand, Svolvær* ☎ *940–97–271* 🌐 *hovgard.no.*

WINTER SPORTS

Lofoten Aktiv

TOUR—SPORTS | **FAMILY** | This company has several guides who are extremely skilled and can take you on a variety of tours, from hunting for the elusive northern lights to snowshoeing in quiet Kabelvåg. ✉ *Rødmyrveien 22, Svolvær* ☎ *76–07–30–00* 🌐 *www.lofoten-aktiv.no/en.*

Stamsund

Around 11 km (7 miles) from Leknes is Stamsund, one of the most colorful villages in all of Lofoten. You will find the traditional *rorbuer* (fishermen's cabins) and other historic structures that call to mind this region's rich past.

GETTING HERE AND AROUND

Stamsund is located very close to Leknes Airport. There are no buses between them, so a rental car is perhaps your best option.

Restaurants

Skjærbrygga Restaurant

$$$$ | **NORWEGIAN** | The menu at this eatery focuses on the flavors of the Lofoten Islands, which of course means lots of seafood, wild game, and local meats and cheeses. The staff is laid back, encouraging you to relax and enjoy the view of the harbor. **Known for:** lovely location on the water; weekly quizzes at the bar; spacious terrace in summer. [$] *Average main: NKr 600* ✉ *Skjæret 2, Stamsund* ☎ *76–05–46–00* 🌐 *www.livelofoten.com.*

Hotels

★ Anne Gerd's Lofoten Guesthouse

$$ | **B&B/INN** | Anne Gerd believes in the recharging power of Norwegian nature and established her guesthouse 6 km (4 miles) east of Leknes to provide easy access to it. **Pros:** warm, family feel; outdoor activities on the doorstep; cooking facilities available. **Cons:** shared bathrooms; some hallway noise; cash only. [$] *Rooms from: NKr 800* ✉ *Hagskarveien 330, Stamsund* ☎ *99–52–99–45* 🌐 *www.lofoten-guesthouse.com* ▭ *No credit cards* *4 rooms* *Free breakfast.*

Live Lofoten

$$$$ | **HOTEL** | Right on the water, this group of *rorbuer* (fishermen's cabins) offers a glimpse of life back in the days where Lofoten was famous for its fish.

Pros: free Wi-Fi and other amenities; children can stay free; convenient fitness center. **Cons:** separate check-in location; no cribs for infants. *Rooms from: NKr 2000* *J. M. Johansens Vei 49, Stamsund* *76–05–46–00* *www.livelofoten.com* *16 cabins, 28 rooms* *No meals.*

Activities

HIKING

★ Steinetind

HIKING/WALKING | While it may not offer the most spectacular views in Lofoten, this mountain on the island of Vestvågøy has hikes that are manageable even for novices. While not at all difficult, the trails hug the cliffs and can be a challenge to those who are afraid of heights. *Stamsund.*

Leknes

If there's any place in Norway that proves the tourist board's slogan—"Powered by Nature"—it must be Leknes. Set in the center of the Lofoten Islands on the country's northwest coast, the administrative center for the region is surrounded by dramatic landscapes of rock thrusting up from the water to form fjords at every turn.

GETTING HERE AND AROUND

Leknes has one of the few airports in Lofoten Islands. Getting around is easy via public transportation.

Sights

★ Lofotr Viking Museum

MUSEUM VILLAGE | **FAMILY** | One of the top historical sites in Europe, this museum 13 km (8 miles) north of Leknes portrays the lifestyle and culture of the Vikings through magical reconstructions of typical buildings and ships. The re-created Viking chieftain's longhouse, on the foundations of a real chieftain's home, has been built according to authentic methods, including grass-turf walls, load-bearing poles, and fireplaces. Inside, it's divided, just like the original, into a lobby, living quarters, great hall, and *byre* (barn). Nearby, several other reconstructed buildings include a smithy and boathouse, and three ships that can be boarded in summer. The exhibition halls display more Viking artifacts and show a 12-minute film about the history and people of the region. Artisans are at work on site, and there's a chance to taste Viking food. There's even an activity area for kids, which makes the museum a popular choice for families. *Vikingveien 539, Bøstad* *76–08–49–00, 76–15–40–00* *www.lofotr.no/en* *NKr 170* *Closed Sun. Feb.–Apr., Sept., and Oct.*

Nasjonal turistveg Lofoten (*Lofoten National Tourist Route*)

SCENIC DRIVE | One of the most scenic road trips in the world, this route stretches 230 km (142 miles) between Raftsundet in the north and the village of Å in the south. Whether heading north or south from Leknes, the craggy rock peaks, white sand beaches, and emerald green seas make it difficult to keep your attention on the road, especially when seen as a backdrop to seaside fishing villages. At regular intervals and particularly scenic spots, rest areas, viewing platforms, observation towers, and restaurants encourage further exploration. *Leknes* *www.nasjonaleturistveger.no/en/routes.*

Beaches

Uttakleiv Beach

BEACH—SIGHT | **FAMILY** | One of the most photogenic beaches in northern Norway, Uttakeiv Beach is 12 kilometers (7 miles) from Leknes. This beach has unmatched aurora shows during winter and a spectacular midnight sun in the summer. **Amenities:** parking. **Best for:** walking. *Uttakleivveien 238, Leknes.*

Restaurants

Himmel og Havn

$$$ | **NORWEGIAN** | As the name translates, "Heaven and Harbor" play lead roles in the spirit of this restaurant in the village of Ballstad. Sitting on a dock moored with fishing boats, the harbor is right outside, and as picturesque as they come. **Known for:** menu that changes regularly; great views over the harbor; excellent wine selection. *Average main: NKr 259* *Moloveien 45, Ballstad* *19 km (12 miles) south of Leknes* *904–70–004* *www.himmeloghavn.no.*

Hotels

Eliassen Rorbuer

$$$ | **RENTAL** | The little red and yellow fishermen's huts (*rorbuer*) that populate the villages of Lofoten and appear on so many postcards also house many tourists in summer—these, dating back to the 19th century, sit along the coast of a tiny rocky island 48 km (30 miles) south of Leknes. **Pros:** pristine location; well-equipped kitchens; excellent base for outdoor activities. **Cons:** weather can be variable; price doesn't include linens; inconsistent Wi-Fi signal. *Rooms from: NKr 1890* *Hamnøya* *45–81–48–45* *www.rorbuer.no/en* *35 cabins* *No meals.*

Scandic Leknes Lofoten

$$$ | **HOTEL** | The only major hotel in Leknes itself, the Scandic Leknes Lofoten sits at the midpoint of the Lofoten National Tourist Route, with most major sights along the way. **Pros:** central location; friendly staff; parking available. **Cons:** additional charge for pets; rooms near restaurant are loud; no elevator. *Rooms from: NKr 1590* *Lillevollveien 15, Leknes* *76–05–44–31* *www.scandichotels.no/hotell/norge/lofoten/lekneslofoten* *60 rooms* *Free breakfast.*

Activities

SURFING

Unstad Arctic Surf

SURFING | Surfing has been popular at Unstad Bay since the early 1960s. In 2003, Thor Frantzen and his wife, Randi, decided to open up a camping area on this beach known for its glassy waves and breaks. Over the years, it expanded into the northernmost surf resort in the world and a great place to go surfing or take a lesson. *Unstadveien 105, Bøstad* *www.unstadarcticsurf.com.*

Nusfjord

One of the smallest villages in Lofoten is Nusfjord. It's immensely popular because its old fishing cabins that are now used as guesthouses. Hidden between rocks and the sea, this small village is a bit of a challenge to reach without a rental car.

GETTING HERE AND AROUND

To get here by car, drive along the E10 until you need to turn off at the Fv 807. No buses service this route, so a rental car is a must.

Restaurants

Restaurant Karoline

$$$ | **NORWEGIAN** | On the harbor in Nusfjord, Restaurant Karoline serves up the best of Lofoten on a plate. Whether it be lamb, cod, or even truffle seaweed, this waterfront restaurant prepares each dish with flair. **Known for:** stockfish is a signature dish; great views of the ocean; informative cooking classes. *Average main: NKr 400* *Nusfjordveien 110, Nusfjord* *76–09–30–20* *nusfjordarcticresort.com/cuisine.*

Hotels

Nusfjord Arctic Resort

$$$$ | **HOTEL** | Nestled in a tranquil fishing village with a population of only 19, the Nusfjord Arctic Resort is home to fishermen's cabins built right on a pier. **Pros:** on-site sauna; amenities like free Wi-Fi; spacious cabins. **Cons:** poor Wi-Fi in some cabins; no 24-hour reception; a bit isolated. *Rooms from: NKr 2500* *Nusfjord N, Nusfjord* *76–09–30–20* *nusfjordarcticresort.com* *19 cabins* *Free breakfast.*

Reine

Reine and the surrounding villages benefit from some of the most beautiful scenery in the Lofoten Islands. Reine was once a commercial center starting back in the 18th century, and in recent years has become a magnet for travelers. During the summer it is renowned for hiking, while winter brings northern lights glory.

GETTING HERE AND AROUND

Connected by the E10, Reine is another fishing village where a rental car is a plus. Once you're here, it's possible to get around by foot.

Beaches

★Kvalvika Beach

BEACH—SIGHT | Hidden on the northern side of Moskenesøy, the only way to reach this beautiful beach is by walking. Wedged between the mountains, this golden-sand beach is a gem. Once you are parked, the hike here takes around 45 minutes. **Amenities:** parking. **Best for:** walking. *Fv 808, Fredvang, Reine.*

Quick Bites

Bringen

$ | **CAFÉ** | **FAMILY** | One of the coziest spots for coffee and light bites in Reine, this café puts you right in the center of the action. It has a highly trained staff and several tables if you want to sit and enjoy your shot of caffeine. **Known for:** delicious coffee; lovely gift shop; the best views. *Average main: NKr 100* *Reine* *76–09–13–00* *Closed Sun.*

Restaurants

Gammelbua Restaurant

$$$$ | **NORWEGIAN** | This restaurant in one of the region's most beautiful villages takes you back in time by serving superb local dishes. From the cozy and rustic dining room you have views of the ocean and mountains beyond. **Known for:** a little bit of history; vegan options available; tasty stockfish with local seaweed. *Average main: NKr 500* *Reine Rorbeurer N, Reine* *76–09–22–22* *www.classic-norway.no/hotell/reine-rorbuer/restaurant.*

Hotels

Catogården

$$ | **HOTEL** | In the beautiful village of Reine you'll find Catogården, a newly renovated lodging with eye-popping views and a location near the water. **Pros:** great activities; nice picnic area; spacious rooms. **Cons:** only two showers available; no kitchen areas; books up fast. *Rooms from: NKr 900* *Sverdrupsvei 9, Reine* *992–23–228* *www.cato-garden.no* *10 rooms* *No meals.*

Reine Rorbuer

$$$ | **HOTEL** | Taking full advantage of one of the most renowned settings in all the Lofoten Islands, these 39 cabins painted a ravishing shade of red sit right beside the sea. **Pros:** amenities like free Wi-Fi; beautiful terraces; secluded location. **Cons:** regular housekeeping only on

request; walls can be thin; a bit isolated. *Rooms from: NKr 1800* *Reine i Lofoten, Reine* *76–09–22–22* *www.classicnorway.no/hotell/reine-rorbuer* *Closed Nov. and Dec.* *39 cabins* *No meals.*

Å

One of the last little fishing villages in the Lofoten Islands, photogenic Å is where you'll find some of the most epic views in the region. There is even a museum dedicated to fishing.

GETTING HERE AND AROUND

To get to Å, you can fly into Leknes Airport or take the ferry over from Bodø. You can also take the 18-742 bus or opt to drive.

Sights

Norsk Fiskeværsmuseum

MUSEUM | This museum is dedicated to the industry that fortified this village for decades. It takes you back to a simpler time when the whole population's livelihood depended solely on what the seas brought in. It re-enacts (in a realistic manner) the old life in the Lofoten Islands, showing how people baked, worked, and did the hard labor that built the islands to what they are today. There is a café on the premises. *Å i Lofoten, Å* *76–09–14–88* *www.museumnord.no/fiskevarsmuseum* *NKr 100* *Closed weekends Sept.–June.*

Quick Bites

★ **Bakeriet på Å**

$ | **NORWEGIAN** | **FAMILY** | If you drive to the end of the Lofoten Islands, you absolutely must stop at this traditional Norwegian bakery famous for its cinnamon buns. The bakers use traditional methods, so the pastries are always their freshest. **Known for:** locals say these are the region's best cinnamon buns; traditional flatbreads and other delights; freshly baked breads. *Average main: NKr 60* *Å* *76–09–14–88.*

Restaurants

Brygga Restaurant

$$$$ | **NORWEGIAN** | This local eatery serves some of the region's best seafood, keeping the menu short and always changing depending on what's available in the market. You are almost always going to find some traditional stockfish, served in a variety of ways, as well as local specialties like reindeer. **Known for:** intentionally short menu; stockfish always available; rooms for those who want to stay overnight. *Average main: NKr 600* *Å i Lofoten, Å* *941–33–793* *www.bryggarestaurant.no.*

Hotels

Å Rorbuer

$$$ | **HOTEL** | As with other *rorbuer,* these lodgings offer a rustic and traditional way to experience the northern Norway islands. **Pros:** terraces for warm weather; lovely gardens; one of the best local lodgings. **Cons:** rooms on the small side; walls are thin; heat can be spotty. *Rooms from: NKr 1800* *Å* *76–09–11–21* *arorbuer.no* *25 cabins* *No meals.*

Chapter 10

NORTHERN NORWAY

Updated by
Megan Starr and
Aram Vardanyan

Sights	Restaurants	Hotels	Shopping	Nightlife
★★★★★	★★★★☆	★★★★☆	★★★☆☆	★★☆☆☆

WELCOME TO NORTHERN NORWAY

TOP REASONS TO GO

★ **Enjoy the great outdoors.** If you're looking for hiking, biking, or other activities, Tromsø has more outfitters than any other destination in northern Norway.

★ **Push yourself to the limit.** Hammerfest, Honningsvåg, and the other communities of the North Cape delight anyone looking for that indescribable feeling of being on top of the world.

★ **Catch some rays at midnight.** The summer sun never sets in this part of the world, so it's the perfect place if you're the type of person who doesn't like going to bed early.

★ **Feel like you're walking on the moon.** Don't pass up a trip to Honningsvåg, located on an otherworldly island void of trees and with a tundra landscape.

★ **Experience the northern lights.** Ghostly auroras are dancing in the night sky during winter in this region above the Arctic Circle.

1 **Tromsø.** The cultural capital of northern Norway, Tromsø is filled with interesting museums detailing life here over the years.

2 **Senja.** Norway's second-largest island is known for Segla Mountain, a dramatic peak that gazes out over the Atlantic.

3 **Alta.** Focused on the great outdoors, this town is appealing to more and more travelers for its less-touristy vibe.

4 **Hammerfest.** If you're here to experience the Arctic, the world's northernmost town is the best place to be your base.

5 **Nordkap.** A visit to the continent's northernmost point is a rite of passage for nearly all Scandinavians.

6 **Honningsvåg.** One of the most important harbors in Norway, Honningsvåg is centered around its waterfront.

7 **Kirkenes.** A stone's throw from Russia, this small town has a fascinating history well worth exploring.

BARENTS SEA
Gamvik
Nordkapp
5
Magerøya
Honningsvåg
Laholmen
6
Repvag
Veidnes
Laksefjord
Tanafjord
Svartnes
Varangerhalvoya
Revsbotn
Hammerfest
4
Tanagard
Skallelv
Olderfjord
Porsangen
Soroya
Luovtejok
Vadsø
Hasvik
Kvalsund
Kunes
Skaidi
Borselv
E6
Varangerfjord
Soroysundet
Sirma
Polmak
E6
Vagge
Kirkenes
Nyby
Rafsbotn
3
E6
E6
7
Alteidet
Alta
Port
FINNMARK
E6
Røvisuvanto
Nordrelsa
Karasjok
Kafjordelva
Sousjav ri
RUSSIA
Kautokeino
FINLAND
E8
0
50 mi
E75
SWEDEN
0
50 km
E45

Despite its rugged landscapes and unapologetic weather, northern Norway draws a constant stream of intrepid travelers during both the summer and winter months. From July's glistening midnight sun to colorful auroras dancing across the sky in December, it's one of the world's most mysterious and captivating destinations. If the Arctic Circle is on your bucket list, this is the best place to experience all that it has to offer.

Northern Norwegians still make their living in the fishing villages of the Lofoten Islands, in small, provincial towns, and in modern cities like Tromsø. Tourism plays an important role in the region, especially with those seeking wild landscapes, outdoor activities, and adventure, whether it's mountaineering, dogsledding, skiing, caving, or wreck-diving. Basking in the midnight sun is one of Norway's most popular attractions; every year, thousands of people flock to Nordkapp (the North Cape) for it.

Planning

When to Go

Depending on your interests, northern Norway is desirable all year round. If you're into hiking and other outdoor activities, head here during the summer months. Hiking trails will lead you around epic landscapes and past unforgettable views, all the way from the Lyngen Alps around Tromsø to the world's northernmost pine forest at Stabbursdalen National Park. And since the sun never sets, the days never end and you can continue to explore no matter what time of the day or night. If you're here to see the northern lights—a sight that will remain in your mind for the rest of your life—you'll want to come in winter. Remember that daylight will often be nonexistent, so you're more limited in terms of outdoor activities. Shoulder season is for the more adventurous of travelers because you really don't know what kind of weather you'll encounter. Flexibility and patience are key during spring and autumn, but you will be rewarded with lower prices and fewer tourists.

Getting Here and Around

Northern Norway is a bit of a challenge to navigate without a fair amount of planning. Trains don't run this far north, and buses are infrequent. If you're here in summer, your best option would be to rent a car or boat. If you're around in winter, your best bet is to fly or take a boat.

AIR TRAVEL

Frequent flights to Tromsø on Norwegian and SAS make it possible to explore this region without too much time on the road. From Tromsø, the domestic airline Widerøe connects you to the smaller cities, towns, and villages. Certain routes have extremely long layovers, making your journey much longer than anticipated.

CONTACTS Norwegian. ☎ *815–21–815 in Norway* 🌐 *www.norwegian.no.* **SAS.** ☎ *05400* 🌐 *www.flysas.com.* **Widerøe.** ☎ *810–01–200* 🌐 *www.wideroe.no.*

BOAT TRAVEL

The Hurtigruten cruises up and down the Norwegian coast in summer and winter, making it a viable option for travelers throughout the year.

CONTACTS Hurtigruten. ☎ *810–30–000* 🌐 *www.hurtigruten.com.*

BUS TRAVEL

Bus travel can be a bit challenging in the far north, but it is possible. Snelandia runs frequent service in and around Tromsø and in Nordkapp. Alta, Hammerfest, and Honningsvåg are all connected by bus, albeit with fewer departures.

CAR TRAVEL

With its lightly traveled roads and endless photo ops, the best way to get around northern Norway during the summer is by car. Keep in mind that gas is not cheap in Norway and that you must reserve well ahead of time in far-flung places like Honningsvåg. Renting a car during winter months presents a challenge to anyone unfamiliar with driving in snow, ice, and darkness. And remember you're sharing the road with other creatures, such as reindeer.

Restaurants

Seafood reigns supreme here, ranging from familiar favorites like a huge bowl of mussels steamed in white wine to oddities like crispy cod tongues served with a squeeze of lemon. Atlantic halibut, herring, and haddock all have a place of honor in these kitchens. Nothing is too fancy here—the emphasis is always on the freshest fish possible, prepared simply.

Hotels

Outside of the larger cities, this region is likely to offer just a few options for accommodations wherever you go. The good news is that they are often family-run inns with plenty of charm or one-of-a-kind lodgings like hotels made completely of ice.

Restaurant and hotel reviews have been shortened. For full information, visit Fodors.com.

What It Costs in Norwegian Krone

$	$$	$$$	$$$$
RESTAURANTS			
under NKr 125	NKr 125–NKr 250	NKr 251–NKr 350	over NKr 350
HOTELS			
under NKr 750	NKr 750–NKr 1250	NKr 1251–NKr 1900	over NKr 1900

Tromsø

1,800 km (1,118 miles) north of Bergen, 250 km (155 miles) north of Narvik.

Tromsø surprised visitors in the 1800s: they thought it very sophisticated and cultured for being so close to the North

The breathtaking aurora borealis winds its way through the sky above the city of Tromsø.

Pole—hence its nickname, the Paris of the North. It looks the way a polar town should—with ice-capped mountain ridges and jagged architecture that echoes the peaks. The midnight sun shines from May 21 to July 21, and it is said that the northern lights decorate the night skies over Tromsø more than any other city in Norway. Tromsø is home to only 73,500 people, but it's very spread out—the city's total area, 2,558 square km (987 square miles), is the most expansive in Norway. The downtown area is on a small, hilly island connected to the mainland by a slender bridge. The 13,000 students at the world's northernmost university are one reason the nightlife here is uncommonly busy.

GETTING HERE AND AROUND

Tromsø, a crossroads for air traffic between northern and southern Norway, is served by SAS, Norwegian, and Widerøe. The airport is 3 km (2 miles) northwest of the town center, and easily reachable via the Flybussen airport shuttle or Tromsø Taxi.

The Hurtigruten coastal express boat calls at Tromsø. Cruise ships dock either in the city center at Prostneset or 4 km (2½ miles) north of the city center at Breivika. Step off the ship in Prostneset, and you're in the city center. A shuttle is offered between Breivika and the city center.

When coming from the south, follow the E6 (the main road north) past Narvik before taking the E8 heading west at Nordkjosbotn. Cominor is the local bus operator in the Tromsø area. There is no train station in Tromsø.

CONTACTS Flybussen. (*Airport Bus*) ☎ *40–55–40–55* *www.flybussen.no/en/Tromsø.* **Tromsø Taxi.** ☎ *03011 in Norway* *www.tromso-taxi.no.*

Sights

Fjellheisen (*Fjellheisen Cable Car*) **TRANSPORTATION SITE (AIRPORT/BUS/FERRY/TRAIN)** | **FAMILY** | To get a sense of Tromsø's immensity and solitude, take this cable car from the mainland, just across the bridge and behind the cathedral, up to the island's mountains. Storsteinen (Big Rock), rising 1,386 feet above sea level, has a great city view. In summer a restaurant is open at the top of the lift. ✉ *Sollivn. 12, Tromsdalen* ☎ *77–63–87–37* 🌐 *www.fjellheisen.no/en* 🎫 *NKr 210.*

★ **Ishavskatedralen** (*Arctic Cathedral*)
RELIGIOUS SITE | Tromsø's signature structure was designed by Jan Inge Hovig to evoke the shape of a Sami tent as well as the iciness of a glacier. Opened in 1965, it represents northern Norwegian nature, culture, and faith. Also called the Arctic Cathedral (although not a cathedral at all, but rather a parish church), the building is globally recognized for its interesting structure and how different it is from the Tromsø Cathedral, a wooden church in the center of the city.

The immense stained-glass window depicts the Second Coming. The Cathedral itself sits around 600 people. The glass mosaic on the eastern side was created by Victor Sparre, a Norwegian painter, in 1972. In 2005, the church received an organ from Grönlunds Orgelbyggeri.

There are midnight sun concerts in summer, starting at 11:30 pm. ✉ *Hans Nilsens v. 41, Tromsdalen, Tromsdalen* ☎ *47–68–06–68* 🌐 *www.ishavskatedralen.no/en* 🎫 *NKr 50.*

★ **Nordnorsk Kunstmuseum** (*Northern Norway Art Museum*)
MUSEUM | **FAMILY** | The Northern Norway Art Museum is a visual and interactive art museum in the far north of Norway. It is one of the youngest museums in all of Norway and has exhibitions that cater to visitors and locals of all ages and interests. They also present a lot of local artwork from the last 100 years. ✉ *Sjøgata 1, Tromsø* ☎ *77–64–70–20* 🌐 *www.nnkm.no/en* 🎫 *NKr 80.*

Polaria
MUSEUM | **FAMILY** | Housed in a striking modern building by the harbor, the adventure center Polaria examines life in and around the polar and Barents regions. Explore the exhibits on polar travel and Arctic research, then check out two panoramic films, *Svalbard—Arctic Wilderness* and *Northern Lights in Arctic Norway*. The aquarium has sea mammals, including bearded seals. ✉ *Hjalmar Johansens gt. 12, Tromsø* ☎ *77–75–01–00* 🌐 *www.polaria.no* 🎫 *NKr 140.*

Polarmuseet (*Polar Museum*)
MUSEUM | Inside a customs warehouse from 1830, Polarmuseet documents the history of the polar regions. There are exhibitions on famous Norwegian polar explorers like Fridtjof Nansen and Roald Amundsen as well as the history of seal hunting and surviving in this often hostile climate. Part of the University of Tromsø, the museum opened in 1978, on the 50th anniversary of Amundsen leaving Tromsø for the last time, in search of his missing explorer colleague Umberto Nobile. ✉ *Søndre Tollbodgt. 11B, Tromsø* ☎ *77–62–33–60* 🌐 *www.polarmuseum.no* 🎫 *NKr 70.*

Telegrafbukta Beach
BEACH—SIGHT | **FAMILY** | South of Tromsø, this popular beach attracts locals and travelers when temperatures reach a tolerable level during the summer months. It's a family-friendly spot surrounded by beautiful nature. ✉ *Tromsø.*

★ **Tromsø Botaniske Hage** (*Tromsø Botanical Garden*)
GARDEN | **FAMILY** | With plants from the Antarctic and Arctic as well as mountainous regions all over the world, the 4-acre Tromsø Botanical Garden has a natural landscape that includes terraces, a stream, and a pond. It is open all year and has no set hours, so you can visit it by the glow of the northern lights or while basking in the midnight sun. Guides are available with advance arrangement.

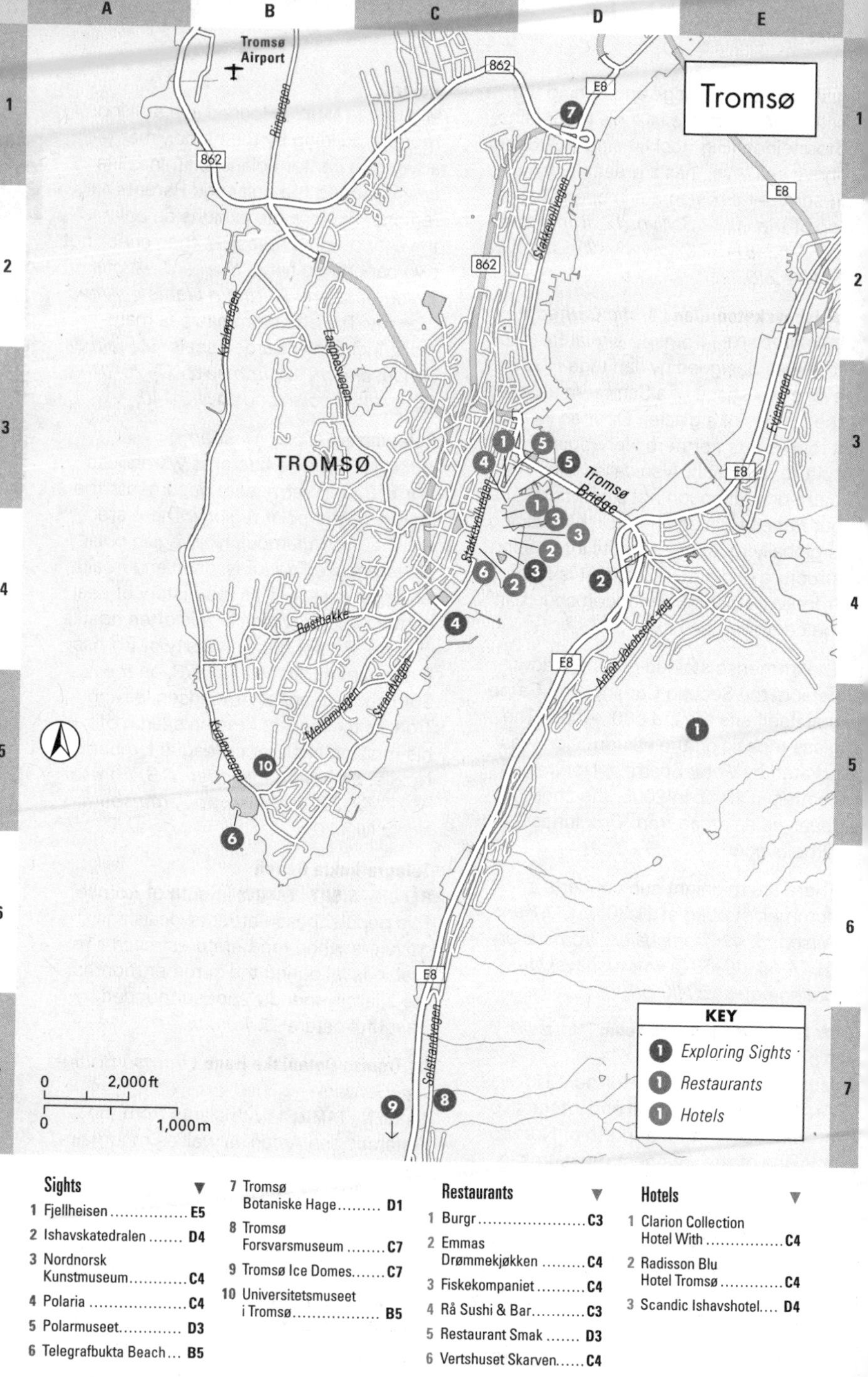

Sights

1 Fjellheisen E5
2 Ishavskatedralen D4
3 Nordnorsk Kunstmuseum............ C4
4 Polaria C4
5 Polarmuseet............. D3
6 Telegrafbukta Beach... B5
7 Tromsø Botaniske Hage......... D1
8 Tromsø Forsvarsmuseum C7
9 Tromsø Ice Domes....... C7
10 Universitetsmuseet i Tromsø................. B5

Restaurants

1 Burgr...................... C3
2 Emmas Drømmekjøkken C4
3 Fiskekompaniet C4
4 Rå Sushi & Bar........... C3
5 Restaurant Smak D3
6 Vertshuset Skarven...... C4

Hotels

1 Clarion Collection Hotel With C4
2 Radisson Blu Hotel Tromsø C4
3 Scandic Ishavshotel.... D4

✉ *Stakkevollvegen 200, Tromsø* ☎ *77–64–50– 01* 🌐 *uit.no/tmu/botanisk.*

Tromsø Forsvarsmuseum
MILITARY SITE | Founded in 1993, the Tromsø Defense Museum exists because locals strongly feel the need to safeguard the region's history around World War II. Everyone working here is a volunteer. ✉ *Solstrandvegen 370, Tromsdalen* ☎ *77–65–54–40* 🌐 *www.tromsoforsvarsmuseum.no* ⊙ *Closed Mon. and Tues.*

★ **Tromsø Ice Domes**
HOTEL—SIGHT | Located in Tamok Valley, the one-of-a-kind Tromsø Ice Domes are constructed entirely with ice and snow. You can enjoy a bar, restaurant, and even a cinema carved out of ice, and if you're taken with the place you can even arrange an overnight stay. Skilled guides explain the building's history and other interesting facts about this remarkable place. Dress warmly, because the temperature inside is always just below freezing. ✉ *Tromsø* ☎ *413–55–333* 🌐 *www.tromsoicedomes.com* 🎫 *NKr 879 (day visit)* ⊙ *Closed Apr.–mid-Dec.*

Universitetsmuseet i Tromsø (*Tromsø University Museum*)
MUSEUM | FAMILY | Dating from 1872, northern Norway's oldest scientific institution is dedicated to the nature and culture of the region. Learn about the northern lights, wildlife, fossils and dinosaurs, minerals and rocks, and church art from 1300 to 1800. Outdoors you can visit a Sami *gamme* (turf hut), and a replica of a Viking longhouse. The pretty Arctic-Alpine botanical garden is the northernmost in the world, at roughly the same latitude as Alaska's north coast. ✉ *Lars Thørings v. 10, Tromsø* ☎ *77–64–50–00* 🌐 *uit.no/tmu* 🎫 *NKr 70.*

Restaurants

Burgr
$$ | **BURGER** | Decorated like a vintage video game—look for characters from Pac Man and other favorites in the mosaic tiles—Burgr is the hippest place in Tromsø. There are plenty of beefy choices on the menu, from traditional varieties with lettuce and tomato to one topped with a habanero sauce that will knock your socks off. **Known for:** great milk shakes; play computer games; fun atmosphere. [$] *Average main: NKr 200* ✉ *Skippergata 6A, Tromsø* 🌐 *www.burgr.no.*

★ **Emmas Drømmekjøkken**
$$$ | **NORWEGIAN** | Emma's Dream Kitchen specializes in the freshest seafood imaginable, attracting both locals and travelers who have heard about it from fellow foodies. On the menu you'll find everything from stockfish to whale steak and more, all of it pleasingly presented. **Known for:** tasty fish soup; small but varied menu; friendly staff. [$] *Average main: NKr 300* ✉ *Kirkegata 8, Tromsø* ☎ *77–63–77–30* 🌐 *www.emmasdrommekjokken.no* ⊙ *Closed Sun.*

★ **Fiskekompaniet**
$$$$ | **NORWEGIAN** | With an ideal location on the harbor, this well-regarded eatery offers some of the freshest seafood in Tromsø. The menu is always changing, offering the sea's bounty in everything from hearty soups to tasty fillets. **Known for:** seafood platter; amazing wine list; idyllic views. [$] *Average main: NKr 385* ✉ *Killengreens gt., Tromsø* ☎ *77–68–76–00* 🌐 *fiskekompani.no.*

Rå Sushi & Bar
$$$ | **JAPANESE** | This well-known sushi bar combines the freshest Norwegian seafood with inventive Asian cooking techniques. You can find everything on the menu from fresh-caught salmon to whale sashimi. **Known for:** wide range of sushi; great decor; great views. [$] *Average main: NKr 349* ✉ *Stortorget 1, Tromsø* ☎ *77–68–46–00* 🌐 *raasushi.no.*

★ **Restaurant Smak**
$$$$ | **NORWEGIAN** | You'll be impressed by the attention to detail shown by the chefs at this elegant dining room, with

well-composed dishes that blend exciting and unexpected flavors. The menu changes with the season and takes advantage of the freshest ingredients available, with meats and cheeses from nearby farms. **Known for:** great set menu; impressive wine selection; local cheeses. *Average main: NKr 795 Skippergata 16B, Tromsø 941–76–110 www.restaurant-smak.no Closed Sun. and Mon.*

Vertshuset Skarven

$$$ | SEAFOOD | The menus at this cluster of eateries mostly emphasize seafood, but there's also a steak house serving an impressive array of local meat cooked over a charcoal grill. Specials might include soup of Kamchatka crab, delicious halibut and coalfish, Arctic reindeer, or whale carpaccio. **Known for:** large selection of craft beers; extensive meat selection; lunchtime fish soup buffet. *Average main: NKr 300 Strandtorget 1, Tromsø 77–60–07–20 www.skarven.no/en.*

Hotels

★ Clarion Collection Hotel With

$$$ | HOTEL | Often ranked as Tromsø's best place to stay, this comfortable lodging in a twin-gabled building facing the harbor puts you within walking distance of the best of the city's sights. **Pros:** breakfast and dinner included; relaxing sauna; lovely views. **Cons:** some rooms have little storage space; hard to block out light on bright summer nights; some rooms have better views than others. *Rooms from: NKr 1700 Sjøgt. 35–37, Tromsø 77–66–42–00 www.nordicchoicehotels.no/ 76 rooms Some meals.*

★ Radisson Blu Hotel Tromsø

$$ | HOTEL | At this hip, streamlined hotel with splendid fjord views, the well-outfitted rooms are decorated in soothing Arctic blues and greens. **Pros:** central location on the harbor; fitness center with fab views; good breakfast. **Cons:** some rooms are on the small side; service gets mixed reviews; not every view is stellar. *Rooms from: NKr 1000 Sjøgt. 7, Tromsø 77–60–00–00 www.radissonblu.com/ 269 rooms No meals.*

Scandic Ishavshotel

$$ | HOTEL | Shaped like an ocean liner docked at the harbor—there's even a slender mast topped by a Norwegian flag—Tromsø's snazziest hotel stretches over the sound toward Ishavskatedralen. **Pros:** near the city and the harbor; excellent breakfast buffet; great views of the waterfront. **Cons:** breakfast can get crowded with people on bus tours; service gets mixed reviews; not all views are created equal. *Rooms from: NKr 850 Fr. Langesgt. 2, Tromsø 77–66–64–00 www.scandichotels.no/hotell/norge/tromso/scandic-ishavshotel/ 214 rooms Free breakfast.*

Nightlife

Blå Rock Café

BARS/PUBS | The city's largest selection of beers can be found at the Blå Rock Café, which has a popular jukebox, frequent live concerts, and DJs on weekends. It's also famous for its burgers. *Strandgt. 14, Tromsø 77–61–00–20.*

★ Bryggeri 13

BREWPUBS/BEER GARDENS | This place brews beer right on the premises, and also offers a diverse menu for both lunch and dinner. A former garage, , the grittiness and hip feel of Bryggeri 13 give it a different vibe than other places around Tromsø. *Skippergata 15, Tromsø 404–50–190 bryggeri13.no/pub/ Closed Sun. and Mon.*

★ Magic Ice Bar

BARS/PUBS | Everything on the premises is made of ice, down to the barstools, the tables, and even the glasses. Ice sculptures of some of Norway's most intrepid explorers make you feel like you're getting a history lesson along with your beer. If you're a little chilly, the staff will loan you a parka. ✉ *Kaigata 4, Tromsø* ☎ *413–01–050* 🌐 *www.magicice.no/listings/tromso-norway/.*

Ølhallen

BARS/PUBS | Since 1928, polar explorers, Arctic skippers, hunters, whalers, and sealers have been meeting at this popular bar. ✉ *Storgt. 4, Tromsø* ☎ *77–62–45–80* 🌐 *www.olhallen.no* ⊗ *Closed Sun.*

Activities

Tromsø has more than 100 km (62 miles) of trails for walking and hiking in the mountains above the city. They're reachable by funicular.

BOATING

Arctic Cruise in Norway

BOATING | Arctic Cruise in Norway is a high-quality tour provider that offers a lot of extras on your boat trip such as prepping and cooking your own self-caught fish and much more. They offer several different packages that will give guests a wonderful taste of the Arctic, whether it be under the northern lights or midnight sun. ✉ *Brinkvegen 41, Tromsø* ☎ *90–54–99–97* 🌐 *www.acinorway.com/.*

HIKING

Troms Turlag (*Troms trekking Association*)

HIKING/WALKING | **FAMILY** | The local trekking association organizes tours and courses and rents out overnight cabins. ✉ *Kirkegt. 2, Tromsø* ☎ *77–68–51–75* 🌐 *troms.dnt.no.*

WHALE-WATCHING

★ **Arctic Explorers**

WHALE-WATCHING | **FAMILY** | One of the most reputable whale-watching excursions in Tromsø and northern Norway. You'll travel in speedy boats with small groups and see humpback whales, orcas, and other species. If you're lucky, you may be able to see these majestic creatures under the northern lights. ✉ *Stortorget 1, Tromsø* ☎ *954–78–500* 🌐 *arcticholidays.org/whale-rib-tour.*

WINTER SPORTS

★ **Chasing Lights**

TOUR—SPORTS | One of the main draws to northern Norway is the magical northern lights, and Chasing Lights is a Tromsø-based tour company that offers diverse packages to help you witness this amazing natural phenomenon. As the name suggests, the company will chase the lights with you rather than standing still in one spot and allowing them to come—or not come—to you. The company also has other activities such as snowmobile adventures and trips to the fjords. ✉ *Storgata 64, Tromsø* ☎ *455–17–551* 🌐 *chasinglights.com.*

Lyngsfjord Adventure

LOCAL SPORTS | This tour company offers dogsledding, reindeer sledding, snowmobile safaris, snowshoeing, northern lights viewing, and the chance to sleep in Sami tents. ☎ *77–71–55–88* 🌐 *www.lyngsfjord.com.*

Svensby Tursenter

LOCAL SPORTS | **FAMILY** | About an hour from Tromsø (including a 20-minute ferry crossing), Svensby Tursenter offers accommodation in small, self-service cabins at the foot of the Lyngen Alps. The company can arrange dogsledding, fjord fishing, horsesledding, moonlight tours, northern lights safaris, and *skikjøring* (skiing behind a snowmobile). ☎ *91–70–99–36* 🌐 *www.svensbytursenter.no.*

Tromsø Lapland

TOUR—SPORTS | **FAMILY** | Surrounded by the majestic Lyngen Alps, this snow-covered camp is run by indigenous people who have been living and working with reindeer for centuries. Visitors can stay in native tents called *lavvu*, participate in reindeer feedings, and enjoy the hopefully not-so-elusive northern lights. ✉ *Sjursnesvegen 144, Tromsø* ☎ *918–57–635* 🌐 *www.tromsolapland.no.*

★ **Tromsø Safari**

TOUR—SPORTS | **FAMILY** | In business for more than 20 years, this outfitter offers a

One of Norway's iconic sights is the craggy coastline at Tungeneset, which in Norwegian means "Devil's Teeth."

wide range of tours throughout the year. Focusing on the region's natural beauty, excursions can range from whale-watching to sea kayaking to husky sledding. ✉ *Radisson Blu Hotel Tromsø, Fredrik Langes gt., Tromsø* ☎ *953–03–888* 🌐 *www.tromsosafari.no.*

Tromsø Villmarkssenter (*Tromsø Wilderness Centre*)
LOCAL SPORTS | FAMILY | Located half an hour outside the city, this outfitter organizes dogsledding trips, northern lights safaris, glacier walking, kayaking, summit tours, and Sami-style dinners, which take place around a campfire inside a *lavvu* (a Sami tent). ✉ *Straumsvegen 603, Marisletta* ☎ *77–69–60–02* 🌐 *www.villmarkssenter.no.*

Senja

The second-largest island in Norway, Senja is well known to outdoor enthusiasts because of Segla Mountain, a dramatic peak that gazes out over the Atlantic. Hiking here is enormously popular, so much so that the trails can be crowded in summer. But many of northern Norway's other natural wonders, including Ånderdalen National Park, are also on Senja.

GETTING HERE AND AROUND

Departing from the mainland town of Finnsnes, buses are a good option for reaching the larger towns on the western edge of the island. Traveling to smaller towns can be more difficult, as local buses depart once or twice a day. The best way to get around this part of northern Norway is by car. There are no major airports on Senja, and the closest one on the mainland is at Bardufoss. Flybussen operates buses from the airport to Finnsnes, where you can transfer to a bus to your destination on Senja.

Sights

Ånderdalen National Park
NATIONAL/STATE PARK | FAMILY | Open to the public in 1970 and expanded in 2004, this national park protects a wide swath

of coastline in northern Norway. Thanks to preservation efforts, moose and other animals have returned to the area. You will find plenty of seabirds along the rocky coast, along with seals in the fjords and otters in the rivers. Transportation options are limited, so rent a car and then explore on foot. Bring a good pair of walking shoes. ✉ *Senja* ☎ *48–15–22–90* 🌐 *www.nasjonalparkstyre.no.*

Segla

HIKING/WALKING | One of the most popular hiking trails in all of northern Norway, Senja attracts a mix of locals and travelers for the stunning views from its rocky promontory. The hike from the fishing village of Fjordgård is moderately difficult, with a fairly steep ascent to the top. This five-hour round-trip may not be for those with a fear of heights, as on one side of the trail there is a steep cliff that plunges down to the sea. ✉ *Fv 275, Senja.*

★ Tungeneset

MOUNTAIN—SIGHT | **FAMILY** | Easily reachable from the road that runs along the coast, this scenic overlooks offers the best views of the rugged and dramatic peaks that locals call the Devil's Teeth. It's accessible to everyone, with a boardwalk that accommodates strollers and wheelchairs. Nearby is a small beach where you can explore tidal pools and watch waves crash over the rocks. It can get crowded in summer, but is worth a stop for the small picnic area and public toilets. ✉ *Rte. 862, Senja.*

Restaurants

Senjastua

$$$$ | **NORWEGIAN** | Originally a roadside café, this popular restaurant in the coastal community of Silsand offers a wide variety of local dishes. Set inside a log cabin, the dining room has a relaxed and cozy vibe. **Known for:** great place to sample lutefisk; delicious desserts; fine dining in a cozy cabin. $ *Average main: NKr 400* ✉ *Laukhellaveien 2, Senja* ☎ *77–84–40–10* 🌐 *www.senjastua.com* ⏲ *Closed weekends.*

Skreien Spiseri

$$$ | **NORWEGIAN** | **FAMILY** | Close to the harbor in Gryllefjord—making it an ideal spot to stop for a bite while waiting for the ferry—this casual eatery serves a wide range of traditional Norwegian dishes, including specialties like boknafisk. Spread over several floors of a clapboard building, it has a cozy and warm atmosphere. **Known for:** great views; comfortable outdoor seating; unusual offerings like seagull eggs. $ *Average main: NKr 350* ✉ *Spiraveien 53, Senja* ☎ *908–93–324* ⏲ *Closed Mon. and Tues.*

Hotels

★ Aurora Borealis Observatory

$$$$ | **RENTAL** | When you're on the lookout for the northern lights, you can't do better than these spacious but cozy apartments with expansive bay windows where you can enjoy one of the world's most impressive natural phenemenons. **Pros:** relaxing spa area; rooms are nicely soundproofed; accommodates special diets. **Cons:** decor is a bit bland; books up quickly; not really an observatory. $ *Rooms from: NKr 4500* ✉ *Torsmoveien 14, Senja* ☎ *970–32–300* 🌐 *aurorabore-alisobservatory.com* *14 apartments* 🍽 *Free breakfast.*

Norwegian Wild

$$ | **RENTAL** | Thiis waterfront lodging is miles from the closest village, giving you the feeling of being far from civilization. **Pros:** ski to your door; barbecue facilities; free parking. **Cons:** pets not allowed; some spartan rooms; a bit isolated. $ *Rooms from: NKr 1200* ✉ *Tranøyveien 2002, Senja* ☎ *916–35–760* 🌐 *norwegianwild.no* *11 cabins, 110 campsites* 🍽 *No meals.*

Senja Hotell

$$$ | **HOTEL** | In the mainland community closest to Senja, this hotel is within walking distance of the Hurtigruten cruise ship terminal and other points of interest in the town of Finnsnes. **Pros:** luggage storage available; pleasant decor; free parking. **Cons:** not all rooms have decent views; bland exterior; not on Senja. *Rooms from: NKr 1445 Storgata 8, Senja 77–85–11–60 www.senjahotell.no 21 rooms Free breakfast.*

Nightlife

Pila Pub and Kultur

BARS/PUBS | This lovely pub offers great views over the bay. With a vast selection of local craft beers, delicious pub food, and live music, it's a great nighttime destination. During the day it also serves tasty coffee and homemade cakes. *Torsmoveien 14 905–14–249.*

Alta

Most travelers spend the night here before ascending to the North Cape. The small community of Alta has three centers—Bossekop, which keeps old trading and market traditions; Elvebakken, where you'll find the harbor; and the city center itself. One of the most up-and-coming destinations in northern Norway, Alta appeals to travelers because it has a less-touristy vibe and access to plenty of outdoor activities.

GETTING HERE AND AROUND

The Alta Airport is about 10 minutes from the city center, with buses making the trip several times an hour. From Alta, with a little advance planning you can reach many of the surrounding towns and areas by bus or ferry.

Sights

Alta Canyon

CANYON | The largest canyon in northern Europe, this open expanse is abundant in its natural beauty. The area is perfect for hiking, cruising along the river, or taking a scenic drive. If you're lucky, you'll see plenty of reindeer frolicking around the canyon. *Alta.*

Alta Museum

MUSEUM | On the outskirts of the city, the Alta Museum has an amazing location overlooking a fjord. Perhaps more impressive than the scenery are the ancient rock carvings created between 3,000 and 7,000 years ago by the Sami tribes, to depict the everyday life of the people who lived here and worked on the land. The museum itself has both indoor and outdoor exhibits about the Sami people. *Altaveien 19, Alta 417–56–330 www.altamuseum.no/en NKr 120.*

★ Cathedral Of the Northern Lights

RELIGIOUS SITE | This ribbon-like church, more formally referred to as the Alta Kirke, embraces modern design while still being a majestic place of worship. There is a small museum at the site along with a café selling coffee and freshly made waffles. *Markedsgata 30, Alta 78–44–42–70 NKr 40 www.nordlyskatedral.no.*

Restaurants

Du Verden Matbar

$$$ | **NORWEGIAN** | In the center of Alta, Du Verden is a fantastic place to try traditional Norwegian dishes. The kitchen takes pride in highlighting the region's finest ingredients like king crab legs. **Known for:** reindeer and other locally sourced meats; lovely dining room; Norwegian-style tapas. *Average main: NKr 315 Markedsgata 21-25, Alta 459–08–213 www.duverden.no/alta.*

Stakeriet Mat og Vinhus

$$$$ | **NORWEGIAN** | Along with delicious local dishes like king crab soup and dried cod, this modern eatery serves you a hearty helping of the region's culinary traditions. Although this is definitely a fine-dining destination, it has a relaxed and casual ambiance. **Known for:** reindeer in its various forms; juicy burgers; great interior design. *Average main: NKr 500*

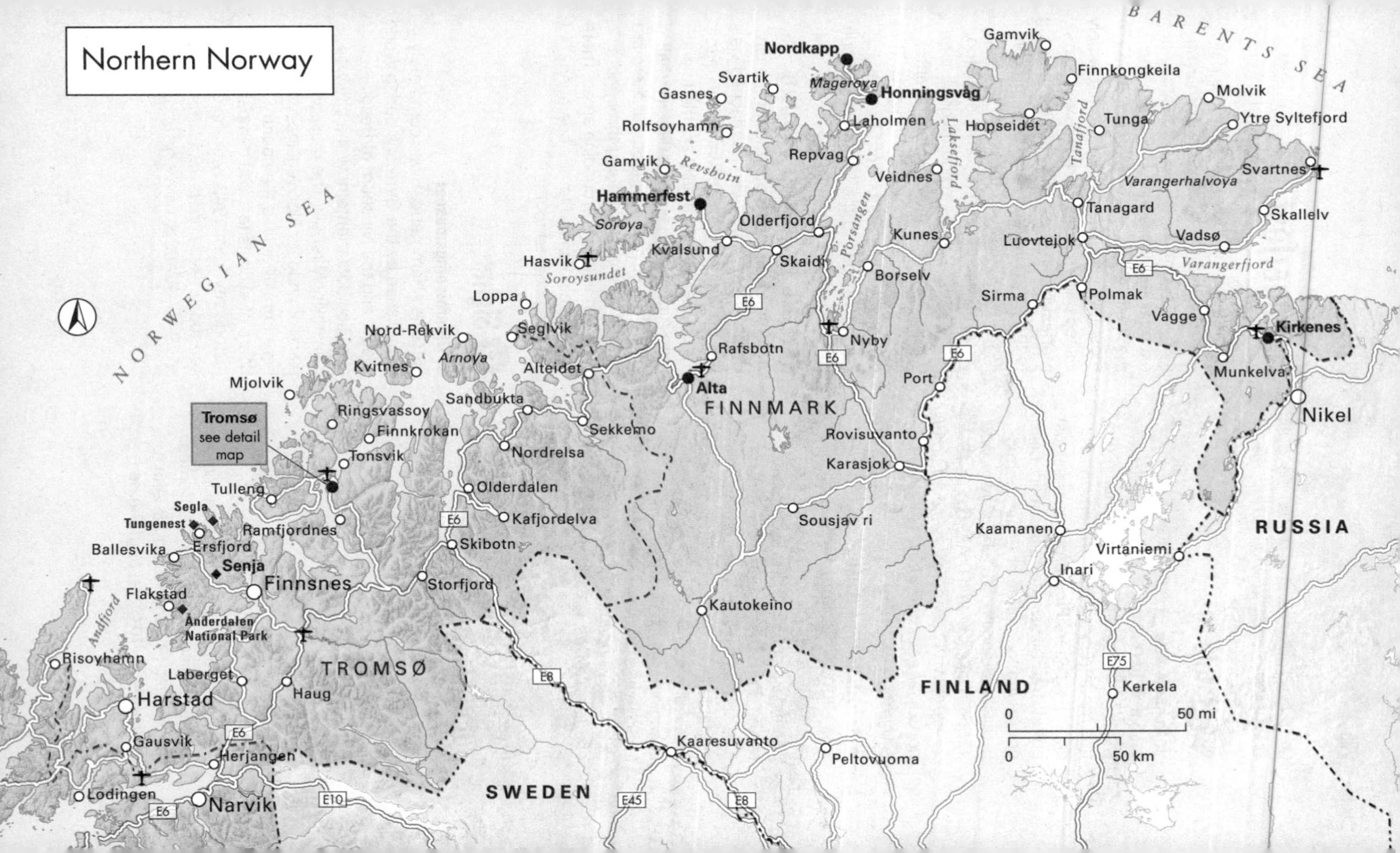

Northern Norway
NORWEGIAN SEA
BARENTS SEA
Gamvik
Nordkapp
Svartik
Magerøya
Honningsvåg
Finnkongkeila
Molvik
Gasnes
Laholmen
Hopseidet
Tanafjord
Tunga
Ytre Syltefjord
Rolfsoyhamn
Repvag
Laksefjord
Gamvik
Revsbotn
Veidnes
Svartnes
Varangerhalvoya
Hammerfest
Soroya
Olderfjord
Porsangen
Tanagard
Skallelv
Kunes
Luovtejok
Vadsø
Kvalsund
Skaidi
Hasvik
Soroysundet
Borselv
E6
Varangerfjord
Loppa
Sirma
Polmak
Vagge
Kirkenes
Seglvik
Nord-Rekvik
Nyby
Arnoya
Rafsbotn
E6
E6
Kvitnes
Alteidet
Alta
Port
Munkelva
Mjolvik
FINNMARK
Nikel
Sandbukta
Ringsvassoy
Tromsø
see detail
map
Sekkemo
Finnkrokan
Rovisuvanto
Nordrelsa
Tonsvik
Karasjok
Olderdalen
Tulleng
Segla
Sousjav ri
Tungenest
Kafjordelva
E6
Ramfjordnes
Kaamanen
RUSSIA
Skibotn
Ballesvika
Ersfjord
Virtaniemi
Senja
Finnsnes
Inari
Storfjord
Flakstad
Andfjord
Kautokeino
Anderdalen
National Park
Risoyhamn
TROMSØ
E75
Laberget
Haug
E8
FINLAND
Kerkela
Harstad
0
50 mi
E6
Gausvik
Kaaresuvanto
Herjangen
0
50 km
Peltovuoma
Lodingen
Narvik
SWEDEN
E10
E45
E8
E6

✉ *18 Markedsgata, Alta* ☎ *400–05–585* 🌐 *www.stakeriet.no/eng.*

Hotels

★ Scandic Alta
$$$ | HOTEL | FAMILY | A short walk from many of the most famous sights in Alta, this modern lodging has a convenient central location. **Pros:** amazing breakfast buffet; free bikes; central location. **Cons:** no parking; no coffee or tea in rooms; no air-conditioning. *$ Rooms from: NKr 1286* ✉ *Løkkeveien 61, Alta* ☎ *78–48–27–00* 🌐 *www.scandichotels.com/hotels/norway/alta/scandic-alta* *241 rooms* *Free breakfast.*

★ Sorrisniva Igloo Hotel
$$$$ | HOTEL | This hotel is magical, melting away each spring and reappearing when winter settles in over the region. **Pros:** free sauna; free parking; free shuttle service. **Cons:** sauna only available in the morning; no luggage allowed in rooms; shared bathroom and changing area. *$ Rooms from: NKr 4820* ✉ *Sorrisniva 20, Alta* ☎ *78–43–33–78* 🌐 *sorrisniva.no/igloo-hotel* *Closed late spring–mid-Dec.* *30 rooms* *Free breakfast.*

Activities

DOGSLEDDING

★ Trasti and Trine
SNOW SPORTS | FAMILY | One of the most recommended tour companies in Alta, Trasti and Trine specializes in sledding excursions that focus on the health and well-being of the dogs. Guides bring the relationship between huskies and humans to the forefront. The company also offers overnight accommodations and a restaurant that uses local ingredients ranging from mountain berries to reindeer. ✉ *Gargiaveien 29, Alta* ☎ *78–40–30–40* 🌐 *trastiogtrine.no.*

Hammerfest

Hammerfest is the gateway to the Barents Sea and the Arctic Ocean, making it an ideal jumping-off point for Arctic expeditions. More than 600 miles above the Arctic Circle, the world's northernmost town is also one of the most widely visited places in northern Norway. Hammerfest means "mooring place," referring to the town's natural harbor (remarkably free of ice year-round thanks to the Gulf Stream). This place has plenty of history to explore. In 1891, residents grew tired of the months of darkness each winter and decided to brighten their nights. They purchased a generator from Thomas Edison, becoming the first city in Europe to have electric street lamps.

GETTING HERE AND AROUND

Just minutes from the center of the city, Hammerfest Airport can be reached via the 132 bus from the downtown bus terminal. There's also a daily shuttle to and from Alta Airport. Hammerfest is small enough to navigate on foot, but there are several bus routes running throughout the town and to surrounding areas. There are also high-speed ferries operating between coastal towns.

Sights

★ Gjenreisningsmuseet
MUSEUM | Hammerfest was completely demolished by the Germans during World War II, and the Museum of Reconstruction documents how the city was painstakingly rebuilt. The museum is a place of pride for Norwegians, who flock here from all across the country. The two floors of exhibits lets you compare the historic city from 1943 with the one you see today. ✉ *Kirkegata 19, Hammerfest* ☎ *78–47–72–00* 🌐 *www.kystmuseene.no.*

Gjenreisningsmuseet for Finnmark og Nord-Troms (*Museum of Reconstruction for Finnmark and North Troms*)
MUSEUM | Although it covers the county of Finnmark's history since the Stone Age, this museum primarily focuses on World War II, when the German army burned the community to the ground as part of a scorched-earth policy. Through photographs, videos, and sound effects, the museum recounts the residents' struggle to rebuild their lives. The interesting exhibit includes dwellings that were built inside caves after the town was evacuated. ✉ *Kirkegt. 21, Hammerfest* ☎ *78–40–29–30* 🌐 *www.kystmuseene.no/the-museum-of-reconstruction* 🎫 *Nkr 80.*

Hammerfest Church
RELIGIOUS SITE | Burned down by the Germans in World War II, this house of worship was on the massive list of buildings that were reconstructed in 1961. Designed by Oslo architect Hans Magnus, the striking modern structure is the most popular attraction in the city. ✉ *Corn Moes gt., Hammerfest* ☎ *78–40–29–20* 🌐 *www.visitnorway.com/listings/hammerfest-church/126230.*

★ **Isbjørnklubben** (*The Royal and Ancient Polar Bear Society*)
MUSEUM | Founded by two business leaders whose goal was to share the town's history as a center of hunting and commerce, the Royal and Ancient Polar Bear Society depicts the skill and daring required to hunt polar bears, seals, lynx, puffins, and wolves. You have to become a member to visit, so this is a very exclusive club open only to those who have visited the world's northernmost city. Members get a document signed by the mayor and a sought-after silver-and-enamel polar bear pin. ✉ *Havnegt. 3, Hammerfest* ☎ *78–41–31–00* 🌐 *www.isbjornklubben.no* 🎫 *NKr 220.*

Meridianstøtten
HISTORIC SITE | A UNESCO World Heritage Site, the Struve Geodetic Arc was the northernmost of 265 survey points mapped out between 1816 and 1855 by the astronomer Friedrich Georg Wilhelm Struve. This graceful column commemorates his attempt to measure the size and shape of the Earth in the 19th century. ✉ *Industrigata 5, Hammerfest.*

 Restaurants

Brygga Mathus
$$$$ | NORWEGIAN | Specializing in local seafood, seasonal produce, and northern Norwegian flavors, this storefront eatery in a charming brick building is a great place to sample local cuisine. Long tables encourage you to get to know your neighbors, and floor-to-ceiling windows let you gaze out at what's happening in the port. **Known for:** daily lunch specials; tasty small plates; local meats and produce. Ⓢ *Average main: NKr 400* ✉ *Strandgata 16, Hammerfest* ☎ *401–89–600* 🌐 *bryggamathus.no* ⏲ *Closed Sun.*

Niri Sushi and Dinner
$$$$ | JAPANESE | One of the most popular places in Hammerfest to grab a bite, this Japanese eatery creates amazing rolls using the freshest local seafood, from salmon to whale. During the day, the place thrives as a sushi bar, but at night DJs transform it into a happening club. **Known for:** unique varieties of sushi; vegetarian options; plenty of options available to go. Ⓢ *Average main: NKr 400* ✉ *Storgata 22, Hammerfest* ☎ *455–00–200* 🌐 *www.nirihammerfest.no* ⏲ *Closed Sun. and Mon.*

Scandic Hammerfest
$$ | HOTEL | This modern hotel in the city center offers comfortable rooms at reasonable prices. **Pros:** breakfast options abound; pleasant fitness center; central location. **Cons:** not all rooms have good views; charge for parking; bland exterior. Ⓢ *Rooms from: NKr 1000* ✉ *Søroygata 15, Hammerfest* ☎ *78–42–57–00*

Gazing out to the Barents Sea, Nordcapp is the northernmost point in continental Europe.

www.scandichotels.com/hotels/norway/hammerfest/scandic-hammerfest *85 rooms* *Free breakfast.*

Smarthotel Hammerfest

$$ | **HOTEL** | Known for its budget-friendly accommodations, this no-nonsense lodging focuses on what you need for a great stay and jettisons the rest. **Pros:** beds are like sleeping on a cloud; architecture is bold and beautiful; free Wi-Fi and other amenities. **Cons:** no maid service on weekends; doesn't accept cash; some small rooms. *Rooms from: NKr 900* *Strandgata 32, Hammerfest* *415–36–500* *https://smarthotel.no/en/hammerfest* *160 rooms* *No meals.*

Thon Hotel Hammerfest

$$$ | **HOTEL** | One of the most popular places for for weary travelers in this part of northern Norway, the centrally located Thon Hotel Hammerfest has amenities that attract corporate clients as well as vacationers. **Pros:** eye-catching exterior design; rooms have splashes of color; best rooms have great views. **Cons:** charges for parking; no cribs for infants; some tiny rooms. *Rooms from: NKr 1300* *Strandgata 2-4, Hammerfest* *78–42–96–31* *www.thonhotels.no/hoteller/norge/hammerfest/thon-hotel-hammerfest* *103 rooms* *Free breakfast.*

Nightlife

Jernteppet

BARS/PUBS | Iron Curtain is one of Hammerfest's most popular pubs, offering great local beers and a social atmosphere. You can watch the midnight sun from the spacious deck during the summer and duck into the candlelit interior in the winter. *Strandgata 24, Hammerfest* *www.jernteppet.no.*

Activities

★ **Hammerfest Turistkontor** (*Hammerfest Tourist information*)

TOUR—SPORTS | **FAMILY** | Stop at the tourist office to learn about activities in the region, including walking tours, bird-watching excursions, and boating trips. A popular activity is taking a catamaran to the small fishing villages on Sørøya Island. ✉ *Havnegt. 3, Hammerfest* ☎ *78–41–21–85* 🌐 *www.hammerfest-turist.no/en.*

Nordkapp

34 km (21 miles) north of Honningsvåg.

Searching for a northeastern passage to India, British navigator Richard Chancellor came upon this impressive promontory in the Barents Sea in 1553. He named it North Cape, or *Nordkapp*. Europe's northernmost point is a rite of passage for nearly all Scandinavians, as well as many other adventurous types from around the world. Honningvåg's northerly location makes for long, dark winter nights and perpetually sun-filled summer days. The village serves as the gateway to Arctic exploration and the beautiful Nordkapp Plateau.

This region has an otherworldly landscape, at once rugged and delicate. You'll see an incredible treeless tundra with crumbling mountains and sparse vegetation. The subarctic environment is very vulnerable, so don't disturb the plants. Walk only on marked trails and don't remove stones, disturb the plants, or make campfires. Because the roads are closed in winter, the only access is from the tiny fishing village of Skarsvåg via Sno-Cat, a thump-and-bump ride that's as unforgettable as the desolate view.

GETTING HERE AND AROUND

Honningsvåg Airport, 30 km (18.6 miles) south of North Cape, has direct flights from Tromsø, Kirkenes, and other towns in the far north, operated by Widerøe. Hurtigruten, the ship company, stops at Honningsvåg on its way to Kirkenes from Bergen.

The E69 goes all the way to the North Cape, with a 6.8-km (4-mile)-long underwater tunnel linking the mainland with the island of Magerøya. The North Cape is 236 km (147 miles) north of Alta, and the journey takes about three hours.

Most cruise passengers visit Nordkapp from Honningsvåg, a fishing village on Magerøya Island. The journey from Honningsvåg to Nordkapp covers about 35 km (22 miles) across a landscape characterized by rocky tundra and grazing reindeer.

CONTACTS Visit North Cape. ✉ *Fiskerivn. 4D, Honningsvåg* ☎ *78–47–70–30* 🌐 *www.nordkapp.no/en.* **Widerøe.** ☎ *810–01–200* 🌐 *www.wideroe.no.*

CRUISE TRAVEL

One of northern Norway's largest ports welcomes about 100 cruise ships annually during the summer season. The port itself has no services, but within 100 yards are shops, museums, tourist information, post office, banks, restaurants, and an ice bar.

VISITOR INFORMATION

CONTACTS Nordkapp Reiseliv. ✉ *Fiskerivn. 4, Honningsvåg* ☎ *78–47–70–30* 🌐 *www.nordkapp.no/en.*

Nordkapphallen (*North Cape Hall*)
MUSEUM | Tucked away into the plateau, North Cape Hall is housed in a cave and includes exhibits tracing the history of the cape, from Richard Chancellor, an Englishman who sailed around it in 1553, to Oscar II, king of Norway and Sweden, who climbed to the top of the plateau in 1873. Celebrate your pilgrimage to 71° North at one of the cafés. The hefty admission charge covers both the exhibits and entrance to the plateau itself. If you arrive on foot or by bike, admission is free. ✉ *Nordkapp* ☎ *78–47–68–60* 🌐 *www.visitnordkapp.net/en/* 🎫 *NKr 285.*

Nordkappmuseet (*North Cape Museum*)
MUSEUM | This museum documents the history of the Arctic fishing industry and the history of tourism at North Cape. You

can learn about the development of society and culture in this region. ✉ *Holmen 1, Honningsvåg* ☎ *78–47–72–00* 🌐 *www.kystmuseene.no/north-cape-museum.107296.en.html* 🎫 *NKr 60* ⏲ *Closed Sun. mid-Sept.–mid-June.*

Restaurants

★ Corner Spiseri

$$$ | NORWEGIAN | The catch of the day often dictates the menu here, but crispy cod tongue is always available. For less adventurous eaters, there's also a variety of pasta dishes. **Known for:** lovely location; incredibly tasty reindeer; great craft beers at the bar. 💲 *Average main: NKr 259* ✉ *Fiskeriveien 2A, Honningsvåg* ☎ *78–47–63–40* 🌐 *www.corner.no.*

Honningsvåg

Honningsvåg was completely destroyed at the end of World War II, when the Germans burned everything as they retreated. The town's northerly location and infrastructure have since made it one of the most important harbors in Norway. Many people make an 18-km (11-mile) round-trip hike to Knivskjelodden (Crooked Knife), Europe's northernmost point. It has a spectacular view toward the North Cape Plateau. You can write your name in the hiking association's minute book and buy a diploma attesting to your visit.

GETTING HERE AND AROUND

Honnigsvåg Airport has regular buses to the city center during the day. There are only a few daily buses to Honnigsvåg—the five departures from Nordkapp in summer dwindle to one in winter. If you really want to explore the region, rent a car during the summer months.

Sights

Gallery West of the Moon

MUSEUM | Located a short walk from the harbor, this gallery displays the work of artists from Honningsvåg and the surrounding region. ✉ *Storgata 4A, Honningsvåg* ☎ *418–41–030* 🌐 *www.evart.no/home_EN.html.*

Stabbursdalen National Park

NATIONAL/STATE PARK | An easy day trip by car from Honningsvåg, this national park is home to the northernmost pine forest in the world. The park wraps around the Stabburselva River, and there is a lovely waterfall that is a great destination for hikers. ✉ *Tromsø* ☎ *78–95–03–77* 🌐 *www.stabbursnes.no/home.*

Restaurants

Arctic Sans

$$$$ | NORWEGIAN | FAMILY | Close to the harbor in Honnigsvåg, this innovative eatery serves dishes that blend Norwegian recipes with Asian touches. The menu changes frequently, with weekly specials highlighting seasonal produce. **Known for:** local king crab; fried cod tongues; rotating menu highlighting seasonal ingredients. 💲 *Average main: NKr 500* ✉ *Storgata 22, Honningsvåg* ☎ *952–28–821.*

★ Havly

$$$$ | NORWEGIAN | In the heart of Honnigsvåg, Havly utilizes the freshest local ingredients to create European dishes that are just as delicious as they are beautiful. The atmosphere is cozy and comfortable, with original art enhancing the fairly utilitarian space. **Known for:** authentic ceviche; dishes are artfully presented; tasty reindeer carpaccio. 💲 *Average main: NKr 500* ✉ *Storgata 12, Honningsvåg* ☎ *458–58–307.*

★ Honni Bakes

$ | CAFÉ | FAMILY | One of the top spots for coffee in Honningsvåg, this French-inspired bakery is known far and wide for its freshly baked pastries. Honni Bakes is located very close to the harbor, making it a good place to stock up on supplies. **Known for:** French-style baking; excellent pastries; mouthwatering cakes. $ *Average main: NKr 100* ✉ *Storgata 1B, Honningsvåg.*

Nordkapp Vandrerhjem

$ | **HOTEL** | Although it's technically a hostel, Nordkapp Vandrerhjem has rooms for budget-minded travelers of all ages. **Pros:** affordable rates; friendly staff; fully equipped kitchen. **Cons:** thin walls—bring earplugs; shared bathrooms; not all rooms have views. $ *Rooms from: NKr 600* ✉ *Kobbhullveien 10, Honningsvåg* ☎ *918–24–156* 🌐 *www.nordkapp.no/en/services/accommodation/item/nordkapp-vandrerhjem* *72 rooms* *No meals.*

★ **Scandic Bryggen**

$$$$ | **HOTEL** | The comfortable, contemporary rooms at this harborside hotel offer a great glimpse of the sea (and even the northern lights, if they decide to come out). **Pros:** fitness center; free Wi-Fi; free parking. **Cons:** some small rooms; the views are not equal; dated decor. $ *Rooms from: NKr 2000* ✉ *Vågen 1, Honningsvåg* ☎ *78–47–72–50* 🌐 *www.scandichotels.com/hotels/norway/honningsvag/scandic-bryggen* *42 rooms* *Free breakfast.*

Gjesvær Bird Safari

BIRD WATCHING | **FAMILY** | One of the best-known tour operators in the region, Gjesvær Bird Safari offers a boat tour to the Gjesværstappan Nature Reserve to see one of Norway's largest groups of kittiwakes and puffins. ✉ *Nygårdsveien 38, Alta* ☎ *78–47–57–73* 🌐 *birdsafari.no.*

Kirkenes

On the border with Russia, Kirkenes is known for its shared history with its eastern neighbor and the pristine nature just beyond its borders. Kirkenes has fantastic displays of the northern lights and lots of outdoor activities, attracting visitors who are looking to get away from the larger cities.

GETTING HERE AND AROUND

No matter how you get here, it's going to take a while. This is the last stop on the Hurtigruten coastal ferry from Bergen, and the end of E6 that travels up most of the coast. To fly here from almost anywhere else in the country you'll have to change planes in Tromsø. Once you're here, a car is the best way to get around.

Grenselandmuseet (*Borderland Museum*)

MUSEUM | One of the must-visit sights in Kirkenes, this museum details the extensive history and often-complicated relationship between Norway, Russia, and Finland. The showpiece here is an Ilyushin IL2M3M, a Soviet-era aircraft that made an emergency landing into a nearby lake in 1944. During World War II the town was occupied by Nazi Germany and relentlessly bombed by Russia, and the local air raid warning went off more than 1,000 times. This was the first Norwegian town to be liberated in 1944. ✉ *Førstevannslia, Kirkenes* ☎ *78–99–48–80* 🌐 *www.varangermuseum.no/besok-oss/besokssteder/grenselandmuseet.*

Restaurants

★ **Gapahuken Restaurant by Sollia**

$$$$ | **NORWEGIAN** | Visited by the Norwegian royal family, this award-winning restaurant sits on the shore of a gorgeous lake that has views all the way to Russia. The modern architecture is by Mia

Hamborg, who says the natural wood and massive windows were inspired by the region's natural wonders. **Known for:** local specialties; first-class kitchen; rooms are available. *Average main: NKr 600 ⊠ Storskog, Kirkenes ☎ 78–99–08–20 ⊕ www.storskog.no/gapahuken-restaurant ⊙ Closed Mon.*

Hotels

Scandic Kirkenes
$$ | HOTEL | In the center of Kirkenes, this hotel with a rather uninspiring facade puts you close to all of the town's most popular attractions. **Pros:** award-winning breakfast; convenient location; spa services. **Cons:** not all rooms have views; basic accommodations; no food options if you arrive late. *Rooms from: NKr 1182 ⊠ Kongens gt. 1-3, Kirkenes ☎ 78–99–59–00 ⊕ www.scandichotels.com/hotels/norway/kirkenes/scandic-kirkenes ⇆ 90 rooms ⦾ Free breakfast.*

Snowhotel Kirkenes
$$$$ | HOTEL | In the middle of a forest, this seasonal hotel made completely out of ice and snow gazes out at a pristine fjord. **Pros:** beautiful location; eye-catching bar; plenty of winter excursions. **Cons:** short season; expensive rates; a bit isolated. *Rooms from: NKr 6000 ⊠ Sandnesdalen 14, Kirkenes ☎ 78–97–05–40 ⊕ www.snowhotelkirkenes.com ⇆ 20 rooms ⦾ No meals.*

Chapter 11

SVALBARD

Updated by
Vanessa Brune

Sights	Restaurants	Hotels	Shopping	Nightlife
★★★★★	★★★★☆	★★★☆☆	★★☆☆☆	★★☆☆☆

WELCOME TO SVALBARD

TOP REASONS TO GO

★ **Arctic wildlife:** Join a boat trip into the Arctic wilderness to get a glimpse of walruses, whales, and maybe even polar bears.

★ **Breathtaking treks:** Whether you opt for mountain scrambling or glacier hiking, Svalbard offers spectacular landscapes and views for days.

★ **Remote settlements:** Discover the remote Russian mining settlements of Barentsburg (still in operation) and Pyramiden (now a ghost town).

★ **Cultural heritage:** All buildings and artefacts from before 1945 are protected on Svalbard, so there is lots of history waiting to be explored.

★ **Polar night and midnight sun:** Experience winter's endless nights illuminated by the northern lights and summer days when midnight is as bright as midday.

In the Arctic Sea halfway between the North Pole and the Norwegian mainland, Svalbard consists of nine larger islands and many smaller islands ones that are uninhabited and unnamed. The biggest island of the archipelago is Spitsbergen, where you'll find the permanent settlement of Longyearbyen.

1 Longyearbyen. The main settlement of Svalbard is the small town of Longyearbyen. On the island of Spitsbergen, the community has approximately 2,000 inhabitants and is home to several museums, as well as hotels, restaurants and shops.

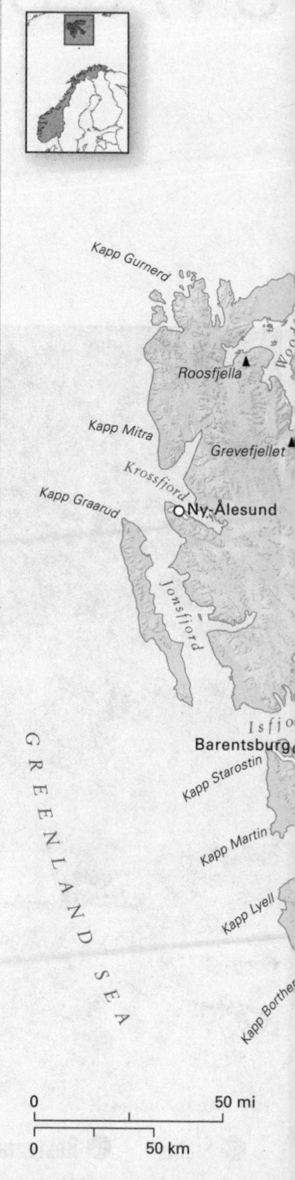

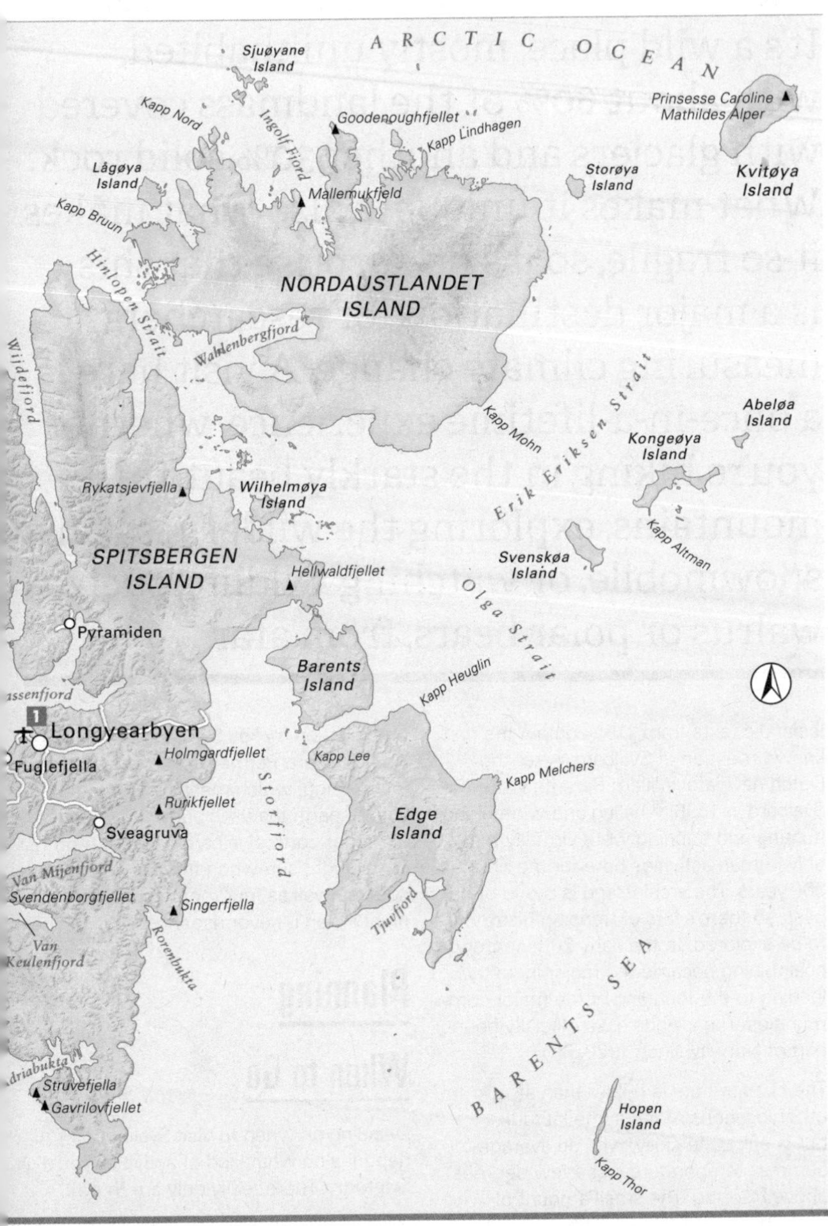
ARCTIC OCEAN
Sjuøyane Island
Kapp Nord
Ingolf Fjord
Goodenoughfjellet
Kapp Lindhagen
Prinsesse Caroline Mathildes Alper
Lågøya Island
Mallemukfjeld
Storøya Island
Kvitøya Island
Kapp Bruun
Hinlopen Strait
NORDAUSTLANDET ISLAND
Wahlenbergfjord
Widefjord
Erik Eriksen Strait
Kapp Mohn
Abeløya Island
Kongeøya Island
Rykatsjevfjella
Wilhelmøya Island
Kapp Altman
SPITSBERGEN ISLAND
Hellwaldfjellet
Svenskøya Island
Olga Strait
Pyramiden
Barents Island
Kapp Heuglin
Longyearbyen
Holmgardfjellet
Fuglefjella
Kapp Lee
Kapp Melchers
Storfjord
Rurikfjellet
Sveagruva
Edge Island
Van Mijenfjord
Svendenborgfjellet
Singerfjella
Tjuvfjord
Van Keulenfjord
Rorenbukta
BARENTS SEA
Struvefjella
Gavrilovfjellet
Hopen Island
Kapp Thor

One of the most remote places on Earth, this cluster of rocky islands and skerries rise dramatically out of the Arctic Sea. It's a wild place, mostly uninhabited, with about 60% of the landmass covered with glaciers and another 30% solid rock. What makes it unique is also what makes it so fragile, so it's no surprise that this is a major destination for researchers measuring climate change. A visit here is a once-in-a-lifetime experience, whether you're hiking in the starkly beautiful mountains, exploring the wilderness on a snowmobile, or watching wildlife, such as walrus or polar bears, from afar.

Icelandic texts from 1194 contain the first known mention of Svalbard. After the Dutch navigator Willem Barents visited Svalbard in 1596, whaling and winter-long hunting and trapping were virtually the only human activities here for the next 300 years. The archipelago is proud of its past, so there's lots of trapping history to be explored. In the early 20th century, coal mining became the major industry, leading to the founding of the major communities. The islands have officially been part of Norway since 1920.

The climate here is milder than at other locations of the same latitude, but is still quite chilly, with an average summer temperature just a few degrees above freezing. The small amount of precipitation makes Svalbard a sort of Arctic desert. Permafrost covers all of the archipelago, which means only the top yard of earth thaws in summer. Because it's so far north, Svalbard has four months of midnight sun when the sun never sets, as well as four months of polar night when it never rises.

Planning

When to Go

Deciding on when to visit Svalbard depends on what kind of activities you'd like to try. There really only are three seasons: the dark winter (between October and February, when you get to see the splendor of the northern lights), the bright winter (March to May, when the sun returns but there's still lots of snow around), and summer (the relatively temperate time from June to September). While winter is usually quite cold, with temperatures well below freezing, summer is still quite chilly. Tour providers work year-round, though the busiest seasons are bright winter and summer—the latter is when most cruise ships stop in the largest community of Longyearbyen. Each season has its own particular pros and cons, but generally speaking you should visit in winter for the best chances of seeing the northern lights, between March and May if you'd like to try snowmobiling and other winter sports, and during the summer if you'd rather freeze a little less and take advantage of the great hiking, kayaking, and mountain biking.

Getting Here and Around

The only way of getting to Svalbard is by plane or boat. You can fly from mainland Norway or find a cruise that heads north from England, Germany, or the Netherlands. Once you arrive on the main island of Spitsbergen, you can easily explore the town of Longyearbyen on foot. Venturing out of town is forbidden except with a guided tour. There are no roads that connect the handful communities on Svalbard—locals visit their neighbors by boat or snowmobile.

AIR TRAVEL

Svalbard Airport (LYR) is approximately 5 km (3 miles) north of the main community of Longyearbyen. There are only two direct flights, from Tromsø in northern Norway and Oslo in eastern Norway. Scandinavian Airlines System flies from both of these cities, while Norwegian Air Shuttle flies from Oslo.

BOAT TRAVEL

There's no shortage of cruises to Svalbard: P&O, Fred. Olsen, Princess, Holland America, Aida, MSC, and Hapag-Lloyd all offer voyages that stop in Longyearbyen, but usually only for a day or two before heading to Iceland or Norway. If you'd like to explore more of the island of Spitsbergen (and have the best chance of spotting wildlife), Hurtigruten is your best bet. This Norwegian cruise company offers expeditions from Longyearbyen that will take you around all of Spitsbergen, with stops in Longyearbyen, Ny-Ålesund (the world's northernmost permanent settlement), Kvitøya (the easternmost island of the Svalbard archipelago), as well as the North-East and South Spitsbergen national parks where you'll have the highest chances of spotting polar bears hunting on ice floes.

CONTACTS Hurtigruten. ✉ *Fredrik Langes gt. 14, Tromsø* ☎ *2038/113947* 🌐 *global.hurtigruten.com.*

CAR TRAVEL

Although Longyearbyen has 50 km (30 miles) of roads, you won't get very far by car as the network only connects the town with the airport, several research facilities, and weekend homes in Advent Valley. You can take the airport shuttle or a taxi to your hotel, where tour operators will pick you up for excursions. And any travel outside of town requires that you hire a guide. If you still insist on renting a car, Arctic Autorent, Longyearbyen's only car rental agency, offers 4x4 vehicles for daily, weekend, or weekly rental at triple the cost for locals.

CONTACTS Arctic Autorent. ✉ *Svalbard Airport, Longyearbyen* ☎ *91–70–22–58* 🌐 *english.autorent.no.*

Restaurants

For a town with only 2,000 inhabitants, Longyearbyen has quite the array of restaurants, bars and cafés. As is the case with the rest of Norway, most restaurants are fairly informal and don't require you to dress up; however smart-casual clothes are the right choice when dining at Longyearbyen's more sophisticated establishments. During peak tourist season in spring and summer, reservations are recommended. Credit cards are accepted everywhere, and most restaurants are open until 10 pm—many until well after midnight. Bars generally close at 2 am.

Hotels

There are a dozen different accommodations in Longyearbyen, including hotels, guesthouses, hostels, and even a campsite by the airport. Most are located downtown, but a few are situated in Nybyen, 2 km (1 mile) away. The airport bus and all tour providers serve Nybyen, so the distance shouldn't matter. There is also a hotel and a hostel in the Russian mining settlement Barentsburg, only reachable by snowmobile or boat. The same applies to the ghost town of Pyramiden, where there's one hotel.

Restaurant and hotel reviews have been shortened. For full information, visit Fodors.com.

What It Costs in Norwegian Krone

$	$$	$$$	$$$$
RESTAURANTS			
under NKr 125	NKr 125–NKr 250	NKr 251–NKr 350	over NKr 350
HOTELS			
under NKr 750	NKr 750–NKr 1250	NKr 1251–NKr 1900	over NKr 1900

Tours

While Longyearbyen can be easily explored on foot, sightseeing tours let you to explore nearby areas that are off-limits due to the danger of polar bears. Svalbard Buss og Taxi offers a two-hour sightseeing tour that heads into Advent Valley and up to Eiscat Radar for a scenic view. Visit Svalbard books walking tours of Longyearbyen and photography tour of the region.

Svalbard Buss og Taxi
Skilled local guides show you the best of what Longyearbyen has to offer while filling you in on the region's history. ✉ *Sjøområdet, Longyearbyen* ☎ *79–02–10–52* 🌐 *svalbardbuss.no/home.html.*

Visitor Information

Visit Svalbard
LOCAL SPORTS | Most of Svalbard's tour providers require advance reservations. You can get more information and book tours at Visit Svalbard. ✉ *Vei 221–1, Longyearbyen* ☎ *79–02–55–50* 🌐 *en.visitsvalbard.com.*

Longyearbyen

Longyearbyen provides you with easy access to nature—the Longyear Glacier, for instance, can be found just outside the neighborhood of Nybyen—but that's not the only reason to explore Svalbard's administrative center, research hub, and tourism magnet. This was a coal mining town until the industry moved to nearby Svea, but the old mines still exist and can be visited, as can historic structures like the Svalbard Church.

SAFETY

The polar bear warning signs on the edges of town aren't just popular props for selfies. Polar bears pose a very real danger, occasionally foraging for food

Svalbard's icy expanse is easily accessible from the colorful village of Longyearbyen.

along the shore or even in Longyearbyen. Never leave Longyearbyen without a knowledgeable guide, no matter what time of year you're visiting. Longyearbyen is otherwise a very safe place.

Sights

Galleri Svalbard (*Svalbard Art Gallery*)
MUSEUM | If the weather is frosty, head to this popular gallery. One of Norway's most admired artists, Kåre Tveter, donated 40 illustrations to this collection. The "Arctic Light Over Svalbard" slide show is an eye-opening look at what makes this area special. Centuries-old maps and books fill an adjacent exhibition room, and copies of many can be purchased in the unique gift shop. ✉ *Vei 100 , Nybyen, Longyearbyen* ☎ *79–02–23–40* 🌐 *www.gallerisvalbard.no* 🕒 *Closed Mon. Oct.–Feb.*

★ **Gruve 3** (*Coal Mine No. 3*)
MINE | Opening in 1971, this coal mine was abandoned in 1996 with all the old equipment still in place, making Gruve 3 the ideal place to learn more about the history of coal mining in Svalbard. Tours last three hours and venture deep into the main tunnel. You'll also get the chance to wear authentic uniforms, including overalls, helmets, headlamps, and gloves. No need to drive, as tours pick you up at your hotel. ✉ *Hotellneset, Longyearbyen* ☎ *481–00–640* 🌐 *www.gruve3.no* 🎟 *NKr 690.*

Kunsthall Svalbard (*Svalbard Art Museum*)
MUSEUM | This gallery focusing on contemporary art is part of the Northern Norwegian Art Museum based in Tromsø and offers interesting changing exhibits. ✉ *University Centre in Svalbard, Longyearbyen* ✣ *Adjacent to Svalbard Museum* ☎ *77–64–70–20* 🌐 *www.nnkm.no/nb/kunsthall-svalbard* 🕒 *Closed Oct.–Dec.*

North Pole Expedition Museum
MUSEUM | This museum presents the history of expeditions to the North Pole that started from Svalbard, namely the story of three airships: *America* (1906–09), *Norge* (1926), and *Italia* (1928). It

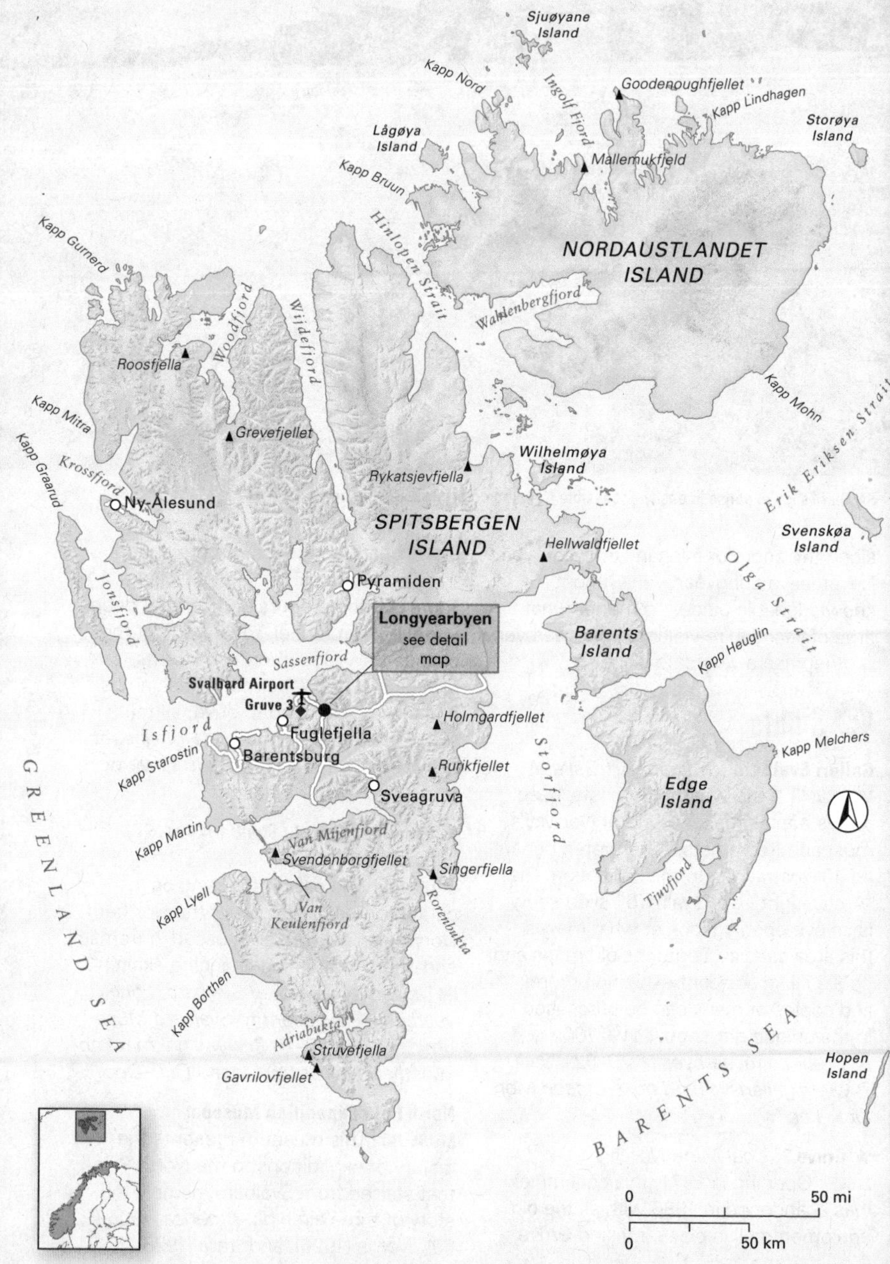
Svalbard
ARCTIC OCEAN
Sjuøyane Island
Kapp Nord
Ingolf Fjord
Goodenoughfjellet
Kapp Lindhagen
Storøya Island
Lågøya Island
Mallemukfjeld
Kapp Bruun
Hinlopen Strait
NORDAUSTLANDET ISLAND
Wahlenbergfjord
Kapp Gurnerd
Woodfjord
Wijdefjord
Roosfjella
Kapp Mitra
Grevefjellet
Kapp Mohn
Erik Eriksen Strait
Kapp Graarud
Krossfjord
Wilhelmøya Island
Rykatsjevfjella
Ny-Ålesund
SPITSBERGEN ISLAND
Svenskøa Island
Hellwaldfjellet
Jonsfjord
Pyramiden
Olga Strait
Longyearbyen
see detail map
Barents Island
Sassenfjord
Kapp Heuglin
Svalbard Airport
Gruve 3
Holmgardfjellet
Isfjord
Fuglefjella
Barentsburg
Storfjord
Kapp Melchers
Kapp Starostin
Rurikfjellet
GREENLAND SEA
Sveagruva
Edge Island
Kapp Martin
Van Mijenfjord
Svendenborgfjellet
Singerfjella
Tjuvfjord
Kapp Lyell
Van Keulenfjord
Rorenbukta
Kapp Borthen
BARENTS SEA
Adriabukta
Struvefjella
Hopen Island
Gavrilovfjellet
0
50 mi
0
50 km

also documents the search-and-rescue expeditions that caused Roald Amundsen and others to lose their lives. Kids love the models ships, airplanes, and airships on display and may pester you to get one of their own in the museum shop. ✉ *Longyearbyen* ✥ *Behind University Centre in Svalbard* ☎ *913–83–467* 🌐 *www.northpolemuseum.com* 🎫 *NKr 100* ⏲ *Closed Oct.–Jan.*

Svalbard Kirke (*Svalbard Church*)
RELIGIOUS SITE | In addition to being used for services, the only church on Svalbard also serves as a cozy place to relax with a cup of coffee or tea at any point during your visit. Completely destroyed during World War II, this new church was a symbol of the city's rebirth, and baptismal font was a gift to the town by Norwegian King Haakon VII. The candlesticks on the altar are the only thing that remains from the original church. ✉ *Longyearbyen* ✥ *Across the Longyearbyen River* ☎ *79–02–55–60* 🌐 *kirken.no/svalbard.*

Svalbard Museum
MUSEUM | This museum portrays Svalbard's 400-year history from discovery of the archipelago onward, including 17th-century whaling, the life of Norwegian trappers, and the relatively recent coal mining in Longyearbyen and the surrounding area. It's a great introduction to the archipelago, especially when you combine it with local tours and excursions. ✉ *University Centre in Svalbard, Vei 231–1, Longyearbyen* ☎ *79–02–64–90* 🌐 *svalbardmuseum.no* 🎫 *NKr 90.*

WildPhoto Gallery
MUSEUM | The northernmost photo gallery of the world, WildPhoto is owned by two local outdoors photographers, Ole J. Liodden and Roy Mangersnes. On display is an impressive collection of 30 prints; ranging from the town bathed in the blue light of polar night to polar bears roaming the archipelago. ✉ *Elvesletta Nord, Vei 509-1, Longyearbyen* ☎ *405–17–775* 🌐 *wildphoto.com* ⏲ *Closed weekends.*

Restaurants

Barentz Gastropub
$$ | **EUROPEAN** | After a long day out in the snow and ice, you'll appreciate this spot's warm and relaxed atmosphere. You'll also love the hearty pub food, including delectable burgers and what might very well be Longyearbyen's best pizza. **Known for:** friendly staff; fun atmosphere; great value. $ *Average main: NKr 193* ✉ *Vei 500, Longyearbyen* ☎ *94–01–06–65* 🌐 *www.radissonblu.com/en/hotel-spitsbergen/bars.*

Coal Miners' Bar and Grill
$$ | **BARBECUE** | Located in a mess hall for miners dating from 1948, you can't beat this spot's scenic surroundings or casual atmosphere. Combine top-notch pub food with a pint of locally brewed beer and board games and you have the recipe for a very relaxed evening after a day of outdoor adventures. **Known for:** outstanding value; eclectic atmosphere; great choice of beer. $ *Average main: NKr 170* ✉ *Vei 100, Longyearbyen* ☎ *94–00–58–33* 🌐 *hurtigrutensvalbard.com/no/restauranter/coal-miners-grill.*

Fruene
$ | **CAFÉ** | **FAMILY** | Called the "northernmost chocolate factory of the world," this cafe offers unusual handmade chocolates shaped like snowballs, ice crystals, and polar bears that you can take home (or, more likely, eat right away). It's a family-run business that focuses on creating a welcoming atmosphere for locals and visitors alike, which is why it draws in the crowd for its lunchtime soups and salads. **Known for:** girl-power packaging featuring local women; unique souvenirs; good value. $ *Average main: NKr 65* ✉ *Lompensenteret, Longyearbyen* ☎ *79–02–76–40* 🌐 *fruene.mystore4.no.*

★ **Funktionærmessen**
$$$ | **NORWEGIAN** | Housed in a former cafeteria for the town's coal miners, Longyearbyen's finest restaurant offers northern Norwegian cuisine with a twist.

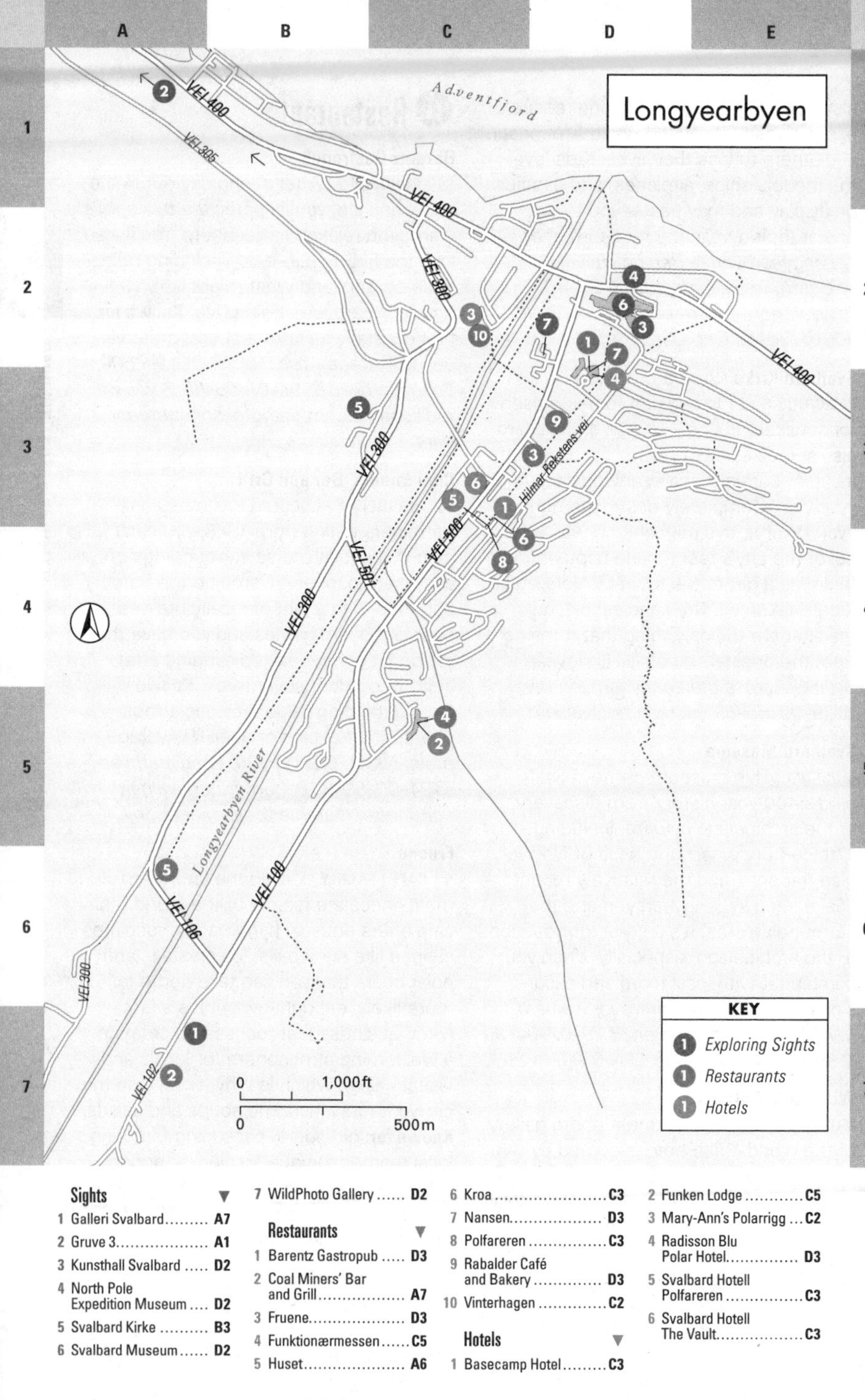

Sights

1 Galleri Svalbard A7
2 Gruve 3 .... A1
3 Kunsthall Svalbard D2
4 North Pole Expedition Museum D2
5 Svalbard Kirke B3
6 Svalbard Museum D2
7 WildPhoto Gallery D2

Restaurants

1 Barentz Gastropub D3
2 Coal Miners' Bar and Grill A7
3 Fruene D3
4 Funktionærmessen C5
5 Huset A6
6 Kroa C3
7 Nansen D3
8 Polfareren C3
9 Rabalder Café and Bakery D3
10 Vinterhagen C2

Hotels

1 Basecamp Hotel C3
2 Funken Lodge C5
3 Mary-Ann's Polarrigg C2
4 Radisson Blu Polar Hotel D3
5 Svalbard Hotell Polfareren C3
6 Svalbard Hotell The Vault C3

Polar Bears: The Kings of the Arctic

Polar bears got their nickname—the Kings of the Arctic, for a reason. Weighing 1,500 pounds or more, they are among the largest bears on the planet. They are distantly related to the more common brown bear, but evolved to thrive in the snowy landscape and icy waters in the Arctic Circle. Unlike other species, polar bears don't hibernate, instead roaming around on land during the winter. There's a population of around 3,000 polar bears in the Barents Sea, which is more than the number of humans living in the area.

Habitat and Habits

In winter, polar bears head to the island of Spitsbergen, where females give birth to their cubs in snow caves. They make their way back to the coast in spring and then roam from one ice floe to another hunting ringed seals. But if temperatures are too warm in spring, polar bears might not make it over to the pack ice and remain stuck on Spitsbergen. Due to the unpredictability of Svalbard's climate, polar bears can be encountered in and around the community of Longyearbyen any time of the year.

Attacks and Safety

Polar bear attacks make headlines, such as when a 17-year-old boy on a camping trip was killed in 2011, or when a German cruise ship passenger was severely injured during a shore landing in 2018. They are unlikely, but they do happen.

Polar bears can be very difficult to spot in the snowy landscape and can attack very quickly and without warning. Any polar bear that comes close to a settlement has to be scared away using warning shots and other loud noises or occasionally using helicopters. Sightings close to Longyearbyen only happen around 5 to 10 times a year.

In order to protect yourself from polar bears on Svalbard, it is of utmost importance not to roam the wilderness on your own. Always join a guided excursion with an experienced guide who has been trained in polar bear protection and who will always keep an eye out for bears. Tour guides know when and how to defend the group if worse comes to worse.

Spotting a Polar Bear

The best and safest way to see these animals is to hop aboard the Hurtigruten or take a cruise that travels north or east of Spitsbergen. If you don't have the time or resources for such a cruise, full-day boat excursions to Pyramiden or Ny-Ålesund might also enable polar bear sightings.

The menu has a strong focus on quality produce and locally sourced ingredients, such as reindeer from Svalbard and king crab from the Barents Sea. **Known for:** sharing platters; a large selection of Champagne; excellent service. *$ Average main: NKr270 ✉ Funken Lodge, Vei 212-4, Longyearbyen ☎ 79–02–62–00 🌐 hurtigrutensvalbard.com/en/restaurants/funktionaermessen-restaurant.*

Huset

$$$$ | NORWEGIAN | A favorite of many locals since the 1950s, Huset once served as airport terminal, a school, and even a hospital, so the rough exterior can't compare to the elegant interior of dimmed lights, textured wallpaper, and

Did You Know?

Svaldbard is one of the best places to see polar bears in the wild.

a polar bear skin on the wall. You can sample Nordic cuisine in two different settings: a less-formal (and much more affordable) bistro serving such modern Norwegian staples as reindeer burgers and fish soup, and a more sophisticated dining room with an innovative New Nordic nine-course tasting menu featuring game from local hunters and trappers. **Known for:** wine cellar with 15,000 bottles; high-quality ingredients; innovative food pairings. *Average main: NKr 1200* ✉ *Longyearbyen* ✣ *On the other side of Longyearbyen River* ☏ *79–02–50–02* 🌐 *www.huset.com* ⏲ *Dining room closed Mon. and Tues.*

Kroa

$$ | CONTEMPORARY | While the rough-hewn beams, stone fireplaces, and wooden-barrel seating is reminscent of a trapper's cabin, any trapper would have been green with envy at the food that's being served at this cozy eateries in downtown Longyearbyen. You can find classic pizza and burgers on the menu of pub favorites, but also Norwegian specialties like moose and clipfish. **Known for:** live music; generous portions; serves well after midnight. *Average main: NKr 191* ✉ *Hilmar Rekstens vei, Longyearbyen* ☏ *79–02–13–00* 🌐 *kroa-svalbard.no.*

Nansen

$$$ | ASIAN FUSION | Experience what happens when Asia meets the Arctic at this scenic restaurant in downtown Longyearbyen. Gazing out from an expansive wall of windows facing the mountains, you can experience a whole new kind of Asian fusion made from fresh and local ingredients such as cloudberries and reindeer. **Known for:** artsy presentations; good choice of vegetarian dishes; playful cocktail selection. *Average main: NKr 275* ✉ *Radisson Blu Polar Hotel, Vei 229-3, Longyearbyen* ☏ *79–02–34–50* 🌐 *www.radissonblu.com/en/hotel-spitsbergen/restaurants.*

Polfareren

$$$ | CONTEMPORARY | Honoring the young and ambitious Norwegian polar explorer Eivind Astrup—the name means "Polar Explorer"—this eatery sets its sights just as high. Expect a fusion of classic French, traditional Japanese, and New Nordic cuisine in a simple, tasteful setting of walnut tables and leather benches. **Known for:** soup buffet at lunch; good wine selection; relaxed atmosphere. *Average main: NKr 278* ✉ *Svalbard Hotell Polfareren, Hilmar Rekstens vei, Longyearbyen* ☏ *79–02–50–01* 🌐 *svalbardadventures.com/foodbeverage#p-37378.*

Rabalder Café and Bakery

$ | CAFÉ | FAMILY | In Longyearbyen Kulturhus, the town's performing arts center, this cozy and quiet café has an exceptional selection of cinnamon buns (said to be "as big as polar bear claws"), pastries, and cakes, but also soups, sandwiches, and salads that make it the perfect lunchtime destination. The downtown location makes it a popular meeting place for locals. **Known for:** reasonable prices; great pastries; popular meeting spot. *Average main: NKr 80* ✉ *Kulturhuset Longyearbyen, Hilmar Rekstens vei, Longyearbyen* ☏ *79–02–23–88* 🌐 *hurtigrutensvalbard.com/en/restaurants/rabalder-cafe-and-bakery.*

Vinterhagen

$$$ | NORWEGIAN | Longyearbyen's most unusual and eclectic restaurant is located in what can only be described as a miniature botanical garden. Try traditional Svalbardian cuisine in the glass-enclosed winter garden that lets in the midnight sun all summer long. **Known for:** Arctic specialities; panoramic views; extraordinary decor. *Average main: NKr 292* ✉ *Mary-Ann's Polarrigg, Longyearbyen* ☏ *79–02–37–02* 🌐 *www.polarriggen.com.*

Hotels

★ Basecamp Hotel
$$$ | **HOTEL** | If you'd like to get a sense of what life was like for Svalbard's trappers back in the day, Basecamp Hotel gives you just that with rooms are tastefully decorated with driftwood walls and slate floors, just like the lodgings of yore. **Pros:** great attention to detail; contributes to nature conservation projects; large selection of tours and excursions. **Cons:** rather small rooms (and bathrooms); some rooms have bunk beds with steep ladders; very basic breakfast selection. *Rooms from: NKr 1790 Hilmar Rekstens vei, Longyearbyen 79–02–46–00 www.basecampexplorer.com/spitsbergen/hotels/basecamp-hotel/ 16 rooms Free breakfast.*

★ Funken Lodge
$$$$ | **HOTEL** | A top-to-bottom renovation of the town's finest hotel resulted in very comfortable and chic rooms with stunning views of the surrounding mountains. **Pros:** sauna and gym; fine in-house restaurant; delicious drinks at the bar. **Cons:** not quite downtown; on the pricy side; extra charge for cappuccino. *Rooms from: NKr 2034 Vei 212-4, Longyearbyen 79–02–62–00 www.nordicchoicehotels.com/hotels/norway/svalbard/funken-lodge 88 rooms Free breakfast.*

Mary-Ann's Polarrigg
$$$ | **B&B/INN** | In the former barracks of local mine workers, this one-of-a-kind hotel offers basic, yet charming, rooms, suites, and apartments and suites only 10 minutes from downtown Longyearbyen. **Pros:** spa, sauna, and outdoor hot tub; great in-house restaurant; warm and welcoming atmosphere. **Cons:** small standard rooms; Wi-Fi only available in the lobby; some rooms have shared bathrooms. *Rooms from: NKr 1395 Longyearbyen Across Longyearbyen River 79–02–37–02 www.polarriggen.com 27 rooms No meals.*

Radisson Blu Polar Hotel
$$$$ | **HOTEL** | Longyearbyen's largest hotel isn't resting on its laurels: a multimillion-kroner renovation updated the lobby with a gorgeous fireplace and added a sauna and outdoor hot tub that makes it the perfect spot to relax after a day exploring the Arctic. **Pros:** central location; sauna and outdoor whirlpool; good breakfast selection. **Cons:** uneven service; some rooms can be noisy; not always the best value. *Rooms from: NKr 2740 Vei 500, Longyearbyen 79–02–34–50 www.radissonblu.com/en/hotel-spitsbergen 95 rooms Free breakfast.*

Svalbard Hotell Polfareren
$$$$ | **HOTEL** | This modern and stylish boutique hotel in downtown Longyearbyen invites guests to relax warm up by the fireplace in the expansive lobby. **Pros:** outstanding breakfast; half-board option available; very comfortable beds. **Cons:** poor sound isolation; no safe available; you may have to drag your luggage across snow or gravel. *Rooms from: NKr 1990 Hilmar Rekstens vei, Longyearbyen 79–02–50–01 svalbardadventures.com/accommodation 31 rooms Free breakfast.*

Svalbard Hotell The Vault
$$$$ | **HOTEL** | Inspired by the massive entrace to the Global Seed Vault, this centrally located hotel offers basic, yet comfortable, accommodations in an industrial atmosphere. **Pros:** half-board available; 24-hour reception; comfortable beds. **Cons:** relatively small rooms and windows; little space to put clothes and toiletries; cramped breakfast room. *Rooms from: NKr 1990 Longyearbyen 79–02–50–04 svalbardadventures.com/accommodation 35 rooms Free breakfast.*

Nightlife

★ Funken Bar

WINE BARS—NIGHTLIFE | Longyearbyen's only cocktail lounge, this spot in the stylish Funken Lodge offers inspired drinks in an intimate and sophisticated atmosphere. Sitting by the fireplace, you can taste vintage wines or exquisite Champagnes—either with snacks from the bar menu or as a prelude to dinner at the adjacent Funktionærmessen Restaurant. ✉ *Funken Lodge, Vei 212-4, Longyearbyen* ☎ *79–02–62–00* 🌐 *www.nordicchoicehotels.com/hotels/norway/svalbard/funken-lodge/facilities/funken-bar/.*

★ Karlsberger Pub

BARS/PUBS | A must for anyone who loves cognac and whisky, this centrally located pub has more than 1,000 from which to choose. It's the largest selection in all of Norway, and (so they say) the world. The intimate space pays tribute to Longyearbyen's long history as a mining town with portraits of local miners decorating the walls. ✉ *Lompesenteret, Longyearbyen* ☎ *79–02–22–00* 🌐 *www.karlsbergerpub.no.*

Svalbard Bryggeri

BREWPUBS/BEER GARDENS | Svalbard's very own brewery produces IPAs, pale ales, wheat beers, stouts, and pilsners, all available right at the source. Made with ice from the 2,000-year-old Bogerbreen Glacier, Svalbard Bryggeri's beer is deeply rooted in the archipelago: former miner Robert Johansen had to get the local liquor laws changed in order the start the business. Drop by on Friday night or book a tour (tours given three times a week). ✉ *612, Svalbardgata 7, Longyearbyen* ☎ *90–28–62–05* 🌐 *www.svalbardbryggeri.no.*

Svalbar Pub

BARS/PUBS | Locals and visitors alike meet here for a pint of beer, occasional live music, and to watch soccer on TV. The laid-back atmosphere lets you relax after a long day outdoors, perhaps while enjoying a hearty burger or a brick-oven baked pizza of generous proportions. The place is open until 2 am—not that it will actually feel that late in the summer when the sun never sets. ✉ *Next to Svalbard Lodge, Longyearbyen* ☎ *79–02–50–03* 🌐 *www.svalbar.no.*

Performing Arts

Dark Season Blues Festival

MUSIC FESTIVALS | In the bluish twilight that precedes polar night, blues musicians from all over the world perform in Longyearbyen's bars and pubs over the course of a weekend during October's Dark Season Blues Festival. ✉ *Longyearbyen* 🌐 *www.svalbardblues.com.*

Shopping

Gullgruva Arctic Design

JEWELRY/ACCESSORIES | This is the best Svalbard has to offer when it comes to gold and silver jewelry, from archipelago-shaped necklaces to polar bear rings to snowflake earrings. The store also sells an array of unique souvenirs like Svalbarði Water, made from Svalbard's smaller icebergs and produced only twice a year. ✉ *Lompensenteret, Longyearbyen* ☎ *79–02–18–16.*

Longyear78 Outdoor and Expeditions

CLOTHING | Longyearbyen's best-known outdoor clothing and equipment store, Longyear78 sells everything from waterproof jackets to hiking boots. As there's no value added tax on Svalbard, all items cost a lot less than on the Norwegian mainland. ✉ *Hilmar Rekstens vei, Longyearbyen* ☎ *79–00–21–00* 🌐 *www.nordskog.com/longyear-78-outdoor-&-expeditions/.*

Activities

BIKING

Longyearbyen is such a small town that biking is a great way to get just about anywhere. Because of the terrain, fat biking (bikes outfitted with extra-thick wheels) is a great way to discover the surrounding landscapes throughout the year.

FatBike Spitsbergen

BICYCLING | This well-regarded company specializes in fat biking tours of various lengths and difficulty levels. The panorama tour—an easy, two-hour sightseeing trip on a gravel road with plenty of stops for pictures—is best for people of average fitness, while more serious bikers might enjoy the four-hour "bike and barbecue" tours. In winter, guides lead fat biking tours on snow. ✉ *Longyearbyen* ☎ *948–05–400* 🌐 *fatbikespitsbergen.com.*

BOATING

Travelling by boat—often the only way to get from one settlement to another—is a great way to discover more of the archipelago in the summer. Explore the Russian mining towns Barentsburg and Pyramiden (the latter a ghost town that's frequently visited by polar bears), or go even farther afield to Ny-Ålesund, Isfjord Radio Station, or one of Svalbard's many impressive glaciers.

Arctic Expedition

BOATING | This company's high-speed catamaran transports you to Barentsburg and Pyramiden. A half-day trip travels to one of the mining communities, while a full-day trip heads along the coast to Barentsburg in the morning and stops in Longyearbyen before heading to Pyramiden in the afternoon. Along the way you'll see the bird-nesting grounds at Fuglefjella and the Nordenskiöld Glacier. ✉ *Longyearbyen* ☎ *918–00–000* 🌐 *www.arcticexpedition.no.*

Better Moments

BOATING | Hop aboard a RIB (rigid-hulled inflatable boat) for daylong excursions to spot walruses or explore the research community of Ny-Ålesund. Two-day trips to Pyramiden include a night's stay in the ghost town and a hike around the local area. ✉ *Longyearbyen* ☎ *400–95–965* 🌐 *www.bettermoments.no.*

DOGSLEDDING

Svalbard's trappers have journeyed into the wilderness using dogsleds for hundreds of years. Today you can join an organized trip in winter or summer (when the sleds are on wheels).

Basecamp Explorer

TOUR—SPORTS | **FAMILY** | Affiliated with Longyearbyen's Basecamp Hotel, this outfit offers dog-sledding tours at their Trapper's Station in Advent Valley. Here you'll meet 100 Alaskan huskies who seem eager to take you on half-day, full-day, and multiple day tours into the wilderness. ✉ *Basecamp Hotel, Vei 223, 6, Longyearbyen* ☎ *79–02–46–00* 🌐 *www.basecampexplorer.com.*

HIKING

A great way to take in the spectacular scenery, organized hikes in the area usually require an above-average fitness because of the height of the nearby mountains.

Svalbard Wildlife Expeditions

HIKING/WALKING | Half- and full-day hikes to several mountains close to Longyearbyen—including Platåfjellet, Trollsteinen, Lindholmhøgda, Sarkofagen, and Foxfonna— are on the itinerary here. Be prepared for steep inclines and patches of bare rocks or snow, even in summer. ✉ *Vei 608 Hus 2, Longyearbyen* ☎ *79–02–22–22* 🌐 *www.wildlife.no.*

KAYAKING

Paddling around Advent Bay while admiring the stunning mountains of Advent Valley doesn't require prior training or more than an average fitness level.

Spitsbergen Outdoor Activities

KAYAKING | You have a choice between half-day kayak trips around Advent Bay and full-day excursions that include plenty of hiking in Advent Valley. ✉ *Longyearbyen* ☎ *917–76–595* 🌐 *www.spitsbergenoutdooractivities.com/en.*

SKIING

Ski trips around Svalbard aren't for beginners: they require previous cross-country skiing experience and above-average fitness levels. Excursions usually last several days, either traversing the glaciers and tundra of Spitsbergen or climbing mountains so you can ski down.

Poli Arctici

SKIING/SNOWBOARDING | Founded by Italian Stefano Poli in the 1990s, Poli Arctici offers a limited number of individual and group excursions across Svalbard. His 4- to 12-day trips explore places such as Nordenskiöldland and Atomfjella. ✉ *Longyearbyen* ☎ *79–02–17–05* 🌐 *www.poliarctici.com/english.*

SNOWMOBILING

Due to the limited road network in Svalbard, snowmobiling is the best and easiest way to get around in winter. Prior experience is not always necessary, but a valid driver's licence and good fitness levels certainly are.

Spitzbergen Adventures

SNOW SPORTS | Offering snowmobile excursions of various lengths and difficulty levels in the winter months, Spitzbergen Adventures takes you to Pyramiden, Barentsburg, Isfjord Radio Station, or the eastern coast of Spitsbergen where there's a chance to spot polar bears. ✉ *Longyearbyen* ☎ *480–61–091* 🌐 *spitzbergen-adventures.com.*

Index

A

B

C

D

E

F

G

U

V

W

Z

Photo Credits

Front Cover: Tatsiana Volskaya [Description: Panoramic seascape near Reine, Moskenes, Lofoten Islands, Norway.]. **Back cover, from left to right:** Ryhor Bruyeu/iStockphoto, Andrey Armyagov/Shutterstock, maradon_333/Shutterstock. **Spine:** Haidamac/Shutterstock. **Interior, from left to right:** Anetlanda/Shutterstock (1), nicky39/iStockphoto (2). **Chapter 1: Experience Norway:** Andrey Armyagov/iStockphoto (6-7). Grisha Bruev/Shutterstock (8). Francesco Bonino/Shutterstock (9). Ondrej Prosicky/Shutterstock (9). BAAS/Shutterstock (10). Rob Kints/Shutterstock (10). Therato/Shutterstock.com (11). Pedal-Power-Photos/iStockphoto (12). Viktor Hladchenko/Shutterstock (12). Maxim Grohotov/Shutterstock (12). Øyvind Heen/Visitnorway.com (12). Olga Miltsova/Shutterstock (13). Anibal Trejo/Shutterstock (13). AlexSN_Photography/Shutterstock (13). Margreet De Groot/Dreamstime (13). my nordic/Shutterstock (14). Diego Fiore/iStockphoto (14). vladacanon/istockphoto (14). Mykhailo Brodskyi/Shutterstock (14). TPopova/iStockphoto (15). Kert/Shutterstock (15). Asgeir Helgestad/Artic Light AS/visitnorway.com (16). alexemanuel/iStockphoto (16). Valentina Photo/Shutterstock (16). Marius Dobilas/Shutterstock (16). Haidamac/Shutterstock (17). Natalya Grisik/Dreamstime (20). Poring Studio/Shutterstock (21). Nancy Bundt/Innovation Norway (22). Jan-Tore Egge (22). Kiev.Victor/Shutterstock (22). Christian Houge/Innovation Norway (22). Pelikh Alexey/Shutterstock (22). Vaitekune/Dreamstime (23). Didrick Stenersen/VisitOSLO (23). Aleksandra Suzi/Shutterstock (23). Shyamal (23). MIR (illustr.)/Statsbygg (23). Irene Libano/Shutterstock (24). Avani/Visitnorway.com (24). Natalia Kabliuk/Shutterstock (24). s.tomas/Shutterstock (24). Kloeg008/iStockphoto (24). Andrey Armyagov/Shutterstock (25). Chris Arnesen/Visitnorway.com (25). Thomas Rasmus Skaug / Visitnorway.com (25). CHUNYIP WONG/iStockphoto (25). reisegraf/iStockphoto (25). Jon Magne Bøe/Dalane Folkemuseum (26). Mr_Karesuando/Shutterstock (26). Sverre Hjornevik/Visit Flam (26). Bard Basberg/Loen Skylift (26). Vichaya Kiatyingangsulee/Dreamstime (26). Dmitry Tkachenko Photo/Shutterstock (27). Robert Bårdsen (27). diephotodesigner.de OHG (27). Fortidsminneforeningen (27). IVAR KVAAL (27). Edalin Photography/Shutterstock (28). Nataliya Nazarova/Shutterstock (29). Dmitry Chulov/Dreamstime (34). **Chapter 3: Oslo:** Murphy1975/Shutterstock (55). saiko3p/Shutterstock (63). Nanisimova/Shutterstock (82). paparazzza/Shutterstock (88). Matt Makes Photos/Shutterstock (90). Emilianocavolina/Dreamstime (96). **Chapter 4: Oslofjord:** Sergey Kamshylin/Shutterstock (101). 0399778584/Shutterstock (109). Petroos/iStockphoto (111). **Chapter 5: Southern Norway:** balipadma/Shutterstock (115). Mariuszks/Dreamstime (123). Lillian Tveit/Dreamstime (132-133). **Chapter 6: Central Norway:** RobKints/iStockphoto (141). Bernhard Richter/Dreamstime (147). Kloeg008/iStockphoto (162). LightField Studios/Shutterstock (168). **Chapter 7: Bergen:** StreetFlash/iStockphoto (171). maylat/iStockphoto (178). TTphoto/Shutterstock (182). Issaurinko/iStock Editorial (193). **Chapter 8: The Western Fjords:** Smit/Shutterstock (197). snapshopped/Shutterstock (210-211). Byvalet/Dreamstime (223). Patryk Kosmider/Shutterstock (234). **Chapter 9: Trondheim to the Lofoten Islands:** Alexander Groffen/Dreamstime (239). Zalka/iStockphoto (250). Sara Winter/Dreamstime (264-265). **Chapter 10: Northern Norway:** Adam Knauz/Shutterstock (271). Kuznetsova Julia/Shutterstock (276). lowpower225/Shutterstock (282). Anibal Trejo/Shutterstock (288). **Chapter 11: Svalbard:** Polina Bublik/Dreamstime (293). Tyler Olson/Dreamstime (299). Don Landwehrle/Shutterstock (304-305). **About Our Writers:** All photos are courtesy of the writers.

*Every effort has been made to trace the copyright holders, and we apologize in advance for any accidental errors. We would be happy to apply the corrections in the following edition of this publication.

Notes

Fodor's ESSENTIAL NORWAY

Publisher: Stephen Horowitz, *General Manager*

Editorial: Douglas Stallings, *Editorial Director*; Jacinta O'Halloran, Amanda Sadlowski, *Senior Editors*; Kayla Becker, Alexis Kelly, Teddy Minford, Rachael Roth, *Editors*

Design: Tina Malaney, *Director of Design and Production*; Jessica Gonzalez, *Graphic Designer;* Mariana Tabares, *Design & Production Intern*

Production: Jennifer DePrima, *Editorial Production Manager*, Carrie Parker, *Senior Production Editor*, Elyse Rozelle, *Production Editor;* Jackson Pranica, *Editorial Production Assistant*

Maps: Rebecca Baer, *Senior Map Editor*, Mark Stroud (Moon Street Cartography), *Cartographer*

Photography: Viviane Teles, *Senior Photo Editor;* Namrata Aggarwal, Ashok Kumar, Carl Yu, *Photo Editors;* Rebecca Rimmer, *Photo Intern*

Business & Operations: Chuck Hoover, *Chief Marketing Officer*, Robert Ames, *Group General Manager*, Tara McCrillis, *Director of Publishing Operations;* Victor Bernal, *Business Analyst*

Public Relations and Marketing: Joe Ewaskiw, *Senior Director Communications & Public Relations*; Esther Su, Senior *Marketing Manager*

Fodors.com: Jeremy Tarr, *Editorial Director*; Rachael Levitt, *Managing Editor*

Technology: Jon Atkinson, *Director of Technology;* Rudresh Teotia, *Lead Developer*, Jacob Ashpis, *Content Operations Manager*

Writers: Vanessa Brune, Cecilie Hauge Eggen, Janicke Hansen, Alexandra Pereira, Megan Starr, Lisa Stentvedt, Aram Vandanyan, Barbara Woolsey

Editors: Margaret Kelly, Mark Sullivan

Production Editor: Elyse Rozelle

1st Edition

ISBN 978-1-64097-238-4

ISSN 2644–3481

Library of Congress Control Number 2019952396

SPECIAL SALES

This book is available at special discounts for bulk purchases for sales promotions or premiums. For more information, e-mail SpecialMarkets@fodors.com.

PRINTED IN CANADA

10 9 8 7 6 5 4 3 2

About Our Writers

Vanessa Brune is a travel writer and tour guide in Norway. After several years of living in the Arctic, she now calls the city of Stavanger in western Norway home. She regularly travels across the region in search of hidden gems and views for days. For this book she wrote the Svalbard chapter.

Oslo-based **Cecilie Hauge Eggen** is a nature-loving freelance journalist and yoga instructor. Born in Ålesund, she has traveled through the scenic region of central Norway more times than she can count. She was editor for the magazine *Shape Up* and other publications. Since 2016 she has been freelancing, enjoying the freedom to travel, write, and teach yoga.

Janicke Hansen is a travel writer, photographer, and destination marketing specialist working with customers from around the world from her home in Bergen, Norway. She loves teaching international travelers about the Nordic way of living, leading adventurous trips around Norway, Sweden, Denmark, and Finland. She updated the Bergen chapter.

Alexandra Pereira is a Scandinavia-based writer originally from Worcester, England. She worked in film and television and has written about travel and the arts for *Condé Nast Traveler, Vanity Fair, Suitcase, Playboy, The Paris Review,* and a host of international inflight magazines. For this book she updated the Oslo and Oslofjord chapters.

Lisa Stentvedt is a travel writer and blogger from the beautiful fjords of Norway. She shares her adventures from around the world, along with her best travel tips, on her blog called "Fjords and Beaches." In addition to writing, she is passionate about diving and wine. She brought her knowledge to the Southern Norway and Western Fjords chapters.

Aram Vardanyan and **Megan Starr** are travel writers and bloggers hailing from Armenia and the United States. Their websites and projects focus on developing tourism in Scandinavia, eastern Europe, the Caucasus, and central Asia. They both passionately love promoting the beauty of Norway. They wrote the Trondheim and the Lofoten Islands and the Northern Norway chapters.

Barbara Woolsey is a Canadian journalist who has been to over 50 countries by plane, train, and motorbike. Born and raised on the prairies to a Filipino mother and Irish-Scottish father, her multicultural upbringing has ignited her passion for travel and storytelling. Her work has been published by Reuters, *The Guardian,*and *USA Today.* She updated the Travel Smart chapter.